Introducing Fortran 95

Springer
London
Berlin
Heidelberg
New York
Barcelona
Hong Kong
Milan
Paris
Singapore
Tokyo

Ian Chivers and Jane Sleightholme

Introducing Fortran 95

 Springer

Ian Chivers, BSc, PGCEd, MSc
Jane Sleightholme, MSc
The Computer Centre, Kings College Strand Campus, London WC2R 2LS, UK

ISBN 1-85233-276-X Springer-Verlag London Berlin Heidelberg

British Library Cataloguing in Publication Data
Chivers, I. D. (Ian David), 1952-
  Introducing Fortran 95
  1. Fortran 95 (Computer language)
  I. Title II. Sleightholme, Jane
  005.1' 33
ISBN 185233276X

Library of Congress Cataloging-in-Publication Data
Chivers, I. D. (Ian David), 1952-
    Introducing Fortran 95 / Ian Chivers and Jane Sleightholme
      p. cm.
    Includes bibliographical references and index.
    ISBN 1-85233-276-X (alk. paper)
    1. Fortran 95 (Computer program language) I. Sleightholme, Jane, 1950- II. Title.

QA76.73.F29 C48 2000
005.13' 3—dc21

                                                            00-034505

Typesetting: Camera ready by authors
Printed and bound at the Athenæum Press Ltd., Gateshead, Tyne & Wear
34/3830-543210 Printed on acid-free paper SPIN 10756213

Contents

Contents

1

Overview

'I don't know what the language of the year 2000 will look like, but it will be called Fortran.'

C.A.R. Hoare.

Aims

The aims of the chapter are to provide a background to the organization of the book.

1   Overview

The book aims to provide coverage of a recommended subset of the full Fortran language. The subset that is chosen is one that fits most closely with the theory and practice of structured programming, data structures and software engineering.

The book has been written for both complete beginners with little or no programming background and existing Fortran programmers wanting to update their skills and move to a modern version of the language.

Chapters 2–5 provide a short background to computer systems and their use.

Chapter 2   This chapter looks at the basics of computer systems from the hardware point of view.

Chapter 3   This chapter provides a short history of operating system developments and looks at some commonly used operating systems.

Chapter 4   This chapter looks at some of the fundamentals of using a computer system.

These three chapters provide information that will be very useful in the longer term for the successful use of computer systems for programming.

Chapters 5 and 6 provide a coverage of problem solving and the history and development of programming languages. Chapter 5 is essential for the beginner as the concepts introduced here are used and expanded on throughout the rest of the book. Chapter 6 must be read at some time but can be omitted initially. Programming languages evolve and some understanding of where Fortran has come from and where it is going will prove valuable in the longer term.

Chapter 5   This chapter looks at problem solving in some depth, and there is a coverage of the way we define problems, the role of algorithms, the use of both top-down and bottom-up methods, and the requirement for formal systems analysis and design for more complex problems.

Chapter 6   This chapter looks at the history and development of programming languages. This is essential as Fortran has evolved considerably from its origins in the mid-1950s, through the first standard in 1966, the Fortran 77 standard, the Fortran 90 standard, the Fortran 95 standard and beyond. It helps to put many of the current and proposed features of Fortran into context. There is also a coverage of parallel Fortrans, and the C, C++ and Java family of languages.

Chapters 7 through 11 cover the major features provided in Fortran for numeric programming in the first instance and for general purpose programming in the second. Each chapter has a range of problems. It is essential that a reasonable range of problems are attempted and completed. It is impossible to learn any language without practice.

Chapter 7 This chapter provides an introduction to programming with some simple Fortran examples. For people with a knowledge of programming this chapter can be covered fairly quickly.

Chapter 8 This chapter looks at arithmetic in some depth, with a coverage of the various numeric data types, expressions and assignment of scalar variables. There is also a thorough coverage of the facilities provided in Fortran in helping to write programs that work on quite widely differing hardware.

Chapter 9 This chapter is an introduction to arrays and DO loops. The chapter starts with some examples of tabular structures that one should be familiar with. There is then an examination of what concepts we need in a programming language to support manipulation of tabular data.

Chapter 10 Here we take the ideas introduced in the previous chapter and extend them to higher dimensioned arrays, additional forms of the DIMENSION attribute and corresponding form of the DO loop, and the use of looping for the control of repetition and manipulation of tabular information without the use of arrays.

Chapter 11 Here we look at more of the facilities offered for the manipulation of whole arrays and array sections, ways in which we can initialize arrays using constructors, look more formally at the concepts we need to be able to accurately describe and understand arrays, and finally look at the differences between the way Fortran allows us to use arrays and the mathematical rules governing matrices.

Chapters 9 through 11 provide a coverage of some of the more important features and uses of arrays in the field of numerical problem solving. The framework provided here is drawn upon in later chapters in the book, with more complex and realistic examples.

Chapters 12 and 13 look at input and output (I/O) in Fortran. An understanding of I/O is necessary for the development of so-called production, non-interactive programs. These are essentially fully developed programs that are used repeatedly with a variety of data inputs and results.

Chapter 12   This chapter looks at output of results and how to generate something that is more comprehensible and easy to read than that available with free format output, and also how to write the results to a file rather than the screen.

Chapter 13   This chapter extends the ideas introduced in chapter 12 on output to cover input of data, or reading data into a program and considers file I/O also.

Chapter 14 introduces the first building block available in Fortran for the construction of programs for the solution of larger more complex problems.

Chapter 14   This chapter looks at the functions available in Fortran, the so-called intrinsic functions and procedures (over 100 of them) and also covers how you can define and use your own functions.

It is essential to develop an understanding of the functions provided by the language and when it is necessary to write your own.

Chapter 15 introduces more formally the concept of control structures and their role in structured programming. Some of the control structures available in Fortran have been introduced in earlier chapters, but there is a summary here of those already covered plus several new ones that complete our coverage of a minimal working set.

Chapter 15   This chapter looks at the control structures available, from the viewpoint of established theory and practice in structured programming.

Chapters 16 through 20 complete our coverage of the data typing and structuring facilities provided by Fortran, both pre-defined and user-defined. Fortran has now caught up with some of the major developments in the data structuring area of the last twenty years, and which have been available in other languages for some time.

Chapter 16   This chapter looks at the character data type in Fortran. There is a coverage of I/O again, with the operators available – only one in fact.

Chapter 17   This chapter looks at the last numeric data type in Fortran, the complex data type. This data type is essential to the solution of a small class of problems in mathematics and engineering.

Chapter 18   Logical. The material covered here helps considerably in increasing the power and sophistication of the way we use and construct logical expressions in Fortran. This proves invaluable in the construction and use of logical expressions in control structures.

Chapters 19   User defined. This introduces another major new feature of Fortran. Previous versions of the language lacked any facilities here. This meant that in many applications earlier versions of Fortran were not the language of first choice for many people.

Chapter 20   This chapter looks at the dynamic data structuring facilities now available in Fortran. Examples are drawn from a range of sources.

These chapters conclude coverage of the data structuring facilities provided by Fortran. There are problems that will require facilities not provided, but it is surprising what can be achieved with the set now provided in Fortran. The material covered is extended into more realistic examples when we look at the construction of larger and more complex programs in the last few chapters in the book.

Chapter 21   Here we provide a more formal coverage of files than has been provided in the earlier chapters on input and output.

Chapter 22–27   These chapters look at program structure, subroutines, procedures and modules from the viewpoint of software engineering. Chapter 22 provides a gentle introduction to some of the fundamental concepts of subroutine definition and use; Chapter 23 extends these ideas. Chapter 24 introduces the concept of a module and the range of things that this brings to Fortran. Chapter 25 looks at IEEE arithmetic. Chapter 26 looks at a number of concepts more formally and thoroughly than earlier coverages. This chapter also provides a coverage of some of the more advanced features of Fortran. Chapter 27 has a small number of case studies helping to pull together the ideas presented in the earlier chapters.

Chapter 28   This chapter looks at language features of Fortran 77 and how to convert (where necessary) to the newer and better features of Fortran 95.

Chapter 29   This chapter looks at Fortran 2000 and the various (non-standard) dialects.

Chapter 30   This provides an overview to the complete coverage of the material in the rest of the book. It looks at program development and software engineering, modules, programming style, data structures, algorithms, structured programming, recursion and recursion removal, efficiency in space and time, program testing, simple debugging techniques, software tools and numerical software sources. There is also coverage of the various internet resources available for Fortran.

Many of the chapters have an annotated bibliography. These provide pointers and directions for further reading. The coverage provided cannot be seen in isolation. The concepts introduced are by intention brief, and fuller coverage must be sought where necessary.

Appendix A   This is a glossary which provides coverage of both the new concepts provided by Fortran and a range of computing terms and ideas.

Appendix B   Provides an example of a simple program in a number of the languages described in the chapter on program language development. There is also coverage of the standards that apply.

Appendix C   The ASCII character set.

Appendix D   Contains a list of all of the intrinsic procedures in Fortran. This contains a full explanation of each intrinsic procedure with a coverage of the rules and restrictions that apply and examples of use.

Appendix E   Contains the English and Latin text extracts used in one of the problems in the chapter on characters.

Appendix F   Contains the coded text extract used in one of the problems in the chapter on characters.

The book is not and cannot possibly be completely self contained and exhaustive in its coverage of the Fortran language. Our first intention has been to produce a coverage of the features that will get you started with Fortran, and enable you to solve quite a wide range of problems successfully.

Fortran, like most languages, has features that are of relatively little use or make the construction of larger scale programs more difficult, especially when moving between hardware platforms. We have deliberately avoided these features.

Another problem is backwards compatibility with Fortran 77. Existing Fortran 77 programs have to be maintained, and there is much in that language that is *deprecated* or *obsolescent* in terms of Fortran 95.

We have aimed to introduce a working subset of the new language that emphasizes the better constructs provided in Fortran over its predecessors, Fortran 77 and Fortran 66.

All in all Fortran is an exciting language, and has *caught up* with language developments of the 1970s, 1980s, and 1990s.

1.1 Miscellanea

This book has evolved from our combined experience of working in Computing Services at the University of London (for the last fourteen years at King's College and before that eight years at Imperial College and seven years at Chelsea College) in the teaching, advice and support of Fortran and related areas.

Thanks are due to:

- The staff and students at King's College London because without them none of this would have been possible; also the support and facilities provided by the Computer Centre.

- The patience of our families during the lengthy period required to develop the courses upon which this book is based and whilst preparing the camera ready copy.

- The staff at NAG, Compaq (née DEC) and Salford Fortran. Special thanks to Steve Lionel at Compaq, Robert Murrels and Malcolm Cohen at NAG, Tim Bartle at Salford, for the opportunity to take part in the beta testing of their compilers. The lessons to be learnt from moving programs between their compilers has been invaluable.

- The people on the Fortran 90 list and comp.lang.fortran Access to the expertise of several hundred people involved in the use and development of Fortran on a daily basis across a wide range of disciplines is inestimable.

- Finally Rebecca Mowat and Beverley Ford at Springer for their enthusiasm and encouragement during the gestation period and birth!

The course notes and book were prepared on a range of PCs using a variety of versions of Corel Ventura Publisher. The facilities provided by Ventura for book production are superb.

A range of hardware platforms, operating systems and Fortran compilers were used. These were:

- DEC VAX under VMS and later Open VMS using the NAG Fortran 90 compiler.

- DEC Alpha under Open VMS using the DEC/Compaq Fortran 90 compiler.

- IBM PC under DOS and Windows using DEC/Compaq Fortran 90.

- IBM PC under DOS and Windows using NAG/Salford Fortran 90.

- Sun UltraSparc under Solaris using NAGWare F90.

- Sun UltraSparc under Solaris using NAGACE F90.

- Sun UltraSparc under Solaris using NAGWare F95.

- Sun UltraSparc under Solaris using Sun F90.

We are the current owners of the Fortran 90 list, and quoting the introduction '*This list covers all aspects of Fortran 90 and HPF, the new standard(s) for Fortran. The emphasis should be on the *new* features of Fortran 90. It welcomes contributions from people who write Fortran 90 applications, teach it in courses, want to port programs and use it on (super)computers.*'

Visit:

- http://www.mailbase.ac.uk/lists-a-e/comp-fortran-90/

for more information.

Our home page is:

- http://www.kcl.ac.uk/kis/support/cc/fortran/f90home.html

All of the program examples can be found there.

Ian D Chivers: ian.chivers@kcl.ac.uk

Jane Sleightholme: jane.sleightholme@kcl.ac.uk

2

Introduction to Computer Systems

'Don't Panic.'

Douglas Adams, *The Hitch Hiker's Guide to the Galaxy*

Aims

The aims of this chapter are to introduce the following:

- The components of a computer – the hardware.

- The components of a complete computer system – the other devices that you need to do useful work with a computer.

- The software needed to make the hardware do what you want.

2   Introduction to Computer Systems

A computer is an electronic device, and can be thought of as a tool, like the lever or the wheel, which can be made to do useful work. At the fundamental level it works with *bits* (binary digits or sequences of zeros and ones). Bits are generally put together in larger configurations, e.g. 8, 16, 32, or 64. Hence computers are often referred to as 8-bit, 16-bit, 32-bit, or 64-bit machines.

2.1   The core of a computer system

The heart of most computer systems will comprise a motherboard, CPU, memory, one or more busses and a power supply. We will look at the CPU, memory and bus in more depth below.

2.1.1   Central Processor Unit – CPU

This is the brains of the computer. All of the work that the computer does is organized here.

2.1.2   Memory

The computer will also have a memory. Memory on a computer is a solid state device that comprises an ordered collection of bits/bytes/words that can be read or written by the CPU. A byte is generally 8 bits (as in *8-bit byte*), and a word is most commonly accepted as the minimum number of bits that can be referenced by the CPU. This referencing is called *addressing*. The memory typically contains programs and data.

The two most common word sizes are 32 and 64 bit.

A computer memory is often called random access memory, or RAM. This simply means that the access time for any part of memory is the same; in order to examine location (say) 97, it is not necessary to first look through locations 1 to 96. It is possible to go directly to location 97. A slightly better term might have been *access at random*. The memory itself is highly ordered.

2.1.3   Bus

A *bus* is a set of connections between the CPU and other components. The bus will be used for a variety of purposes. These include address signals which tell the memory which words are wanted next; data lines which are used to transfer data to and from memory, and to and from other parts of the computer system. This is typical of many systems, but systems do vary considerably; while the information above may not be true in specific cases, it provides a general model.

2.2 Other components of a computer system

So far the computer we have described is not sufficiently versatile. We have to add on other pieces of electronics to make it really useful.

2.2.1 Disks

These are devices for storing collections of *bits*, which are inevitably organized in reality into bytes and files. One advantage of adding these to our computer system is that we can switch the machine off, go away and come back at a later time and continue with what we were doing.

Memory is expensive and fast whereas disks are slower but cheaper. Most computer systems balance speed against cost, and have a small memory in relation to disk capacity.

Most people would be familiar with the two main type of disks on personal computers (PCs) or microcomputers, and these are floppy disks and hard disks. Floppy disks now come in one main physical size, 3 1/2 inch, and smaller sizes are also used. Hard disks are inside the system, and most people do not see this type of disk.

CD-ROM drives are an essential part of present day systems. They exist in a variety of flavours including simple read only CD, rewriteable CD and DVD forms.

2.2.2 Others

There are a large number of other input and output devices. These vary considerably from system to system depending on the work being carried out. These include:

- Network or ethernet cards for access to local and wide area networks.
- Modems for access from home, mainly to the internet.
- Printers of a variety of types.
- Colour plotters.
- Photo-typesetters.
- Pens.
- Sound interfaces, both for speech recognition and sound production.
- Scanners.
- Digital cameras.
- Joy sticks.
- Zip drives.

Figure 1 shows a simple model of the above for a pc.

Figure 1 Simple model of a PC.

The most important I/O devices are the keyboard and screen, whether you use a terminal, PC or workstation. This book has been written assuming that most of your work will be done at one of these devices.

Terminals fall into two categories, character based devices (and the DEC VT series is a very popular one) and graphical devices (and the X-Windows terminals are the most popular). Terminal access to remote systems is often provided on PCs using terminal emulation software, e.g. Telnet, WinQVT and X-Windows access to Unix systems via software like Vista Exceed.

PCs provide the opportunity of cheap and powerful desktop computing facilities, where the processing is done locally.

Workstations are more powerful than microcomputers but this division is becoming rather blurred with the recent generations of processors. Screens on these devices are graphically oriented. Access to these systems is via a graphical or windows interface.

This means that the device we use looks rather like an ordinary typewriter key-board, although some of the keys are different. However, the location of the letters, numbers and common symbols is fairly standard. Don't panic if you have never met a keyboard before. You don't have to know much more than where the keys are. Few programmers, even professionals, advance beyond the stage of using two index fingers and a thumb for their typing. You will find that speed of typing is rarely important, it's accuracy that counts.

One thing that people unfamiliar with keyboards often fail to realise is that what you have typed in is not sent to the computer until you press the *carriage return* key. To achieve any sort of communication you must press that key; it will be somewhere on the right hand side of the keyboard, and will be marked *return, c/r, send, enter*, or something similar.

2.3 Software

So far we have not mentioned software. Software is the name given to the programs that *run* on the hardware. Programs are written in *languages*. Computer languages are frequently divided into two categories; *high-level* and *low-level*. A low level language (e.g. assembler) is closer to the hardware, while a high level language (e.g. Fortran) is closer to the problem statement. There is typically a one to one correspondence between an assembly language statement and the actual hardware instruction. With a high level language there is a one to many correspondence; one high level statement will generate many machine level instructions.

A certain amount of general purpose software will have been provided by the manufacturer. This software will typically include the basic operating system, one or more *compilers*, an *assembler*, an *editor*, and a *loader* or *link editor*.

- A *compiler* translates high level statements into machine instructions.

- An *assembler* translates low level or assembly language statements into machine instructions.

- An *editor* makes changes to text files, e.g. program sources.

- A *loader* or *link editor* takes the output from the compiler and completes the process of generating something that can be executed on the hardware.

These programs will vary considerably in size and complexity. Certain programs that make up the operating system will be quite simple and small (like copying utilities), while certain others will be relatively large and complex (like a compiler).

In this book we concentrate on software or programs that you write for your research work or course work. As the book progresses you will be introduced to ways of building on what other people have written, and how to take advantage of the vast amount of software already written, tested and documented.

2.4   Problems

1. Distinguish between a memory address and memory contents.

2. What does RAM stand for?

3. What would a WOM (write only memory) do? How would you use it?

4. What does CPU stand for? What does it do?

5 What does a compiler do?

6 What does a linker do?

2.5   Bibliography

Baer J.L., *Computer Systems Architecture*, Computer Science Press.

> Extremely readable coverage of this whole area. The version could do with an update, but it is still a very impressive coverage. Highly recommended.

Bhandarkar D.P., *Alpha Implementation and Architecture: Complete Reference and Guide*, Digital Press, 1996.

> Excellent source of information on the Alpha architecture.

Intel, *i486 Microprocessor Hardware Reference Manual,* Intel, 1990.

> Most if not all processor manufacturers provide publications that describe their hardware. Intel are no exception. This is one of the last paper publications on the i86 family of processors.
>
> Intel currently make a lot of material available on their web site. Two useful URLs are:
>
> - http://www.intel.com/
>
> and
>
> - http://developer.intel.com/
>
> Well worth a look. Many publications are available in Adobe Acrobat Portable Document Format – PDF.

Reeves C.M., *An Introduction to Logical Design of Digital Circuits*, CUP, 1972.

> This book provides coverage of the construction of the very simple electronic building blocks, from which most modern computer systems are made of. Relatively theoretical.

Tannenbaum A.S., *Structured Computer Organisation*, Prentice Hall, 1976.

> Very good coverage looking at a computer system in terms of a hierarchy of levels. An easy read.

3

Introduction to Operating Systems

'Where shall I begin your Majesty' he asked.
'Begin at the beginning,' the King said, graveley 'and go
on till you come to the end then stop.'

Lewis Carroll, *Alice's Adventures in Wonderland*.

Aims

The aims of this chapter are to introduce the following:

- To provide a brief history of operating system development.
- To look briefly at some commonly used operating systems
  - DOS and Windows.
  - Unix and X-Windows.
  - VMS and Open VMS.

3   Introduction to Operating Systems

A simple definition of an operating system is the suite of programs that make the hardware usable. Most computer systems provide one. They vary considerably from those available on early microcomputers, like CP/M, to DOS and the various versions of Microsoft Windows on PCs, UNIX and X-Windows on workstations and supercomputers.

From the designer's point of view they are mainly resource manages. They allow management of the CPU, disks and I/O devices. They have to provide a user interface for computer operators, professional programmers (whether systems or applications), administrators of the system, and finally the casual end user. As can be imagined, these groups have different functional requirements. It is therefore useful to look at the development of operating systems, and see a shift from satisfying the requirements of the professional to satisfying the requirements of the casual end user.

3.1   History of operating systems

3.1.1   The 1940s

Early computer systems had no operating systems in the modern sense of the word. An early commercially available machine was the IBM 604. This machine could undertake some 60 program steps before using punch cards as backing store. The end user had intimate knowledge of the machine and programmed at a very low level.

3.1.2   The 1950s

This era saw a rapid change in the capabilities of operating systems. They were designed to make efficient use of an expensive resource. Jobs were *batched* so that the time between jobs was minimized. The end user was now distanced from the machine. This era saw rapid development in program language design and a notable end to the period was the design of Algol 60.

3.1.3   The 1960s

The next milestone was the introduction of multiprogramming. Probably initially seen as a way of making efficient use of hardware it heralded the idea of time sharing. A time sharing systems is characterized by the conversational nature of the interaction, and the use of a keyboard. This had a tremendous impact on the range of uses that a computer system had and on the program development process.

3.1.4   The 1960s and 1970s

The realization that computer systems could be used in a large range of human activities saw the development of large general purpose systems, and probably the most famous of these was the IBM 360 series. These systems were some of the most complex programming endeavours undertaken, and most projects were late and well over budget. These costly mistakes helped lead to the establishment of software engineering as a discipline.

The contribution of the time sharing system to program development was quickly realized to be considerable. A system that was developed during this period was UNIX – and this operating system has a very sharp set of tools to aid in program development.

3.1.5 The 1970s, 1980s and 1990s

The 70s represented a period of relative stability with newer and more complex versions of existing systems.

During this period the importance of graphical interfaces emerged and with dropping hardware costs graphical interfaces started to dominate.

The Apple Macintosh heralded a new era and became a popular choice for many people. At the same time graphical interfaces were being added to existing major operating systems, with X-Windows and associated higher level systems hiding raw UNIX from many users, and Microsoft Windows on the Intel family of processors.

Linux (a free Unix variant) is popular in the scientific field, and an alternative to DOS and Windows on the Intel family of processors.

3.2 Networking

Networking simplistically is a way of connecting two or more computer systems, and networking computer systems is not new one of the first was the SAGE military network, funded by the US DoD in the 1950s.

Networking capability has undergone a massive increase during the computer age. Local networks of two or three systems, through tens of systems in small research groups and organizations are now extremely common place. It is not uncommon now to have in excess of a thousand network connected devices on one local area network.

Wide area networking is also quite common, and most major organizations now have networks spanning a country or even the whole world.

One of the most widely used wide area networks in the academic and scientific world is the Internet, and there are over thirty million systems on the Internet at the time of writing this book.

A number of books on networking are included in the bibliography.

3.3   Problems

1. What type of system do you use, i.e. is it a stand alone microcomputer, terminal, workstation etc?

2. Is it networked, and if so in what way?

3. Is wide area networking available?

4. Is a graphical interface available?

3.4   Bibliography

Brooks F.P., *The Mythical Man Month: Essays on Software Engineering,* Addison Wesley, 1982.

> A very telling coverage of the development of the operating system for the IBM 360 series of systems. A must for any one involved in the longer term in program development.

Deitel H.M., *An Introduction to Operating Systems*, Addison Wesley, 1984.

> One of the most accessible books on operating systems with coverage of process management, storage management, processor management, auxiliary storage management, performance, networks and security, with case studies of the major players including UNIX, VMS, CP/M, MVS, VM, DOS and Windows.

Feit S., *TCP/IP, Architecture, Protocols, and Implementation,* McGraw Hill.

> A more technical book than Kroll, well written with a wealth of information for the more inquisitive reader.

Kroll E., *The Whole Internet User's Guide and Catalog,* O'Reilly, 1994.

> **The** Internet book. Written with very obvious enthusiasm by Mister Internet himself!

4

Introduction to Using a Computer System

'Maybe one day we will be glad to remember even these things.'

Virgil

Aims

The aims of this chapter are to introduce some of the fundamentals of using a computer system including:

- Files.

- Editors.

- Systems access and networking.

4 Introduction to Using a Computer System

There are a number of concepts that underpin your use of any computing system. Sitting at a high resolution colour screen with a myriad of icons this may not be immediately apparent, but developing an appreciation of this will help considerably in the long term, and when inevitably moving from one system to another.

4.1 Files

A file is a collection of information that you refer to by name, e.g. if you were to use a word processor to prepare a letter then the letter would exist independently as a file on that system, generally on a disk. With graphical interfaces there will be a systematic iconic representation of files.

There will be many ways of manipulating files on the operating system that you work on. You will use an editor to make changes to a file. This file might be the source of a program and you could then use a compiler to compile your program. The compiler will generate a number of files, some of interest to you, others for its own use. There will be commands in the operating system to make copies of files, back files up onto a variety of media, etc.

4.2 Editors

All general purpose computer systems have at least one editor so that you can modify programs and data. Screen editors are by far the easiest to use, with changes you make to the file being immediately visible on the screen in front of you.

Some editors will have sophisticated command modes of operation with pattern matching allowing very powerful text processing capabilities. These can automate many common tasks, taking away the manual, repetitive drudgery of screen based editing.

4.3 Single user systems

These are becoming increasingly common, in use both at work and in the home. The IBM PC and compatibles is a very popular choice in the scientific community. They offer ease of use and access to a considerable amount of raw processing power for computer intensive applications.

4.4 Networked systems

It is quite common to interconnect the above to local and wide area networks. This same network would also have file servers, printers, plotters, mail gateways etc. Both authors have PCs with modems at home and have access via the telephone to the Internet.

Workstations are generally networked in an environment like the above, providing very powerful processing capability.

4.5 Multi-user systems

One step above microcomputers and workstations are multi-user systems. The dividing line between microcomputers, individual workstations and multi-user systems is rapidly becoming blurred.

Multi-user systems, especially the larger ones, are very popular as they take away from the casual end user much of the drudgery of the day to day tasks of backing up disks, installing new versions of the software, locating and fixing problems with software that doesn't work quite as it should, etc to a system manager or operator.

Here we find one person with the role of registering new users, backing up the file system, sorting out printer problems, networking problems, etc. This also means that all of the users of the system do not have to remember rather arcane and sometimes rather magical commands! They can get on with solving their actual problem.

4.6 Other useful things to know

You will soon need to know what files you are working with and there will be commands to do this. There will be a need to get rid of files and there will be commands to achieve this.

There will be ways of getting on-line help, and *help* as a command is (for once!) used by a variety of operating systems. On UNIX systems the rather more unintelligible *man* command is available.

There will be commands to print program listings and data files

With networked and multiuser systems there will be commands to send and receive electronic mail to/from other users. It is easy to send and reply to mail from people across the world, often in hours and even minutes. Table 4.1 has examples of some common operating system commands in DOS, UNIX and VMS.

Operating System and Command	DOS	UNIX	VMS
What files are there	dir	ls	dir
Get rid of a file	del	rm	del
Copy a file	copy	cp	copy
Display a file on the screen	type	cat	type
Print a file	print	pr	print
Create or make changes to a file	edit	ed	edit
		vi	edit/tpu
Make a sub-directory	mkdir, md	md	create/dir
Change to another directory	chdir, cd	cd	set default

Table 4.1 Common operating system commands.

4.7   Bibliography

The main source here are the manuals and documentation provided by the supplier of whatever system you use. These are increasingly of a very high standard. However they are inevitably written to highlight the positive and downplay the negative aspects of the systems. The next source are the many third party books written and widely available throughout the world. These vary considerably in price from basic introductory coverages to very comprehensive reference works. These are a very good complement to the first. The following url is a very good source of UNIX information.

http://unixhelp.ed.ac.uk/

Gilly D., *UNIX in a Nutshell,* O'Reilly and Associates, 1992.

A very good quick reference guide. Assumes some familiarity with UNIX. Current edition (at the time of writing this book) was System V Release IV, with Solaris 2.0. Also provides coverage of the various shells, Bourne, Korn and C.

Microsoft, *Windows User's Guide*, Microsoft Press.

Good coverage of Windows and suitable for the beginner and intermediate level user. Sufficient for most users. A massive improvement over earlier versions.

Introduction to Problem Solving

They constructed ladders to reach to the top of the enemy's wall, and they did this by calculating the height of the wall from the number of layers of bricks at a point which was facing in their direction and had not been plastered. The layers were counted by a lot of people at the same time, and though some were likely to get the figure wrong the majority would get it right... Thus, guessing what the thickness of a single brick was, they calculated how long their ladder would have to be.

Thucydides, *The Peloponnesian War*

'When I use a word,' Humpty Dumpty said, in a rather scornful tone, 'it means just what I choose it to mean - neither more nor less'
'The question is,' said Alice, 'whether you can make words mean so many different things.'

Lewis Carroll, *Through the Looking Glass and What Alice Found There.*

Aims

The aims are:

- To examine some of the ideas and concepts involved in problem solving.

- To introduce the concept of an algorithm.

- To introduce two ways of approaching algorithmic problem solving.

- To introduce the ideas involved with systems analysis and design, i.e. to show the need for pencil and paper study before using a computer system.

5 Introduction to Problem Solving

It is informative to consider some of the dictionary definitions of problem:

- A matter difficult of settlement or solution, *Chambers*.
- A question or puzzle propounded for solution, *Chambers*.
- A source of perplexity, *Chambers*.
- Doubtful or difficult question, *Oxford*.
- Proposition in which something has to be done, *Oxford*.
- A question raised for enquiry, consideration, or solution, *Webster's*.
- An intricate unsettled question, *Webster's*.

and a common thread seems to be a question that we would like answered or solved. So one of the first things to consider in problem solving is how to pose the problem. This is often not as easy as is seems. Two of the most common methods are:

- In natural language.
- An artificial language or stylized language.

Both methods have their advantages and disadvantages.

5.1 Natural language

Most people use natural language and are familiar with it, and the two most common forms are the written and spoken word. Consider the following language usage:

- The difference between a three year old child and an adult describing the world.
- The difference between the way an engineer and a physicist would approach the design of a car engine.
- The difference between a manager and worker considering the implications of the introduction of new technology.

Great care must be taken when using natural language to define a problem and a solution. It is possible that people use the same language to mean completely different things, and one must be aware of this when using natural language whilst problem solving.

Natural language can also be ambiguous:

Old men and women eat cheese.

Are both the men and women old?

5.2 Artificial language

The two most common forms of artificial language are technical terminology and notations. Technical terminology generally includes both the use of new words and alternate use of existing words. Consider some of the concepts that are useful when examining the expansion of gases in both a theoretical and practical fashion:

- Temperature.
- Pressure.
- Mass.
- Isothermal expansion.
- Adiabatic expansion.

Now look at the following:

- A chef using a pressure cooker.
- A garage mechanic working on a car engine.
- A doctor monitoring blood pressure.
- An engineer designing a gas turbine.

Each has a particular problem to solve, and each will approach their problem in their own way; thus they will each use the same terminology in slightly different ways.

5.2.1 Notations

Some examples of notations are:

- Algebra.
- Calculus.
- Logic.

All of the above have been used as notations for describing both problems and their solutions.

5.3 Resumé

We therefore have two ways of describing problems and they both have a learning phase until we achieve sufficient understanding to use them effectively. Having arrived at a satisfactory problem statement we next have to consider how we get the solution. It is here that the power of the algorithmic approach becomes useful.

5.4   Algorithms

An algorithm is a sequence of steps that will solve part or all of a problem. One of the most easily understood examples of an algorithm is a recipe. Most people have done some cooking, if only making toast and boiling an egg.

A recipe is made up of two parts:

- A check list of things you need.

- The sequence or order of steps.

Problems can occur at both stages, e.g. finding out halfway through the recipe that you do not have an ingredient or utensil; finding out that one stage will take an hour when the rest will be ready in ten minutes. Note that certain things can be done in any order – it may not make any difference if you prepare the potatoes before the carrots.

There are two ways of approaching problem solving when using a computer. They both involve *algorithms*, but are very different from one another. They are called *top-down* and *bottom-up*.

5.4.1   Top-down

In a *top down* approach the problem is first specified at a high or general level: prepare a meal. It is then refined until each step in the solution is explicit and in the correct sequence, e.g. peel and slice the onions, then brown in a frying pan before adding the beef. One drawback to this approach is that it is very difficult to teach to beginners because they rarely have any idea of what *primitive* tools they have at their disposal. Another drawback is that they often get the sequencing wrong, e.g. *now place in a moderately hot oven* is frustrating because you may have not lit the oven (sequencing problem) and secondly because you may have no idea how hot *moderately hot* really is. However as more and more problems are tackled top-down becomes one of the most effective methods for programming.

5.4.2   Bottom-up

Bottom-up is the reverse to top-down! As before you start by defining the problem at a high level, e.g. prepare a meal. However, now there is an examination of what tools, etc. you have available to solve the problem. This method lends itself to teaching since a repertoire of tools can be built up and more complicated problems can be tackled. Thinking back to the recipe there is not much point trying to cook a six course meal if the only thing that you can do is boil an egg and open a tin of beans. The bottom-up approach thus has advantages for the beginner. However there may be a problem when no suitable tool is available. One of the authors' colleague and friend learned how to make Bechamel sauce, and was so pleased by his success that every other meal had a course with a Bechamel sauce. Try it on your eggs one morning. Here was a case of specifying a problem *prepare a meal,* and using an inappropriate but plausible tool *Bechamel sauce.*

The effort involved in tackling a realistic problem, introducing the constructs as and when they are needed and solving it is considerable. This approach may not lead to a reasonably comprehensive coverage of the language, or be particularly useful from a teaching point of view. Case studies do have great value, but it helps if you know the elementary rules before you start on them. Imagine learning French by studying Balzac, before you even look at a French grammar. You can learn this way but even when you have finished, you may not be able to speak to a Frenchman and be understood. A good example of the case study approach is given in the book *Software Tools*, by Kernighan and Plauger.

In this book our aim is to gradually introduce more and more tools until you know enough to approach the problem using the top-down method, and also realize from time to time that it will be necessary to develop some new tools.

5.4.3 Stepwise refinement

Both the above techniques can be combined with what is called *step-wise refinement.* The original ideas behind this technique are well expressed in a paper by Wirth entitled *Program Development by Stepwise Refinement,* published in 1971. This means that you start with a global problem statement and break the problem down in stages, into smaller and smaller sub-problems, that become more and more amenable to solution. When you first start programming the problems you can solve are quite simple, but as your experience grows you will find that you can handle more complex problems.

When you think of the way that you solve problems you will probably realize that, unless the problem is so simple that you can answer it straight away some thinking and pencil and paper work is required. An example that some may be familiar with is in practical work in a scientific discipline, where coming unprepared to the situation can be very frustrating and unrewarding. It is therefore appropriate to look at ways of doing analysis and design before using a computer.

5.4.4 Modular programming

As the problems we try solving become more complex we need to look at ways of managing the construction of programs that comprise many parts. Modula 2 was one of the first languages to support this methodology and we will look at modular programming in more depth in the subsequent chapter.

5.4.5   Object oriented programming

There are a class of problems that are best solved by the treatment of the components of these problems as objects. We will look at the concepts involved in object oriented programming and object oriented languages in the next chapter.

5.5   Systems analysis and design

When one starts programming it is generally not apparent that one needs a methodology to follow to become successful as a programmer. This is generally because the problems are reasonably simple, and it is not necessary to make explicit all of the stages one has gone through in arriving at a solution. As the problems become more complex it is necessary to become more rigorous and thorough in one's approach, to keep control in the face of the increasing complexity and to avoid making mistakes. It is then that the benefit of systems analysis and design becomes obvious. Broadly we have the following stages in systems analysis and design:

- Problem definition.

- Feasibility study and fact finding.

- Analysis.

- Initial system design.

- Detailed design.

- Implementation.

- Evaluation.

- Maintenance.

and each problem we address will entail slightly different time spent in each of these stages. Let us look at each stage in more detail.

5.5.1   Problem definition

Here we are interested in defining what the problem really is. We should aim at providing some restriction on both the scope of the problem, and the objectives we set ourselves. We can use the methods mentioned earlier to help out. It is essential that the objectives are:

- Clearly defined.

- When more than one person is involved, understood by all people concerned, and agreed by all people concerned.

- Realistic.

5.5.2 Feasibility study and fact finding

Here we look to see if there is a feasible solution. We would try and estimate the cost of solving the problem and see if the investment was warranted by the benefits, i.e. cost benefit analysis.

5.5.3 Analysis

Here we look at what must be done to solve the problem. Note we are interested in finding what we need to do, but we do not actually do it at this stage.

5.5.4 Design

Once the analysis is complete we know what must be done, and we can proceed to the design. We may find there are several alternatives, and we thus examine alternate ways in which the problem can be solved. It is here that we use the techniques of top-down and bottom-up problem solving, combined with step-wise refinement to generate an algorithm to solve the problem. We are now moving from the logical to the physical side of the solution. This stage ends with a choice between one of several alternatives. Note that there is generally not one ideal solution, but several, each with their own advantages and disadvantages.

5.5.5 Detailed design

Here we move from the general to the specific, The end result of this stage should be a sufficiently tightly defined specification to generate actual program code from.

It is at this stage that it is useful to generate *pseudo-code*. This means writing out in detail the actions we want carried out at each stage of our overall algorithm. We gradually expand each stage (step-wise refinement) until it becomes Fortran – or whatever language we want in fact.

5.5.6 Implementation

It is at this stage that we actually use a computer system to create the program(s) that will solve the problem. It is here that we actually need to know sufficient about a programming language to use it effectively to solve our problems. This is only one stage in the overall process, and mistakes at any of the stages can create severe difficulties.

5.5.7 Evaluation and testing

Here we try to see if the program(s) we have produced actually do what they are supposed to. We need to have data sets that enable us to say with confidence that the program really does work. This may not be an easy task, as quite often we only have numeric methods to solve the problem, which is why we are using the computer to solve the problem – hence we are relying on the computer to provide the proof; i.e. we have to use a computer to determine the veracity of the programs – and as Heller says *Catch 22*.

5.5.8   Maintenance

It is rare that a program is run once and thrown away. This means that there will be an on-going task of maintaining the program, generally to make it work with different versions of the operating system, compiler, and to incorporate new features not included in the original design. It often seems odd when one starts programming that a program will need maintenance as we are reluctant to regard a program in the same way as a mechanical object like a car that will eventually fall apart through use. Thus maintenance means keeping the program working at some tolerable level, with often a high level of investment in manpower and resources. Research in this area has shown that anything up to 80% of the manpower investment in a program can be in maintenance.

5.6   Conclusions

A drawback, inherent in all approaches to programming, and to problem solving in general, is the assumption that a solution is indeed possible. There are problems which are simply insoluble – not only problems like balancing a national budget, weather forecasting for a year, or predicting which radioactive atom will decay, but also problems which are apparently computationally solvable.

Knuth gives the example of a chess problem – determining whether the game is a forced victory for white. Although there is an algorithm to achieve this, it requires an inordinately large amount of time to complete. For practical purposes it is unsolvable.

Other problems can be shown mathematically to be undecidable. The work of Gödel in this area has been of enormous importance, and the bibliography contains a number of references for the more inquisitive and mathematically orientated reader. The Hofstader coverage is the easiest, and least mathematical.

As far as possible we will restrict ourselves to solvable problems, like learning a programming language.

Within the formal world of Computer Science our description of an algorithm would be considered a little lax. For our introductory needs it is sufficient, but a more rigorous approach is given by Hopcroft and Ullman in *Introduction to Automata Theory, Languages and Computation*, and by Beckman in *Mathematical Foundations of Programming*.

5.7   Problems

1. What is an algorithm?

2. What distinguishes top-down from bottom-up approaches to problem solving? Illustrate your answer with reference to the problem of a car, motor-cycle or bicycle having a flat tire.

5.8 Bibliography

Aho A.V., Hopcroft J.E., Ullman J.D., *The Design and Analysis of Computer Algorithms*, Addison Wesley, 1982.

Theoretical coverage of the design and analysis of computer algorithms.

Beckman F.S., *Mathematical Foundations of Programming*, Addison Wesley, 1981

Good clear coverage of the theoretical basis of computing.

Bulloff J.J., Holyoke T.C., Hahn S.W., *Foundations of Mathematics – Symposium Papers Commemorating the 60th Birthday of Kurt Gödel*, Springer Verlag, 1969.

The comment by John von Neumann highlights the importance of Gödel's work, .. *Kurt Gödel's achievement in modern logic is singular and monumental – indeed it is more than a monument, it is a landmark which will remain visible far in space and time. Whether anything comparable to it has occurred in the logic of modern times may be debated. In any case, the conceivable proxima are very, very few. The subject of logic has certainly changed its nature and possibilities with Gödel's achievement.*

Dahl O.J., Dijkstra E.W., Hoare C.A.R., *Structured Programming*, Academic Press, 1972.

This is the seminal book on structured programming.

Davis M., *Computability and Unsolvability*, Dover, 1982.

The book is an introduction to the theory of computability and non-computability – the theory of recursive functions in mathematics. Not for the mathematically faint hearted!

Davis W.S., *Systems Analysis and Design*, Addison Wesley, 1983.

Good introduction to systems analysis and design, with a variety of case studies. Also looks at some of the tools available to the systems analyst.

Fogelin R.J., *Wittgenstein*, Routledge and Kegan Paul, 1980.

The book provides a gentle introduction to the work of the philosopher Wittgenstein, who examined some of the philosophical problems associated with logic and reason.

Gödel K., *On Formally Undecidable Propositions of Principia Mathematica and Related Systems*, Oliver and Boyd, 1962.

An English translation of Gödel's original paper by Meltzer, with quite a lengthy introduction by R.B. Braithwaite, then Knightbridge Professor of Moral

Philosophy at Cambridge University, England, and classified under philosophy at the library at King's, rather than mathematics.

Hofstadter D.,*The Eternal Golden Braid*, Harvester Press, 1979.

A very readable coverage of paradox and contradiction in art, music and logic, looking at the work of Escher, Bach and Gödel respectively.

Hopcroft J.E., Ullman J.D., *Introduction to Automata Theory, Languages and Computation*, Addison Wesley, 1979.

Comprehensive coverage of the theoretical basis of computing.

Kernighan B.W., Plauger P.J., *Software Tools,* Addison Wesley, 1976.

Interesting essays on the program development process, originally using a non-standard variant of Fortran. Also available using Pascal.

Knuth D.E., *The Art of Computer Programming*, Addison Wesley,

Vol 1. *Fundamental Algorithms*, 1974

Vol 2. *Semi-numerical Algorithms*, 1978

Vol 3. *Sorting and Searching*, 1972

Contains interesting insights into many aspects of algorithm design. Good source of specialist algorithms, and Knuth writes with obvious and infectious enthusiasm (and erudition).

Millington D., *Systems Analysis and Design for Computer Applications*, Ellis Horwood, 1981.

Short and readable introduction to systems analysis and design.

Wirth N., *Program Development by Stepwise Refinement*, Communications of the ACM, April 1971, Volume 14, Number 4, pp. 221-227.

Clear and simple exposition of the ideas of stepwise refinement.

6

Introduction to Programming Languages

'We have to go to another language in order to think clearly about the problem.'

Samuel R. Delany, *Babel-17*

Aims

The primary aim of this chapter is to provide a short history of program language development and provide some idea as to the concepts that have had an impact on Fortran 95. It concentrates on some but not all of the major milestones of the last 40 years, in rough chronological order. The secondary aim is to show the breadth of languages available. The chapter concludes with coverage of a small number of more specialized languages.

6 Introduction to Programming Languages

It is important to realize that programming languages are a recent invention. They have been developed over a relatively short period – 45 years – and are still undergoing improvement. Time spent gaining some historical perspective will help you understand and evaluate future changes. This chapter starts right at the beginning and takes you through some, but not all, of the developments during this 45 year span. The bulk of the chapter restricts itself to languages that are reasonably widely available commercially, and therefore ones that you are likely to meet. The chapter concludes with a coverage of some more specialized and/or recent developments.

6.1 Some early theoretical work

Some of the most important early theoretical work in computing was that of *Turing* and *von Neumann*. Turing's work provided the base from which it could be shown that it was possible to get a machine to solve problems. The work of von Neumann added the concept of storage and combined with Turing's work to provide the basis of most computers designed to this day.

6.2 What is a programming language ?

For a large number of people a programming language provides the means of getting a digital computer to solve a problem. There are a wide range of problems, and an equally wide range of programming languages, with particular programming languages being suited to a particular class of problems. Thus there are a wide variety of programming languages, which often appears bewildering to the beginner.

6.3 Program language development and engineering

There is much in common between the development of programming languages and the development of anything from the engineering world. Consider the car: old cars offer much of the same functionality as modern ones, but most people prefer driving newer ones. The same is true of programming languages, where you can achieve much with the older languages, but the newer ones are easier to use.

6.4 The early days

A concept that proves very useful when discussing programming languages is that of the level of a machine. By this is meant how close a language is to the underlying machine that the program *runs* on. In the early days of programming (up to 1954) there were only two broad categories, machine languages and assemblers. The language that a digital machine uses is that of 0 and 1, i.e. they are binary devices. Writing a program in terms of patterns of 0 and 1 was not particularly satisfactory and the capability of using more meaningful mnemonics was soon introduced. Thus it was realized quite quickly that one of the most important aspects of programming languages is that they have to be read and understood by *both* machines and humans.

6.4.1 Fortran

The next stage was the development of higher level languages. The first of these was *Fortran* and it was developed over a three year period from 1954 to 1957 by an IBM team led by John Backus. This group achieved considerable success, and helped to prove that the way forward lay with high level languages for computer based problem solving. Fortran stands for *for*mula *trans*lation and was used mainly by people with a scientific background for solving problems that had a significant arithmetic content. It was thus relatively easy, for the time, to express this kind of problem in Fortran.

By 1966 and the first standard Fortran was:

- Widely available.

- Easy to teach.

- Had demonstrated the benefits of subroutines and independent compilation.

- Was relatively machine independent.

- Often had very efficient implementations.

Possibly the single most important fact about Fortran was and still is its widespread usage in the scientific community.

6.4.2 Cobol

The business world also realised that computers were useful and several languages were developed including FLOWMATIC, AIMACO, Commercial Translator and FACT, leading eventually to Cobol – *Common Business Orientated Language*. There is a need in commercial programming to describe data in a much more complex fashion than for scientific programming, and thus Cobol had far greater capability in this area than Fortran. The language was unique at the time in that a group of competitors worked together with the objective of developing a language that would be useful on machines used by other manufacturers.

The contributions made by Cobol include:

- Firstly the separation between:
  - The task to be undertaken.
  - The description of the data involved.
  - The working environment in which the task is carried out.

- Secondly a data description mechanism that was largely machine independent.

- Thirdly its effectiveness for handling large files.

- Fourthly the benefit to be gained from a programming language that was easy to read.

Modern developments in computing, of report generators, file handling software, fourth generation development tools, and especially the increasing availability of commercial relational database management systems are gradually replacing the use of Cobol, except where high efficiency and or tight control are required.

6.4.3   Algol

Another important development of the 1950s was Algol. It had a history of development from Algol 58, the original Algol language, through Algol 60 eventually to the Revised Algol 60 Report. Some of the design criteria for Algol 58 were:

- The language should be as close as possible to standard mathematical notation and should be *readable* with little further explanation.

- It should be possible to use it for the description of computing processes in publications.

- The new language should be mechanically translatable into machine programs.

A sad feature of Algol 58 was the lack of any input/output facilities, and this meant that different implementations often had incompatible features in this area.

The next important step for Algol occurred at a UNESCO sponsored conference in June 1959. There was an open discussion on Algol and the outcome of this was Algol 60, and eventually the Revised Algol 60 Report.

It was at this conference that John Backus gave his now famous paper on a method for defining the syntax of a language, called Backus Normal Form, or BNF. The full significance of the paper by Backus was not immediately recognized. However BNF was to prove of enormous value in language definition, and helped provide an interface point with computational linguistics.

The contributions of Algol to program language development include:

- Block structure.

- Scope rules for variables because of block structure.

- The BNF definition by Backus – most languages now have a formal definition.

- The support of recursion.

- Its offspring.

and thus Algol was to prove to make a contribution to programming languages that was never reflected in the use of Algol 60 itself, in that it has been the parent of one of the main strands of program language development.

6.5 Chomsky and program language development

Programming languages are of considerable linguistic interest, and the work of Chomsky in 1956 in this area was to prove of inestimable value. Chomsky's system of transformational grammar was developed in order to give a precise mathematical description to certain aspects of language. Simplistically Chomsky describes grammars and these grammars in turn can be used to define or generate corresponding kinds of languages. It can be shown that for each type of grammar and language there is a corresponding type of machine. It was quickly realized that there was a link with the earlier work of Turing.

This link helped provide a firm scientific base for programming language development, and modern compiler writing has come a long way from the early work of Backus and his team at IBM. It may seem unimportant when playing a video game at home or in an arcade, but for some it is very comforting that there is a firm theoretical basis behind all that fun.

6.6 Lisp

There were developments in very specialized areas also. List processing was proving to be of great interest in the 50s and saw the development of IPLV between 1954 and 1958. This in turn lead to the development of Lisp at the end of the 50s. It has proved to be of considerable use for programming in the areas of artificial intelligence, playing chess, automatic theorem proving and general problem solving. It was one of the first languages to be interpreted rather than compiled. Whilst interpreted languages are invariably slower and less efficient in their use of the underlying computer systems than compiled languages, they do provide great opportunities for the user to explore and try out ideas whilst sat at a terminal. The power that this gives to the computational problem solver is considerable.

Possibly the greatest contribution to program language development made by Lisp was its functional notation. One of the major problems for the Lisp user has been the large number of Lisp flavours, and this has reduced the impact that the language has had and deserved.

6.7   Snobol

Snobol was developed to aid in string processing which was seen as an important part of many computing tasks, e.g. parsing of a program. Probably the most important thing that Snobol demonstrated was the power of pattern matching in a programming language, e.g. it is possible to define a pattern for a title that would include Mr, Mrs, Miss, Rev, etc. and search for this pattern in a text using Snobol. Like Lisp it is generally available as an interpreter rather than a compiler, but compiled versions do exist, and are often called Spitbol. Pattern matching capabilities are now to be found in many editors and this makes them very powerful and useful tools. It is in the area of text manipulation that Snobol's greatest contribution to program language development lies.

6.8   Second generation languages

6.8.1   PL/1 and Algol 68

It is probably true that Fortran, Algol 60 and Cobol are the three main first generation high level languages. The 60s saw the emergence of PL/1 and Algol 68. PL/1 was a synthesis of features of Fortran, Algol 60 and Cobol. It was soon realized that whilst PL/1 had great richness and power of expression this was in some ways offset by the greater difficulties involved in language definition and use.

These latter problems were true of Algol 68 also. The report introduced its own syntactic and semantic conventions and thus forced upon the prospective user another stage in the learning process. However it has a small but very committed user population who like the very rich facilities provided by the language.

6.8.2   Simula

Another strand that makes up program language development is provided by Simula. It is a general purpose programming language developed by Dahl, Myhrhaug and Nygaard of the Norwegian Computing Centre. The most important contribution that Simula makes is the provision of language constructs that aid the programming of complex, highly interactive problems. It is thus heavily used in the areas of simulation and modelling. It was effectively the first language to offer the opportunity of object orientated programming, and we will come back to this very important development in programming languages later in this chapter.

6.8.3   Pascal

The designer of Pascal, Niklaus Wirth, had participated in the early stages of the design of Algol 68 but considered that the generality and complexity of Algol 68 was a move in the wrong direction. Pascal (like Algol 68) had its roots in Algol 60 but aimed at providing expressive power through a small set of straightforward concepts. This set is relatively easy to learn and helps in producing readable and hence more comprehensible programs.

It became the language of first choice within the field of computer science during the 1970s and 1980s, and the comment by Wirth sums up the language very well: *'although Pascal had no support from industry, professional societies, or government agencies, it became widely used. The important reason for this success was that many people capable of recognising its potential actively engaged themselves in its promotion. As crucial as the existence of good implementations is the availability of documentation. The conciseness of the original report made it attractive for many teachers to expand it into valuable textbooks. Innumerable books appeared between 1977 and 1985, effectively promoting Pascal to become the most widespread language used in introductory programming courses. Good course material and implementations are the indispensable prerequisites for such an evolution.'*

6.8.4 APL

APL is another interesting language of the 60s. It was developed by Iverson in the early 1960s and was available by the mid to late 60s. It is an interpretive vector and matrix based language with an extensive set of operators for the manipulation of vectors, arrays, etc. of whatever data type. As with Algol 68 it has a small but dedicated user population. A possibly unfair comment about APL programs is that you do not debug them, but rewrite them!

6.8.5 Basic

Basic stands for *B*eginners *A*ll Purpose *S*ymbolic *I*nstruction *C*ode, and was developed by Kemeny and Kurtz at Dartmouth during the 1960s. Its name gives a clue to its audience and it is very easy to learn. It is generally interpreted, though compiled versions do exist. It is probably the most heavily used language on micros and home computers. It has proved to be well suited to the rapid development of small programs. It is much criticized because it lacks features that encourage or force the adoption of sound programming techniques.

6.8.6 C

There is a requirement in computing to be able to access directly or at least efficiently the underlying machine. It is therefore not surprising that computer professionals have developed high level languages to do this. This may well seem a contradiction, but it can be done to quite a surprising degree. Some of the earliest published work was that of Martin Richards and the development of BCPL.

This language directly influenced the work of Ken Thompson and can be clearly seen in the programming languages B and C. The UNIX operating system is almost totally written in C and demonstrates very clearly the benefits of the use of high level languages wherever possible.

With the widespread use of UNIX within the academic world C gained considerable ground during the 1970s and 1980s. UNIX systems also offered much to the professional software developer, and became widely used for large scale software development, and as Ritchie says: '*C is quirky, flawed, and an enormous success. While accidents of history surely helped, it evidently satisfied a need for a system implementation language efficient enough to displace assembly language, yet sufficiently abstract and fluent to describe algorithms and interactions in a wide variety of environments.*'

6.9   Some other strands in language development

There are many strands that make up program language development and some of them are introduced here.

6.9.1   Abstraction, stepwise refinement and modules

Abstraction has proved to be very important in programming. It enables a complex task to be broken down into smaller parts concentrating on *what* we want to happen rather than *how* we want it to happen. This leads almost automatically to the ideas of stepwise refinement and modules, with collections of modules to perform specific tasks or steps.

6.9.2   Structured programming

Structured programming in its narrowest sense concerns itself with the development of programs using a small but sufficient set of statements and in particular control statements. It has had a great effect on program language design and most languages now support the minimal set of control structures.

In a broader sense structured programming subsumes other objectives including simplicity, comprehensibility, verifiability, modifiability and maintenance of programs.

6.9.3   Standardization

The purposes of a standard are quite varied and include:

- **Investment in people:** by this we mean that the time spent in learning a standard language pays off in the long term, as what one learns is applicable on any hardware/software platform that has a standard conformant compiler.

- **Portability:** one can take the code one has written for one hardware/software platform and move it to any hardware/software platform that has a standard conformant compiler.

- **Known reference point:** when making comparisons one starts with reference to the standard first, and then between the additional functionality.

and these are some but not all of the reasons for the use of standards. Their importance is summed up beautifully by Ronald G. Ross in his introduction to the Cannan and Otten book on the SQL standard: '*Anybody who has ever plugged in an electric cord into a wall outlet can readily appreciate the inestimable benefits of workable standards. Indeed, with respect to electrical power, the very fact that we seldom even think about such access (until something goes wrong) is a sure sign of just how fundamentally important a successful standard can be.*'

Appendix A contains notes on what standards apply at this time for the languages covered.

6.10 Ada

Ada represents the culmination of many years of work in program language development. It was a collective effort and the main aim was to produce a language suitable for programming large scale and real time systems. Work started in 1974 with the formulation of a series of documents by the American Department of Defence (DoD), which lead to the Steelman documents. It is a modern algorithmic language with the usual control structures, and facilities for the use of modules and allows separate compilation with type checking across modules.

Ada is a powerful and well engineered language. Its widespread use is certain as it has the backing of the DoD. However it is a large and complex language and consequently requires some effort to learn. It seems unlikely to be widely used except by a small number of computer professionals.

6.11 Modula

Modula was designed by Wirth during the 1970's at ETH, for the programming of embedded real time systems. It has many of the features of Pascal, and can be taken for Pascal at a glance. The key new features that Modula introduced were those of processes and monitors.

As with Pascal it is relatively easy to learn and this makes it much more attractive than Ada for most people, achieving much of the capability without the complexity.

6.12 Modula 2

Wirth carried on developing his ideas about programming languages and the culmination of this can be seen in Modula 2, and in his words: '*In 1977, a research project with the goal to design a computer system (hardware and software) in an integrated approach, was launched at the Institut fur Informatik of ETH Zurich. This system (later to be called Lilith) was to be programmed in a single high level language, which therefore had to satisfy requirements of high level system design as well as those of low level programming of parts that closely interact with the given hardware. Modula 2 emerged from careful design deliberations as a language that includes all aspects of Pascal and extends them with the important module concept and those of multi-programming. Since its syntax was more in line with Modula than Pascal's the chosen name was Modula 2.'*

The language's main additions with regard to Pascal are:

- The module concept, and in particular the facility to split a module into a definition part and an implementation part.

- A more systematic syntax which facilitates the learning process. In particular, every structure starting with a keyword also ends with a keyword, i.e. is properly bracketed.

- The concept of process as the key to multi-programming facilities.

- So-called low level facilities which make it possible to breach the rigid type consistency rules and allow one to map data with Modula 2 structure onto a store without inherent structure.

- The procedure type which allows procedures to be dynamically assigned to variables.

A sad feature of Modula 2 has been the long time taken to arrive at a standard for the language.

6.13 Other language developments

The following is a small selection of language developments that the authors find interesting – they may well not be included in other people's coverage.

6.13.1 Logo

Logo is a language that was developed by Papert and colleagues at the Artificial Intelligence Laboratory at MIT. Papert is a professor of both mathematics and education, and has been much influenced by the psychologist Piaget. The language is used to create learning environments in which children can communicate with a computer. The language is primarily used to demonstrate and help children develop fundamental concepts of mathematics. Probably the *turtle* and *turtle geometry* are known by educationalists outside of the context of Logo. Turtles have been incorporated into the Smalltalk computer system developed at Xerox Palo Alto Research Centre – Xerox PARC.

6.13.2   Postscript, TeX and LaTeX

The 80s saw a rapid spread in the use of computers for the production of printed material. The above languages are each used in this area quite extensively.

Postscript is a low level interpretive programming language with good graphics capabilities. Its primary purpose is to enable the easy production of pages containing text, graphical shapes and images. It is rarely seen by most end users of modern desk-top publishing systems, but underlies many of these systems. It is supported by an increasing number of laser printers and typesetters.

TeX is a language designed for the production of mathematical texts, and was developed by Donald Knuth. It linearizes the production of mathematics using a standard computer keyboard. It is widely used in the scientific community for the production of documents involving mathematical equations.

LaTex is Leslie Lamport's version of TeX, and is regarded by many as more friendly. It is basically a set of macros that hide raw TeX from the end user. The TeX/LaTeX ration is probably 1 to 9 (or so I'm reliably informed by a TeXie).

6.13.3   Prolog

Prolog was originally developed at Marseille by a group lead by Colmerauer in 1972/73. It has since been extended and developed by a variety of people including Pereira (L.M.), Pereira (F), Warren and Kowalski. Prolog is unusual in that it is a vehicle for *logic* programming. Most of the languages described here are basically algorithmic languages and require a specification of *how* you want something done. Logic programming concentrates on the *what* rather than the *how*. The language appears strange at first, but has been taught by Kowalski and others to 10 year old children at schools in London.

6.13.4   SQL

SQL stands for Structured Query Language, and was originally developed by a variety of people mainly working for IBM in the San Jose Research Laboratory. It is a relational database language, and enables programmers to define, manipulate and control data in a relational database. Simplistically a relational database is seen by a user as a collection of tables, comprising rows and columns. It has become the most important language in the whole database field.

6.13.5   ICON

ICON is in the same family as Snobol, and is a high-level general purpose programming language that has most of the features necessary for efficient processing of non-numeric data. Griswold (one of the original design team for Snobol) has learnt much since the design and implementation of Snobol, and the language is a joy to use in most areas of text manipulation.

It is available for most systems via anonymous FTP from a number of sites on the Internet.

6.14 Object orientated programming – OOP

OOP represents a major advance in program language development. The concepts that this introduces include:

- Classes.
- Objects.
- Messages.
- Methods.

and these in turn draw on the ideas found in more conventional programming languages and correspond to

- Extensible data types.
- Instances of a class.
- Dynamically bound procedure calls.
- Procedures of a class.

Inheritance is a very powerful high level concept introduced with OOP. It enables an existing data type with its range of valid operations to form the basis for a new class, with additional data types added with corresponding operations, and the new type is compatible with the original.

As was mentioned earlier the first language to offer functionality in this area was Simula, and thus the ideas originate in the 1960s. The book *Simula Begin* by Birtwistle, Dahl, Myhrhaug and Nygaard is well worth a read as it represents one of the first books to introduce the concepts of OOP.

6.14.1   Oberon and Oberon 2

As Wirth says: *'The programming language Oberon is the result of a concentrated effort to increase the power of Modula-2 and simultaneously to reduce its complexity. Several features were eliminated, and a few were added in order to increase the expressive power and flexibility of the language.'*

Oberon and Oberon 2 are thus developments beyond Modula 2. The main new concept added to Oberon was that of type extension. This enables the construction of new data types based on existing types and to take advantage of what has already been done for that existing type.

Language constructs removed included:

- Variant records.

- Opaque types.

- Enumeration types.

- Sub-range types.

- Local modules.

- WITH statement.

- Type transfer functions.

- Concurrency.

The short paper by Wirth provides a fuller coverage. It is available at ETH via anonymous FTP.

6.14.2 Smalltalk

Language plus use of a computer system.

Smalltalk has been under development by the Xerox PARC Learning Research Group since the 1970s. In their words: *'Smalltalk is a graphical, interactive programming environment. As suggested by the personal computer vision, Smalltalk is designed so that every component in the system is accessible to the user and can be presented in a meaningful way for observation and manipulation. The user interface issues in Smalltalk revolve around the attempt to create a visual language for each object. The preferred hardware system for Smalltalk includes a high resolution graphical display screen and a pointing device such as a graphics pen or mouse. With these devices the user can select information viewed on the screen and invoke messages in order to interact with the information.'* Thus Smalltalk represents a very different strand in program language development. The ease of use of a system like this has long been appreciated and was first demonstrated commercially by the Macintosh microcomputers.

Wirth has spent some time at Xerox PARC and has been influenced by their work, and in his own words *the most elating sensation was that after sixteen years of working for computers the computer now seemed to work for me.* This influence can be seen in the design of the Lilith machine, the original Modula 2 engine and in the development of Oberon as both language and operating system.

6.14.3 C++

Stroustrup did his Ph.D thesis at the Computing Laboratory, Cambridge University England, and worked with Simula. He had previously worked with Simula at the University of Aarhus in Denmark. His comments are illuminating: *'but was pleasantly surprised by the way the mechanisms of the Simula language became increasingly helpful as the size of the program increased. The class and co-routine mechanisms of Simula and the comprehensive type checking mechanisms ensured that problems and errors did not (as I - and I guess most people - would have expected) grow linearly with the size of the program. Instead, the total program acted like a collection of very small (and therefore easy to write, comprehend and debug) programs rather than a single large program.'*

He designed C++ to provide Simula's functionality within the framework of C's efficiency, and he has succeeded in this goal. C++ is the most widely used OOP at this time. The major disadvantage now concerns the largely incompatible class libraries that exist. It is hoped that the various standards bodies address this problem in the immediate future.

6.15 Fortran 90

Almost as soon as the Fortran 77 standard was complete and published work began on the next version. The language draws on many of the ideas covered in this chapter and these help to make Fortran 90 a very promising language for the future. Some of the new features include

- New source form, with blanks being significant and names being up to 31 characters.
- Better control structures.
- Control of the precision of numerical computation.
- Array processing.
- Pointers.
- User defined data types and operators.
- Procedures.
- Modules.
- Recursion.
- Dynamic storage allocation.

We will look into all of these in turn.

6.15.1 Fortran 1995

Fortran was next standardized in 1996 – yet again out by one! Firstly we have a clear up of some of the areas in the standard that have emerged as requiring clarification. Secondly Fortran 95 has added the following major concepts:

- The FORALL construct.

- PURE and ELEMENTAL procedures.

- Implicit initialization of derived type objects.

- Initial association status for pointers.

and the first two help considerably in parallelization of code.

Minor features include:

- Automatic deallocation of allocatable arrays.

- Intrinsic SIGN functions distinguishes between -0 and +0.

- Intrinsic function NULL returns disconnected pointer.

- Intrinsic function CPU_TIME returns the processor time.

- References to some pure functions are allowed in specification statements.

- Nested WHERE constructs.

- Masked ELSEWHERE construct.

- Small changes to the CEILING, FLOOR, MAXLOC and MINLOC intrinsic functions.

amongst others.

Some of these were added to keep Fortran in-line with High Performance Fortran (HPF). More details are given later.

Part 2 of the standard (ISO/IEC 1539-2:1994) adds the functional specification for varying length character data type, and this extends the usefulness of Fortran for character applications very considerably.

6.15.2   ISO Technical Reports TR15580 and TR15581

There are two additional reports that have been published on Fortran. TR 15580 specifies three modules that provide access to IEE floating point arithmetic and TR15581 allows the use of the ALLOCATABLE attribute on dummy arguments, function results and structure components.

6.15.3   High Performance Fortran – HPF

To quote from the High Performance Fortran Language Specification, Version 1.1, November 10, 1994: *'The High Performance Fortran Forum (HPFF) was founded as a coalition of industrial and academic groups working to suggest a set of standard extensions to Fortran to provide the necessary information. Its intent was to develop extensions to Fortran that provide support for high performance programming on a wide variety of machines, including massively parallel SIMD and MIMD systems and vector processors. From its very beginning, HPFF included most ven-*

dors delivering parallel machines, a number of government laboratories and many university research groups. Public input was encouraged to the greatest extent possible.'

A number of suppliers now provide HPF Fortran extensions, and these are generally based on Fortran 90, rather than Fortran 77.

6.15.4   Internet resources

The Internet provides access to a wealth of information regarding the Fortran family of languages.

The first to look at is the Fortran 90 list. Details can be found at:

http://www.mailbase.ac.uk/lists/comp-fortran-90/

If you subscribe you will have access to people involved in Fortran standardization, language implementors for most of the hardware and software platforms, people using Fortran in many very specialised areas, people teaching Fortran etc.

There is also a comp.lang.fortran list available via USENET news. This provides access to people world-wide with enormous combined expertise in all aspects of Fortran. Someone will inevitably have encountered your problem or one very much like it and have one or more solutions.

There are many people on the Internet who will make the time to provide you with very valuable advice. As a point of network etiquette please do not waste bandwidth with questions that are answered in the FAQ. Please also spend some time developing an understanding of your problem and making some attempt to see if the answer lies in the documentation or manuals. In computing services and technical support many user problems are labelled RTFM – read the fabulous manual.

The following URLs are very useful:

- Fortran 90 FAQ, maintained by Michel Olagnon
    - http://www.ifremer.fr/ditigo/molagnon/fortran90/engfaq.html
    - http://www.kcl.ac.uk/kis/support/cc/fortran/engfaq.html
    - http://www.mailbase.ac.uk/lists/comp-fortran-90/files/f90-faq.html

- The Fortran Market, maintained by Walt Brainerd
    - http://www.fortran.com/fortran/market.html
- Fortran90/95 Information, maintained by Mike Metcalf
    - http://www.fortran.com/fortran/metcalf.html

- Fortran FAQ, maintained by Keith Bierman, Sun

    - http://www.fortran.com/fortran/FAQ/cont.html

6.16 Summary

It is hoped that the reader now has some idea about the wide variety of uses that programming languages are put to.

Fortran now has much more in common with Ada and Modula 2 than one might first have expected from its origins. This is reflected in the UK by the formation under the auspices of the BCS of the Modular Languages Specialist Interest Group, which provides coverage of Ada, Fortran 90, Modula 2, Modula 3, Oberon 2 and Pascal.

6.17 Bibliography

Fortran 90 Standard ISO/IEC 1539:1991

> The definition of the language and the programmers bible. Copies are available for reference in the Computer Centre.

Fortran 96 Standard, ISO/IEC 1539:1996

Varying Length Character Strings in Fortran, ISO/IEC 1539-2:1994.

> Consult the Fortran 90 FAQ for up to date details, or visit the Fortran Market!

High Performance Fortran Language Specification, HPFF, Version 1.1, November 1994.

> This is available via anonymous FTP from a variety of sources. Consult the Fortran 90 FAQ for up to date details, or visit the Fortran Market!

Adobe Systems Incorporated, *Postscript Language: Tutorial and Cookbook*, Addison Wesley, 1985.

Adobe Systems Incorporated, *Postscript Language: Reference Manual,* Addison Wesley, 1985.

Adobe System Incorporated, *Postscript Language: Program Design,* Addison Wesley, 1985.

> The three books provide a comprehensive coverage of the facilities and capabilities of Postscript.

ACM SIG PLAN, *History of Programming Languages Conference – HOPL-II,* ACM Press, 1993.

> One of the best sources of information on programming language developments, from an historical perspective. There is coverage of Ada, Algol 68, C, C++, CLU, Concurrent Pascal, Formac, Forth, Icon, Lisp, Pascal, Prolog,

Smalltalk and Simulation Languages by the people involved in the original design and or implementation. Very highly recommended. This is the second in the HOPL series, and the first was edited by Wexelblat. Details are given later.

Adams J.C., Brainerd W.S., Martin J.T., Smith B.T., Wagener J.L., *Fortran 90 Handbook: Complete ANSI/ISO Reference,* McGraw Hill, 1992.

A complete coverage of the language. As with the Metcalf and Reid book some of the authors were on the X3J3 committee. Originally expensive, but very thorough.

Annals of the History of Computing, *Special Issue: Fortran's 25 Anniversary,* ACM, Article 6,1, 1984.

Very interesting comments, some anecdotal, about the early work on Fortran.

Barnes J., *Programming in Ada 95,* Addison Wesley, 1996.

One of the best Ada books. He was a member of the original design team

Birtwistle G.M., Dahl O. J., Myhrhaug B., Nygaard K., *SIMULA BEGIN*, Chartwell-Bratt Ltd, 1979.

A number of chapters in the book will be of interest to programmers unfamiliar with some of the ideas involved in a variety of areas including systems and models, simulation, and co-routines. Also has some sound practical advice on problem solving.

Brinch-Hansen P., *The Programming Language Concurrent Pascal,* IEEE Transactions on Software Engineering, June 1975, 199-207.

Looks at the extensions to Pascal necessary to support concurrent processes.

Cannan S., Otten G., *SQL – The Standard Handbook*, McGraw Hill, 1993.

Very thorough coverage of the SQL standard, ISO 9075:1992(E).

Chivers I.D., Clark M.W., *History and Future of Fortran,* Data Processing, vol. 27 no 1, January/February 1985.

Short article on an early draft of the standard, around version 90.

Date C.J., *A Guide to the SQL Standard*, Addison Wesley, 1997.

Date has written extensively on the whole database field, and this book looks at the SQL language itself. As with many of Date's works quite easy to read. Appendix F provides a useful SQL bibliography.

Deitel H.M., Deitel P.J., *Java How to Program*, Prentice Hall, 1999.

A very good introduction to Java.

Eckstein R., Loy M., Wood D., *Java Swing*, O'Reilly, 1998.

Comprehensive coverage of the visual interface features available in Java.

Flanagan D., *Java in a Nutshell*, O'Reilly, 1996.

Just what you would expect from this series. Very useful reference text.

Geissman L.B., *Separate Compilation in Modula2 and the structure of the Modula2 Compiler on the Personal Computer Lilith*, Dissertation 7286, ETH Zurich

Jacobi C., *Code Generation and the Lilith Architecture,* Dissertation 7195, ETH Zurich

Fascinating background reading concerning Modula2 and the Lilith architecture.

Goldberg A., Robson D., *Smalltalk 80: The Language and its Implementation*, Addison Wesley, 1983.

Written by some of the Xerox PARC people who have been involved with the development of Smalltalk. Provides a good introduction (if that is possible with the written word) of the capabilities of Smalltalk.

Goos G., Hartmanis J. (Eds), *The Programming Language Ada - Reference Manual,* Springer Verlag, 1981.

The definition of the language.

Griswold R.E., Poage J.F., Polonsky I.P., *The Snobol4 Programming Language,* Prentice-Hall, 1971.

The original book on the language. Also provides some short historical material on the language.

Griswold R.E., Griswold M.T., *The Icon Programming Language*, Prentice-Hall, 1983.

The definition of the language with a lot of good examples. Also contains information on how to obtain public domain versions of the language for a variety of machines and operating systems.

Hoare C.A.R., *Hints on Programming Language Design,* SIGACT/SIGPLAN Symposium on Principles of Programming Languages, October 1973.

The first sentence of the introduction sums it up beautifully: *'I would like in this paper to present a philosophy of the design and evaluation of programming languages which I have adopted and developed over a number of years, namely that the primary purpose of a programming language is to help the programmer in the practice of his art.'*

Jenson K., Wirth N., *Pascal: User Manual and Report*, Springer Verlag, 1975.

The original definition of the Pascal language. Understandably dated when one looks at more recent expositions on programming in Pascal.

Kemeny J.G., Kurtz T.E., *Basic Programming*, Wiley, 1971.

The original book on Basic by its designers.

Kernighan B.W., Ritchie D.M., *The C Programming Language,* Prentice Hall: Englewood Cliffs, New Jersey, 1978.

> The original work on the C language, and thus essential for serious work with C.

Kowalski R., *Logic Programming in the Fifth Generation*, The Knowledge Engineering Review, The BCS Specialist Group on Expert Systems.

> A short paper providing a good background to Prolog and logic programming, with an extensive bibliography.

Knuth D. E., *The TeXbook*, Addison Wesley, 1986.

> Knuth writes with an tremendous enthusiasm and perhaps this is understandable as he did design TeX. Has to be read from cover to cover for a full understanding of the capability of TeX.

Lyons J., *Chomsky*, Fontana/Collins, 1982.

> A good introduction to the work of Chomsky, with the added benefit that Chomsky himself read and commented on it for Lyons. Very readable.

Malpas J., *Prolog: A Relational Language and its Applications*, Prentice-Hall, 1987.

> A good introduction to Prolog for people with some programming background. Good bibliography. Looks at a variety of versions of Prolog.

Marcus C., *Prolog Programming: Applications for Database Systems, Expert Systems and Natural Language Systems,* Addison Wesley.

> Coverage of the use of Prolog in the above areas. As with the previous book aimed mainly at programmers, and hence not suitable as an introduction to Prolog as only two chapters are devoted to introducing Prolog.

Metcalf M. and Reid J., *Fortran 90 Explained*, Oxford Science Publications, 1992.

> A clear compact coverage of the main features of Fortran 8x. Reid was secretary of the X3J3 committee.

Mossenbeck H., *Object-Orientated Programming in Oberon-2,* Springer–Verlag, 1995.

> One of the best introductions to OOP. Uses Oberon-2 as the implementation language. Highly recommended.

Papert S., *Mindstorms - Children, Computers and Powerful Ideas*, Harvester Press, 1980.

> Very personal vision of the uses of computers by children. It challenges many conventional ideas in this area.

Sammet J., *Programming Languages: History and Fundamentals*, Prentice Hall, 1969.

> Possibly the most comprehensive introduction to the history of program language development – ends unfortunately before the 1980s.

Sethi R., *Programming Languages: Concepts and Constructs*, Addison Wesley, 1989.

> The annotated bibliographic notes at the end of each chapter and the extensive bibliography make it a useful book.

Reiser M., Wirth N., *Programming in Oberon – Steps Beyond Pascal and Modula*, Addison Wesley, 1992.

> Good introduction to Oberon. Revealing history of the developments behind Oberon.

Reiser M., *The Oberon System: User Guide and Programmer's Manual*, Addsion Wesley, 1991.

> How to use the Oberon system, rather than the language.

Stroustroup B., *The C++ Programming Language, 3rd Edition*, Addison Wesley, 1997.

> **The** C++ book. Written by the designer of the language. Massive improvement over the earlier editions.

Young S. J., *An Introduction to Ada, 2nd Edition*, Ellis Horwood, 1984.

> A readable introduction to Ada. Greater clarity than the first edition.

Wexelblat, *History of Programming Languages, HOPL I*, ACM Monograph Series, Academic Press, 1978.

> Very thorough coverage of the development of programming languages up to June 1978. Sessions on Fortran, Algol, Lisp, Cobol, APT, Jovial, GPSS, Simula, JOSS, Basic, PL/I, Snobol and APL, with speakers involved in the original languages. Very highly recommended.

Wirth N., *An Assessment of the Programming Language Pascal*, IEEE Transactions on Software Engineering, June 1975, 192-198.

Wirth N., *History and Goals of Modula2*, Byte, August 1984, 145-152.

> Straight from the horse's mouth!

Wirth N., *On the Design of Programming Languages*, Proc. IFIP Congress 74, 386-393, North Holland, Amsterdam.

Wirth N., *The Programming Language Pascal*, Acta Informatica 1, 35-63, 1971.

Wirth N., *Modula: a language for modular multi- programming*, Software Practice and Experience, 7, 3-35, 1977.

Wirth N., *Programming in Modula2*, Springer Verlag, 1983.

> The original definition of the language. Essential reading for anyone considering programming in Modula2 on a long term basis.

Wirth N. *Type Extensions*, ACM Trans. on Prog. Languages and Systems, 10, 2 (April 1988), 2004-214

Wirth N. *From Modula 2 to Oberon*, Software – Practice and Experience, 18,7 (July 1988), 661-670

Wirth N., Gutknecht J., *Project Oberon: The Design of an Operating System and Compiler*, Addison Wesley, 1992.

> Fascinating background to the development of Oberon. Highly recommended for anyone involved in large scale program development, not only in the areas of programming languages and operating systems, but more generally.

7

Introduction to Programming

'Though this be madness, yet there is method in't'
Shakespeare.

'Plenty of practice' he went on repeating, all the time that Alice was getting him on his feet again. 'plenty of practice.'
The White Knight, *Through the Looking Glass and What Alice Found There,* Lewis Carroll.

Aims

The aims of the chapter are:

- To introduce the idea that there is a wide class of problems that may be solved with a computer, and that there is a relationship between the kind of problem to be solved and the choice of programming language that is used to solve that problem.

- To give some of the reasons for the choice of Fortran.

- To introduce the fundamental components or kinds of statements to be found in a general purpose programming language.

- To introduce the three concepts of name, type and value.

- To illustrate the above with sample programs based on three of the five intrinsic data types:

  - character, integer and real

- To introduce some of the formal syntactical rules of Fortran.

7 Introduction to Programming

We have seen that an algorithm is a sequence of steps that will solve a part or the whole of a problem. A program is the realization of an algorithm in a programming language, and there are at first sight a surprisingly large number of programming languages. The reason for this is that there are a wide range of problems that are solved using a computer, e.g. the telephone company generating itemized bills or the meteorological centre producing a weather forecast. These two problems make different demands on a programming language, and it is unlikely that the same language would be used to solve both.

The range of problems that you want to solve will therefore have a strong influence on the programming language that you use. FORTRAN stands for FORmula TRANslation, which gives a hint of the expected range of problems.

7.1 Language standardisation

Fortran is the subject of on-going standardisation.

7.1.1 Fortran 66

The first was in 1966, and established Fortran as the major language for numerical programming.

7.1.2 Fortran 77

The next standard in 1977 (actually 1978, and thus out by one – a very common programming error, more of this later!) added character handling, but little else in the way of major new features, really tidying up some of the deficiencies of the 1966 standard.

7.1.3 Fortran 90

The 1990 standard altered the language considerably. Some of the major improvements are covered below.

7.1.3.1 Source form

Free source form, names can be up to 31 characters in length, blanks are significant, lines up to 132 characters in length (can be continued up to 39 lines using the continuation character &), ; as statement separator for multiple statements per line, ! as comment symbol; include option for source text from files;

This offers much that is taken for granted within the Algol family of languages.

7.1.3.2 Control structures

The 77 standard offered little in the way of accepted control structures. Fortran 90 has a modern DO statement, with CYCLE and EXIT options and the control part of the DO can be conventional iteration, WHILE or no control clause. There is also a CASE statement.

7.1.3.3 Numeric precision

For anyone involved in moving between different hardware platforms and in some instances simply between different compilers on the same hardware platform the specification of precision has always been a problem. This has been quite cleanly addressed in the new standard.

7.1.3.4 Array processing

It is now possible to treat arrays as whole objects and simply write statements like

   A = B + C

where **A**, **B** and **C** are arrays. Array slicing has been introduced, arrays may be allocated dynamically, and there is a large new set of intrinsic functions to process arrays.

7.1.3.5 Dynamic behaviour

Fortran now supports recursion, pointers and allocate/deallocate. This makes algorithms much clearer and understandable, and considerably increases the range of problems that can be easily solved in Fortran.

7.1.3.6 User defined data types and operators

The Algol family has had user defined data types for a long time and there have been many extra hours spent coding round the lack of these facilities in Fortran, prior the 90 standard. This has now been added, with the ability to define the action of operators on these types.

7.1.3.7 Procedures

The power of functions and subroutines has been extended greatly with the addition of extra features in this area. Functions can be used to extend existing operators, or add new ones; procedure argument is optional, and keywords can be used; generic procedures can be created.

7.1.3.8 Modules

Modules can declare global data, and this is a big improvement over the use of common blocks. A module can make a type definition available; information hiding has been added; interface blocks have been introduced and their use in conjunction with modules aids considerably in the construction of secure large scale programs.

7.1.4   Fortran 95

This standard cleaned up a number of areas that emerged as Fortran 90 experience grew. It also increased support for parallelisation of code, and added a number of minor features.

ISO Technical Reports TR 15580 and TR 15581 have also been published and will be included in the next standard. Some companies have already implemented these reports as part of their current compilers.

7.1.5   Fortran 2000

Work is already well under way for the next standard. Up to date information can be found at some of the web addresses given throughout the book.

7.2   Language strengths and weaknesses

Some of the reasons for choosing Fortran are:

- It is a modern and expressive language, with much of the power of Ada without the complexity.

- The language is now suitable for a very wide class of both numeric and non-numeric problems.

- The language is widely available in both the educational and scientific sectors.

- A lot of software already exists, written in either Fortran 77 or its, predecessor, Fortran 66. Fortran 66 is also known as Fortran IV. This code can be recompiled with standard conforming Fortran 90 compilers. This thus protects the major investment there is in existing code. Some 15% of code world-wide is estimated to be in Fortran.

There are a few warts however. Given that there has to be backwards compatibility with Fortran 77 some of the syntax is clumsy to say the least. However a considerable range of problems can now be addressed quite cleanly, if one sticks to a subset of the language and adopts a consistent style.

7.3   Elements of a programming language

As with ordinary (so-called *natural*) languages, e.g. English, French, Gaelic German, etc., programming languages have rules of syntax, grammar and spelling. The application of the rules of syntax, grammar and spelling in a programming language are more strict. A program has to be unambiguous, since it is a *precise* statement of the actions to be taken. Many everyday activities are rather vaguely defined — *Buy some bread on your way home* — but we are generally sufficiently adaptable to cope with the variations which occur as a result. If, in a program to calculate wages, we had an instruction *Deduct some money* for tax and insurance we could have an awkward problem when the program calculated completely different wages for the same person for the same amount of work every time it was run. One of the implications of the strict syntax of a programming language for the novice is that apparently silly error messages will appear when first writing programs. As with many other *new* subjects you will have to learn some of the jargon to understand these messages.

Programming languages are made up of statements. We will look at the various kinds of statements briefly below.

7.3.1 Data description statements

These are necessary to describe what kinds of data are to be processed. In the wages program for example, there is obviously a difference between peoples names and the amount of money they earn, i.e. these two things are not the same, and it would not make any sense adding your name to your wages. The technical term for this is *data type;* a wage would be of a different data type (a number) to a surname (a sequence of characters).

7.3.2 Control structures

A program can be regarded as a sequence of statements to solve a particular problem, and it is common to find that this sequence needs to be varied in practice. Consider again the wages program. It will need to select between a variety of circumstances (say married or single, paid weekly or monthly etc), and also to repeat the program for everybody employed. So there is the need in a programming language for statements to vary and/or repeat a sequence of statements.

7.3.3 Data processing statements

It is necessary in a programming language to be able to process data. The kind of processing required will depend on the kind or type of data. In the wages program, for example, you will need to distinguish between names and wages. Therefore there must be different kinds of statements to manipulate the different types of data, i.e. *wages* and *names*.

7.3.4 Input and output (I/O) statements

For flexibility, programs are generally written so that the data that they work on exists *outside* the program. In the wages example the details for each person employed would exist in a *file* somewhere, and there would be a *record* for each person in this file. This means that the program would not have to be modified each time a person left, was ill, etc., although the individual records might be updated. It is easier to modify data than to modify a program, and less likely to produce unexpected results. To be able to vary the action there must be some mechanism in a programming language for getting the data *into* and *out of* the program. This is done using input and output statements, sometimes shortened to I/O statements.

Let us now consider a simple program which will read in somebody's name and print it out.

```
PROGRAM Chapter7_Ex01
!
! This program reads in and prints out a name
!
IMPLICIT NONE
CHARACTER (20) :: Name
!
   PRINT *,' Type in your first name.'
   PRINT *,' up to 20 characters'
   READ *,Name
   PRINT *,Name
!
END PROGRAM Chapter7_Ex01
```

There are several very important points to be covered here, and they will be taken in turn:

- Each line is a statement.

- There is a sequence to the statements. The statements will be processed in the order that they are presented, so in this example the sequence is *print, read, print.*

- The first statement names the program. It makes sense to choose a name that conveys something about the purpose of the program.

- The next three lines are *comment* statements. They are identified by a !. Comments are inserted in a program to explain the purpose of the program. They should be regarded as an integral part of all programs. It is essential to get into the habit of inserting comments into your programs straight away.

- The IMPLICIT NONE statement means that there has to be explicit typing of each and every data item used in the program. It is good programming practice to include this statement in every program that you write, as it will trap many errors, some often very subtle in their effect. Using an analogy with a play where there is always a list of the persona involved before the main text of the play, this statement serves the same purpose.

- The CHARACTER (20) statement is a *type* declaration. It was mentioned earlier that there are different kinds of data. There must be some way of telling the programming language that this data is of a certain type, and that therefore certain kinds of operation are allowed and others are banned or just plain stupid! It would not make sense to add a name to a number, e.g. what does Fred+10 mean? So this statement defines that the *variable*

NAME to be of type CHARACTER and only character operations are permitted. The concept of a variable is covered in the next section. Character variables of this type can hold up to 20 characters.

- The PRINT statements print out an informative message to the terminal – in this case a guide as to what to type in. The use of informative messages like this throughout your programs is strongly recommended.

- The READ statement is one of the I/O statements. It is an instruction to *read* from the terminal or keyboard; whatever is typed in from the terminal will end up being associated with the variable NAME. Input/output statements will be explained in greater detail in later sections.

- The PRINT statement is another I/O statement. This statement will print out what is associated with the variable NAME and in this case, what you typed in.

- The END PROGRAM statement terminates this program. It can be thought of as being similar to a full stop in natural language, in that it finishes the program, in the same way that a . ends a sentence. Note the use of the name given in the PROGRAM statement at the start of the program.

- Note also the use of the '*' in three different contexts.

- Indentation has been used to make the structure of the program easier to determine. Programs have to be read by human beings and we will look at this in more depth later.

- Lastly, when you do run this program, character input will terminate with the first blank character.

The above program illustrates the use of some of the statements in the Fortran language. Let us consider the action of the READ * statement in more detail. In particular, what is meant by a variable and a value.

7.4 Variables – name, type and value

The idea of a variable is one that you are likely to have met before, probably in a mathematical context. Consider the following

tax payable = gross wages – tax allowances * tax rate

This is a simplified equation for the calculation of wage deductions. Each of the *variables* on the right hand side takes on *a value* for each person, which allows the calculation of the deductions for that person. The above equation expressed in Fortran would be an example of an *arithmetic assignment statement*. There is some arithmetic calculation taking place which yields a value, and this value is then assigned to the variable on the left hand side. This could be expressed in Fortran as

Tax_Payable = Gross_Wages - Tax_Allowances * Tax_Rate

Note the use of the underscore character and capitalization to make the statement (and hence program) understandable. Remember, a program has to be read and understood by human beings.

The following arithmetic assignment statement illustrates clearly the concepts of name and value, and the difference between the = in mathematics and computing:

I=I+1

In Fortran this reads as take the current value of the variable *I* and add one to it, store the new value back into the variable *I*, i.e. *I* takes the value *I+1*. Algebraically,

i=i+1

does not make any sense.

Variables can be of different types, and Table 7.1 shows some of those available in Fortran.

Variable name	Data type	Value stored
Gross_Pay	REAL	9440.30
Tax_Allowances	INTEGER	2042
Tax_Rate	REAL	.7
Name	CHARACTER	ARTHUR

Table 7.1 Name, type and value

The concept of data type seems a little strange at first, especially as we commonly think of integers and reals as numbers. However, the benefits to be gained from this distinction are considerable. This will become apparent after writing several programs.

Let us consider another program now. This program reads in three numbers, adds them up and prints out both the total and the average.

```
PROGRAM Sum_and_Average
!
! This program reads in three numbers and sums and
averages them
!
IMPLICIT NONE
REAL :: N1,N2,N3,Average = 0.0, Total = 0.0
INTEGER :: N = 3
   PRINT *,' Type in three numbers.'
   PRINT *,' Separated by spaces or commas'
   READ *,N1,N2,N3
   Total= N1+N2+N3
   Average=Total/N
   PRINT *,'Total of numbers is ',Total
   PRINT *,'Average of the numbers is ',Average
END PROGRAM Sum_and_Average
```

7.5 Notes

The program has been given a name that means something.

There are comments at the start of the program describing what the program does.

The IMPLICIT NONE statement ensures that all data items introduced have to occur in a type declaration.

The next two statements are type declarations. They define the variables to be of *real* or *integer* type. Remember integers are *whole* numbers, while real numbers are those which have a *decimal point*. For example, 2 is an integer, while 2.7, 2.00000001, and 2.0 are all real numbers. One of the fundamental distinctions in Fortran is between integers and reals. Type declarations must always come at the start of a program, before any *processing* is done. Note that the variables have been given sensible names, to aid in making the program easier to understand.

The variables Average, Total and N are also given initial values within the type declaration. Variables are initially undefined in Fortran.

The first PRINT statement makes a text message, (in this case what is between the apostrophes) appear at the terminal. As was stated earlier it is good practice to put out a message like this so that you have some idea of what you are supposed to type in.

The READ statement looks at the input from the keyboard (i.e. what you type) and in this instance associates these values with the three variables. These values can be separated by commas (,), spaces ( ), or even by pressing the carriage return key, i.e. they can appear on separate lines.

The next statement actually does some data processing. It adds up the *values* of the three variables (N1, N2, and N3), and assigns the result to the variable Total. This statement is called an *arithmetic assignment statement*, and is covered more fully in the next chapter.

The next statement is another data processing statement. It calculates the average of the numbers entered and assigns the result to Average. We could have actually used the value 3 here instead, i.e. written Average=Total/3 and had exactly the same effect. This would also have avoided the type declaration for N. However the original example follows established programming practice of declaring all variables and establishing their meaning unambiguously. We will see further examples of this type throughout the book.

Indentation has been used to make the structure of the program easier to determine.

The sum and average are printed out with suitable captions or headings. **Do not** write programs without putting captions on the results. It is too easy to make mistakes when you do this, or even forget what each number means.

Finally we have the end of the program and again we have the use of the name in the PROGRAM statement.

7.6   Some more Fortran rules

There are certain things to learn about Fortran which have little immediate meaning, and some which have no logical justification at all, other than historical precedence. Why is a cat called a cat? At the end of some of the chapters there will be a brief summary of these *rules* or regulations when necessary. Here are a few:

- Source is free format.

- Multiple statements may appear on one line and are separated by the semi-colon character ';'.

- There is an order to the statements in Fortran. Within the context of what you have covered so far, the order is:

  - PROGRAM statement.

  - Type declarations, e.g. IMPLICIT, INTEGER, REAL or CHARACTER.

  - Processing and I/O statements.

  - END PROGRAM statement.

- Comments may appear anywhere in the program, after PROGRAM and before END, and are introduced with a ! character, and can be in line.

- Names may be up to 31 characters in length and include the underscore character

- Lines may be up to 132 characters

- Up to 39 continuation lines are allowed (using the & as continuation character)

- The syntax of the READ and PRINT statement introduced in these examples is

  - READ *format, input-item-list.*

  - PRINT *format, output-item-list.*

    - where *format* is in the examples *, and called list directed formatting and

    - *input-item-list* is a list of variable names separated by commas.

- *output-item-list* is a list of variables names and or strings enclosed in either ' or " , again separated by commas.

- If the IMPLICIT NONE statement is not used variables that are not explicitly declared will default to REAL if the first letter of the variable name is A-H or O-Z, and to INTEGER if the first letter of the variable name is I-N.

7.7 Good programming guidelines

The following are guidelines, and do not form part of the Fortran language definition.

- Use comments to clarify the purpose of both sections of the program and the whole program.

- Chose meaningful names in your programs.

- Use indentation to highlight the structure of the program. Remember that the program has to be read and understood by both humans and a computer.

- Use IMPLICIT NONE in all programs you write to minimize errors.

- Do not rely on the rules for explicit typing, as this is a major source of errors in programming.

7.8 Fortran character set

Table 7.2 summarizes the Fortran character set.

A–Z	(left bracket	& ampersand
0–9	) right bracket	; semicolon
_ underscore	, comma	< less than
blank	. decimal point or period	
= equal	' apostrophe	> greater than
+ plus	: colon	? question mark
– minus	! exclamation mark	$ currency symbol
* asterisk	" quotation mark	
/ slash or oblique	% percent	

Table 7.2 Fortran character set

7.8.1   Notes

Lowercase letters are permitted, but not required to be recognized.

7.8.2   Compilers

A number of hardware platforms, operating systems and compilers have been used. They include:

- DEC VAX under VMS and later OPEN VMS with the NAG Fortran 90 compiler.

- DEC Alpha under OPEN VMS using the DEC Fortran 90 compiler.

- Sun Ultra Sparc under Solaris using the NAGACE F90 compiler.

- Sun Ultra Sparc under Solaris using the NAGWare F95 compiler.

- Sun Ultra Sparc under Solaris using the Sun (Release 1.x) F90 compiler.

- Sun Ultra Sparc under Solaris using the Sun (Release 2.x) F90 compiler.

- IBM PC and compatibles under DOS and Windows using the NAG Salford Fortran 90 Compiler.

- IBM PC and compatibles under DOS and Windows using the DEC/Compaq Fortran 90 and Fortran 95 compilers.

It is very illuminating to use more than one compiler whilst developing programs.

7.9   Program development

A number of ways of developing programs have been used including:

- Using DEC terminals to log into the DEC VAX and DEC Alpha systems.

- Using PCs running terminal emulation software to log into the DEC VAX and DEC Alpha systems.

- Using terminal emulation software to log into the SUN Ultra Sparc.

- Using X-Windows software to log into the SUN Ultra Sparc systems.

- Using a DOS box and simple command line prompt.

- Using an integrated development environment, e.g. Microsoft Developer Studio.

It is likely that you will end up doing at least one of the above and probably more. The key stages involved are:

- Creating and making changes to the Fortran program source.

- Saving the file.

- Compiling the program.

  - If there are errors you must go back to the Fortran source and make the changes indicated by the compiler error messages.

- Linking if successful to generate an executable

  - Automatic link. This happens behind the scenes and the executable is generated for you immediately.

  - Manual link. You explicitly invoke the linker to generate the executable.

- Running the program.

- Determining whether the program actually works and gives the results expected.

These steps must be taken whatever hardware platform, operating system and compiler you use. Some people like working at the operating system prompt (e.g. DOS or UNIX), others prefer working within a development environment. Both have their strengths and weaknesses.

7.10 Problems

1. Write a program that will read in your name and address and print them out in reverse order.

Think about the following points:

- How many lines are there in your name and address?
- What is the maximum number of characters in the longest line in your name and address?
- What happens at the first blank character of each input line?
- What characters can be used in Fortran to enclose each line of text typed in and hence not stop at the first blank character?
- If you use one of the two special characters to enclose text what happens if you start on one line and then press the return key before terminating the text?

The action here will vary between Fortran implementations.

2. Type in the program Sum_And_Average, given in this chapter.

Think about the following points:

- Is there a difference between separating the input by spaces or commas?
- Do you need the decimal point?
- What happens when you type in too much data?
- What happens when you type in too little?

If you have access to more than one compiler repeat the above and compare the results.

8

Arithmetic

Taking Three as the subject to reason about —
  A convenient number to state —
We add Seven, and Ten, and then multiply out
  By One Thousand diminished by Eight.
The result we proceed to divide, as you see,
  By Nine Hundred and Ninety and Two:
Then subtract Seventeen, and the answer must be
  Exactly and perfectly true.
Lewis Carroll, *The Hunting of the Snark*

Round numbers are always false.
Samuel Johnson.

Aims

The aims of this chapter are to introduce:

- The rules for the evaluation of arithmetic expressions to ensure that they are evaluated as you intend.

- The idea of truncation and rounding applied to reals.

- The use of the PARAMETER statement to define or set up constants.

- The concepts and ideas involved in numerical computation including:

  - Specifying data types using kind type parameters.

  - The concept of numeric models and positional number systems for integer and real arithmetic and their implementation on binary devices.

  - Testing the numerical representation of different kind types on a system.

8 Arithmetic

Most problems in the education and scientific community require arithmetic evaluation as part of the algorithm. As the rules for the evaluation of arithmetic in Fortran may differ from those that you are probably familiar with, you need to learn the Fortran rules thoroughly. In the previous chapter, we introduced the arithmetic assignment statement, emphasising the concepts of name, type and value. Here we will consider the way that arithmetic expressions are evaluated in Fortran.

Table 8.1 has details of the five arithmetic operators available in Fortran:

Mathematical operation	Fortran symbol or operator
Addition	+
Subtraction	−
Division	/
Multiplication	*
Exponentiation	**

Table 8.1 Fortran operators

Exponentiation is raising to a power. Note that the exponentiation operator is the * character *twice*.

The following are some examples of valid arithmetic statements in Fortran:

```
Taxable_Income = Gross_Pay - Deductions
Cost = Bill + Vat + Service
Delta = Deltax/Deltay
Area = Pi * Radius * Radius
Cube = Big ** 3
```

The above expressions are all simple, and there are no problems when it comes to evaluating them. However, now consider the following:

```
Tax_Payable = Gross_Pay - Allowances * Tax_Rate
```

This is ambiguous. There is a choice of doing the subtraction before or after the multiplication. Our everyday experience says that the subtraction should take place before the multiplication. However, if this expression was evaluated in Fortran the *multiplication* would be done before the subtraction.

We need to look at three areas here:

- The rules for forming expressions, the syntax.

- The rules for interpreting expressions, the semantics.

- The rules for evaluating expressions, optimization.

The syntax rules determine what expressions are valid. The semantics determine a valid interpretation, and once this has been done the compiler can replace this expression with any other mathematically equivalent expression, generally in the interests of optimization.

Here are the rules for the evaluation of expressions in Fortran:

- Brackets are used to define priority in evaluation of an expression.

- Operators have a hierarchy of priority – a precedence. The hierarchy of operators is:

  - **exponentiation;** when the expression has multiple exponentiation, they are evaluated right to left. For example,

    L=I**J**K

    is evaluated by first raising J to the power K, and then using this result as the exponent for I; more explicitly therefore

    L=I**(J**K)

    Although this is similar to the way in which we might expect an algebraic expression to be evaluated, it is not consistent with the rules for multiplication and division, and may lead to some confusion. When in doubt, use brackets.

  - **multiplication and division;** within successive multiplications and divisions, the rules regarding any mathematically equivalent expression means that to ensure the evaluation you want brackets must be used. For example with

    A=B*C/D*E

    for non-integer numeric types the compiler does not necessarily evaluate in a left to right manner, i.e. evaluate B times C, then divide the result by D and finally take that result and multiply by

E. Section 7.2.5 of the standard confuses the issue by stating that within the context of equal precedence that left to right scanning would apply.

- **addition and subtraction**; as for multiplication and division the rules regarding any equivalent expression apply. However, it is seldom that the order of addition and subtraction is important, unless other operators are involved. Again section 7.2.5 of the standard confuses the issue by stating in the context of equal precedence that left to right scanning applies.

The following are all examples of valid arithmetic expressions in Fortran:

```
Slope = (Y1-Y2)/(X1-X2)
X1=(-B+((B*B-4*A*C)**0.5))/(2*A)
Q = Mass_D/2*(Mass_A*Veloc_A/Mass_D)**2 + &
      ((Mass_A * Veloc_A)**2)/2
```

Note that brackets have been used to make the order of evaluation more obvious. It is often possible to write involved expressions without brackets, but, for the sake of clarity, it is often best to leave the brackets in, even to the extent of inserting a few extra ones to ensure that the expression is evaluated correctly. The expression will be evaluated just as quickly with the brackets as without. Also note that none of the expressions are particularly complex. The last one is about as complex as you should try: with more complexity than this it is easy to make a mistake.

The rule regarding any equivalent expression therefore means if A, B and C are numeric that the following are true:

A + B = B + A

- A + B = B - A

A + B + C = A + (B + C)

and the last is nominally evaluated left to right, as the additions are of equal precedence.

A * B = B * A

A * B * C = A * (B * C)

and again the last is nominally evaluated left to right, as the multiplications are of equal precedence.

A * B - A * C = A * (B - C)

A / B / C = A / (B * C)

The last is true for non-integer numeric types only.

Problems arise when the value that a *faulty* expression yields lies within the range of expected values and the error may well go undetected. This may appear strange at first, but a computer does exactly what it is instructed to do. If, through a misunderstanding on the part of a programmer, the program is syntactically correct but logically wrong from the point of view of the problem definition, then this will not be spotted by the compiler. If an expression is complex, break it down into successive statements with elements of the expression on each line, e.g.

```
Temp = B * B - 4 * A * C
X1 = ( - B + ( Temp ** 0.5 )) / ( 2 * A )
```

and

```
Moment = Mass_A * Veloc_A
Q = Mass_D / 2 * ( Moment / Mass_D ) **2 + &
    ( Moment **2) / 2
```

8.1 Rounding and truncation

When arithmetic calculations are performed one of the following can occur:

- **Truncation.** This operation involves throwing away part of the number, e.g. with 14.6 truncating the number to two figures leaves 14.

- **Rounding**. Consider 14.6 again. This is rounded to 15. Basically, the number is changed to the nearest whole number. It is still a real number. What do you think will happen with 14.5, will this be rounded up or down?

You must be aware of these two operations. They may occasionally cause problems in division and in expressions with more than one data type.

To see some of the problems that can occur consider the examples below:

```
REAL :: A,B,C
INTEGER :: I
   A = 1.5
   B = 2.0
   C = A/B
   I = A/B
```

After executing these statements C has the value 0.75, and I has the value zero! This is an example of type conversion across the = sign. The variables on the right are all real, but the last variable on the left is integer. The value is therefore made into an integer by truncation. In this example, 0.75 is real, so I becomes zero when truncation takes place.

Consider now an example where we assign into a real variable (so that no truncation due to the assignment will take place), but where part of the expression on the right hand side involves integer division.

```
INTEGER  ::  I,J,K
REAL  ::  Answer
   I=5
   J=2
   K=4
   Answer=I/J*K
```

The value of ANSWER is 8, because the I/J term involves integer division. The expected answer of 10 is not that different from the actual one of 8, and it is cases like this that cause problems for the unwary, i.e. where the calculated result may be close to the actual one. In complicated expressions it would be easy to miss something like this.

To recap, truncation takes place in Fortran

- across an = sign, when a real is assigned to an integer;

- in integer division

It is very important to be careful when attempting *mixed mode arithmetic* – that is, when mixing reals and integers. If a real and integer are together in a division or multiplication, the result of that operation will be real; when addition or subtraction takes place, in a similar situation, the result will also be real. The problem arises when some parts of an expression are calculated using integer arithmetic, and other parts with real arithmetic:

```
C = A + B - I / J
```

The integer division is carried out before the addition and subtraction, hence the result of I/J is integer, although all the other parts of the expression will be carried out with real arithmetic.

8.2   Example 1: Time taken for light to travel from the Sun to Earth

How long does it take for light to reach the Earth from the Sun? Light travels 9.46 10^{12} km in one year. We can take a year as being equivalent to 365.25 days. (As all school-children know, the astronomical year is 365 days, 5 hours, 48 minutes and 45.9747 seconds – hardly worth the extra effort.) The distance between the Earth and Sun is about 150,000,000 km. There is obviously a bit of imprecision involved in these figures, not least since the Earth moves in an elliptical orbit, not a circular one. One last point to note before presenting the program is that the elapsed time will be given in minutes and seconds. Few people readily grasp fractional parts of a year.

```fortran
PROGRAM Time
IMPLICIT NONE
REAL :: Light_Minute, Distance, Elapse
INTEGER :: Minute, Second
REAL , PARAMETER :: Light_Year=9.46*10**12
! Light_year   : Distance travelled by light
! in one year in km
! Light_minute : Distance travelled by light
! in one minute in km
! Distance : Distance from sun to earth in km
! Elapse : Time taken to travel a
! distance (Distance) in minutes
! Minute : Integer number part of elapse
! Second : Integer number of seconds
! equivalent to fractional part of elapse
!
   Light_minute = Light_Year/(365.25*24.0*60.0)
   Distance = 150.0*10**6
   Elapse = Distance / Light_minute
   Minute = Elapse
   Second = ( Elapse - Minute)*60
   Print *,' Light takes ' , Minute,' Minutes'
   Print *,'                ' , Second,' Seconds'
   Print *,' To reach the earth from the sun'
END PROGRAM Time
```

The calculation is straightforward; first we calculate the distance travelled by light in one minute, and then use this value to find out how many minutes it takes for light to travel a set distance. Separating the time taken in minutes into whole number minutes and seconds is accomplished by exploiting the way in which Fortran will truncate a real number to an integer on type conversion. The difference between these two values is the part of a minute which needs to be converted to seconds. Given the inaccuracies already inherent in the exercise, there seems little point in giving decimal parts of a second.

It is worth noting that some structure has been attempted by using comment lines to separate parts of the program into fairly distinct chunks. Note also that the comment lines describe the variables used in the program.

Final note: type this program in and compile it. It will generate an error on certain systems. Can you think where the error will occur?

8.3   The PARAMETER statement

This statement is used to provide a way of associating a meaningful name with a *constant* in a program. Consider a program where π was going to be used a lot. It would be silly to have to type in 3.14159265358, etc. every time. There would be a lot to type and it is likely that a mistake could be made typing in the correct value. It therefore makes sense to set up π once and then refer to it by name. However, if PI was just a variable then it would be possible to do the following:

```
REAL :: LI,PI
.
PI=3.14159265358
.
PI=4*ALPHA/BETA
```

The PI=4*ALPHA/BETA statement should have been LI=4*ALPHA/BETA. What has happened is that, through a typing mistake (P and L are close together on a keyboard), an error has crept into the program. It will not be spotted by the compiler. Fortran provides a way of helping here with the PARAMETER statement, which should be preceded with a type declaration. The following are correct examples of the PARAMETER statement:

```
REAL , PARAMETER :: Pi=3.14159265358 , C=2.997925
```

and

```
REAL , PARAMETER :: Charge=1.6021917
```

The advantage of the PARAMETER statement is that you could not then assign another value to Pi, C or Charge. If you tried to do this, the compiler would generate an error message.

A PARAMETER statement may contain an arithmetic expression, so that some relatively simple arithmetic may be performed in setting up these constants. The evaluation must be confined to addition, subtraction, multiplication, division and integer exponentiation. The following examples help to demonstrate the possibilities:

```
REAL , PARAMETER :: Parsec = 3.08*10**16 , &
                    Pi = 3.14159265358 , &
                    Radian = 360./Pi
```

8.4   Precision and size of numbers

The precision and the size of a number in computing is directly related to the number of bits allocated to its internal representation. On a large number of computers this is the same as the word size. Table 8.2 summarizes this information for a number of machines, operating systems and compilers.

Machine and word size (bits)	Maximum Integer	Smallest real Largest real
DEC Alpha	(2**63) - 1	0.5562684646268004E-308
(64)	9223372036854774807	0.89884656743115785407E+308
DEC VAX	(2**31) - 1	0.29E-38
(32)	2,147,483,647	1.7E38
SUN SPARC	(2**31)-1	0.29E-38
(32)	2,147,483,647	1.7E38
IBM PC	(2**31) - 1	0.29E-38
(8, 16 and 32)	2,147,483,647	1.7E38

Table 8.2 Word size and reals and integers

Note that access to what the hardware supports is dependent on the operating system and compiler as well.

Precision is not the same as accuracy. In this age of digital time-keeping, it is easy to provide an extremely precise answer to the question *What time is it*? This answer need not be accurate, even though it is reported to tenths (or even hundredths!) of a second. Do not be fooled into believing that an answer reported to ten places of decimals must be accurate to ten places of decimals. The computer can only retain a limited precision. When calculations are performed, this limitation will tend to generate inaccuracies in the result. The estimation of such inaccuracies is the domain of the branch of mathematics known as Numerical Analysis.

To give some idea of the problems, consider an imaginary *decimal* computer, which retains two significant digits in its calculations. For example, 1.2, 12.0, 120.0 and 0.12 are all given to two digit precision. Note therefore that 1234.5 would be represented as 1200.0 in this device. When any arithmetic operation is carried out, the result (including any intermediate calculations) will have two significant digits. Thus:

```
130+12 = 140  (rounding down from 142)
```

and similarly:

```
17/3 = 5.7  (rounding up from 5.666666...)
```

and:

```
16*16 = 260
```

Where there are more involved calculations, the results can become even less attractive. Assume we wish to evaluate:

```
(16*16) / 0.14
```

We would like an answer in the region of 1828.5718, or, to two significant digits, 1800.0. If we evaluate the terms within the brackets first, the answer is 260/0.14, or 1857.1428; 1900.0 on the two digit machine. Thinking that we could do better, we could re-write the fraction as:

```
(16/0.14) * 16
```

This gives a result of 1800.0.

Algebra shows that all these evaluations are equivalent if unlimited precision is available.

Care should also be taken when is one is near the numerical limits of the machine. Consider the following:

```
z = B * C / D
```

where B, C and D are all 10^{30} and we are using a VAX or IBM PC where the maximum real is approximately 10^{38}. Here the product B * C generates a number of 10^{60} – beyond the limits of the machine. This is called *overflow* as the number is too large. Note that we could avoid this problem by retyping this as:

```
z = B * (C/D)
```

where the intermediate result would now be $10^{30}/10^{30}$, i.e. 1.

There is an inverse called *underflow* when the number is too small, which is illustrated below:

```
Z = X1 * Y1 * Z1
```

where X1 and Y1 are 10^{-20} and Z1 is 10^{20}. The intermediate result of X1 * Y1 is 10^{-40} – again beyond the limits of the machine. This problem could have been overcome by retyping as:

```
Z = X1 * (Y1 * Z1)
```

This is a particular problem for many scientists and engineers with all machines that use 32-bit arithmetic for integer and real calculations. This is because many physical constants, etc are around the limits of the magnitude (large or small) supported by single precision. This is rarely a problem with machines with hardware support for 64-bit arithmetic.

How we get round this problem and how we move our programs from one platform to another making sure that we are working with the same precision and same range of numbers is covered in detail in the next section.

8.5 Health warning: optional reading, beginners are advised to leave until later

It is very important in scientific programming to know the range and precision of data on the hardware platform on which we are working. The facilities provided in Fortran 95 now allow the programmer to specify the range and precision they wish to use and the compiler will chose an appropriate type.

If it is not possible to offer the precision and range requested the compiler returns an error code. To avoid this happening the programmer needs to query the computer first for details of its data representations, before trying to run a program which specifies range and precision.

In order to do this we use the KIND intrinsic function. (Intrinsic functions are covered in depth in Chapter 14, and Appendix C), e.g.:

```
REAL :: X
PRINT *,'Kind number for X = ',KIND(X)
```

This will print out the *kind* number used by your system to represent default REAL variables. These kind numbers are arbitrary and there is usually no meaning attached to them.

Consider the following program which demonstrates the use of the KIND function.

```
PROGRAM Chapter8_01
IMPLICIT NONE
INTEGER          :: i
REAL             :: r
CHARACTER (1) :: c
LOGICAL             :: l
COMPLEX          :: cp
   PRINT *,' Integer  ',KIND(i)
   PRINT *,' Real     ',KIND(r)
   PRINT *,' Char     ',KIND(c)
   PRINT *,' Logical ',KIND(l)
   PRINT *,' Complex ',KIND(cp)
END PROGRAM Chapter8_01
```

It is worthwhile actually typing this program in and seeing what answers you get for the system you are working on. Output from a PC compiler is given below:

```
[FTN90 Version 1.12 Copyright (c)SALFORD SOFTWARE LTD
1992  &  ]
[                       (c)THE NUMERICAL ALGORITHMS
GROUP 1991,1992]
    NO ERRORS   [FTN90]
Program entered
  Integer   3
  Real      1
  Char      1
  Logical   2
  Complex   1
```

The following is the output from the DEC Fortran 90 compiler under OPEN VMS on an Alpha 2100:

```
Program entered
  Integer   4
  Real      4
  Char      1
  Logical   4
  Complex   4
```

Thus it is up to each compiler implementation to decide what kind numbers are associated with each type and kind variation. Thus the kind value on its own should not be used across platforms to try and achieve portability.

In fact, specifying a kind number actually is not what is intended by the Fortran 95 standard, so two intrinsic functions:

SELECTED_INT_KIND

and

SELECTED_REAL_KIND

are available instead. They are used to specify the range of numbers for integers and the range and precision of numbers for reals, and the compiler will return the appropriate kind numbers that it has assigned to such representations. These kind numbers can be assigned to parameters which we call *kind type parameters* and they can be used with REAL and INTEGER type declarations. Let's consider the two main numeric types to see how this works.

8.5.1 Selecting different INTEGER kinds

The Fortran 95 standard specifies that only one **integer** kind needs to be available, but often a machine's architecture or compiler implementation will offer more. Most compiler implementations will offer the following:

- 8-bit or one byte integers
- 16-bit or two byte integers
- 32-bit or four byte integers

and 64-bit or 8 byte integers will be available on certain platforms and implementations, e.g. the DEC alpha. The most common reason for choosing 8-bit or 16-bit integers is to reduce the memory requirements of your program and the most common reason for choosing 64-bit integers is to solve specialised problems in mathematics requiring large integer numbers.

To choose an integer kind other than the default, you specify the range of the numbers you require it to lie in, in terms of a power of 10, e.g.:

```
INTEGER, PARAMETER :: First = SELECTED_INT_KIND (2)
INTEGER (First) :: I,J
. . .
```

selects an integer kind parameter, First, with representation which includes all integers between -10^2 and 10^2, i.e. numbers in the range -100 to 100. The integer kind parameter can be used in brackets after the integer type statement, to specify variables of this integer kind, e.g. I and J.

If there is no integer kind representation for the range specified, the SE-LECTED_INT_KIND function returns -1. Unfortunately it is not possible to then test for -1 in a type statement, i.e. you will get a compile time error. We suggest that you run the program in section 8.5.9 to find the limits of your machine's architecture before trying to specify a kind parameter that it can't support.

8.5.2   Selecting different REAL kinds

The Fortran 95 standard specifies that there must be at least two representations of the real type, the default plus one other. Often there are more depending on what the underlying hardware can support. When working with real data there are two things to specify, range and precision. The precision is the minimum number of significant digits (all floating point numbers are normalized) to which real numbers are stored, and the range is the power of 10 of the largest number to be represented. So, for example, to specify that a variable R has a kind type that supports 15 significant figures and a range $\pm 10^{-307}$ to $\pm 10^{307}$ we define a real kind parameter, *Long* and then use this with the REAL type declaration for R as follows:

```
INTEGER, PARAMETER :: Long=SELECTED_REAL_KIND(15,307)
REAL (Long) :: R
```

The only problem is if the underlying hardware can't support this specification, in which case the function will return -1 if the requested precision is unavailable, - 2 if the range is unavailable, and -3 if both are unavailable. As we mentioned earlier with integer kinds, it is not possible to test for negative values in a type declaration, so before trying to use different kind types, or even just the default types, you need to know what kind types your machine supports and the range and precision of them.

8.5.3   Specifying kind types for literal integer and real constants

A literal constant is a data object whose value cannot change. An integer constant 1 is of default integer kind and a real constant 10.3 is a default real constant. If in a program you have chosen a real kind type, other than the default, then to be consistent and also to make sure that all real arithmetic is done to the precision specified, you need to declare all real constants to be of this kind type. This is done by giving the literal constant followed by an underscore and a kind number or kind type parameter, e.g.:

```
constant_kind
```

For the earlier example with a kind type parameter Long a real literal constant of this type would be given as:

```
-22.36_Long
```

It is not recommended to use the actual kind number because, as we have seen, these are not portable across machines.

The convention we use throughout the book if we require a numeric kind type other than the defaults is to specify a kind type parameter, e.g.::

```
INTEGER, PARAMETER :: Long=SELECTED_REAL_KIND(15,307)
```

and then use it with REAL type declarations, e.g.

```
REAL (Long) :: R
```

This still doesn't make programs completely portable across different hardware platforms, so you will firstly need to run a program which tests the range of data representations. Before doing this we need to know a bit more about the underlying representation of numerical data on computer systems.

8.5.4 Positional number systems

Most people take arithmetic completely for granted, and rarely think much about the subject. It is necessary to look in a bit more depth at this subject if we are to understand what the computer is doing in this area.

Our way of working with numbers is essentially a positional one. When we look at the number 1024 for example we rarely think of it in terms of 1 * 1000 + 0 * 100 + 2 * 10 + 4 * 1. Thus the normal decimal systems we use in everyday life is a positional one, with a base of 10.

We are probably aware that we can use other number bases, and 2, 8 and 16 are fairly common alternate number bases. As the computer is a binary device it uses base 2.

We are also reasonably familiar with a mantissa exponent or floating point combination when the numbers get very large or very small, e.g. a parsec is commonly expressed as 3.08*10**16, and here the mantissa is 3.08, and the exponent is 10**16.

The above information will help in understanding the way in which integers and reals are represented on computer systems.

8.5.5 Bit data type and representation model

The model is only defined for positive integers (or cardinal numbers), where they are represented as a sequence of binary digits, and is based on the model:

$$i = \sum_{k=0}^{n-1} b_k \, 2^k$$

where i is the integer value, n is the number of bits, and b_k is a bit value of 0 or 1, with bit numbering starting at 0, and reading right to left. Thus the integer 43 and bit pattern 101011 is given by:

$43 = (1*32) + (0*16) + (1*8) + (0*4) + (1*2) + (1*1)$

or

$43 = (1*2^5) + (0*2^4) + (1*2^3) + (0*2^2) + (1*2^1) + (1*2^0)$

8.5.6   Integer data type and representation model

The integer data type is based on the model:

$$i = s \sum_{k=1}^{q} l_k \, r^{k-1}$$

where i is the integer value, s is the sign, q is the number of digits (always positive), r is the radix or base (integer greater than 1), and l_k is a positive integer (less than r).

A base of 2 is typical so 1023 is:

$1023 = (1*2^9) + (1*2^8) + (1*2^7) + (1*2^6) + (1*2^5) + (1*2^4) + (1*2^3) + (1*2^2) +$
$(1*2^1) + (1*2^0)$

8.5.7   Real data type and representation model

The real data type is based on the model:

$$x = s \, b^e \sum_{k=1}^{m} f_k \, b^{-k}$$

where x is the real number, s is the sign, b is the radix or base (greater than 1), m is the number of bits in the mantissa, e is an integer in the range e_{min} to e_{max} and f_k is a positive number less than b.

This means that with, for example, a 32-bit real there would be 8 bits allocated to the exponent and 24 to the mantissa. One of these bits in each part would be used to represent the sign and is hence called the sign bit. This reduces the numbers of bits that actually can be used to represent the mantissa and exponent to 31 and 7 respectively. There is also the concept of normalization, where the exponent is adjusted so that the most significant bit is in position 22 – bits are typically numbered 0–22, rather than 1–23. This form of representation is not new, and is documented around 1750 BC, when Babylonian mathematicians used a sexagesimal (radix 60) positional notation. It is interesting that the form they used omitted the exponent!

This is the theoretical basis of the representation of these three data types in Fortran. Remember from chapter 2 that the computer is essentially a binary device, and works at the lowest level with sequences of zeros and ones.

This information together with the following provides a good basis for writing portable code across a range of hardware.

8.5.8 IEEE 754

For many people there will also be access to floating point arithmetic as defined in IEEE 754. For example all Sun Sparc and Sun x86 based computers use IEEE arithmetic. The DEC F90 compiler also provides an option to allow specification of IEEE floating point arithmetic.

For a description of IEEE 754 the bibliography should be consulted, and is essential reading when working on Sun hardware.

8.5.9 Example 2: Testing the numerical representation of different kind types on a system

You are now ready to write or adapt a program to run on your system in order to test the range of integer kind types, and the range and precision of real kind types.

The following program selects several integer and real kind types and by calling the intrinsic functions KIND, HUGE, PRECISION and EPSILON it produces most of the information you need to know about these kind types.

Table 8.3 provides details of what these functions do.

Function	Action
KIND(X)	returns kind type number for X.
HUGE(X)	returns largest number in the numerical model representing numbers of the same type kind as X.
PRECISION(X)	returns the decimal precision in the numerical model representing real numbers of the same kind type as X.
EPSILON(X)	returns a positive model number that is almost negligible compared to unity in the model representing numbers of the same kind type as X.

Table 8.3 Function description

```
PROGRAM C8_ex04
!
! Examples of the use of the kind
! function and the numeric inquiry functions
!
! Integer arithmetic
! -----------------
!
! 32 bits is a common word size,
! and this leads quite cleanly
! to the following
! 8 bit integers
! -128 to 127 10**2
! 16 bit integers
! -32768 to 32767 10**4
! 32 bit integers
! -2147483648 to 2147483647 10**9
!
!
INTEGER                              :: I
INTEGER ( SELECTED_INT_KIND( 2))     :: I1
INTEGER ( SELECTED_INT_KIND( 4))     :: I2
```

```
INTEGER ( SELECTED_INT_KIND( 9))    ::  I3

! Real arithmetic
! --------------
! 32 bits is a common word size,
! but 64 bits is also available
!
! 32 bit integers 8 bit exponent, 24 bit mantissa
! This applies on both DEC VAX and the Intel family
! of processors, i.e. 80386, 80486.
!
! 64 bits. Two choices here,
! simply double the precision
! and keep the mantissa the same or alter both.
!
! 64 bit   8/56 exponent/mantissa
! same as for 32 bit
! 64 bit 11/53 exponent/mantissa
! now got approximately the same
! precision as for 56 bit mantissa,
! but the range is now ~ 10**308
! much more useful in the scientific world.

REAL :: R
REAL ( SELECTED_REAL_KIND(6,37)) :: R1
!
! The next has to be commented out on the PC.
!
!REAL ( SELECTED_REAL_KIND(15,38)) :: R2
!
REAL ( SELECTED_REAL_KIND(15,307)) :: R3
   PRINT *,' '
   PRINT *,' Integer values'
   PRINT *,' Kind      Huge'
   PRINT *,' '
   PRINT *,' ',KIND(I  ),' ',HUGE(I  )
   PRINT *,' '
   PRINT *,' ',KIND(I1 ),' ',HUGE(I1 )
   PRINT *,' ',KIND(I2 ),' ',HUGE(I2 )
   PRINT *,' ',KIND(I3 ),' ',HUGE(I3 )
   PRINT *,' '
   PRINT *,' Real values'
```

```
   PRINT *,' Kind      Huge                    ',&
 'Precision        epsilon'
   PRINT *,' '
   PRINT *,' ',KIND(R  ),' ',HUGE(R  ),&
   '              ',PRECISION(R),' ',EPSILON(R)
   PRINT *,' '
   PRINT *,' ',KIND(R1 ),' ',HUGE(R1 ),&
   '              ',PRECISION(R1),' ',EPSILON(R1)
! PRINT *,' ',KIND(R2 ),' ',HUGE(R2 ),&
!    ' ',PRECISION(R2),' ',EPSILON(R2)
   PRINT *,' ',KIND(R3 ),' ',HUGE(R3 ),&
   ' ',PRECISION(R3),' ',EPSILON(R3)

END PROGRAM C8_ex04
```

and the result of running this program on a PC follows:

```
[FTN90 Version 2.0 Copyright (c)SALFORD SOFTWARE LTD
1992-1994   &  ]
[                      (c)THE NUMERICAL ALGORITHMS
GROUP 1991,1992,1993]
   NO ERRORS  [FTN90]
Program entered

  Integer values
  Kind    Huge

   3    2147483647

   1    127
   2    32767
   3    2147483647

  Real values
  Kind    Huge                  Precision        epsilon

  1      3.4028235E+38              6
1.1920929E-07

  1      3.4028235E+38              6
1.1920929E-07
```

```
    2       1.7976931348623157E+308       15
2.2204460492503131E-16
```

Run this program on whatever system you have access to and compare the output.

8.5.10   Example 3: Binary representation of different integer kind type numbers

For those who wish to look at the internal binary representation of integer numbers, with a variety of kinds we have included the following program.

SELECTED_INT_KIND(2) means provide at least an integer representation with numbers between -10^2 and $+10^2$.

SELECTED_INT_KIND(4) means provide at least an integer representation with numbers between -10^4 and $+10^4$.

SELECTED_INT_KIND(9) means provide at least an integer representation with numbers between -10^9 and $+10^9$.

We use the INT function to convert from one integer representation to another.

We use the logical function BTEST to determine whether the binary value at that position within the number is a zero or a one, i.e. if the bit is set.

I_in_Bits is a character string that holds a direct mapping from the internal binary form of the integer and a text string that prints as a sequence of zeros or ones.

```
PROGRAM Integer_Representation
!
! Use the bit functions in Fortran to write out a
! 32 bit integer number as a sequence of
! zeros and ones
!
INTEGER :: J
INTEGER :: I
INTEGER ( SELECTED_INT_KIND( 2)) :: I1
INTEGER ( SELECTED_INT_KIND( 4)) :: I2
INTEGER ( SELECTED_INT_KIND( 9)) :: I3
CHARACTER (LEN=32) :: I_in_Bits
   PRINT *,' Type in an integer '
   READ * , I
   I1=INT(I,KIND(2))
   I2=INT(I,KIND(4))
   I3=INT(I,KIND(9))
```

```
    I_in_Bits=' '
    DO J=0,7
       IF (BTEST(I1,J)) THEN
          I_in_Bits(8-J):8-J)='1'
       ELSE
          I_in_Bits(8-J):8-J)='0'
       END IF
    END DO
    PRINT *,'            1         2         3'
    PRINT *,'12345678901234567890123456789012345678901234567890'
    PRINT *,I1
    PRINT *,I_in_Bits
    DO J=0,15
       IF (BTEST(I2,J)) THEN
          I_in_Bits(16-J:16-J)='1'
       ELSE
          I_in_Bits(16-J:16-J)='0'
       END IF
    END DO
    PRINT *,I2
    PRINT *,I_in_Bits
    DO J=0,31
       IF (BTEST(I3,J)) THEN
          I_in_Bits(32-J:32-J)='1'
       ELSE
          I_in_Bits(32-J:32-J)='0'
       END IF
    END DO
    PRINT *,I3
    PRINT *,I_in_Bits
END PROGRAM Integer_Representation
```

The DO loop indices follow the convention of an 8-bit quantity starting at bit 0 and ending at bit 7, 16-bit quantities starting at 0 and ending at 15 etc.

The numbers written out follow the conventional mathematical notation of having the least significant quantity at the right hand end of the digit sequence, i.e. with 127 in decimal we have 1 * 100, 2 * 10 and 7 * 1, so 00100001 in binary means 1 * 32 + 1 * 1 decimal.

Try running this program on the system you are using. Does it produce the results you expect? Experiment with a variety of numbers. Try at least the following 0, +1, -1, -128, 127, 128, -32768, 32767, 32768.

8.5.11 Summary of how to select the appropriate KIND type

To write programs that will perform arithmetically in a similar fashion on a variety of hardware therefore requires an understanding of:

- The integer data representation model, and in practice the word size of the various integer kind types.

- The real data representation model, and in practice the word size of the various real kind types and the number of bits in both the mantissa and exponent.

Armed with this information we can then choose a kind type that will ensure minimal problems when moving from one platform to another. End of health warning!

8.6 Variable status

Fortran has two concepts regarding the status of a variable, and these are defined and undefined. If a program does not provide an initial value (in a type statement) for a variable then its status is said to be undefined. Consider the following code segment taken from the earlier example that calculated the sum and average of three numbers:

```
REAL :: N1, N2, N3, Average=0.0, Total=0.0
INTEGER :: N=3
```

In the above the variables Average, Total and N all have a defined status. However N1, N2 and N3 are said to be undefined. The use of undefined values is implementation dependent and therefore not portable. Care must be taken when writing programs to ensure that your variables have a defined status wherever possible. We will look at this area again in later chapters.

8.7 Summary

The following are some practical rules and guidelines:

- Learn the rules for the evaluation of arithmetic expressions.

- Break expressions down where necessary to ensure that the expressions are evaluated in the way you want.

- Take care with truncation due to integer division in an expression. Note that this will only be a problem where both parts of the division are INTEGER.

- Take care with truncation due to the assignment statement when there is an integer on the left hand side of the statement, i.e. assigning a real into an integer variable.

- When you want to set up constants, which will remain unchanged throughout the program, use the PARAMETER statement.

- Do not confuse precision and accuracy.

- Learn what the default KINDs are for the numeric types you work with, and what the maximum and minimum values and precision are for REAL data, and what the maximum and minimum are for INTEGER data.

- You have been introduced to the use of the functions DIGITS, HUGE and PRECISION, and some of the concepts involved in their use. We will look at functions in much greater depth later on.

8.8   Problems

1. Modify the program that read in your name and address to also read in and print out your age, telephone number and sex.

2. One of the easiest ways to write a program is to modify an existing one. The example given earlier, dealing with the time taken for light to travel from the Sun to the Earth, could form the basis of several other programs.

(i) Many communications satellites follow a geosynchronous orbit, some 35,870 km above the Earth's surface. What is the time lag incurred in using one such satellite for a telephone conversation?

(ii) The Moon is about 384,400 km from the Earth on average. What implications does this have for control of experiments on the Moon? What is the time lag?

(iii) The following table gives the distance in 10^9m from the Sun to the planets in the Solar System:

Mercury	57.9	Venus	108.2
Earth	149.6	Mars	227.9
Jupiter	778.3	Saturn	1427.0
Uranus	2869.6	Neptune	4496.6
Pluto	5900.0		

Table 8.4 The planets

Use this information to find the greatest and least time taken to send a message from Earth to the other planets. Assume that all orbits are in the same plane and circular (if it was good enough for Copernicus, it's good enough for this example). For all practical purposes, the speed of light in vacuum is a constant, and therefore an excellent candidate for a PARAMETER statement. Use it.

3. Write a program to read in, sum and average five numbers.

4. Write a program to calculate the period of a pendulum. Use the following formula:

```
T=2*PI*(LENGTH/9.81)**.5
```

Calculate the period for at least 5 values of the length. The length (LENGTH) is in metres, and the time (T) in seconds. π was given a value earlier in this chapter.

Repeat the above using two other methods. Try a hand held calculator and a spreadsheet. Do you get the same answers?

5. Unit pricing: Table 8.4 gives the price and weight of various cereals available in the local supermarket.

Cereal	Price	Weight (grams)
Rice Crispys	71	295
Bran Bits	85	625
Coco Puffs	77	280
Huffa Puffa Rice	76	230
Friends Oats	74	750
Welsh Porage Oats	74	750
More	61	250
Korn Flakes	81	500
Korn Flakes	65	375

Table 8.5 Cereal pricing

Which of these gives best value for money, in terms of cost per gram (i.e. unit pricing)? Which gives the poorest value, on the same criterion?

6. Write a program that tests the precision and size of numbers of the system you use. Finding out the word size of the machine you work with is the first step. Then try some multiplication and division, and see what sort of error messages you get as the numbers become too small and too large.

Hint: Try reading in a value (try both 1.0E37 and 1.0E-37) and multiplying by 10, 100 and 1000, and dividing by 10, 100 and 1000.

If you have access to more than one Fortran 95 compiler try the program out on the other platforms and look at the differences in error reporting.

7. Base conversion.

In this chapter you have seen a brief coverage of base conversion. The following program illustrates some of the problems that can occur when going from base 10 to base 2 and back again. Which numbers will convert without loss?

```
program base_conversion
real  :: x1=1.0
real  :: x2=0.1
real  :: x3=0.01
real  :: x4=0.001
real  :: x5=0.0001
   print *,'  ',x1
   print *,'  ',x2
   print *,'  ',x3
   print *,'  ',x4
   print *,'  ',x5
end program base_conversion
```

Which do you think will provide the same number as originally entered?

8. Simple subtraction. In this chapter we looked at representing floating point numbers in a finite number of bits.

Try the following program:

```
program subtract
real  :: a=1.0002
real  :: b=1.0001
real  :: c
   c=a-b
   print *,a
```

```
   print *,b
   print *,c
end program subtract
```

9. Expression equivalence. We introduced some of the rules that apply in Fortran for expression evaluation. In mathematics the following is true.

$$(x^2-y^2) = (x*x-y*y) = (x-y)*(x*y)$$

Try the following program:

```
program expression_equivalence
!
! simple evaluation of x*x-y*y
! when x and y are similar
!
! we will evaluate in three ways.
!
real :: x=1.002
real :: y=1.001
real :: t1,t2,t3,t4,t5
   t1=x-y
   t2=x+y
   print *,t1
   print *,t2
   t3=t1*t2
   t4=x**2-y**2
   t5=x*x-y*y
   print *,t3
   print *,t4
   print *,t5
end program expression_equivalence
```

Solve the problem with pencil and paper, calculator and Excel.

The last three examples show that you must be careful when using a computer to solve problems.

8.9 Bibliography

Some understanding of numerical analysis is essential for successful use of Fortran when programming. As Froberg says *'numerical analysis is a science – computation is an art.'* The following are some of the more accessible books available.

Froberg C.E., *Introduction to Numerical Analysis*, Addison Wesley, 1969.

The short chapter on numerical computation is well worth a read, and it covers some of the problems of conversion between number bases, and some of the errors that are introduced when we compute numerically. The Samuel Johnson quote owes its inclusion to Froberg!

IEEE, *IEEE Standard for Binary Floating-Point Arithmetic, ANSI/IEEE Std 754-1985*, Institute of Electrical and Electronic Engineers Inc.

The formal definition of IEEE 754.

Knuth D., *Seminumerical Algorithms*, Addison Wesley, 1969.

A more thorough and mathematical coverage than Wakerly. The chapter on positional number systems provides a very comprehensive historical coverage of the subject. As Knuth points out the floating point representation for numbers is very old, and is first documented around 1750 B.C. by Babylonian mathematicians. Very interesting and worthwhile reading.

Sun, *Numerical Computation Guide*, SunPro, 1993.

Very good coverage of the numeric formats for IEEE Standard 754 for Binary Floating-Point Arithmetic. All SunPro compiler products support the features of the IEEE 754 standard .

Wakerly J.F., *Microcomputer Architecture and Programming*, Wiley, 1981.

The chapter on number systems and arithmetic is surprisingly easy. There is a coverage of positional number systems, octal and hexadecimal number system conversions, addition and subtraction of non-decimal numbers, representation of negative numbers, two's complement addition and subtraction, one's complement addition and subtraction, binary multiplication, binary division, bcd or binary coded decimal representation and fixed and floating point representations. There is also coverage of a number of specific hardware platforms, including DEC PDP-11, Motorola 68000, Zilog Z8000, TI 9900, Motorola 6809 and Intel 8086. A little old but quite interesting nevertheless.

9

Arrays 1
Some Fundamentals

Thy gifts, thy tables, are within my brain
Full charactered with lasting memory

William Shakespeare, *The Sonnets*.

Here, take this book, and peruse it well:
The iterating of these lines brings gold;

Christopher Marlowe, *The Tragical History of Doctor Faustus*

Aims

The aims of the chapter are to introduce the fundamental concepts of arrays and DO loops, in particular:

- To introduce the ideas of tables of data and some of the formal terms used to describe them:

    - Array.

    - Vector.

    - List and linear list

- To discuss the array as a random access structure where any element can be accessed as readily as any other and to note that the data in an array is all of the same type.

- To introduce the twin concepts of data structure and corresponding control structure.

- To introduce the statements necessary in Fortran to support and manipulate these data structures.

9 Arrays 1: Some Fundamentals

9.1 Tables of data

Consider the following examples.

9.1.1 Telephone directory

A telephone directory consists of the following kinds of entries:

Name	Address	Number
Adcroft A.	61 Connaught Road, Roath, Cardiff	223309
Beale K.	14 Airedale Road, Balham	745 9870
Blunt R.U.	81 Stanlake Road, Shepherds Bush	674 4546
...		
...		
...		
Sims Tony	99 Andover Road,Twickenham	898 7330

This *structure* can be considered in a variety of ways, but perhaps the most common is to regard it as a *table* of data, where there are 3 columns and as many rows as there are entries in the telephone directory.

Consider now the way we extract information from this table. We would scan the name column looking for the name we are interested in, and then read along the row looking for either the address or telephone number, i.e. we are using the name to *look up* the item of interest.

9.1.2 Book catalogue

A catalogue could contain:

Author(s)	Title	Publisher
Carroll L.	Alice through the Looking Glass	Penguin
Steinbeck J.	Sweet Thursday	Penguin
Wirth N.	Algorithms plus Data Structures = Programs	Prentice Hall

Again, this can be regarded as a *table* of data, having 3 columns and many rows. We would follow the same procedure as with the telephone directory to extract the information. We would use the *Name* to *look up* what books are available.

9.1.3 Examination marks or results

This could consist of:

Name	Physics	Maths	History	Geography	French
Fowler L.	50	47	89	30	46
Barron L.W	37	67	65	68	98
Warren J.	25	45	48	10	36
Mallory D.	89	56	45	30	65
Codd S.	68	78	76	98	65

This can again be regarded as a *table* of data. This example has 6 columns and 5 rows. We would again *look up* information by using the Name.

9.1.4 Monthly rainfall

Typically this would consist of:

Month	Rainfall
January	10.4
February	11.1
March	8.3
April	7.5
May	3.2
June	4.6
July	3.2
August	4.5
September	2.1
October	3.1
November	10.1
December	11.1

In this table there are 2 columns and 12 rows. To find out what the rainfall was in July, we scan the table for July in the Month column and locate the value in the same row, i.e. the rainfall figure for July.

These are just some of the many examples of problems where the data that is being considered has a tabular structure. Most general purpose languages therefore have mechanisms for dealing with this kind of structure. Some of the special names given to these structures include:

- Linear list.

- List.

- Vector.

- Array.

The term used most often here, and in most books on Fortran programming, is *array*.

9.2   Arrays in Fortran

There are three key things to consider here:

- The ability to refer to a set or group of items by a single name.

- The ability to refer to individual items or members of this set, i.e. look them up.

- The choice of a control structure that allows easy manipulation of this set or array.

9.3   The DIMENSION attribute

The DIMENSION attribute defines a variable to be an array. This satisfies the first requirement of being able to refer to a set of items by a single name. Some examples are given below:

```
REAL , DIMENSION(100)  :: Wages
INTEGER , DIMENSION(10000)  ::   Sample
```

For the variable Wages it is of type REAL and an array of dimension or size 100, i.e. the variable array Wages can hold up to 100 real items.

For the variable Sample it is of type INTEGER and an array of dimension or size 10,000, i.e. the variable Sample can hold up to 10,000 integer items.

9.4   An index

An index enables you to refer to or select individual elements of the array. In the telephone directory, book catalogue, exam marks table and monthly rainfall examples we used the name to index or look up the items of interest. We will give concrete Fortran code for this in the example of monthly rain fall.

9.5   Control structure

The statement that is generally used to manipulate the elements of an array is the DO statement. It is typical to have several statements controlled by the DO statement, and the block of repeated statements is often called a *DO loop*. Let us look at two complete programs that highlight the above.

9.6   Monthly rainfall

Let us look at this earlier example in more depth now. Consider the following:

Month	Associated integer representation	Array and index	Rainfall value
January	1	RainFall(1)	10.4
February	2	RainFall(2)	11.1
March	3	RainFall(3)	8.3
April	4	RainFall(4)	7.5
May	5	RainFall(5)	3.2
June	6	RainFall(6)	4.6
July	7	RainFall(7)	3.2
August	8	RainFall(8)	4.5
September	9	RainFall(9)	2.1
October	10	RainFall(10)	3.1
November	11	RainFall(11)	10.1
December	12	RainFall(12)	11.1

Most of you should be familiar with the idea of the use of an integer as an alternate way of representing a month, e.g. in a date expressed as 1/3/2000, for 1st March 2000 (anglicized style) or 3rd January (americanized style). Fortran, in common with other programming languages, only allows the use of integers as an index into an array. Thus when we write a program to use arrays we have to map between whatever construct we use in everyday life as our index (names in our examples of telephone directory, book catalogue, and exam marks) to an integer representation in Fortran. The following is an example of an assignment statement showing the use of an index.

```
RainFall(1)=10.4
```

We saw earlier that we could use the DIMENSION attribute to indicate that a variable was an array. In the above example Fortran statement our array is called RainFall. In this statement we are assigning the value 10.4 to the first element of the array, i.e. the rainfall for the month of January is 10.4 We use the index 1 to represent the first month. Consider the following statement:

```
SummerAverage  =  (RainFall(6)  +  RainFall(7)  +  &
                    RainFall(8))/3
```

This statement says take the values of the rainfall for June, July and August, add them up and then divide by 3, and assign the result to the variable SummerAverage, thus providing us with the rainfall average for the three summer months – northern hemisphere of course.

9.6.1   Example 1: Rainfall

The following program reads in the 12 monthly values from the terminal, computes the sum and average for the year, and prints the average out.

```
PROGRAM Rain
IMPLICIT NONE
REAL :: Total=0.0, Average=0.0
REAL , DIMENSION(12) :: RainFall
INTEGER :: Month
   PRINT *,' Type in the rainfall values'
   PRINT *,' one per line'
   DO Month=1,12
      READ *, RainFall(Month)
   ENDDO
   DO Month=1,12
      Total = Total + RainFall(Month)
   ENDDO
   Average = Total / 12
   PRINT *,' Average monthly rainfall was'
   PRINT *, Average
END PROGRAM Rain
```

RainFall is the *array name*. The variable Month in brackets is the index. It takes on values from 1 to 12 inclusive, and is used to pick out or select elements of the array. The index is thus a variable and this permits dynamic manipulation of the array at *run time.* The general form of the DO statement is:

```
DO Counter = Start, End, Increment
```

The block of statements that form the loop are contained between the DO statement, which marks the beginning of the block or loop, and the ENDDO statement , which marks the end of the block or loop.

In this program, the DO loops take the form:

```
DO Month=1,12          start
    ...                      body
ENDDO                  end
```

The body of the loop in the program above has been indented. This is *not* required by Fortran. However it is good practice and will make programs easier to follow.

The number of times that the DO loop is executed is governed by the last part of the DO statement, i.e. by the:

```
Counter = Start, End, Increment
```

Start as it implies, is the initial value which the counter (or index, or control variable) takes. Each time the loop is executed, the value of the counter will be increased by the value of *increment,* until the value of *end* is reached. If *increment* is omitted, it is assumed to be 1. No other element of the DO statement may be omitted. In order to execute the statements within the loop (the *body*) it must be possible to reach *end* from *start.* Thus zero is an illegal value of *increment.* In the event that it is not possible to reach *end,* the loop will not be executed and control will pass to the statement after the end of the loop.

In the example above both loops would be executed 12 times. In both cases, the first time round the loop the variable MONTH would have the value 1, the second time round the loop the variable MONTH would have the value 2, etc., and the last time round the loop MONTH would have the value 12.

9.7 People's weights

Consider the following:

Person	Associated integer representation	Array and index	Associated value
Andy	1	Weight(1)	48.7
Barry	2	Weight(2)	76.5
Cathy	3	Weight(3)	58.5
Dawn	4	Weight(4)	65.3
Elaine	5	Weight(5)	88.7
Frank	6	Weight(6)	67.5
Gordon	7	Weight(7)	56.7
Hannah	8	Weight(8)	66.7
Ian	9	Weight(9)	70.6
Jatinda	10	Weight(10)	65.5

We have ten people, with their names as shown. We associate each name with a number – in this case we have ordered the names alphabetically, and the numbers therefore reflect their ordering. WEIGHT is the *array name*. The number in brackets is called the *index*. The index is used to pick out or select elements of the array. Therefore the table is read as 'the first element of the array WEIGHT has the value 48.7, the second element of the array WEIGHT has the value 76.5

9.7.1   Example 2: People's weights

There are two examples in the program below:

```
PROGRAM SumAndAverage
! The program reads up to 10 weights
! into the array Weight
! Variables used
! Weight, holds the weight of the people
! Person, an index into the array
! Total, total weight
! Average, average weight of the people
! Parameters used
! NumberOfPeople ,10 in this case.
! The weights are written out so that they can be
checked
!
IMPLICIT NONE
INTEGER , PARAMETER :: Number_Of_People = 10
```

```
REAL ::   Total = 0.0, Average = 0.0
INTEGER :: Person
REAL , DIMENSION(Number_of_People) :: Weight
   DO Person=1,Number_Of_People
      PRINT *, ' Type in the weight for person ',Person
      READ *,Weight(Person)
      Total = Total + Weight(Person)
   ENDDO
   Average = Total / Number_Of_People
   PRINT *,' The total of the weights is ',Total
   PRINT *,' Average Weight is ',Average
   PRINT *,' 10 Weights were '
   DO Person=1,Number_Of_People
      PRINT *,Weight(Person)
   ENDDO
END PROGRAM SumAndAverage
```

9.8 Summary

The DIMENSION attribute declares a variable to be an array. The DIMENSION attribute must come at the start of a program unit, with other *declarative* statements.

The PARAMETER attribute declares a variable to have a fixed value that cannot be changed during the execution of a program. In our example above note that this statement occurs before the other declarative statements that depend on it. To recap the statements covered so far, the order is summarized below.

PROGRAM	first statement	
INTEGER REAL CHARACTER	*declarative*	in any order and the DIMENSION and PARAMETER attributes are added here
Arithmetic assignment PRINT * READ * DO ENDDO	*executable*	in any order
END PROGRAM	last statement	

We choose individual members using an index, and these are always of integer type in Fortran.

The DO loop is a very convenient control structure to manipulate arrays, and we use indentation to clearly identify loops.

9.9 Problems

1. Using a DO loop and an array rewrite the program which calculated the average of five numbers (Question 3 in Chapter 8) and increase the number of values read in from 5 to 10.

2. Modify the program that calculates the total and average of people's weights to additionally read in their heights and calculate the total and average of their height. Use the data given below. This has been taken from a group of first year under-graduates.

```
1.85    85
1.80    76
1.85    85
1.70    90
1.75    69
1.67    83
```

```
1.55    64
1.63    57
1.79    65
1.78    76
```

Your body mass index is given by your height (in metres) squared divided by your weight in kilos. Calculate the BMI for each person..

Grades of obesity according to Garrow as follows:

Grade 0 (desirable) 20–24.9

Grade 1 (overweight) 25–29.9

Grade 2 (obese) 30–40

Grad 3 (morbidly obese) >40

Ideal BMI range,

Men, Range 20.1 – 25 kg/m^2

Women, Range 18.7 – 23.8 kg/m^2

When working on either a Unix system or a PC in a DOS box it is possible to use the following characters to enable you to read data from a file or write output to a file when running your program.

Character	Meaning
<	read from file
>	write to file

On a typical Unix system we could use:

```
a.out < data.dat > results.txt
```

to read the data from the file called data.dat and write the output to a file called results.txt.

On a PC in a DOS box the equivalent would be:

```
program.exe < data.dat > results.txt
```

This is a quick and dirty way of developing programs that do simple I/O, and we don't have to keep typing in the data and we also have a record of the behaviour of the program.

3. Modify the program that read in your name to read in 10 names. Use an array and a DO loop. When you have read the names into the array write them out in reverse order on separate lines.

Hint: Look at the formal syntax of the DO statement.

4. Modify the rainfall program (which assumes that the measurement is in inches) to convert the values to centimetres. One inch equals 2.54 centimetres. Print out the two sets of values as a table.

Hint: Use a second array to hold the metric measurements.

5. Combine the programs that read in and calculate the average weight with the one that reads in peoples names. The program should read in the weights into one array, and the names into another. Allow 20 characters for the length of a name. Print out a table linking names and weights.

6. In an earlier chapter we used the following formula to calculate the period of a pendulum:

T=2*PI*(LENGTH/9.81)**.5

Write a program that uses a DO loop to make the length go from 1 to 10 metres in 1 metre increments.

Produce a table with 2 columns, the first of lengths and the second of periods.

10

Arrays 2
Further Examples

Sir, In your otherwise beautiful poem (The Vision of Sin) there is a verse which reads

Every moment dies a man,
every moment one is born.

Obviously this cannot be true and I suggest that in the next edition you have it read

Every moment dies a man,
every moment 1 1/16 is born.

Even this value is slightly in error but should be sufficiently accurate for poetry.

Charles Babbage in a letter to Lord Tennyson.

Aims

The aims of the chapter are to extend the concepts introduced in the previous chapter and in particular:

- To introduce the idea of an array with more than one dimension.

- To introduce the corresponding control structure to permit easy manipulation of higher dimensioned arrays.

- To introduce an extended form of the DIMENSION attribute declaration.

- To introduce the corresponding alternative form to the DO statement, to help manipulate the array in this new form.

- To introduce the DO loop as a mechanism for the control of repetition in general, not just for manipulating arrays.

- To formally define the block DO syntax.

10 Arrays 2: Further Examples

10.1 Higher dimension arrays

There are many instances where it is necessary to have arrays with more than one dimension. Consider the following examples:

10.1.1 Example 1: A map

Consider the representation of height of an area of land expressed as a two dimensional table of numbers, e.g. we may have some information represented in a simple table as shown below:

	Longitude		
	1	2	3
Latitude			
1	10.0	40.0	70.0
2	20.0	50.0	80.0
3	30.0	60.0	90.0

The values in the *array* are the heights above sea level. The example is obviously artificial, but it does highlight the concepts involved. For those who have forgotten their geography lines of latitude run east–west (the equator is a line of latitude) and lines of longitude run north–south (they go through the poles and are all of the same length). In the above table therefore the latitude values are ordered by row and the longitude values are ordered by column.

A program to manipulate this data structure would involve something like the following:

```
PROGRAM C1001
! Variables used
! Height - used to hold the heights above sea level
! Long - used to represent the longitude
! Lat - used to represent the latitude
!     both restricted to integer values.
! Correct - holds the correction factor
IMPLICIT NONE
INTEGER , PARAMETER :: Size = 3
INTEGER   :: Lat , Long
REAL , DIMENSION(Size,Size) :: Height
```

```
REAL , PARAMETER :: Correct = 10.0
  DO Lat = 1,Size
    DO Long = 1,Size
      PRINT *,' Type in value at ',Lat,' ',Long
      READ * , Height(Lat,Long)
    ENDDO
  ENDDO
  DO Lat = 1,Size
    DO Long = 1,Size
      Height(Lat,Long) = Height(Lat,Long) + Correct
    ENDDO
  ENDDO
  PRINT * , ' Corrected data is '
  DO Lat = 1,Size
    DO Long = 1,Size
      PRINT * , Height(Lat,Long)
    ENDDO
  ENDDO
END PROGRAM C1001
```

Note the way in which indentation has been used to highlight the structure in this example. Note also the use of a textual prompt to highlight which data value is expected. Running the program highlights some of the problems with the simple I/O used in the example above. We will address this issue in the next example.

The *inner* loop is said to be *nested* within the outer one. It is very common to encounter problems where nesting is a natural way to express the solution. Nesting is permitted to any depth. Here is an example of a valid nested DO loop:

```
        DO                      ! Start of outer loop

          .

          DO                    ! Start of inner loop

            .

            .

          ENDDO                 ! End of inner loop

          .

        ENDDO                   ! End of outer loop
```

This example introduces the concept of two indices, and can be thought of as a row and column data structure.

10.1.2   Example 2: Sensible tabular output

The first example had the values printed in a format that wasn't very easy to work with. In this example we introduce a so-called implied DO loop, which enables us to produce neat and humanly comprehensible output.

```
PROGRAM C1002
! Variables used
! Height - used to hold the heights above sea level
! Long - used to represent the longitude
! Lat - used to represent the latitude
!     both restricted to integer values.
IMPLICIT NONE
INTEGER , PARAMETER :: Size = 3
INTEGER   :: Lat , Long
REAL , DIMENSION(Size,Size) :: Height
REAL , PARAMETER :: Correct = 1.5
  DO Lat = 1,Size
    DO Long = 1,Size
      READ * , Height(Lat,Long)
      Height(Lat,Long) = Height(Lat,Long) + Correct
    ENDDO
  ENDDO
  DO Lat = 1,Size
    PRINT * , (Height(Lat,Long),Long=1,3)
  ENDDO
END PROGRAM C1002
```

The key statement in this example is:

```
PRINT * , (Height(Lat,Long),Long=1,3)
```

This is called an implied DO–loop, as the longitude variable takes on values from 1 through 3 and will write out all three values on one line.

We will see other examples of this statement in later examples.

10.1.3   Example 3: Average of three sets of values

This example extends the previous one, and now we have three sets of measurements and we are interested in calculating the average of these three sets. The two new data sets are:

```
        9.5        39.5        69.5
       19.5        49.5        79.5
```

```
     29.5        59.5        89.5
```

and

```
     10.5        40.5        70.5
     20.5        50.5        80.5
     30.5        60.5        90.5
```

and we have chosen the values to enable us to quickly check that the calculations for the averages are correct.

```
PROGRAM C1003
! Variables used
! H1,H2,H3 - used to hold the heights above sea level
! H4 - used to hold the average of the above
! Long - used to represent the longitude
! Lat - used to represent the latitude
!     both restricted to integer values.
IMPLICIT NONE
INTEGER , PARAMETER :: Size = 3
INTEGER   :: Lat , Long
REAL , DIMENSION(Size,Size) :: H1,H2,H3,H4
  DO Lat = 1,Size
    DO Long = 1,Size
      READ * , H1(Lat,Long)
    ENDDO
  ENDDO
  DO Lat = 1,Size
    DO Long = 1,Size
      READ * , H2(Lat,Long)
    ENDDO
  ENDDO
  DO Lat = 1,Size
    DO Long = 1,Size
      READ * , H3(Lat,Long)
    ENDDO
  ENDDO
  DO Lat = 1,Size
    DO Long = 1,Size
      H4(Lat,Long)=( H1(Lat,Long) + H2(Lat,Long) + &
                  H3(Lat,Long) ) / Size
    ENDDO
  ENDDO
```

```
   DO Lat = 1,Size
       PRINT * , (H4(Lat,Long),Long=1,3)
   ENDDO
END PROGRAM C1003
```

The original data was accurate to 3 figures. The output from the above has spurious additional accuracy. We will look at how to correct this in the later chapter on output.

10.1.4   Example 4: Booking arrangements in a theatre or cinema

A theatre or cinema consists of rows and columns of seats. In a large cinema or a typical theatre there would also be more than one level or storey. Thus, a program to represent and manipulate this structure would probably have a two or three dimensional array. Consider the following program extract:

```
PROGRAM Theatre
IMPLICIT NONE
INTEGER   , PARAMETER :: NRows=30, NColumns=30,
NFloors=3
INTEGER :: Row,Column,Floor
? , DIMENSION(NRows, NColumns, NFloors) :: Seats
   . . .
   DO  Floor=1,NFloors
      DO  Column=1,NCols
         DO  Row=1,NRows
             PRINT *,Seats(Row,Column,Floor)
         ENDDO
      ENDDO
   ENDDO
   . . .
END PROGRAM Theatre
```

Note here the use of the term PARAMETER in conjunction with the INTEGER declaration. This is called an entity orientated declaration. An alternative to this is attribute orientated declarations, e.g.

```
INTEGER :: NRows,NColumns,NFloors
PARAMETER :: NRows=30,NColumns=30,NFloors
```

and we will be using the entity orientated declaration method throughout the rest of the book. This is our recommended method as you only have to look in one place to determine everything that you need to know about an entity.

An interesting question here is what is the best data type for *Seats*. We will leave the choice to you.

10.2 Additional forms of the DIMENSION attribute and DO loop statement

10.2.1 Example 5: Voltage from -20 to +20 volts

Consider the problem of an experiment where the independent variable voltage varies from −20 to +20 volts and the current is measured at 1 volt intervals. Fortran has a mechanism for handling this type of problem:

```
PROGRAM C10_03
IMPLICIT NONE
REAL , DIMENSION(-20:20) :: Current
REAL :: Resistance
INTEGER :: Voltage
   ...
   DO   Voltage=-20,20
      ...
      Current(Voltage)=Voltage/Resistance
      ...
   ENDDO
   ...
END PROGRAM C10_03
```

We appreciate that, due to experimental error, the voltage will not have exact integer values. However, we are interested in representing and manipulating a set of values, and thus from the point of view of the problem solution and the program this is a reasonable assumption. There are several things to note here:

• This form of the DIMENSION attribute:

```
DIMENSION(First:Last)
```

is of considerable use when the problem has an effective index which does not start at 1 (as implied by the original form of the statement).

• There is a corresponding form of the DO statement which allows processing of problems of this nature. This is shown in the above program. The general form of the DO statement is therefore:

```
DO counter=start, end, increment
```

where *start, end* and *increment* can be positive or negative. Note that zero is a legitimate value of the dimension limits and of a DO loop index.

10.2.2 Example 6: Longitude from -180 to +180

Consider the problem of the production of a table linking time difference with longitude. The values of longitude will vary from −180 to +180 degrees, and the time will vary from +12 hours to −12 hours. A possible program segment is:

```
PROGRAM Zone
IMPLICIT NONE
REAL , DIMENSION(-180:180) :: Time
INTEGER :: Degree,Strip
REAL :: Value
   ...
   DO Degree=-180,170,10
      Value=Degree/15.
      DO Strip=0,9
         Time(Degree+Strip)=Value
        ENDDO
   ENDDO
   ...
END PROGRAM Zone
```

10.2.3 Notes

The values of the time are **not** being calculated at every degree interval.

The variable Time is a real variable. It would be possible to arrange for the time to be an integer by expressing it in either minutes or seconds.

This example takes no account of all the wiggly bits separating time zones, or of British Summer Time.

What changes would you make to the program to accommodate +180? What is the time at -180 and +180?

10.3 The DO loop and straight repetition

10.3.1 Example 7: Table of temperatures

Consider the production of a table of temperatures. The independent variable is the Fahrenheit value; the Celsius temperature is the dependent variable. Strictly speaking, a program to do this does not have to have an array, i.e. the DO loop can be used to control the repetition of a set of statements that make no reference to an array. The following shows complete but simple conversion program.

```
PROGRAM Convert
IMPLICIT NONE
INTEGER :: Fahrenheit
REAL :: Celsius
   DO Fahrenheit=-50,250
      Celsius=(Fahrenheit-32)*5./9.
      PRINT *, Fahrenheit , Celsius
   ENDDO
END PROGRAM Convert
```

Note here that the DO statement has been used *only* to control the repetition of a block of statements. In the conversion of Fahrenheit to Celsius, we multiply by 5./9. rather than 5/9; do you recall why? If you can't remember have a look at Question 3 in the problems and try running it.

This is the other use of the DO statement. The DO loop thus has two functions, its use with arrays as a control structure, and its use solely for the repetition of a block of statements.

10.3.2   Example 7: Means and standard deviations

In the calculation of the mean and standard deviation of a list of numbers, we may use the following formulae. It is not actually necessary to store the values, nor to accumulate the sum of the values and their squares. In the first case, we would possibly require a large array, while in the second, it is conceivable that the accumulated values (especially of the squares) might be too large for the machine. The following example uses an *updating* technique which avoids these problems, but is still accurate. The DO loop is simply a control structure to ensure that all the values are read in, with the index being used in the calculation of the updates.

```
PROGRAM MeansAndStandardDeviation
! Variables used are
!    Mean  - for the running mean
!    SSQ   - The running corrected sum of squares
!    X     - Input values for which
! mean and sd required
!    W     - Local work variable
!    SD    - Standard Deviation
!    R     - Another work variable
IMPLICIT NONE
REAL :: Mean=0.0,SSQ=0.0,X,W,SD,R
INTEGER :: I,N
   PRINT *,' ENTER THE NUMBER OF READINGS'
   READ*,N
```

```
    PRINT*,' ENTER THE ',N,' VALUES, ONE PER LINE'
    DO I=1,N
        READ*,X
        W=X-Mean
        R=I-1
        Mean=(R*Mean+X)/I
        SSQ=SSQ+W*W*R/I
    ENDDO
    SD=(SSQ/R)**0.5
    PRINT *,' Mean is ',Mean
    PRINT *,' Standard deviation is ',SD
END PROGRAM MeansAndStandardDeviation
```

10.4 Summary

* Arrays can have up to 7 dimensions.

* DO loops may be nested, but they must not overlap.

* The DIMENSION attribute allows limits to be specified for a block of information which is to be treated in a common way. The limits must be integer, and the second limit must exceed the first, e.g.

```
REAL , DIMENSION(-123:-10) :: List
REAL , DIMENSION(0:100,0:100) :: Surface
REAL , DIMENSION(1:100) :: Value
```

The last example could equally be written:

```
REAL , DIMENSION(100) :: Value
```

where the first limit is omitted, and is given the default value 1. The array LIST would contain 114 values, while X would contain 2001.

* A DO statement and its corresponding ENDDO statement define a loop. The DO statement provides a starting value, terminal value, and, optionally, an increment, for its index or counter.

* The increment may be negative, but should never be zero. If it is not present, the default value is 1. It must be possible for the terminating value to be reached from the starting value.

* The counter in a DO loop is ideally suited for indexing an array, but it may be used anywhere that repetition is needed, and of course the index or counter need not be used explicitly.

The formal syntax of the block DO construct is

```
[ do-construct-name : ] DO [label] [ loop-control ]
    [execution-part-construct ]
[ label ] end-do
```

where the forms of the loop control are:

```
[ , ] scalar-variable-name =
scalar-numeric-expression ,
scalar-numeric-expression
[ , scalar-numeric-expression ]
```

and the forms of the end-do are:

```
END DO [ do-construct-name ]
CONTINUE
```

and [] identify optional components of the block DO construct. This statement is looked at in much greater depth in the chapter on control structures.

10.5 Problems

0. Compile and run the first three examples in this chapter if you haven't already done so to get familiar with what is happening with two dimensional arrays.

1. Modify the first example to convert the height in feet to height in metres. The conversion factor is one foot equals 0.305 metres.

Hint: You can either overwrite the height array or introduce a second array.

2. Of what data type should the array Seats be in the theatre example?

3. The following is a slight variation on the original temperature conversion program. What do you think the output will be?

```
PROGRAM Convert
IMPLICIT NONE
INTEGER :: Fahrenheit
REAL :: Celsius
!   .
  DO Fahrenheit=-50,250
    Celsius=5/9*(Fahrenheit-32)
    PRINT *, Fahrenheit , Celsius
  ENDDO
!   ...
```

END PROGRAM Convert

Now compile and run the program to verify what you thought. Key temperatures are -40, 32 and 212 Fahrenheit.

Is this what you expected? Try replacing 5/9 with 5./9. and run again. Is this any better?

4. Write a program to print out the 12 times table. Typical output would be of the form:

1	*	12	=	12
2	*	12	=	24
3	*	12	=	36

etc.

Hint: You don't need to use an array here.

5. Write a program to read the following data into a two dimensional array.

1	2	3
4	5	6
7	8	9

Produce totals for each row and column and produce a output similar to that below.

1	2	3	6
4	5	6	15
7	8	9	24
12	15	18	

Hint: You need to introduce variables for each row and column total. These can be either scalar variables or arrays.

6. Modify the above to produce averages for each row and column as well as the totals.

7. Write a program to convert from Celsius to Fahrenheit. The equation is:

Fahrenheit=32+9/5*Celsius

Use a DO loop to step the Celsius temperature from -50 to 100.

8. Combine the two temperature conversion programs. The output from the program should be similar to the following:

Celsius	T	Fahrenheit
-45.56	-50	-58.00
-45.00	-49	-56.20
-44.44	-48	-54.40
-43.89	-47	-52.60
-43.33	-46	-50.80
-42.78	-45	-49.00
-42.22	-44	-47.20
-41.67	-43	-45.40
-41.11	-42	-43.60
-40.56	-41	-41.80
-40.00	-40	-40.00
-39.44	-39	-38.20
-38.89	-38	-36.40
-38.33	-37	-34.60
-37.78	-36	-32.80
-37.22	-35	-31.00
-36.67	-34	-29.20
-36.11	-33	-27.40
-35.56	-32	-25.60
-35.00	-31	-23.80
-34.44	-30	-22.00

This enables the middle column to be treated as either Celsius or Fahrenheit and the corresponding temperature read off easily.

The actual output from your program will probably line up in a reasonable tabular form, but will have rather too much precision in most cases, and there will be the odd line where the output will be in a scientific numeric notation.

We will look at ways of achieving the above in later chapters.

9. Using the following data from Problem 2 in Chapter 9:

1.85	85
1.80	76
1.85	85
1.70	90
1.75	69
1.67	83
1.55	64
1.63	57
1.79	65

```
1.78      76
```

use the program that evaluated the mean and standard deviation to do so for these heights and weights.

In the first case use the program as is and run the program twice, first with the heights then with the weights.

What changes would you need to make to the program to read a height and a weight in pairs?

Hint: You could introduce separate scalar variables for the heights and weights.

Whole Array and Additional Array Features

A good notation has a subtlety and suggestiveness which at times make it seem almost like a live teacher.

Bertrand Russell.

Aims

The aims of the chapter are:

- To look more formally at the terminology required to precisely describe arrays.

- To introduce ways in which we can manipulate whole arrays and parts of arrays (sections).

- ALLOCATABLE arrays – ways in which the size of an array can be deferred until execution time.

- To introduce the concept of array element ordering and physical and virtual memory.

- To introduce ways in which we can initialize arrays using array constructors.

- To introduce the WHERE statement and array masking.

- To introduce the FORALL statement and construct.

11 Whole Array and Additional Array Features

11.1 Terminology

Fortran 95 introduces an abundance of array handling features. In order to make the description of these features more precise a number of additional terms have been introduced.

11.1.1 Rank

The number of dimensions of an array is called its rank. A one-dimensional array has rank 1, a two-dimensional array has rank 2 and so on.

11.1.2 Bounds

The bounds of an array are the upper and lower limits of the index in each dimension.

11.1.3 Extent

The number of elements along a dimension of an array is called the extent.

```
INTEGER, DIMENSION(-10:15) :: Current
```

has bounds -10 and 15 and an extent of 26.

11.1.4 Size

The total number of elements in an array is its size.

11.1.5 Shape

The shape of an array is determined by its rank and its extents in each dimension.

11.1.6 Conformable

Two arrays are said to be conformable if they have the same shape, that is they have the same rank and the same extents in each dimension.

11.2 Whole array manipulation

The examples of arrays so far have shown operations on arrays via array elements. One of the significant improvements in Fortran 95 is the ability to manipulate arrays as whole objects. This allows arrays to be referenced not just as single elements but also as groups of elements. Along with this ability comes a whole host of intrinsic procedures for array processing. These intrinsic procedures are mentioned in Chapter 14, and listed in alphabetical order, with examples in Appendix D.

11.2.1 Assignment

An array name without any indices can appear on both sides of assignment statements and input and output statements. For example a value can be assigned to all the elements of an array in one statement:

```
REAL, DIMENSION(1:12):: Rainfall
Rainfall=0.0
```

The elements of one array can be assigned to another:

```
INTEGER, DIMENSION(1:50) :: A,B
...
A=B
```

Arrays A and B must be conformable in order to do this.

The following example is **illegal** since X has shape 20 and Z has shape 41:

```
REAL, DIMENSION(1:20) :: X
REAL, DIMENSION(1:41) :: Z
X=50.0
Z=X
```

But the following is legal because both arrays are now conformable, i.e. they are both of rank 1 and an extent of 41:

```
REAL , DIMENSION (-20:20) :: X
REAL , DIMENSION (1:41) :: Y
X=50.0
Y=X
```

11.2.2 Expressions

All the arithmetic operators available to scalars are available to arrays, but care must be taken because mathematically they may not make sense.

```
REAL , DIMENSION (1:50) :: A,B,C,D,E
C=A+B
```

adds each element of A to the corresponding element of B and assigns the result to C.

```
E=C*D
```

multiplies each element of C by the corresponding element of D. This is **not** vector multiplication. To perform a vector dot product there is an intrinsic procedure

DOT_PRODUCT, and an example of this is given under the later section on array constructors.

For higher dimensions:

```
REAL ,DIMENSION (1:10,1:10) :: F,G,H
F=F**0.5
```

takes the square root of every element of F.

```
H=F+G
```

adds each element of F to the corresponding element of G.

```
H=F*G
```

multiplies each element of F by the corresponding element of G. The last statement is **not** matrix multiplication. An intrinsic procedure MATMUL performs matrix multiplication; further details are in Appendix D.

The following program demonstrates the power of these whole array features.

```
PROGRAM Temperatures
! This program reads in a grid of temperatures
! (degrees Fahrenheit) at 25 grid references
! and converts them to degrees Celsius
IMPLICIT NONE
REAL, DIMENSION (1:5,1:5) :: Fahrenheit, Celsius
INTEGER :: Long, Lat
!
! Read in the temperatures
!
   DO Lat=1,5
      PRINT *, ' For Latitude= ',Lat
      DO Long=1,5
         PRINT *, ' For Longitude', Long
         READ *,Fahrenheit( Long, Lat)
      END DO
   END DO
!
! Conversion applied to all values
!
   Celsius = 5.0/9.0 * (Fahrenheit - 32.0)
   PRINT * , Celsius
   PRINT * , Fahrenheit
```

```
END PROGRAM Temperatures
```

Note the use of whole arrays in the print statements. The output does look rather messy though, and also illustrates array element ordering.

11.3 Array sections

Often it is necessary to access part of an array not the whole, and this is possible with Fortran 95's powerful array manipulation features.

11.3.1 Example 1: Ages

```
INTEGER, DIMENSION (1:20) :: Ages
  Ages(1:5) = 0
! Sets elements 1 to 5 to value 0
  Ages(6:20) = 1
! Sets elements 6 to 20 to value 1
```

11.3.2 Example 2: Examination results

```
REAL, DIMENSION (1:20,1:10) :: Exam_Results
!
! Rows represent pupils
! Columns represent subjects
!
! Scale column 3 by 2.5 to change
! original mark out of 40
! to a mark out of 100
!
   Exam_Results(1:20,3) = 2.5 * Exam_Results(1:20,3)
```

11.4 Allocatable arrays

The sample program in Chapter 9 to read in, sum and average people's weights is restricted to ten people. This means that if we wish to run the program with a different number of people we would have to change the program, albeit only altering the parameter Number_Of_People. This is a common problem in programming and so Fortran 95 provides a facility to handle it. Instead of using:

```
INTEGER , PARAMETER :: Number_of_People=10
REAL, DIMENSION (Number_of_People) :: Weight
```

The compiler can be told to defer allocating space to this array until execution time, using:

```
REAL, DIMENSION (:), ALLOCATABLE :: Weight
READ *, Number_of_people
ALLOCATE(Weight(1:Number_of_people))
```

This is done by giving an array a deferred shape by using the ALLOCATABLE attribute and declaring only the rank of the array on the DIMENSION statement. The array can then be allocated space at run time using the ALLOCATE statement.

Arrays with the allocatable attribute are called deferred-shape arrays.

11.4.1 Example 3: Height above sea level

Taking the example in Chapter 10 of heights above sea level measured in feet, amend the program so that it converts to metres and then prints out the newly converted heights.

```
PROGRAM Locate
! Variables used
! Conversion - a constant holding the feet to metres
! conversion factor
! Height - used to hold heights above sea level
! Lat - used to represent latitude
! restricted to integer values
! Nzones - the number of degrees
IMPLICIT NONE
INTEGER :: Lat , Nzones
REAL, PARAMETER:: Conversion=0.305
REAL, DIMENSION(:,:), ALLOCATABLE :: Heights
!
! Read in the number of zones and
! allocate array Heights
!
   PRINT *, 'Input the number of zones'
   READ *, Nzones
   ALLOCATE (Heights ( 1:Nzones, 1:Nzones) )
!
! Read in heights by latitude
!
   DO Lat = 1, Nzones
      PRINT *, 'heights for latitude = ', Lat
      READ *, Heights(Lat, 1:Nzones)
   END DO
!
! Convert heights from feet to metres
```

```
!
   Heights = Conversion * Heights
!
! Print out newly converted heights
!
   DO Lat = 1, Nzones
      PRINT *, Heights(Lat, 1:Nzones)
   END DO
END PROGRAM Locate
```

11.5 Array element ordering

When whole array operations take place there is no stated order in which the evaluations are performed, although Fortran 95 does specify an ordering of the elements of an array. For a lot of operations this is not important, but it is required for the input and output of whole arrays, and for certain intrinsic functions.

Array element ordering states that the elements of an array, regardless of rank, form a linear sequence. The sequence is such that the subscripts along the first dimension vary most rapidly, and those along the last dimension vary most slowly. This is best illustrated by considering for example, a rank two array A defined by:

```
REAL , DIMENSION(1:4,1:2) :: A
```

A has 8 real elements whose array element order is:

A(1,1), A(2,1), A(3,1), A(4,1), A(1,2), A(2,2), A(3,2), A(4,2)

i.e. mathematically by column, and not row. This is illustrated graphically in Figure 11.1

Figure 11.1 Array memory ordering

11.5.1 Array element ordering and physical and virtual memory

Fortran compilers will store arrays in memory according to the array element ordering scheme above. Whilst the standard says nothing about how this is implemented this generally means in contiguous memory locations.

There will be a limit to the amount of physical memory available on any computer system. To enable problems that require more than the amount of physical memory available to be solved most implementations will provide access to virtual memory, which in reality means access to a portion of a physical disk.

Access to virtual memory is commonly provided by a paging mechanism of some description. Paging is a technique whereby fixed sized blocks of data are swapped between real memory and disk as required.

In order to minimize paging (and hence reduce execution time) array operations should be performed according to the array element order.

Some common page sizes are:

- Sun UltraSparc – 4Kb, 8Kb.

- DEC Alpha – 8Kb, 16Kb, 32Kb., 64Kb.

- Intel 80x86 – 4Kb.

- Intel Pentium PIII – 4Kb

The Intel PIII also supports large pages (2Mb and 4Mb) – see the reference at the end of the chapter for more details.

11.6 Array constructors

Values can be assigned to rank one arrays using an array constructor. For example an integer array with element values (1,3,5,7,9) could be constructed as follows:

```
INTEGER, DIMENSION (1:5)  :: Odd
Odd=(/1,3,5,7,9/)
```

The general form of the array constructor is (/ a list of expressions/) where each expression is of the same type.

To construct arrays of higher rank than one the intrinsic function RESHAPE must be used. (An introduction to intrinsic functions is given in Chapter 14, and an alphabetic list with a full explanation of each function is given in Appendix D) To use it in its simplest form:

Matrix = RESHAPE (Source, Shape)

where Source is a rank one array containing the values of the elements required in the new array, Matrix, and Shape is a rank one array containing the shape of the new array Matrix.

Let's consider the rank one array B=(1,3,5,7,9,11) and we wish to store these values in a rank two array A, such that A is the matrix:

$$A = \begin{pmatrix} 1 & 7 \\ 3 & 9 \\ 5 & 11 \end{pmatrix}$$

The following code extract is needed:

```
INTEGER, DIMENSION(1:6)  ::  B
INTEGER, DIMENSION(1:3,  1:2)  ::  A
B  =  (/1,3,5,7,9,11/)
A  =  RESHAPE(B,(/3,2/))
```

Note that the elements of the source array B must be stored in the array element order of the required array A.

The following example uses an array constructor and the intrinsic procedure DOT_PRODUCT:

```
INTEGER  ,  DIMENSION(1:3)  ::  X,Y
INTEGER  ::  Result
X=(/1,3,5/)
Y=(/2,4,6/)
Result=DOT_PRODUCT(X,Y)
```

and Result has the value 44, i.e. is obtained by the normal mathematical dot product operation, $1*2 + 3*4 + 5*6$.

11.7 Masked array assignment and the where statement

Fortran 95 has array assignment both on an element by element basis and on a whole array basis. There is an additional form of assignment based on the concept of a logical mask.

Consider the earlier example of time zones in Chapter 10. The Time array will have values that are both negative and positive. We can then associate with the positive values the concept of east of the Greenwich meridian, and with the negative values the concept of west of the Greenwich meridian, e.g.:

```
REAL  ,  DIMENSION(-180:180)  ::  Time
CHARACTER  (LEN=1)  ,  DIMENSION(-180:180)  ::  Direction
```

```
...
WHERE (Time > 0.0)
   Direction='E'
ELSEWHERE (Time < 0.0)
   Direction='W'
ENDWHERE
...
```

11.7.1   Notes

The arrays must be conformable, i.e. in our example Time and Direction are the same shape.

The selective assignment is achieved through the WHERE statement.

Both the WHERE and ELSEWHERE blocks can be executed therefore.

The formal syntax is:

```
WHERE (array logical assignment)
   array assignment block
ELSEWHERE
   array assignment block
END WHERE
```

The first array assignment is executed where Time is positive.

The second array assignment is executed where Time is negative.

For further coverage of logical expressions see chapters 15 and 18.

11.8 The FORALL statement and FORALL construct

The FORALL statement and FORALL construct have been introduced into Fortran 95 to keep it in-line with High Performance Fortran – HPF. They indicate to the compiler that the code can be optimized on a parallel processor. Consider the following example where a value is subtracted from the diagonal elements of a square matrix A.

```
FORALL (I=1:N)
  A(I,I) = A(I,I) - Lamda
END FORALL
```

The FORALL construct allows the calculations to be carried out simultaneously in a multiprocessor environment.

11.8.1 Syntax

```
FORALL ( triplet  [ , triplet ] ... [ , mask ] )
variable = expression
FORALL ( triplet  [ , triplet ] ... [ , mask ] )
pointer => target
```

The triplet specifies a value set for an index variable. It has the following syntax

```
index = first : last [ : stride ]
```

First, last and stride are scalar integer expressions.

Mask is a scalar logical expression.

```
[ name : ] FORALL ( triplet [ , triplet ] ... [ ,
mask ] )
...
END FORALL [ name ]
```

Name is an optional name, which identifies the FORALL construct.

11.9 Summary

We can now perform operations on whole arrays and part arrays (array sections) without having to refer to individual elements. This shortens program development time, and greatly clarifies the meaning of programs.

Array constructors can be used to assign values to rank one arrays within a program unit. The RESHAPE functions allows us to assign values to a two or higher rank array when used in conjunction with an array constructor.

We have introduced the concept of a deferred-shape array. Arrays do not need to have their shape specified at compile time, only their rank. Their actual shape is deferred until run-time. We achieve this by the combined use of the ALLOCAT-ABLE attribute on the variable declaration, and the ALLOCATE statement. This makes Fortran a very flexible language for array manipulation.

11.10 Problems

1. Give the rank, bounds, extents and size of the following arrays:

```
REAL , DIMENSION(1:15) :: A
INTEGER , DIMENSION(1:3,0:4) :: B
REAL , DIMENSION(-2:2,0:1,1:4) :: C
INTEGER , DIMENSION(0:2,1:5) :: D
```

Which two of these arrays are conformable?

2. Use the SUM intrinsic function (see Appendix D) to calculate the total rainfall in the rainfall program example in Chapter 9.

3. Write a program to read in five rank one arrays, A, B, C, D, E and then store them as five columns in a rank two array TABLE.

4. Take the first part of Problem 2 in Chapter 10 and rewrite it using the SUM intrinsic function.

11.11 Bibliography

Bhandarkar D.P., *Alpha Implementation and Architecture: Complete Reference and Guide,* Digital Press.

Intel, *Intel Architecture Software Developer's Manual Volume 3: System Programming*

This is available as a PDF file from Intel. Try:

http://developer.intel.com/design/PentiumIII/manuals/

12

Output of Results

Why, sometimes I've believed as many as six impossible things before breakfast.

Lewis Carroll, *Through the Looking-Glass and What Alice Found There*

All the persons in this book are real and none is fictitious even in part.

Flann O'Brien, *The Hard Life.*

Aims

The aims here are to introduce the facilities for producing neat output, and to show how to write results to a file, rather than to the terminal. In particular:

- The A, I, E, F, and X layout or edit descriptors.
- The OPEN, WRITE, and CLOSE statements.

12 Output of Results

When you have used PRINT * a few times it becomes apparent that it is not always as useful as it might be. The data is written out in a way which makes some sense, but may not be especially easy to read. Real numbers are written out with all their significant places, which is very often rather too many, and it is often difficult to line up the columns for data which is notionally tabular. It is possible to be much more precise in describing the way in which information is presented by the program. To do this, we use FORMAT statements. Through the use of the FORMAT we can:

- Specify how many columns a number should take up.

- Specify where a decimal point should lie.

- Specify where white space appears.

- Specify titles.

The FORMAT statement has a label associated with it; through this label, the PRINT statement associates the data to be written with the form in which to write it.

12.1 Integers, I format

Integer format is reasonably straightforward, and offers clues for formats used in describing other numbers. I3 is an integer taking three columns. The number is right justified, a bit of jargon meaning that it is written as far to the right as it will go, so that there are no trailing or following blanks. Consider the following example:

```
PROGRAM TwelveTimesTable
INTEGER :: I
   PRINT *,' '
   PRINT *,' Twelve times table'
   PRINT *,' '
   DO I=1,12
     PRINT 100, I,I*12
     100 FORMAT(' ',I3,' *   12 = ',I3)
   END DO
END PROGRAM TwelveTimesTable
```

12.2 Reals, F format

The F format can be seen as an extension of the integer format. But here we have to deal with the decimal point. The form of the F format specifies where the decimal point will occur, and how many digits follow it. Thus, F7.4 means:

- There is a total width of 7.

- A decimal point

- 4 digits after the decimal point.

This means that since the decimal point is also written out, there may be up to 2 digits before the decimal point. As in the case of the integer, any minus sign is part of the number, and would take up one column. Thus, the format F7.4 may be used for numbers in the range

      -9.9999   to   99.9999

Let us look at the last example more closely. When a number is written out, it is rounded; that is to say, if we write out 99.99999 in an F7.4 format, the program will try to write out 100.0000! This is bad news, since we have not left enough room for all those digits before the decimal point. What happens? Asterisks will be printed. In the example above, a number out of range of the format's capabilities would be printed as:

****

What would a format of F7.0 do? Again, seven columns have been set aside to accommodate the number and its decimal point, but this time no digits follow the point:

```
    99.
-21375.
```

are examples of numbers written in this format. With an F format, there is no way of getting rid of the decimal point.

The numbers making up the parts of the descriptors must all be positive integers. The definition of a real format is therefore; F followed by two integer numbers, separated by a decimal point. The first integer must exceed the second, and the second must be greater than or equal to zero. The following are valid examples:

```
F4.0
F6.2
F12.2
F16.8
```

but these are *not* valid:

```
F4.4
F6.8
F-3.0
F6
F.2
```

The following two programs illustrate the use of both I format and F format.

12.2.1   Litres to Pints

```
PROGRAM ltop
IMPLICIT NONE
INTEGER :: litres
REAL :: pints
  DO litres=1,10
    pints=litres*1.75
    PRINT 10,litres,pints
    10 FORMAT(' ',I3,' * 1.75 = ',F7.3)
  END DO
END PROGRAM ltop
```

Run the program to see what output is produced.

12.2.2   Pints To Litres

```
PROGRAM ptol
IMPLICIT NONE
INTEGER :: pints
REAL    :: litres
  DO pints=1,10
    litres=pints/1.75
    PRINT 10,pints,litres
    10 FORMAT(' ',I3,' / 1.75 = ',F7.3)
  END DO
END PROGRAM ptol
```

As with the previous example run the program to see what output is produced.

12.3 Reals, E format

The exponential or scientific notation is useful in cases where we need to provide a format which may encompass a wide range of values. If likely results lie in a very wide range, we can ensure that the most significant part is given. It is possible to give a very large F format, but alternatively, the E format may be used. This takes a form such as

```
E10.4
```

which looks something like the F, and may be interpreted in a similar way. The 10 gives the total *width* of the number to be printed out, that is the number of columns it will take. The number after the decimal point indicates the number of positions to be written after the decimal point; since all exponent format numbers are written so that the number is between 0.1 and 0.9999..., with the exponent taking care of scale shifts, this implies that the first four significant digits are to be printed out.

Taking a concrete example, 1000 may be written as 10**3, or as 0.1 * 10**4. This gives us the two parts; 0.1 gives the significant digits (in this case only one significant digit), while the 10**4 gives the exponent, namely 4 or +4. In a form that looks more like Fortran, this would be written .1E+04 where the E+04 means 10**4.

There is a minimum *size* for an exponential format. Because of all the extra bits and pieces it requires:

- The decimal point.

- The sign of the entire number.

- The sign of the exponent.

- The magnitude of the exponent.

- The E.

the width of the number, less the number of significant places should not be less than 6. In the example given above, E10.4 meets this requirement. When the exponent is in the range zero to 99, the E will be printed as part of the number; when the exponent is greater, the E is dropped, and its place is taken by a larger value; however, the sign of the exponent is always given, whether it is positive or negative. The sign of the whole number will usually only be given when it is negative. This means that, if the numbers are always positive, the *rule of six* given above can be modified to a *rule of five*. It is safer to allow six places over, since, if the format is insufficient, all you will get are asterisks.

The most common mistake with an E format is to make the edit descriptor too small, so that there is insufficient room for all the *padding* to be printed. Formats like E8.4 just don't work (on output anyway). The following are valid E formats on output:

```
E9.3
E11.2
E18.7
E10.4
```

but the following would not be acceptable as output formats, for a variety of reasons:

```
E11.7
E6.3
E4.0
E10
E7.3
```

12.3.1   Simple E format example

```
PROGRAM eformat
IMPLICIT NONE
INTEGER :: i
REAL     :: b,s
  b=1.0
  s=1.0
  DO i=1,10
    b=b*10
    s=s/10
    PRINT 10,i,b,s
    10 FORMAT(' ',I3,'   ',E10.4,'   ',E10.4)
  END DO
END PROGRAM eformat
```

12.4 Spaces

There is a shorthand way of expressing spaces (or blanks) in your output – the X descriptor, e.g.

```
PRINT 100, ALPHA,BETA
100 FORMAT(1X,F10.4,10X,F10.3)
```

The 10X is read rather like any of the other format elements – logically it should have been X10, to correspond to I10 or F10.4, but that would be allowing intuition to run away with you. Clearly the X3J3 committee felt it important that Fortran should have inconsistencies, just like a natural language.

There are other ways of achieving the same thing – having a large space delimited by apostrophes, or by manipulating character variables. What you use is your choice. Remember that these blanks are in addition to any generated as a result of the leading blanks on numbers (if any are present). If you wish to leave a single space, you must still precede the X by a number (in this case, 1); simply writing X is illegal. The general form is therefore; positive integer followed by X.

12.5 Alphanumeric or character format, A

This is perhaps the simplest output of all. Since you will already have declared the length of a character variable in your declarations:

```
CHARACTER (10) :: B
```

when you come to write out B, the length is known – thus you need only specify that a character string is to be output:

```
PRINT 100,B
100 FORMAT(1X,A)
```

If you feel you need a little extra control, you can append an integer value to the A, like A10 (A9 or A1) and so on. If you do this, only the first 10 (9 or 1) characters are written out; the remainder are ignored. Do note that 10A1 and A10 are not the same thing. 10A1 would be used to print out the first character of ten character variables, while A10 would write out the first ten characters of a single character variable. The general form is therefore just A, but if more control is required, this may be followed by a positive integer.

Within a FORMAT statement you may also write out anything within apostrophes. These strings of characters will be written out with no modification; e.g.

```
PRINT 100,X
100 FORMAT(' THE ANSWER IS',F10.4)
```

will be written out as something like:

```
THE ANSWER IS    12.3457
```

12.5.1 Headings

A partial program segment to output a 3 column table with an informative heading could be:

```
PRINT *,' NUMBER : X READING : Y READING'
DO I=1,100
   PRINT 100,I,XVALUE(I),YVALUE(I)
   100   FORMAT(1X,I3,3X,E10.4,3X,E10.4)
END DO
```

12.6 Mixed type output in a FORMAT statement

The following example shows how to mix and match character, integer and real output in one FORMAT statement:

```
PROGRAM mixedio
IMPLICIT NONE
CHARACTER (LEN=15) :: Firstname
INTEGER :: age
REAL :: weight
CHARACTER (LEN=1) :: sex
  PRINT *,' Type in your first name '
  READ *,Firstname
  PRINT *,' type in your age in years'
  READ *,age
  PRINT *,' type in your weight in kilos'
  READ *,weight
  PRINT *,' type in your sex (f/m)'
  READ *,sex
  PRINT *,' your personal details are'
  PRINT *
  PRINT 100
  100 FORMAT(4x,'first name', 4x , 'age' , 1x , &
      'weight' , 2x , 'sex')
  PRINT 200 , firstname, age , weight , sex
  200 FORMAT(1x , a , 2x , i3 , 2x , f5.2 , 2x, a)
END PROGRAM mixedio
```

Take care to match up the variables with the appropriate edit descriptors. You also need to count the number of characters and spaces when lining up the heading.

12.7 Common mistakes

It must be stressed that an integer can only be printed out with an I format, and a real with an F (or E) format. You cannot mix integer and F, or real and I. If you do, unpredictable results will follow. There are (at least) two other sorts of errors you might make on writing out a value. You may try to write out something which has never actually been assigned a value; this is termed an indefinite value. You may find that the letter I is written out. In passing, note that many loaders and link editors will preset all values to zero — i.e. unset (indefinite) values are actually set to zero. On better systems there is generally some way of turning this facility off, so that undefined is really indefinite. More often than not, indefinite values are the result of mis-typing, rather than never setting values. It is not uncommon to type O for 0, or 1 for either I or l. The other likely error is to try to print out a value greater than that which the machine can calculate – *out of range* values. Some machines will print out such values as R; some machines will actually print out something which looks right, and such *overflow* and *underflow* conditions can go unnoticed. Be wary.

12.8 OPEN (and CLOSE)

One of the particularly powerful features of Fortran is the way it allows you to manipulate files. Up to now, most of the discussion has centred on reading from and writing to the terminal. It is also possible to read and write to one or more files. This is achieved using the OPEN, WRITE, READ and CLOSE statements. We will consider *reading* from files in a later chapter, and concentrate on *writing* in this chapter.

12.8.1 The OPEN statement

This statement sets up a file for either reading or writing. A typical form is:

```
OPEN  (UNIT=1,FILE='DATA')
```

The file will be known to the operating system as DATA (or will have DATA as the first part of its name), and can be written to by using the UNIT number. This statement should come *before* you first read from or write to the file DATA.

It is not possible to write to the file DATA directly; it must be referenced through its unit number. Within the Fortran program you write to this file using a statement like

```
WRITE(UNIT=1,FMT=100)  XVAL,YVAL
```

or

```
WRITE(1,100)  XVAL,YVAL
```

These two statements are equivalent. Besides opening a file, we really ought to CLOSE it when we have finished writing to it:

```
CLOSE(UNIT=1)
```

In fact, on many systems it is not obligatory to OPEN and CLOSE all your files. Almost certainly, the terminal will not require this, since INPUT and OUTPUT units will be there by default. At the end of the job, the system will CLOSE all your files. Nevertheless, explicit OPEN and CLOSE cannot hurt, and the added clarity generally assists in understanding the program.

The following program segment contains all of the above statements.

```
PROGRAM Redo
...
   OPEN (UNIT=1,FILE='DATA')
   ...
   DO I=1,100
      PRINT (UNIT=1,FMT=200) X(I)
      200 FORMAT(E10.3)
   END DO
   ...
   CLOSE(1)
   ...
END PROGRAM Redo
```

12.8.2   Writing

PRINT is always directed to the file OUTPUT; in the case of interactive working, this is the terminal. This is not a very flexible arrangement. WRITE allows us to direct output to any file, including *OUTPUT*. The basic form of the WRITE is

```
WRITE(6,100) X,Y,Z
```

or

```
WRITE(UNIT=6,FMT=100) X,Y,Z
```

The latter form is more explicit, but the former is probably the one most widely used. We have an example here of the use of positionally dependent parameters in the first case and equated keywords in the second. With the exceptions of the PRINT statement and the READ * form of the READ, all of the input/output statements allow the unit number and the format labels to be specified either by an equated keyword (or specifier), or in a positionally dependent form. If you use the explicit UNIT= and FMT= it does not matter what order the elements are placed in, but if you omit these keywords, the unit number must come first, followed by the format label.

UNIT=6 means that the output will be written to the file given the unit number 6. In the next chapter we will cover the way in which you may associate file names and unit numbers, but, for the moment, we will assume that the default is being used. The name of the file, as defined by the system, will depend on the particular system you use; a likely name is something like DATA06, TAPE6, or FILE0006. One *easy* way to find out (apart from asking someone), is to create such a file from a program, and then look at the names of your files after the program has finished. A great many of computing's minor complexities can be clarified by simple experimentation.

FMT=100 simply gives the label of the format to be used.

The overworked asterisk may be used, either for the unit, or for the format:

UNIT=* will write to OUTPUT (the terminal), and

FMT=* will produce output controlled by the list of variables, often called *list directed output.*

The following three statements are therefore equivalent:

```
WRITE(UNIT=*,FMT=*) X,Y,Z
WRITE(*,*) X,Y,Z
PRINT*,X,Y,Z
```

There are other controls possible on the WRITE, which will be elaborated later.

12.9 Repetition

Often we need to print more than one number on a line and want to use the same layout descriptor. Consider the following:

```
PRINT 100,A,B,C,D
```

If each number can be written with the same layout descriptor, we can abbreviate the FORMAT statement to take account of the pattern:

```
100 FORMAT(1X,4F8.2)
```

is equivalent to:

```
100 FORMAT(1X,F8.2,F8.2,F8.2,F8.2)
```

as you might anticipate. If the pattern is more complex, we can extend this approach:

```
PRINT 100,I,A,J,B,K,C
100 FORMAT(1X,3(I3,F8.2))
```

Bracketing the description ensures that we repeat the whole entity:

```
100 FORMAT(1X,3(I3,F8.2))
```

is equivalent to:

```
100 FORMAT(1X,I3,F8.2, I3,F8.2, I3,F8.2)
```

Repetition with brackets can be rather more complex. In order to give some overview of formatted Fortran output, it is helpful to delve a little into the history of the language. Many of the attributes of Fortran can be traced back to the days of single user mainframes (with often a fraction of the power of many contemporary micro-computers and workstations). These would generally take input from punched cards (the traditional 80-column Hollerith card), and would generate output on a line printer. In this sort of environment, the individual punched card had a significance which lines in a file do not have today. Each card could be seen as a single entity – a physical record unit. The *record* was seen as an element of subdivision within a file. Even then, there was some confusion between the notion of physical records and files split into logically distinct sub-units, since these sub-units might also be termed records. The present Fortran standard merely says that a record *does not necessarily correspond to a physical entity*, although *a punched card is usually considered to be a record*. This leaves us sitting at our terminals in a bemused state, especially since we may have no idea what a punched card looks like (an ideal state of affairs!)

It is important to have some notion of a record, since most of the formal definitions dealing with output (and input) are couched in terms of records. Every time an input or output statement is executed your nominal position in the file changes. If we think in terms of individual records (which may be cards), the notions of *current, preceding* and *next* record seem fairly straightforward. The current record is simply the one we have just read or written, and the other definitions follow natu-rally.

The situation becomes less clear when we realize that a single output statement may generate many lines of output.

```
WRITE(UNIT=6,FMT=101)    A,B,C
101 FORMAT(1X,F10.4)
```

writes out three separate lines. Looking at the output alone, there is no way to distinguish this from the output generated by:

```
WRITE(UNIT=6,FMT=101)    A
WRITE(UNIT=6,FMT=101)    B
WRITE(UNIT=6,FMT=101)    C
101 FORMAT(1X,F10.4)
```

In the latter case we would probably be happy to consider each line a *record,* although in the previous example we might swither between considering all three lines (generated by a single statement) a single record or three records. Consider the first of these two examples more closely; each time the format is exhausted — that is to say, each time we run out of format description, we start again on a new line (a new record). A new record is begun as each F10.4 is begun. The correct interpre-tation is therefore that three records have been written.

The same sort of thing happens in more complex FORMAT statements:

```
WRITE(UNIT=6,FMT=105)  X,I,Y
105  FORMAT(1X,F8.4,I3,(F8.4))
```

would write out a single record containing a real, an integer and a real. Using the same format statement with WRITE (UNIT=6, FMT=105) X,I,Y,Z would write out two records. The first containing the values of X, I and Y, the second containing only Z. If there were still more values

```
WRITE(UNIT=6,FMT=105)  X,I,Y,Z,A
```

would print out three records. The group in brackets – the (F8.4) – is repeated until we run out of items.

12.10 Some more examples

Since it is the last open bracket which determines the position at which the format is repeated, simply writing:

```
WRITE(UNIT=6,FMT=100)   A,I,B,C,J
100  FORMAT(1X,F8.4,I3,F8.2)
```

would imply that A, I and B would be written on one line, then, returning to the last open brackets, (in this case the only open brackets), a new record (or line) is begun to write out C and J. A statement like:

```
100  FORMAT(1X,(F8.4),I3,F8.2)
```

would return to the (F8.4) group, and then continue to the I3 and F8.2 before repeating again (if necessary). The same thing happens if the (F8.4) had no brackets around it. On the other hand:

```
100  FORMAT(1X,(F8.4),I3,(F8.2))
```

contains superfluous brackets around the F8.4, since the repeat statement will never return to that group. Are you confused yet? This seems all very esoteric, and really, we have only hinted at the complexity which is possible. It is seldom that you have to create complex FORMAT statements, and clarity is far more important than brevity.

When patterned or repeated output is used, we may want to stop when there are no more numbers to write out. Take the following example:

```
WRITE(UNIT=1,FMT=100)  A,B,C,D
100  FORMAT(1X,4(F6.1,','))
```

This will give output which looks like:

```
 37.4,    29.4,    14.2,    -9.1,
```

The last comma should not be there. We can suppress these unwanted elements by using the colon:

```
100 FORMAT(1X,4(F6.1:','))
```

which would then give us:

```
 37.4,    29.4,    14.2,    -9.1
```

Since we run out of data at the fourth item, D, the output following is not written out. It is a small point, but it does look a lot tidier. There are other ways of achieving the same thing.

This helps to illustrate another point, namely that you may have formats which are more extensive than the lists which reference them:

```
WRITE(UNIT=1,FMT=100)  A,B,C
WRITE(UNIT=1,FMT=100)  X,Y
100 FORMAT(1X,6F8.2)
```

Both WRITE statements use the format provided, although they write out different amounts of data, and neither uses up the whole format.

12.11 Implied DO loops and array sections for array output

In reading and writing it is possible to use more compact ways of indicating that an array is being referenced, since it is often rather tedious to declare each element which is involved, e.g.

```
WRITE(UNIT=6,FMT=100)Y(1),Y(2),Y(3),Y(4)
100 FORMAT(1X,F8.4)
```

Clearly we could improve this slightly by making it into a loop:

```
DO I=1,4
   WRITE(UNIT=6,FMT=100)  Y(I)
   100 FORMAT(1X,F8.4)
END DO
```

and equally we can simplify this to:

```
WRITE(UNIT=6,FMT=100)(Y(I),I=1,4)
100  FORMAT(1X,F8.4)
```

where the DO loop is subsumed into the expression (the syntax is just the same as for the counter part of a DO loop, with the same rules for starting, ending and incrementing).

The following shows how to achieve the same result using the array section facility.

```
WRITE(UNIT=6,FMT=100)  Y(1:4)
100  FORMAT(1X,F8.4)
```

An alternative, and yet more compact, form is:

```
REAL  ,  DIMENSION(4)  ::   Y
   . . .
   . . .
WRITE(UNIT=6,FMT=100)Y
100  FORMAT(1X,F8.4)
```

In all these cases, the output would be the same – four numbers printed out on separate lines. The FORMAT statement is controlling this layout. Changing the format to:

```
100  FORMAT(1X,4F8.4)
```

would change the layout in three out of the four cases outlined. Which three? Even two (or more) dimensional arrays can be written out or read in by implied loops.

```
REAL  ,  DIMENSION(10,10)  ::  Y
   NROWS=6
   NCOLS=7
   DO I=1,NROWS
      WRITE(UNIT=6,FMT=100)(Y(I,J),J=1,NCOLS)
      100  FORMAT(1X,10F10.4)
   END DO
```

The write statement may be written as :

```
WRITE(UNIT=6,FMT=100)  Y(I,1:NCOLS)
```

using an array section.

Take care when using whole arrays. Consider the following program:

```
PROGRAM RC
REAL , DIMENSION(10,10) :: Y
INTEGER :: NROWS=6
INTEGER :: NCOLS=7
INTEGER :: I,J
INTEGER :: K=0

  DO I=1,NROWS
    DO J=1,NCOLS
      K=K+1
      Y(I,J)=K
    END DO
  END DO

  WRITE(UNIT=*,FMT=100)Y
  100 FORMAT(1X,10F10.4)

END PROGRAM RC
```

There are several points to note with this example. Firstly, this is a whole array reference, and so the entire contents of the array will be written; there is no scope for fine control. Secondly, the order in which the array elements are written is according to Fortran's array element ordering, i.e. the first subscript varying 1 to 10 (the array bound), with the second subscript as 1, then 1 to 10 with the second subscript as 2 and so on; the sequence is:

```
Y(1,1)    Y(2,1)    Y(3,1)        Y(10,1)
Y(1,2)    Y(2,2)    Y(3,2)        Y(10,2)
  .
  .
Y(1,10)   Y(2,10)                 Y(10,10)
```

Thirdly we have defined values for part of the array. This program behaves differently with the following compilers:

- Sun Fortran 90
- NagWare F95
- Compaq F95

If you have access to more than one compiler then try this example out.

Another feature to note is that we can generate values from within a WRITE statement:

```
WRITE(UNIT=6,FMT=101)(I,I=0,9)
101  FORMAT(1X,10I3)
```

would produce a line like:

```
 0   1   2   3   4   5   6   7   8   9
```

12.12 Formatting for a line-printer

There is one extension to format specifications which is relevant to line-printers. Fortran defines four special characters which have a particular effect on standard line-printers. They have an effect when they occur in the first character position of a line. This means that a line-printer which is not under your immediate control can be used to produce neat output, by sending a file to be printed on it. This has a variety of names including *spooling*, *queueing* and *routing* depending on the system. You should check with your local system for the exact mechanism to achieve this.

The special characters are +, 0, 1 and blank. To be used, they must be the first character of the output in each line – as if they were to be printed in column 1. In fact, a standard line printer never prints a character that occurs in column 1 at all.

Whenever a WRITE statement is begun, the printer *advances* to a new record; i.e. a new line is begun before any data is transferred. If the first character is a *special character*, then this will be interpreted by the line-printer. If the first character to be printed is a blank, the printer continues printing on that line. The first character is also known as the *carriage control character*.

The blank is a *do nothing special* control. It signifies that the line is to be printed as it is.

The zero indicates that you wish to leave an extra line; this is often useful in spacing out results to make the output more readable.

The 1 makes the output skip down to the top of the next page. This is clearly useful for separating logically distinct chunks of output. If you obtain a line printer listing of your compiled program, each segment will start at the top of a new page.

The plus is a *no advance* or *overprint* character. It suppresses the effect of the line advance which a WRITE generates. No new line is begun and the previous line is over-printed with the new. Overprinting can be useful especially when you wish to print out grey scale maps but its use is rather restricted. In particular, it can be a dangerous control character. If you have a format starting with a plus in a loop, you can make the printer overprint again and again and again .... and again and again, until it has hammered itself into a pulp. This is not a good idea.

Similarly, accidental use of the 1 as a control character in a loop will give you lots of blank pages. It is just a bit embarrassing to be presented with a six inch stack of paper which is (almost) blank, because you had a 1 repeatedly in column 1.

12.12.1 Mechanics of carriage control

The following are all quite reasonable ways of generating the blank in column 1:

```
WRITE(UNIT=6,FMT=100)A
100 FORMAT(' ',F10.4)
```

or

```
WRITE(UNIT=6,FMT=100)A
100 FORMAT(1X,F10.4)
```

or

```
WRITE(UNIT=6,FMT=100)A
100 FORMAT(' THE ANSWER IS ',F10.4)
```

Note, however, that

```
WRITE(UNIT=6,FMT=100)A
100 FORMAT(F8.4)
```

could result in problems. If A contained the value 100.2934, the result on a line printer would be

```
00.2934
```

printed at the top of a new page. The 1 is taken as carriage control, and the rest of the line then printed.

Accidentally printing zeros in column 1 is a little more difficult, but:

```
WRITE(UNIT=6,FMT=100)I
100 FORMAT(I1)
```

might just do it. Don't.

Remember that this only applies to line printer output, and not to the terminal. Since Fortran only defines 4 characters as carriage control, you will find that anything else in column 1 will give unpredictable results. On some systems, a fair number of alternatives may be defined by the installation, and they may do something useful. On other systems, they may do something, but they may also fail to print the rest of the line. This can be very perplexing. Beware.

12.12.2 Generating a new line, on both line-printers and terminals

There are several ways of generating new lines, other than with a 0 in column one of your line printer output. A more general approach, which works on terminals and also line printers, is through the oblique or slash, /. Each time this is encountered in a FORMAT statement, a new line is begun.

```
PRINT 101,A,B
101 FORMAT(1X,F10.4/1X,F10.4)
```

would give output like:

```
100.2317
-4.0021
```

This is the same as (F10.4) would have given, but clearly this opens up lots of possibilities for formatting output more tidily:

```
PRINT 102,NVAL,XMAX,XMIN
102 FORMAT(' NUMBER OF VALUES READ IN WAS: ',I10/ &
           ' MAXIMUM VALUE IS: ',F10.4/            &
           ' MINIMUM VALUE IS: ',F10.4)
```

which may be easier to read than using only one line, and is certainly more compact to write than using three separate print statements. It is not necessary to separate / by commas, although if you do nothing catastrophic will happen.

You may also begin a format description with a /, in order to generate an extra line, or even generate lots of lines with lots of slashes; e.g.

```
WRITE(UNIT=6,FMT=103)A,B
103 FORMAT(//1X,F10.4,4(/),1X,F10.4)
```

will leave two lines before printing A, and then will generate 4 new lines before writing B (i.e. there will be three lines between A and B — the fourth new line will contain B). While a slash by itself, or with another slash, does not have to be separated by commas from other groups, a more complex grouping, 4(/), does have to have commas and brackets to delimit it.

12.13 Summary

You have been introduced in this chapter to the use of format or layout descriptors which will allow greater control over output.

The main features are:

- The I format for integer variables.

- The E and F formats for real numbers.

- The A format for characters.

- The X, which allows insertion of spaces.

Output can be directed to files as well as to the terminal, through the WRITE statement.

The WRITE, together with the OPEN and CLOSE statements, also introduces the class of Fortran statements which use equated keywords, as well as positionally dependent parameters.

The FORMAT statement and its associated layout or edit descriptor are powerful, and allow repetition of patterns of output (both explicitly and implicitly).

When output is to be directed to a line-printer, the following 4 characters:

- +

- 0

- 1

- (blank)

allow reasonable control over the layout. Care must to be taken with these characters, since it is possible to decimate forests with little effort.

12.14 Problems

1. Rewrite the temperature conversion program which was Problem 8 in Chapter 10 to actually produce the output shown.

2. Write a litres and pints conversion program to produce a similar kind of output to the above. Start at 0, and make the central column go up to 50. One pint is 0.568 litres.

3. Information on car fuel consumption is usually given in miles per gallon in Britain and the US, and in litres per 100 km in Europe. Just to add an extra problem US gallons are 0.8 Imperial gallons.

Prepare a table which allows conversion from either US or Imperial fuel consumption figures to the metric equivalent. Use the PARAMETER statement where appropriate.

        1 Imperial gallon = 4.54596 litres
        1 mile = 1.60934 kilometres.

4. The two most commonly used operating systems for Fortran programming are Unix and DOS. It is possible to use the operating system file redirection symbols < and > to read from a file and write to a file respectively. Rerun program 1 to write to a file. Examine the file using an editor.

5. Modify any of the above to write to a file rather than the terminal. What changes are required to produce a general output which will be suitable for both the terminal and a line printer? Is this degree of generality worthwhile?

6. To demonstrate your familiarity with formats, re-format Questions 1, 2 or 3 to use E formats, rather than F (or vice versa).

7. Modify the temperature conversion program to produce output suitable for a line-printer. Use the local operating system commands to send the file to be printed.

8. Repeat for the litres and pints program.

9. What features of Fortran reveal its evolution from punched card input?

10. Try to create a real number greater than the maximum possible on your computer – write it out. Try to repeat this for an integer. You may have to exercise some ingenuity.

11. Check what a number too large for the output format will be printed as on your local system – is it all asterisks?

12. Write a program which stores litres and corresponding pints in arrays. You should now be able to control the output of the table (excluding headings – although this could be done too) in a single WRITE or PRINT statement. If you don't like litres and pints, try some other conversion (sterling to US dollars, leagues to fathoms, Scots miles to Betelgeusian pfnings). The principle remains the same.

13. Fortran is an old programming language and the text formatting functionality discussed in this chapter assumes very dumb printing devices.

The primary assumption is that we are dealing with so-called monospace fonts, i.e. that digits, alphabetic characters, punctuation, etc., all have the same width.

If you are using a PC try using:

- Notepad

and

- Word

to open your programs and some of the files created in this chapter. What happens to the layout?

If you are using Notepad look at the *Word wrap* and *set Font* options under the *edit* menu.

What fonts are available? What happens to the layout when you choose another font?

If you are using Word what fonts are available? What happens when you make changes to your file and exit Word? Is it sensible to save a Fortran source file as a Word document?

13

Reading in Data

Winnie-the-Pooh read the two notices very carefully,
first from left to right, and afterwards,
in case he had missed some of it, from right to left.

A A Milne, *Winnie-the-Pooh*.

For Madmen Only

Hermann Hesse, *Steppenwolf.*

Aims

The aims of this chapter are to introduce some of the ideas involved in reading data
into a program. In particular, using the following:

- reading from fixed fields

- integers, reals and characters

- blanks – nulls or zeros?

- READ – extensions

  - error handling on input

- OPEN – associating unit numbers and file names

  - CLOSE

  - REWIND

  - BACKSPACE

13 Reading in Data

13.1 Reading from the terminal versus reading from files

It is unlikely that you would use fixed formats when reading numeric input from
the keyboard; they are more likely to be used when reading data from a file. However the examples that follow do this. We look at reading from files later in this
chapter.

13.2 Fixed fields on input

All the formats described earlier are available, and again they are limited to particular types. Integers may only be input by the I format, reals with F and E, and
character (alphanumeric) with A.

13.2.1 Integers, the I format

Integers are read in with the I edit descriptor. While, on output, integers appear
right justified, on input they may appear anywhere in the field you have delimited.
Blanks (by default) are considered not to exist, for the purpose of the value read,
although they do contribute to the field width. Apart from the digits 0 to 9, the only
other characters which may appear in an integer field are − and +.

```
READ(UNIT=*,FMT=100)  I,J,K
100 FORMAT(3I4)
```

with the following values:

```
2   -4 0+ 21
```

would result in the values 2, − 40 and 21 being assigned to I, J and K respectively.
This example also introduces yet another flavour of the read statement, which is
covered in more detail later in the chapter.

13.2.2 Reals, the F and E formats

Real numbers may be input using either the E or F format, whether or not the E
descriptor is present in the field. Again, we define a width, and, as with output, the
number of places after the point:

```
F10.4              E12.3              F6.0              E10.0
```

However, if the point is already present in the value being input, this overrides the
definition in the format. Again, blanks are treated as null values.

```
READ(UNIT=*,FMT=100)  A,B,C
100 FORMAT(F10.6,E12.6,F6.0)
```

with

```
1234567890   14              4    .
```

results in A taking the value 1234.56789, B taking the value 14.0, and C the value 4.

The absence of the *E* in the field for B has no adverse affect. As a general rule, it is best to retain the decimal point with real numbers, just as a precaution. Sometimes it is difficult to line up fields properly, and the first sign of trouble may be finding two decimal points in the one field, which will generate an error message, e.g. consider:

```
READ(UNIT=*,FMT=101)  A,B,C,X,Y,Z
101  FORMAT(6F5.2)
```

If this was in a loop to read the following values:

```
2.0   3.0   13.0 6.1   0.9   0.2
12.0   62.   9.  -4.2 2.9  -3.7
```

The second time the READ was used, you would get an error (can you see why and where?)

An exponential format number (which may be read in F or E formats) can take a number of different forms. The most obvious is the explicit form:

```
-1.2E-4
```

where all the components of the value are present – the significant digits to the left of the E, the E itself, and the exponent to the right. We can drop almost any two of these three components, and therefore:

```
-1.2
-1.2E
-1.2-4
-4
```

are all valid values. Only the first two are interpreted as the same numerical value, and just giving the exponent part would be interpreted by the format as just giving the significant digits. If the exponent is to be given, there must be some significant digits also. It is not even enough to give the E and assume that the program will interpret this as 10 to the power *exponent* :

```
E-4
```

is not an acceptable exponential format value, although:

```
1E-4
```

would be.

There are opportunities for confusion with E formats.

```
READ(UNIT=*,FMT=102) X,Y
102 FORMAT(2E10.3)
```

with:

```
10.23 -2
```

This would be interpreted as X taking the value 10.23E-2 and Y taking the value 0.0, while with

```
102 FORMAT(2F8.3)
```

X would be 10.23, and Y would be –2.0.

Although the decimal point may also be dropped, this may generate confusion too. While:

```
4E3
45
45E-4
45-4
```

are all valid forms, if an E format is used, a special conversion takes place. A format, like E10.8, when used with integral significant digits (no decimal point), uses the 8 as a *negative* power of 10 scaling, e.g.

```
3267E05
```

converts to

```
3267*10**-8*10**5
```

or

```
3267*10**3
```

or

```
3.267.
```

Therefore, the interpretation of, say, 136, read in E format, would depend on the format used:

Value	Format		Interpretation
136	E10.0		136.0
136	E10.4		$136.0*10**-4$
		or	0.0136
136	E10.10		$136.0*10**-10$
		or	0.0000000136
136.	any above		136.0

One implication of all this is that the format you use to input a variable may not be suitable to output that same variable.

13.3 Blanks, nulls and zeros

You can control how Fortran treats blanks in input through two special format instructions, BN and BZ. BN is a shorthand form of *blanks become null,* that is, a blank is treated as if it was not there at all. BZ is therefore *blanks become zeros.*

As we have already seen, 1 4 (i.e. the two digits separated by a blank) read in I3 format would be read as 14; similarly, 14 (one-four-blank) is also 14 when the BN format is in operation. All of the blanks are ignored for the purposes of interpreting the number. They help to create the width of the number, but otherwise contribute nothing. This is the default, which will be in operation unless you specify otherwise.

The BZ descriptor turns blanks into zeros. Thus, 1 4 (one-blank-four) read in I3 format is 104, and 14 (one-four-blank) is 140.

There is one place where we must be very careful with the use of the BZ format – when using exponent format input. Consider:

```
5.321E+02
```

read in (BZ,E10.3) format. We have specified a field which is ten characters wide, therefore the blank in column 10, which follows the E+02, is read as a zero, making this E+020. This is probably not what was requi·ed.

13.4 Characters

When characters are read in, it is sufficient to use the A format, with no explicit mention of the size of the character string, since this size (or length) is determined in the program by the CHARACTER declaration. This implies that any *extra* characters would not be read in. You may however read in less:

```
CHARACTER (10) :: LIST
    .
    .
    READ(UNIT=5,FMT=100)LIST
100 FORMAT(A1)
```

would read only the first character of the input. The remaining 9 characters of LIST would be set to blank.

The notion of blanks as nulls or zeros has no meaning for characters. The blank is a legitimate character, and is treated as meaningful, completely distinct from the notion of a null or a zero.

13.5 Skipping spaces and lines

The X format is also useful for input. There may be fields in your data which you do not wish to read. These are easily omitted by the X format:

```
    READ(UNIT=*,FMT=100) A,B
100 FORMAT(F10.4,10X,F8.3)
```

Similarly, you can *jump over* or ignore entire records, by using the oblique. Do note however, that

```
    READ(UNIT=*,FMT=100) A,B
100 FORMAT(F10.4/F10.4)
```

would read A from one line (or record) and B from the next. To omit a record between A and B, the format would need to be:

```
100 FORMAT(F10.4//F10.4)
```

Another way to skip over a record is:

```
    READ(UNIT=*,FMT=100)
100 FORMAT()
```

with no variable name at all.

13.6 Reading

As you have seen already, reading, or the input of information, is accomplished through the READ statement. We have used:

```
READ *,X,Y
```

for list directed input from the terminal, and:

```
READ(UNIT=*,FMT=100) X,Y
```

for formatted input also from the terminal. These forms may be expanded to:

```
READ(UNIT=*,FMT=*) X,Y
```

or

```
READ(UNIT=*,FMT=100) X,Y
```

for input from the terminal, or to:

```
READ(UNIT=5,FMT=*) X,Y
```

or

```
READ(UNIT=5,FMT=100) X,Y
```

when we wish to associate the READ statement with a particular unit number (or format label, for formatted input). As with the WRITE statement, these last two READ statements may be abbreviated to:

```
READ(5,*) X,Y
```

and

```
READ(5,100) X,Y
```

13.7 File manipulation again

The OPEN and CLOSE statements are also relevant to files which are used as input, and they may be used in the same ways. Besides introducing the notion of manipulating lots of files, the OPEN statement allows you to change the default for the treatment of blanks. The default is to treat blanks as null, but the statement BLANK='ZERO' changes the default to treat blanks as zeros. There are other parameters on the OPEN, which are considered elsewhere.

Once you have OPENed a file, you may not issue another OPEN for the same file until it has been CLOSEd, except in the case of the BLANK= parameter. You may change the default back again with:

```
OPEN(UNIT=10,FILE='Example.dat')
READ(UNIT=10,FMT=100) A,B
...
OPEN(UNIT=10,FILE='Example.dat',BLANK='ZERO')
READ(UNIT=10,FMT=100) A,B
```

This implies that, within the same input file, you may treat some records as blank for null, and some as blank for zero. This sounds very dangerous, and would be better done by manipulating individual formats if it had to be done at all.

Given that you may write a file, you may also *rewind* it, in order to get back to the beginning. The syntax is similar to the other commands:

```
REWIND(UNIT=1)
```

This often comes in useful as a way of providing backing storage, where intermediate data can be stored on file and then used at a later part of the processing.

The notion of records in Fortran input and output has been introduced. If you are confident in your understanding of this ambiguous and nebulous concept, you can *backspace* through a file, using the statement

```
BACKSPACE(UNIT=1)
```

which moves back over a single record on the designated file. There is no point in trying to BACKSPACE or REWIND input, if that input is the terminal.

13.8 Errors when reading

In discussing some aspects of input, it has been pointed out that errors may be made. Where such errors are noticed, in the sense that something illegal is being attempted, there are two options

- Print a diagnostic message, and allow correction of the mistake.
- Print a diagnostic message, and terminate the program.

The only time that the first makes sense is when you are interacting with a program at a terminal. Some Fortran implementations provide correction facilities in a case like this, but most do not.

We will look in Chapter 21 at how we handle errors in input data, together with a more in-depth coverage of file I/O.

13.9 Summary

• Values may be read in from the terminal or from another file through fixed formats.

• Much of the structure of input format statements is very similar to that of the output formats. Broadly speaking, data written out in a particular format may be read in by the same format. However, there is greater flexibility, and quite a variety of forms can be accepted on input.

• A key distinction to make is the interpretation of blanks, as either nulls or zeros; alternative interpretations can radically alter the structure of the input data

• Fortran allows file names to be associated with unit numbers through the OPEN statement. This statement allows control of the interpretation of blank, although this can also be done through the BN and BZ formats.

• Files may also be manipulated through REWIND and BACKSPACE.

13.10 Problems

1. Write a program that will read in two reals and one integer, using

```
FORMAT(F7.3,I4,F4.1)
```

and that, in one instance treats blanks as zeros, and in the second treats blanks as nulls. Use PRINT * to print the numbers out immediately after reading them in. What do you notice? Can you think of instances where it is necessary to use one rather than the other?

2. Write a program to read in and write out a real number using

```
FORMAT(F7.2)
```

What is the largest number that you can read in and write out with this format? What is the largest negative number that you can read in and write out with this format? What is the smallest number, other than zero, that can be read in and written out?

3. Rewrite two of the earlier programs that used READ,* and PRINT,* to use FORMAT statements.

4. Write a program to read the file created by either the temperature conversion program or the litres and pints conversion program. Make sure that the programs ignore the line–printer control characters, and any header and title information. This kind of problem is very common in programming (writing a program to read and possibly manipulate data created by another program).

5. Use the OPEN, REWIND, READ and WRITE statements to input a value (or values) as a character string, write this to a file, rewind the file, read in the values again, this time as real variables with blanks treated as null, then repeat with blanks as zeros.

6. Demonstrate that input and output formats are not symmetric — i.e. what goes in does not necessarily come out.

7. Can you suggest why Fortran treats blanks as null rather than zero?

8. What happens at your terminal when you enter faulty data, inappropriate for the formats specified? We will look at how we address this problem in Chapter 21.

14

Functions

I can call spirits from the vasty deep.
Why so can I, or so can any man; but will they come
when you do call for them?

William Shakespeare, *King Henry IV, part 1*

Aims

The aims of this chapter are:

- to consider some of the reasons for the inclusion of functions in a programming language

- to introduce, with examples, some of the predefined functions available in Fortran 95

- to introduce a classification of intrinsic functions, generic, elemental, transformational

- to introduce the concept of a user defined function

- to introduce the concept of a recursive function

- to introduce the concept of user defined elemental and pure functions

- to briefly look at scope rules in Fortran 95 for variables and functions

- to look at internal user defined functions.

14 Functions

The role of functions in a programming language and in the problem solving process is considerable and includes:

- allowing us to refer to an action using a meaningful name, e.g. SINE(X) a very concrete use of abstraction;

- they provide a mechanism that allows us to break a problem down into parts, giving us the opportunity to structure our problem solution;

- they provide us with the ability to concentrate on one part of a problem at a time and ignore the others;

- they allow us to avoid the replication of the same or very similar sections of code when solving the same or similar sub-problem. This has the secondary effect of reducing the memory requirements of the final program;

- they allow us to build up a library of functions or modules for solving particular sub-problems, both saving considerable development time and increasing our effectiveness and productivity.

Some of the underlying attributes of functions are

- they take parameters or arguments;

- the parameter can be an expression;

- a function will normally return a value and the value returned is normally dependent on the parameter(s);

- they can sometimes take arguments of a variety of types;

Most languages provide both a range of predefined functions and the facility to define our own. We will look at the predefined functions first.

14.1 An introduction to predefined functions and their use

Fortran provides over a hundred intrinsic functions and subroutines. A subroutine can be regarded as a variation on a function for the purposes of this chapter. They are covered in more depth in a later chapter. They are used in a straightforward way. If we take the common trigonometric functions, sine, cosine and tangent, the appropriate values may be calculated quite simply by:

```
X=SIN(Y)
Z=COS(Y)
A=TAN(Y)
```

This is in rather the same way that we might say that X is a function of Y, or X is sine Y. Note that the argument, Y, is in *radians* not *degrees*.

14.1.1   Example 1: Simple function usage

A complete example is given below.

```
PROGRAM C14_Example_1
REAL :: X
   PRINT *,' Type in an angle (in radians)'
   READ *,X
   PRINT *,' Sine of ', X ,' = ',SIN(X)
END PROGRAM C14_Example_1
```

These functions are called *intrinsic functions*. A selection is given here:

Function	Action	Example
INT	conversion to integer	J=INT(X)
REAL	conversion to real	X=REAL(J)
ABS	absolute value	X=ABS(X)
MOD	remaindering	K=MOD(I,J)
	remainder when I divided by J	
SQRT	square root	X=SQRT(Y)
EXP	exponentiation	Y=EXP(X)
LOG	natural logarithm	X=LOG(Y)
LOG10	common logarithm	X=LOG10(Y)
SIN	sine	X=SIN(Y)
COS	cosine	X=COS(Y)
TAN	tangent	X=TAN(Y)
ASIN	arcsine	Y=ASIN(X)
ACOS	arccosine	Y=ACOS(X)
ATAN	arctangent	Y=ATAN(X)
ATAN2	arctangent(a/b)	Y=ATAN2(A,B)

A complete list is given in Appendix D.

14.2 Generic functions

All but four of the intrinsic functions and procedures are generic, i.e. they can be called with arguments of one of a number of kind types.

14.2.1 Example 2: The ABS generic function

The following short program illustrates this with the ABS intrinsic function.

```
PROGRAM C14_Example_2
IMPLICIT NONE
COMPLEX :: C=(1,1)
REAL    :: R=10.9
INTEGER :: I=-27
   PRINT *,ABS(C)
   PRINT *,ABS(R)
   PRINT *,ABS(I)
END PROGRAM C14_Example_2
```

The four non-generic functions are LGE, LGT, LLE and LLT – the lexical character comparison functions.

Type this program in and run it on the system you use.

It is now possible with Fortran 95 for the arguments to the intrinsic functions to be arrays. It is convenient to categorize the functions into either elemental or transformational, depending on the action performed on the array elements.

14.3 Elemental functions

These functions work with both scalar and array arguments, i.e. with arguments that are either single or multiple valued.

14.3.1 Example 3: Elemental function use

Taking the earlier example with the evaluation of sine as a basis we have:

```
PROGRAM C14_Example_3
REAL , DIMENSION(5) :: X = (/1.0,2.0,3.0,4.0,5.0/)
   PRINT *,' Sine of ', X ,' = ',SIN(X)
END PROGRAM C14_Example_3
```

In the above example the sine function of each element of the array X is calculated and printed.

14.4 Transformational functions

Transformational functions are those whose arguments are arrays, and work on these arrays to transform them in some way.

14.4.1 Example 4: Simple transformational use

To highlight the difference between an element by element function and a transformational function consider the following examples.

```
PROGRAM C14_Example_4
IMPLICIT NONE
REAL , DIMENSION(5) :: X = (/1.0,2.0,3.0,4.0,5.0/)
! Elemental function
   PRINT *,' Sine of ', X ,' = ',SIN(X)
! Transformational function
   PRINT *,' Sum of ', X ,' = ',SUM(X)
END PROGRAM C14_Example_4
```

The SUM function adds each element of the array and returns the SUM as a scalar, i.e. the result is single valued and not an array.

14.4.2 Example 5: Intrinsic DOT_PRODUCT use

The following program uses the transformational function DOT_PRODUCT:

```
PROGRAM C14_Example_5
IMPLICIT NONE
REAL , DIMENSION(5) :: X = (/1.0,2.0,3.0,4.0,5.0/)
   PRINT *,' Dot product of X with X is'
   PRINT *,' ',DOT_PRODUCT(X,X)
END PROGRAM C14_Example_5
```

Try typing these examples in and running them to highlight the differences between elemental and transformational functions.

14.5 Notes on function usage

You should not use variables which have the same name as the intrinsic functions, e.g. what does SIN(X) mean when you have declared SIN to be a real array?

When a function has multiple arguments care must be taken to ensure that the arguments are in the correct position and of the appropriate kind type;

You may also replace arguments for functions by expressions, e.g.

```
   X = LOG(2.0)
```

or

```
   X = LOG(ABS(Y))
```

or

```
X = LOG(ABS(Y)+Z/2.0)
```

14.6 Example 6: Easter

This example uses only one function, the MOD (or modulus). It is used several
times, helping to emphasize the usefulness of a convenient, easily referenced function. The program calculates the date of Easter for a given year. It is derived from
an algorithm by Knuth, who also gives a fuller discussion of its importance of its
algorithm. He concludes that the calculation of Easter was a key factor in keeping
arithmetic alive during the Middle Ages in Europe. Note that determination of the
Eastern churches' Easter requires a different algorithm.

```
PROGRAM Easter
IMPLICIT NONE
INTEGER :: Year, Metcyc, Century, Error1, Error2, Day
INTEGER :: Epact, Luna, Temp
! A program to calculate the date of Easter
   PRINT *,' Input the year for which Easter'
   PRINT *,' is to be calculated'
   PRINT *,' enter the whole year, e.g. 1978 '
   READ *,Year
! calculating the year in the 19 year
! metonic cycle using variable metcyc
   Metcyc = MOD(Year,19)+1
   IF(Year <= 1582)THEN
      Day = (5*Year)/4
      Epact = MOD(11*Metcyc-4,30)+1
   ELSE
!         calculating the Century-century
      Century = (Year/100)+1
!         accounting for arithmetic inaccuracies
!         ignores leap years etc.
      Error1 = (3*Century/4)-12
      Error2 = ((8*Century+5)/25)-5
!         locating Sunday
      Day = (5*Year/4)-Error1-10
!         locating the epact(full moon)
      Temp = 11 * Metcyc + 20 + Error2 - Error1
      Epact = MOD(Temp,30)
      IF(Epact <= 0) THEN
         Epact = 30 + Epact
```

```
      ENDIF
      IF((Epact  ==  25  .AND.  Metcyc  >  11)  &
      .or.  Epact  ==  24)THEN
         Epact  =  Epact+1
      ENDIF
   ENDIF
!       finding  the  full  moon
   Luna=  44  -  epact
   IF  (Luna  <  21)  THEN
      Luna  =  Luna+30
   ENDIF
!       locating  Easter  Sunday
   Luna  =  Luna+7-(MOD(Day+Luna,7))
!       locating  the  correct  month
   IF(Luna  >  31)THEN
      Luna  =  Luna  -  31
      PRINT  *,'  for  the  year  ',YEAR
      PRINT  *,'  Easter  falls  on  April  ',Luna
   ELSE
      PRINT  *,'  for  the  year  ',YEAR
      PRINT  *,'  Easter  falls  on  march  ',Luna
   ENDIF
END  PROGRAM  Easter
```

We have introduced a new statement here, the IF THEN ENDIF and a variant the IF THEN ELSE ENDIF. A more complete coverage is given in the later chapter on control structures. The main thing of interest is that the normal sequential flow from top to bottom can be varied. In the following case:

IF (expression) THEN

   block of statements

ENDIF

if the expression is true the block of statements between the IF THEN and the ENDIF is executed. If the expression is false then this block is skipped, and execution proceeds with the statements immediately after the ENDIF.

In the following case:

IF (expression) THEN

   block 1

ELSE

block 2

ENDIF

if the expression is true block 1 is executed and block 2 is skipped. If the expression is false then block 2 is executed and block 1 is skipped. Execution then proceeds normally with the statement immediately after the ENDIF.

As well as noting the use of the MOD generic function in this program, it is also worth noting the structure of the decisions. They are *nested*, rather like the nested DO loops we met earlier.

14.7 Complete list of predefined functions

Due to the large number of predefined functions it is useful to classify them, and the following is one classification.

14.7.1   Inquiry functions

These functions return information about their arguments. They can be further subclassified into BIT, CHARACTER, NUMERIC, ARRAY, POINTER, ARGUMENT PRESENCE

Bit	BIT_SIZE
Character	LEN
Numeric	DIGITS, EPSILON, EXPONENT, FRACTION, HUGE, KIND, MAXEXPONENT, MINEXPONENT, NEAREST, PRECISION, RADIX, RANGE, RRSPACING, SCALE, SET_EXPONENT, SELECTED_INT_KIND, SELECTED_REAL_KIND, SPACING, TINY
Array	ALLOCATED, LBOUND, SHAPE, SIZE, UBOUND,
Pointer	ASSOCIATED, NULL
Argument Presence	PRESENT

14.7.2   Transfer and conversion functions

These functions convert data from one type and kind type to another type and kind type. Most of them are by necessity generic.

Transfer and Conversion	ACHAR, AIMAG, AINT, ANINT, CHAR, CMPLX, CONJG, DBLE, IACHAR, IBITS, ICHAR, INT, LOGICAL, NINT, REAL, TRANSFER

14.7.3 Computational functions

These functions actually carry out a computation of some sort and return the result of that computation.

Numeric	ABS, ACOS, ASIN, ATAN, ATAN2, CEILING, COS, COSH, DIM, DOT_PRODUCT, DPROD, EXP, FLOOR, LOG, LOG10, MATMUL, MAX, MIN, MOD, MODULO, SIGN, SIN, SINH, SQRT, TAN, TANH
Character	ADJUSTL, ADJUSTR, INDEX, LEN_TRIM, LGE, LGT, LLE, LLT, REPEAT, SCAN, TRIM, VERIFY
Bit	BTEST, IAND, IBCLR, IBSET, IEOR, IOR, ISHFT, ISHFTC, NOT

14.7.4 Array functions

Reduction	ALL, ANY, COUNT, MAXVAL, MINVAL, PRODUCT, SUM
Construction	MERGE, PACK, SPREAD, UNPACK
Reshape	RESHAPE
Manipulation	CSHIFT, EOSHIFT, TRANSPOSE
Location	MAXLOC, MINLOC

14.7.5 Pre-defined subroutines

Date and Time	CPU_TIME, DATE_AND_TIME, SYSTEM_CLOCK
Random Number	RANDOM_NUMBER, RANDOM_SEED
Other	MVBITS

An alphabetical list of all intrinsic functions and procedures is given in Appendix D. This list provides the following information:

- function name
- description
- argument name and type
- result type
- classification

- examples of use.

This appendix should be consulted for a more complete and thorough understanding of intrinsic functions and their use in Fortran 95.

14.8 Supplying your own functions

There are two stages here, firstly to define the function and secondly to reference or use it. Consider the calculation of the greatest common divisor of two integers.

14.8.1 Example 7: Simple user defined function

The following defines a function to achieve this:

```
INTEGER FUNCTION GCD(A,B)
IMPLICIT NONE
INTEGER , INTENT(IN) :: A,B
INTEGER :: Temp
   IF (A < B) THEN
      Temp=A
   ELSE
      Temp=B
   ENDIF
   DO WHILE ((MOD(A,Temp) /= 0) .OR. (MOD(B,Temp) /=0))
      Temp=Temp-1
   END DO
   GCD=Temp
END FUNCTION GCD
```

To use this function, you reference or call it with a form like:

```
PROGRAM GCDExample
IMPLICIT NONE
INTEGER :: I,J,Result
INTEGER :: GCD
   PRINT *,' Type in two integers'
   READ *,I,J
   Result=GCD(I,J)
   PRINT *,' GCD is ',Result
END PROGRAM GCDExample
```

The first line of the function

```
INTEGER FUNCTION GCD(A,B)
```

has a number of things of interest:

- firstly the function has a type, and in this case the function is of type INTEGER, i.e. it will return an integer value

- the function has a name, in this case GGD

- the function takes arguments or parameters, in this case A and B.

The structure of the rest of the function is the same as that of a program, i.e. we have declarations, followed by the executable part. This is because both a program and a function can be regarded as a so-called *program unit*. We will look into this more fully in later chapters.

In the declaration we also have a new attribute for the INTEGER declaration. The two parameters A and B are of type integer, and the INTENT(IN) attribute means that these parameters will NOT be altered by the function.

The value calculated is returned through the function name somewhere in the body of the executable part of the function. In this case GCD appears on the left hand side of an arithmetic assignment statement at the bottom of the function. The end of the function is signified in the same way as the end of a program:

END FUNCTION GCD

We then have the program which actually uses the function GCD. In the program the function is called or invoked with I and J as arguments. The variables are called A and B in the function, and references to A and B in the function will use the values that I and J have respectively in the main program. We will look into the whole area of argument association in much greater depth in later chapters.

Note also here a new control statement, the DO WHILE ENDDO. In the following case:

DO WHILE (expression)

  block of statements

ENDDO

the block of statements between the DO WHILE and the ENDDO is executed whilst the expression is true. There is a more complete coverage in the chapter on control structures.

We have two options here regarding compilation. Firstly, to make the function and the program into one file, and invoke the compiler once. Secondly, to make the function and program into separate files, and invoke the compiler twice, once for each file. With large programs comprising one program and several functions it is probably worthwhile to keep the component parts in different files and compile individually, whilst if it consists of a simple program and one function then keeping things together in one file makes sense.

Try this program out on the system you work with.

14.9 An Introduction to the scope of variables and local variables

One of the major strengths of Fortran is the ability to work on parts of a problem at a time. This is achieved by the use of *program units* (a main program, one or more functions and one or more subroutines) to solve discrete sub-problems. Interaction between them is limited and can be isolated, for example, to the arguments of the function. Thus variables in the main program can have the same name as variables in the function and they are completely separate variables, even though they have the same name. Thus we have the concept of a local variable in a program unit. We will look into this area again after a coverage of recursion and very thoroughly after the coverage of subroutines and modules.

In the example above I, J, Result, are local to the main program. The declaration of GCD is to tell the compiler that it is an integer, and in this case is is an external function.

A and B in the function GCD do not exist in any real sense, rather that they will be replaced by the actual variable values from the calling routine, in this case by whatever values I and J have. Temp is local to GCD.

14.10 Recursive functions

There is an additional form of the function header that must be used when the function is recursive. Recursion means the breaking down of a problem into a simpler but identical sub problem. The concept is best explained with reference to an actual example. Consider the evaluation of a factorial, e.g. 5!. From simple mathematics we know that the following is true:

5!=5*4!

4!=4*3!

3!=3*2!

2!=2*1!

1!=1

and thus 5! = 5*4*3*2*1 or 120.

14.10.1 Example 8: Recursive factorial evaluation

Let us look at a program with recursive function to solve the evaluation of factorials.

```
PROGRAM FactorialEvaluation
IMPLICIT NONE
INTEGER :: I, F, Factorial
   PRINT *,' Type in the number, integer only'
   READ *,I
   DO WHILE(I<0)
      PRINT *,' Factorial only defined for '
      PRINT *,' positive integers: Re-input'
      READ *,I
   END DO
   F=Factorial(I)
   PRINT *,' Answer is', F
END PROGRAM FactorialEvaluation

RECURSIVE INTEGER FUNCTION Factorial(I) RESULT(Answer)
IMPLICIT NONE
INTEGER , INTENT(IN):: I
   IF (I==0) THEN
      Answer=1
   ELSE
      Answer=I*Factorial(I-1)
   END IF
END FUNCTION Factorial
```

Well what additional information is there? Firstly we have an additional attribute on the function header that declares the function to be recursive. Secondly we must return the result in a variable, in this case Answer. Let us look now at what happens when we compile and run the whole program (both function and main program). If we type in the number 5 the following will happen:

- the function is first invoked with argument 5. The ELSE block is then taken and the function is invoked again;

- the function now exists a second time with argument 4. The ELSE block is then taken and the function is invoked again;

- the function now exists a third time with argument 3. The ELSE block is then taken and the function is invoked again;

- the function now exists a fourth time with argument 2. The ELSE block is then taken and the function is invoked again;

- the function now exists a fifth time with argument 1. The ELSE block is then taken and the function is invoked again;

- the function now exists a sixth time with argument 0. The IF BLOCK is executed and Answer=1. This invocation ends and we return to the previous level, with Answer=1*1.

- We return to the previous invocation and now Answer=2*1.

- We return to the previous invocation and now Answer=3*2.

- We return to the previous invocation and now Answer=4*6.

- We return to the previous invocation and now Answer=5*24

The function now terminates and we return to the main program or calling routine. The answer 120 is the printed out.

Add a PRINT *,I statement to the function after the last declaration and type the program in and run it. Try it out with 5 as the input value to verify the above statements.

Recursion is a very powerful tool in programming, and remarkably simple solutions are possible to quite complex problems using recursive techniques. We will look at recursion in much more depth in the later chapters on dynamic data types, and subroutines and modules.

14.11 Example 9: Recursive version of GCD

The following is another example of the earlier GCD function but with the algorithm in the function replaced with an alternate recursive solution.

```
PROGRAM GCDExample
IMPLICIT NONE
INTEGER :: I,J,Result
INTEGER :: GCD
   PRINT *,' Type in two integers'
   READ *,I,J
   Result=GCD(I,J)
   PRINT *,' GCD is ',Result
END PROGRAM GCDExample

RECURSIVE INTEGER FUNCTION GCD(I,J) RESULT(Answer)
IMPLICIT NONE
```

```
INTEGER , INTENT(IN) :: I,J
   IF (J==0) THEN
      Answer=I
   ELSE
      Answer=GCD(J,MOD(I,J))
   ENDIF
END FUNCTION GCD
```

Try this program out on the system you work with, and look at the timing information provided, and compare the timings with the previous example. The algorithm is a much more efficient algorithm than in the original example, and hence should be much faster. On one system there was a twenty-fold decrease in execution time between the two versions.

Recursion is sometimes said to be inefficient, and the following example looks at a non-recursive version of the second algorithm.

14.12 Example 10: After removing recursion

The following is a variant of the above, with the same algorithm, but with the recursion removed.

```
PROGRAM GCDExample
IMPLICIT NONE
INTEGER :: I,J,Result
INTEGER :: GCD
   PRINT *,' Type in two integers'
   READ *,I,J
   Result=GCD(I,J)
   PRINT *,' GCD is ',Result
END PROGRAM GCDExample

INTEGER FUNCTION GCD(I,J)
IMPLICIT NONE
INTEGER , INTENT(INOUT) :: I,J
INTEGER :: Temp
   DO WHILE (J/=0)
      Temp=MOD(I,J)
      I=J
      J=Temp
   END DO
   GCD=I
END FUNCTION GCD
```

14.13 Pure functions

Within the world of mathematics there is the concept of a pure function. This means that the function only returns a value, and has no effect on the arguments. Fortran 95 introduced the ability to write user defined pure functions. We will provide examples in the chapter on case studies, when we have covered the additional syntax that is required.

14.14 Elemental functions

Fortran 77 introduced the concept of generic intrinsic functions. Fortran 95 added elemental intrinsic functions and the ability to write generic user defined functions. Fortran 95 squares the circle and enables us to write elemental user defined functions. We will show how this can be done in the chapter on case studies when we have covered the additional syntax that is required.

14.15 Internal functions

An internal function is a more restricted and hidden form of the normal function definition.

Since the internal function is specified within a program segment, it may only be used within that segment, and cannot be referenced from any other functions or subroutines, unlike the intrinsic or other user-defined functions.

14.15.1 Example 11: Stirling's approximation

In this example we use Stirling's approximation for large n

$$n! = \sqrt{2\pi n}\left(\frac{n}{e}\right)^n$$

and a complete program to use this internal function is given below.

```
PROGRAM Factor
IMPLICIT NONE
REAL :: Result,N,R
    PRINT *,' Type in N and R'
    READ *,N,R
!   NUMBER OF POSSIBLE COMBINATIONS THAT CAN
!   BE FORMED WHEN
!   R OBJECTS ARE SELECTED OUT OF A GROUP OF N
!        N!/R!(N-R)!
    Result=Stirling(N)/(Stirling(R)*Stirling(N-R))
    PRINT *,Result
```

```
    PRINT *,N,R
CONTAINS
REAL FUNCTION Stirling (X)
   REAL , INTENT(IN) :: X
   REAL , PARAMETER :: PI=3.1415927, E =2.7182828
   Stirling=SQRT(2.*PI*X) * (X/E)**X
END FUNCTION Stirling
END PROGRAM Factor
```

The difference between this example and the earlier ones lies in the CONTAINS statement. The function is now an integral part of the program, and could not be used elsewhere in another function for example. This provides us with a very powerful way of information hiding, and making the construction of larger programs more secure and bug free.

14.16 Resumé

There are a large number of Fortran supplied functions and subroutines (intrinsic functions) which extend the power and scope of the language. Some of these functions are of *generic* type, and can take several different types of argument. Others are restricted to a particular type of argument. Appendix D should be consulted for a fuller coverage concerning the rules that govern the use of the intrinsic functions and procedures.

When the intrinsic functions are inadequate, it is possible to write *user defined* functions. Besides expanding the scope of computation, such functions help in problem visualization and logical subdivision, may reduce duplication, and generally help in avoiding programming errors.

In addition to separately defined user functions, internal functions may be employed. These are functions which are used within a program segment.

Although the normal exit from a user defined function is through the END, other, *abnormal,* exits may be defined through the RETURN statement.

Communication with non-recursive functions is through the function name and the function arguments. The function *must* contain a reference to the function name on the left hand side of an assignment. Results may also be returned through the argument list.

We have also covered briefly the concept of scope for a variable, local variables, and argument association. This area warrants a much fuller coverage and we will do this after we have covered subroutines and modules.

14.17 Function syntax

The syntax of a function is:

[function prefix] function_statement &
[RESULT (Result_name)]
[specification part]
[execution_part]
[internal sub program part]
END [FUNCTION [function name]]

and prefix is:

[type specification] RECURSIVE

or

[RECURSIVE] type specification

and the function_statement is:

FUNCTION function_name ([dummy argument name list])

[ ] represent optional parts to the specification.

14.18 Rules and restrictions

The type of the function must only be specified once, either in the function statement or in a type declaration.

The names must match between the function header and END FUNCTION function name statement.

If there is a RESULT clause that name must be used as the result variable, and therefore all references to the function name are recursive calls.

The function name must be used to return a result when there is no RESULT clause.

We will look at additional rules and restrictions in later chapters.

14.19 Problems

1. Find out the action of the MOD function when one of the arguments is negative. Write your own modulus function to return only a positive remainder. Don't call it MOD!

2. Create a table which gives the sines, cosines and tangents for -1 degrees to 91 degrees in 1 degree intervals. Remember that the arguments have to be in radians.

What value will you give π? One possibility is π=4*atan(1.0). Pay particular attention to the following angle ranges:

- -1,0,+1
- 29,30,31
- 44,45,46
- 59,60,61
- 89,90,91

What do you notice about sine and cosine at 0 and 90 degrees? What do you notice about the tangent of 90 degrees? Why do you think this is?

Use a calculator to evaluate the sine, cosine at 0 and 90. Do the same for the tangent at 90 degrees. Does this surprise you?

Repeat using a spreadsheet, e.g. Excel.

Are you surprised?

Repeat the Fortran program using one or more real kind types.

3. Write a program that will read in the lengths a and b of a right angled triangle and calculate the hypotenuse c. Use the Fortran SQRT intrinsic.

4. Write a program that will read in the lengths a and b of two sides of a triangle and the angle between them θ (in degrees). Calculate the length of the third side c using the cosine rule:

$$c^2 = a^2 + b^2 - 2abcos(\theta)$$

5. Write a function to convert an integer to a binary character representation. It should take an integer argument and return a character string that is a sequence of zeros and ones. Use the program in Chapter 8 as a basis for the solution.

14.20 Bibliography

Abramowitz M., Stegun I., *Handbook of Mathematical Functions*, Dover, 1968.

- This book contains a fairly comprehensive collection of numerical algorithms for many mathematical functions, of varying degrees of obscurity. It is a widely used source.

Association of Computing Machinery (ACM)

- *Collected Algorithms*, 1960–1974

- *Transactions on Mathematical Software*, 1975 –
  A good source of more specialized algorithms. Early algorithms tended to
  be in Algol, Fortran now predominates.

14.20.1 Recursion and problem solving

The following are a number of books that look at the role of recursion in problem
solving and algorithms.

Hofstader D. R., *Gödel, Escher, Bach – an Eternal Golden Braid*, Harvester Press.

- The book provides a stimulating coverage of the problems of paradox and
  contradiction in art music and mathematics using the works of Escher,
  Bach and Gödel, and hence the title. There is a whole chapter on recursive
  structures and processes. The book also covers the work of Church and
  Turing, both of whom have made significant contributions to the theory of
  computing.

Kruse R.L., *Data Structures and Program Design*, Prentice Hall, 1994.

- Quite a gentle introduction to the use of recursion and its role in problem
  solving. Good choice of case studies with explanations of solutions. Pascal
  is used.

Sedgewick R., *Algorithms in Modula 3*, Addison Wesley, 1993.

- Good source of algorithms. Well written. The GCD algorithm was taken
  from this source.

Vowels R.A., *Algorithms and Data Structures in F and Fortran,* Unicomp, 1998.

- The only book currently that uses Fortran 90/95 and F. Visit the Fortran
  web site for more details. They are the publishers.

    http://www.fortran.com/fortran/market.html

Wirth N., *Algorithms + Data Structures = Programs*, Prentice Hall, 1976.

- In the context of this chapter the section on recursive algorithms is a very
  worthwhile investment in time.

Wood D., *Paradigms and Programming in Pascal*, Computer Science Press.

- Contains a number of examples of the use of recursion in problem solving.
  Also provides a number of useful case studies in problem solving.

15

Control Structures

Summarizing: as a slow-witted human being I have a very small head and I had better learn to live with it and to respect my limitations and give them full credit, rather than try to ignore them, for the latter vain effort will be punished by failure. Edsger W. Dijkstra, *Structured Programming*.

Aims

The aims of this chapter are to introduce:

- Selection between various courses of action as part of the algorithm.

- The concepts and statements in Fortran needed to support the above:

    Logical expressions and logical operators.

    One or more *blocks* of statements.

- The IF THEN ENDIF construct

- The IF THEN ELSE IF ENDIF construct

- To introduce the CASE statement with examples

- To introduce the DO loop, in three forms with examples, in particular

    The iterative DO loop

    The DO WHILE form

    The DO ... IF THEN EXIT END DO or repeat until form

    The CYCLE statement

    the EXIT statement

15 Control Structures

When we look at this area it is useful to gain some historical perspective concerning what control structures are available in a programming language.

At the time of the development of Fortran in the 1950s there was little theoretical work around and the control structures provided were very primitive and very closely related to the capability of the hardware.

By the time of the first standard in 1966 there was little published work regarding structured programming and control structures. The seminal work by Dahl, Dijkstra and Hoare was not published until 1972.

By the time of the second standard there was a major controversy regarding languages with poor control structures like Fortran which essentially were limited to the GOTO statement. The facilities in the language had led to the development and continued existence of major code suites that were unintelligible, and the pejorative term *spaghetti* was applied to these programs. Developing an understanding of what a program did became an almost impossible task in many cases.

Fortran missed out in 1977 of incorporating some of the more modern and intelligible control structures that had emerged as being of major use in making code more easy to understand and modify.

It was not until the latest standard that a reasonable set of control structures have emerged and become an accepted part of the language. The more inquisitive reader is urged to read at least the work by Dahl, Dijkstra and Hoare to develop some understanding of the importance of control structures and the role of structured programming. The paper by Knuth is also highly recommended and provides a very balanced coverage of the controversy of earlier times over the GOTO statement.

15.1 Selection between courses of action

In most problems you need to chose between various courses of action, e.g.

- if overdrawn, then do not draw money out of the bank

- if Monday, Tuesday, Wednesday, Thursday or Friday, then go to work

- if Saturday, then go to watch Queens Park Rangers

- if Sunday, then lie in bed for another two hours

As most problems involve selection between two or more courses of action it is necessary to have the concepts to support this in a programming language. Fortran has a variety of selection mechanisms, some of which are now introduced.

15.1.1 The BLOCK IF statement.

The following short example illustrates the main ideas:

```
. wake up
.
. check the date and time
IF (Today = = Sunday) THEN
        .
        . lie in bed for another two hours
        .
ENDIF
.
. get up
. make breakfast
```

If today is Sunday then the block of statements between the IF and the ENDIF is executed. After this block has been executed the program continues with the statements after the ENDIF. If today is not Sunday the program continues with the statements after the ENDIF immediately. This means that the statements after the ENDIF are executed whether or not the expression is true.

The general form is:

```
IF (Logical expression) THEN
        .
        Block of statements
        .
ENDIF
```

The logical expression is an expression that will be either true or false, hence its name. Some examples of logical expressions are given below:

```
(Alpha >= 10.1)
```

Test if Alpha is greater than or equal to 10.1

```
(Balance <= 0.0)
```

Test if overdrawn

```
(( Today == Saturday).OR.( Today == Sunday))
```

Test if today is Saturday or Sunday

```
((Actual-Calculated) <= 1.0E-6)
```

Test if Actual minus Calculated is less than or equal to 1.0E-6

Fortran has the following relational and logical operators:

Operator	Meaning	Type
= =	Equal	Relational
/=	Not equal	Relational
>=	Greater than or equal	Relational
<=	Less than or equal	Relational
<	Less than	Relational
>	Greater than	Relational
.AND.	and	Logical
.OR.	or	Logical
.NOT.	not	Logical

The first six should be self-explanatory. They enable expressions or variables to be compared and tested. The last three enable the construction of quite complex comparisons, involving more than one test; in the example given earlier there was a test to see whether today was Saturday or Sunday.

Use of logical expressions and logical variables (something not mentioned so far) are covered again in a later chapter on logical data types.

The 'IF *expression* THEN *statements* ENDIF' is called a BLOCK IF construct. There is a simple extension to this provided by the ELSE statement. Consider the following example:

```
IF (Balance > 0.0) THEN
        . draw money out of the bank
ELSE
        . borrow money from a friend
ENDIF
. Buy a round of drinks.
```

In this instance, one or other of the blocks will be executed. Then execution will continue with the statements after the ENDIF statement (in this case *buy a round*).

There is yet another extension to the BLOCK IF which allows an ELSEIF statement. Consider the following example:

```
IF (Today == Monday) THEN
   .
ELSEIF (Today == Tuesday) THEN
   .
ELSEIF (Today == Wednesday) THEN
   .
ELSEIF (Today == Thursday) THEN
   .
ELSEIF (Today == Friday) THEN
   .
ELSEIF (Today == Saturday) THEN
   .
ELSEIF (Today == Sunday) THEN
   .
ELSE
   there has been an error. The variable Today has
   taken on an illegal value.
ENDIF
```

Note that, as soon as one of the logical expressions is true, the rest of the test is skipped, and execution continues with the statements after the ENDIF. This implies that a construction like:

```
IF(I < 2)THEN
   ...
ELSEIF(I < 1)THEN
   ...
ELSE
   ...
ENDIF
```

is inappropriate. If I is less than 2, the latter condition will never be tested. The ELSE statement has been used here to aid in trapping errors or exceptions. This is recommended practice. A very common error in programming is to assume that the data is in certain well-specified ranges. The program then fails when the data goes outside this range. It makes no sense to have a day other than Monday, Tuesday, Wednesday, Thursday, Friday, Saturday or Sunday.

15.1.2   Example 1: Quadratic roots

A quadratic equation is:

$$a x^2 + b x + c = 0$$

This program is straightforward, with a simple structure. The roots of the quadratic are either real, equal and real, or complex depending on the magnitude of the term B ** 2 − 4 * A * C. The program tests for this term being greater than or less than zero: it assumes that the only other case is equality to zero (from the mechanics of a computer, floating point equality is rare, but we are safe in this instance).

```
PROGRAM Qroots
IMPLICIT NONE
REAL :: A , B , C , Term , A2 , Root1 , Root2
!
!    a b and c are the coefficients of the terms
!    a*x**2+b*x+c
!    find the roots of the quadratic, root1 and root2
!
   PRINT*,' GIVE THE COEFFICIENTS A, B AND C'
   READ*,A,B,C
   Term = B*B - 4.*A*C
   A2 = A*2.
! if term < 0, roots are complex
! if term = 0, roots are equal
! if term > 0, roots are real and different
   IF(Term < 0.0)THEN
      PRINT*,' ROOTS ARE COMPLEX'
   ELSEIF(Term > 0.0)THEN
      Term = SQRT(Term)
      Root1 = (-B+Term)/A2
      Root2 = (-B-Term)/A2
      PRINT*,' ROOTS ARE ',Root1,' AND ',Root2
   ELSE
      Root1 = -B/A2
      PRINT*,' ROOTS ARE EQUAL, AT ',Root1
   ENDIF
END PROGRAM Qroots
```

15.1.3   Note

Given the understanding you now have about real arithmetic and finite precision will the ELSE block above ever be executed?

15.1.4   Example 2: Date calculation

This next example is also straightforward. It demonstrates that, even if the conditions on the IF statement are involved, the overall structure is easy to determine.

The comments and the names given to variables should make the program self-explanatory. Note the use of integer division to identify leap years.

```fortran
PROGRAM Date
IMPLICIT NONE
INTEGER :: Year , N , Month , Day , T
!
! calculates day and month from year and
! day-within-year
! t is an offset to account for leap years.
! Note that the first criteria is division by 4
! but that centuries are only
! leap years if divisible by 400
! not 100 (4 * 25) alone.
!
   PRINT*,' year, followed by day within year'
   READ*,Year,N
!    checking for leap years
   IF ((Year/4)*4 == Year ) THEN
      T=1
      IF ((Year/400)*400 == Year ) THEN
         T=1
      ELSEIF ((Year/100)*100 == Year) THEN
         T=0
      ENDIF
   ELSE
      T=0
   ENDIF
!    accounting for February
   IF(N > (59+T))THEN
      Day=N+2-T
   ELSE
      Day=N
   ENDIF
   Month=(Day+91)*100/3055
   Day=(Day+91)-(Month*3055)/100
   Month=Month-2
   PRINT*,' CALENDAR DATE IS ', Day , Month , Year
END PROGRAM Date
```

15.1.5   The CASE statement

The CASE statement provides a very clear and expressive selection mechanism between two or more course of action. Strictly speaking it could be constructed from the IF THE ELSE IF ENDIF statement, but with considerable loss of clarity. Remember that programs have to read and understood by both humans and compilers!

15.1.6   Example 3: Simple calculator

```
PROGRAM Case01
IMPLICIT NONE
!
! Simple case statement example
!

INTEGER :: I,J,K
CHARACTER :: Operator
   DO
      PRINT *,' Type in two integers'
      READ *, I,J
      PRINT *,' Type in operator'
      READ '(A)',Operator
      Calculator : &
      SELECT CASE (Operator)
         CASE ('+') Calculator
            K=I+J
            PRINT *,' Sum of numbers is ',K
         CASE ('-') Calculator
            K=I-J
            PRINT *,' Difference is ',K
         CASE ('/') Calculator
            K=I/J
            PRINT *,' Division is ',K
         CASE ('*') Calculator
         K=I*J
         PRINT *,' Multiplication is ',K
      CASE DEFAULT Calculator
         EXIT
      END SELECT Calculator
   END DO
END PROGRAM Case01
```

The user is prompted to type in two integers and the operation that they would like carried out on those two integers. The CASE statement then ensures that the appropriate arithmetic operation is carried out. The program terminates when the user types in any other character than +, -, * or /.

The CASE DEFAULT options introduces the EXIT statement. This statement is used in conjunction with the DO statement. When this statement is executed control passes to the statement immediately after the matching END DO statement. In the example above the program terminates, as there are no executable statements after the END DO.

15.1.7   Example 4: Counting vowels, consonants, etc

This example is more complex, but again is quite easy to understand. The user types in a line of text and the program produces a summary of the frequency of the characters typed in.

```
PROGRAM Case02
IMPLICIT NONE
!
! Simple counting of vowels, consonants,
! digits, blanks and the rest
!
INTEGER :: Vowels=0 , Consonants=0, Digits=0
INTEGER :: Blank=0, Other=0, I
CHARACTER :: Letter
CHARACTER (LEN=80) :: Line
   READ '(A)', Line
   DO I=1,80
      Letter=Line(I:I)
! the above extracts one character at position I
      SELECT CASE (Letter)
         CASE ('A','E','I','O','U', &
               'a','e','i','o','u')
            Vowels=Vowels + 1
         CASE ('B','C','D','F','G','H', &
               'J','K','L','M','N','P', &
               'Q','R','S','T','V','W', &
               'X','Y','Z',            &
               'b','c','d','f','g','h', &
               'j','k','l','m','n','p', &
               'q','r','s','t','v','w', &
               'x','y','z')
            Consonants=Consonants + 1
```

```
        CASE ('1','2','3','4','5','6','7','8','9','0')
           Digits=Digits + 1
        CASE (' ')
           Blank=Blank + 1
        CASE DEFAULT
           Other=Other+1
     END SELECT
   END DO
   PRINT *, ' Vowels =   ', Vowels
   PRINT *, ' Consonants =   ', Consonants
   PRINT *, ' Digits = ', Digits
   PRINT *, ' Blanks = ',Blank
   PRINT *, ' Other characters = ', Other
END PROGRAM Case02
```

15.2 The three forms of the DO statement

You have already been introduced in the chapters on arrays to the iterative form of the DO loop, i.e.

DO Variable = Start, End, Increment

>   block of statements

END DO

A complete coverage of this form is given in the three chapters on arrays.

There are two additional forms of the block DO that complete our requirements and these are:

>   DO WHILE (Logical Expression)
>
>>   block of statements
>
>   ENDDO

and

>   DO
>
>>   block of statements
>>
>>   IF (Logical Expression) EXIT
>
>   END DO

The first form is often called a WHILE loop as the block of statements executes whilst the logical expression is true, and the second form is often called a REPEAT UNTIL loop as the block of statements executes until the statement is true.

Note that the WHILE block of statements may never be executed, and the REPEAT UNTIL block will always be executed at least once.

15.2.1 Example 5: Sentinel usage

The following example shows a complete program using this construct.

```
PROGRAM Find
IMPLICIT NONE
! this program picks up the first occurrence
! of a number in a list.
! a sentinel is used, and the array is 1 more
! than the max size of the list.
INTEGER , DIMENSION(101) :: A
INTEGER :: Mark
INTEGER :: End,I
   OPEN (UNIT=1,FILE='DATA')
   PRINT *,' What number are you looking for?'
   READ  *, Mark
   READ (UNIT=1,FMT=*) End
   READ(UNIT=1,FMT=*)  (A(I),I=1,End)
   I=1
   A(End+1)= Mark
   DO WHILE(Mark /= A(I))
      I=I+1
   END DO
   IF(I == (END+1)) THEN
      PRINT*,' ITEM NOT IN LIST'
   ELSE
      PRINT*,' ITEM IS AT POSITION ',I
   ENDIF
END PROGRAM Find
```

The *repeat until* construct is written in Fortran as:

```
   DO
   . . .
   . . .
      IF (Logical Expression) EXIT
   END DO
```

There are problems in most disciplines that require a numerical solution. The two main reasons for this are that either the problem can only be solved numerically, or that an analytic solution involves too much work. Solutions to this type of problem often require the use of the *repeat until* construct. The problem will typically require the repetition of a calculation until the answers from successive evaluations differ by some small amount, decided generally by the nature of the problem. Here is a program extract to illustrate this:

```
REAL , PARAMETER :: TOL=1.0E-6
.
DO
    . . .
    CHANGE=
    . . .
    IF (CHANGE <= TOL) EXIT
END DO
```

The value of the tolerance is set here to 1.0E–6. Note again the use of the EXIT statement. The DO END DO block is terminated and control passes to the statement immediately after the matching END DO.

15.2.2 CYCLE and EXIT

These two statements are used in conjunction with the block DO statement. You have seen examples above of the use of the EXIT statement to terminate the block DO, and pass control to the statement immediately after the corresponding END DO statement.

The CYCLE statement can appear anywhere in a block DO and will immediately pass control to the start of the block DO. Examples of CYCLE and EXIT are given in later chapters.

15.2.3 Example 6: e**x evaluation

The function ETOX illustrates one use of the *repeat until* construct. The function evaluates e**x. This may be written as:

$$1 + x/1! + x^2/2! + x^3/3! \ldots$$

or

$$1 + \sum_{n=1}^{\infty} \frac{x^{n-1}}{(n-1)!} \frac{x}{n}$$

Every succeeding term is just the previous term multiplied by x/n. At some point the term x/n becomes very small, so that it is not sensibly different from zero, and successive terms add little to the value. The function therefore repeats the loop until x/n is smaller than the tolerance. The number of evaluations is not known beforehand, since this is dependent on x.

```
REAL FUNCTION Etox(X)
IMPLICIT NONE
REAL :: Term
REAL , INTENT(IN) :: X
INTEGER :: Nterm
REAL , PARAMETER ::Tol = 1.0E-6
   Etox=1.0
   Term=1.0
   Nterm=0
   DO
      Nterm = Nterm +1
      Term =( X / Nterm) * Term
      Etox = Etox + Term
      IF(ABS(Term) <= Tol)EXIT
   END DO
END FUNCTION Etox
```

Both types of loop are combined in this last example. The algorithm employed here finds the zero of a function. Essentially, it finds an interval in which the zero must lie; the evaluations on either side are of different sign. The *while loop* ensures that the evaluations are of different sign, by exploiting the knowledge that the incident wave height must be greater than the reformed wave height (to give the lower bound). The upper bound is found by experiment, making the interval bigger and bigger. Once the interval is found, its mean is used as a new potential bound. The zero must lie on one side or the other; in this fashion, the interval containing the zero becomes smaller and smaller, until it lies within some tolerance. This approach is rather plodding and unexciting, but is suitable for a wide range of problems.

15.2.4   Example 7: Wave breaking on an offshore reef

This example is drawn from a situation where a wave breaks on an offshore reef or sand bar, and then reforms in the near-shore zone before breaking again on the coast. It is easier to observe the heights of the reformed waves reaching the coast than those incident to the terrace edge.

```
PROGRAM Break
IMPLICIT NONE
REAL :: Hi , Hr , Hlow , High , Half , Xl
REAL :: Xh , Xm , D
REAL , PARAMETER :: Tol=1.0E-6
! problem - find hi from expression given
! in function f
! F=A*(1.0-0.8*EXP(-0.6*C/A))-B
```

```
! HI IS INCIDENT WAVE HEIGHT           (C)
! HR IS REFORMED WAVE HEIGHT           (B)
! D IS WATER DEPTH AT TERRACE EDGE     (A)
  PRINT*,' Give reformed wave height, and water depth'
  READ*,Hr,d
!
! for Hlow- let Hlow=hr
! for high- let high=Hlow*2.0
!
! check that signs of function results are different
!
  Hlow = Hr
  High = Hlow*2.0
  Xl = F( Hlow, Hr, D)
  Xh = F( High, Hr, D)
!
  DO WHILE ((XL*XH)  >= 0.0)
     HIGH = HIGH*2.0
     XH = F(HIGH,HR,D)
  END DO
!
  DO
     HALF=(HLOW+HIGH)*0.5
     XM=F(HALF,HR,D)
     IF((XL*XM) < 0.0)THEN
        XH=XM
        HIGH=HALF
     ELSE
        XL=XM
        HLOW=HALF
     ENDIF
     IF(ABS(HIGH-HLOW)<= TOL)EXIT
  END DO
  PRINT*,' Incident Wave Height Lies Between'
  PRINT*,Hlow,' and ',High,' metres'
CONTAINS
REAL FUNCTION F(A,B,C)
IMPLICIT NONE
REAL , INTENT (IN) :: A
REAL , INTENT (IN) :: B
REAL , INTENT (IN) :: C
  F=A*(1.0-0.8*EXP(-0.6*C/A))-B
```

```
END FUNCTION F
END PROGRAM Break
```

15.3 Summary

You have been introduced in this chapter to several control structures and these include:

- the *block if*

- the *if then else if*

- the *case* construct

- the block *do* in three forms:

  - the *iterative do* or *do variable=start,end,increment ... end do*

  - the *while* construct, or *do while ... end do*

  - the *repeat until* construct, or *do ... if then exit end do*

- the *cycle* and *exit* statements, which can be used with *do* statement in all three forms:

  - the *do variable = start,end,increment ... end do*

  - the *while* construct, or *do while ... end do*

  - the *repeat until* construct, or *do ... if then exit end do*

These constructs are sufficient to solve a wide class of problems. There are other control statements available in Fortran, especially those inherited from Fortran 66 and Fortran 77, but the ones that are covered here are the preferred ones. We will look in Chapter 28 at one more control statement, the so-called GOTO statement, with recommendations as to where its use is appropriate.

The above are more formally described below:

CASE

```
SELECT CASE ( case variable )
   [ CASE case selector
     [executable construct ] ... ] ...
   [ CASE DEFAULT
   [executable construct ]
END SELECT
```

DO

```
DO [ label ]
   [executable construct ] ...
do termination

DO [ label ] [ , ] loop variable = initial value ,
final value , [ increment ]
   [executable construct ] ...
do termination

DO [ label ] [ , ] WHILE (scalar logical expression )
   [executable construct ] ...
do termination
```

IF

```
IF ( scalar logical expression ) THEN
   [executable construct ] ...
[ ELSE IF ( scalar logical expression   THEN
   [executable construct ] ... ] ...]
[ ELSE
     [executable construct ] ...]
END IF
```

15.4 Problems

1. Rewrite the program for the period of a pendulum. The new program should print out the length of the pendulum, and period for lengths of the pendulum from 0 to 100 cm in steps of 0.5 cm. The program should incorporate a function for the evaluation of the period.

2. Write a program to read an integer that must be positive.

Hint. Use a DO WHILE to make the user re-enter the value.

3. Using functions, do the following:

- Evaluate $n!$ from $n=0$ to $n=10$

- Calculate 76!

- Now calculate $(x**n)/n!$, with $x=13.2$ and $n=20$.

- Now do it another way.

4. The program BREAK is taken from a real example. In the particular problem, the reformed wave height was 1 metre, and the water depth at the reef edge was 2

metres. What was the incident wave height? Rather than using an absolute value for the tolerance, it might be more realistic to use some value related to the reformed wave height. These heights are unlikely to be reported to better than about 5 per cent accuracy. Wave energy may be taken as proportional to wave height squared for this example. What is the reduction in wave energy as a result of breaking on the reef or bar, for this particular case.

5. What is the effect of using INT on negative real numbers? Write a program to demonstrate this.

6. How would you find the nearest integer to a real number? Now do it another way. Write a program to illustrate both methods. Make sure you test it for negative as well as positive values.

7. The function ETOX has been given in this chapter. The standard Fortran function EXP does the same job. Do they give the same answers? Curiously the Fortran standard does not specify how a *standard* function should be evaluated, or even how accurate it should be.

The physical world has many examples where processes require some threshold to be overcome before they begin operation: critical mass in nuclear reactions, a given slope to be exceeded before friction is overcome, and so on. Unfortunately, most of these sorts of calculations become rather complex and not really appropriate here. The following problem tries to restrict the range of calculation, whilst illustrating the possibilities of decision making.

8. If a cubic equation is expressed as

$$z^3 + a_2 z^2 + a_1 z + a_0 = 0$$

and we let

$$q = \frac{a_1}{3} - \frac{(a_2 * a_2)}{9}$$

and

$$r = \frac{(a_1 * a_2 - 3 * a_0)}{6} - \frac{(a_2 * a_2 * a_2)}{27}$$

we can determine the nature of the roots as follows:

$q^3 + r^2 > 0$; one real root and a pair of complex;
$q^3 + r^2 = 0$; all roots real, and at least two equal;
$q^3 + r^2 < 0$; all roots real;

Incorporate this into a suitable program, to determine the nature of the roots of a cubic from suitable input.

9. The form of breaking waves on beaches is a continuum, but for convenience we commonly recognize three major types: surging, plunging and spilling. These may be classified empirically by reference to the wave period, T (seconds), the breaker wave height, H_b (metres), and the beach slope, m. These three variables are combined into a single parameter, B, where

$B = H_b/(gmT^2)$

g is the gravitational constant (981 cm s^{-2}). If B is less than 0.003, the breakers are surging; if B is greater than 0.068, they are spilling, and between these values, plunging breakers are observed.

(i) On the east coast of New Zealand, the normal pattern of waves is swell waves, with wave heights of 1 to 2 metres, and wave periods of 10 to 15 seconds. During storms, the wave period is generally shorter, say 6 to 8 seconds, and the wave heights higher, 3 to 5 metres. The beach slope may be taken as about 0.1. What changes occur in breaker characteristics as a storm builds up?

(ii) Similarly, many beaches have a concave profile. The lower beach generally has a very low slope, say less than 1 degree (m=0.018), but towards the high tide mark, the slope increases dramatically, to say 10 degrees or more (m=0.18). What changes in wave type will be observed as the tide comes in?

15.5 Bibliography

Dahl O.J., Dijkstra E.W., Hoare C.A.R., *Structured Programming*, Academic Press, 1972.

- This is the original text, and a must. The quote at the start of the chapter by Dijkstra summarises beautifully our limitations when programming and the discipline we must have to successfully master programming.

Knuth D.E., *Structured Programming with GOTO Statements,* in Current Trends in Programming Methodology, Volume 1, Prentice Hall, 1977.

- The chapter by Knuth provides a very succinct coverage of the arguments for the adoption of structured programming, and dispells many of the myths concerning the use of the GOTO statement. Highly recommended.

16

Characters

These metaphysics of magicians,
And necromantic books are heavenly;
Lines, circles, letters and characters;

Christopher Marlowe, *The Tragical History of Doctor Faustus*

Aims

The aims of this chapter are:

- to extend the ideas about characters introduced in earlier chapters;

- to demonstrate that this enables us to solve a whole new range of problems in a satisfactory way.

16 Characters

For each type in a programming language there are the following concepts:

- values are drawn from a finite domain

- there are a restricted number of operations defined for each type

For the numeric types we have already met, integers and reals:

- the values are either drawn from the domain of integer numbers or the domain of real numbers

- the valid operations are addition, subtraction, multiplication, division and exponentiation.

For the character data type the basic unit is an individual character – any character which is available on your keyboard normally. To ensure portability we should restrict ourselves to the Fortran character set, that is:

- the alphabetic characters A through Z, the digits or numeric characters 0 through 9, and the underscore character _

which may be used in variable names, and the special characters in Table 16.1.

	blank	)	right brackets or parenthesis	"	quotation mark
=	equal			%	percent
+	plus	,	comma	&	ampersand
-	minus	.	decimal point or period	;	semi-colon
*	asterisk	,	apostrophe	<	less than
/	slash or oblique	:	colon	>	greater than
(	left brackets or parenthesis	!	exclamation mark	?	question mark
				$	currency symbol

Table 16.1 Special characters

This provides us with 58 printing characters and omits many commonly used characters, e.g. lower case letters. However if one does work with this set then one can ensure that programs are portable.

As the most common current internal representation for the character data type uses 8 bits this should provide access to 256 (2^8) characters. However there is little agreement over the encoding of these 256 possible characters, and the best you can normally assume is access to the ASCII character set, which is given in Appendix B. One of the problems looks at determining what characters one has available.

The only operations defined are concatenation (joining character strings together) and comparison.

We will look into the area of character sets in more depth later in this chapter.

We may declare our character variables:

```
CHARACTER :: A, String, Line
```

Notice that there is no default typing of the character variable (unlike integer and real data types), and we can use any convenient name within the normal Fortran conventions. In the declaration above, each character variable would have been permitted to store one character. This is limiting, and, to allow character strings which are several units long, we have to add one item of information:

```
CHARACTER (10) :: A
CHARACTER (16) :: String
CHARACTER (80) :: Line
```

This indicates that A holds 10 characters, STRING holds 16, and LINE holds 80. If all the character variables in a single declaration contain the same number of characters, we may abbreviate the declaration to

```
CHARACTER(80) :: LIST, STRING, LINE
```

But we cannot mix both forms in the one declaration. We can now assign data to these variables, as follows:

```
A='FIRST ONE '
STRING='A LONGER ONE
LINE='THE QUICK BROWN FOX JUMPS OVER THE LAZY DOG'
```

The delimiter apostrophe (') or quotation mark(") is needed to indicate that this is a character string (otherwise the assignments would have looked like invalid variable names).

16.1 Character input

In an earlier chapter we saw how we could use the READ * and PRINT * statements to do both numeric and character input and output or I/O. When we use this form of the statement we have to include any characters we type within delimiters (either the apostrophe ' or quotation mark "). This is a little restricting and there is a slightly more complex form of the READ statement that allows one to just type the string on its own. The following two programs illustrate the differences.

```
PROGRAM Chapter16_01
!
! Simple character i/o
!
CHARACTER (80) :: Line
   READ *, Line
   PRINT *, Line
END PROGRAM Chapter16_01
```

This form requires enclosing the string with delimiters. Consider the next form:

```
PROGRAM Chapter16_02
!
! Simple character i/o
!
CHARACTER (80) :: Line
   READ '(A)' , Line
   PRINT *,Line
END PROGRAM Chapter16_02
```

With this form one can just type the string in and input terminates with the carriage return key. The additional syntax involves '(A)' where '(A)' is a character edit descriptor. The simple examples we have used so far have used implied format specifiers and edit descriptors. For each data type we have one or more edit descriptors to choose from. For the character data type only one edit descriptor is available and that is the A edit descriptor.

16.2 Character operators

The first manipulator is a new operator – the concatenation operator //. With this operator we can join two character variables to form a third, as in

```
   CHARACTER (5)  :: FIRST,  SECOND
   CHARACTER (10) :: THIRD
   FIRST='THREE'
```

```
SECOND='BLIND'
...
THIRD=FIRST//SECOND
.
THIRD=FIRST//'MICE'
```

Where there is a discrepancy between the created length of the concatenated string and the declared lengths of the character strings, truncation will occur. For example

```
THIRD=FIRST//' BLIND MICE'
```

will only append the first five characters of the string ' BLIND MICE' – that is ' BLIN', and THIRD will therefore contain 'THREE BLIN'.

What would happen if we assigned a character variable of length 'n' a string which was shorter than n? e.g.

```
CHARACTER (4) :: C2
C2='AB'
```

The remaining two characters are considered to be blank, that is, it is equivalent to saying

```
C2='AB   '
```

However, while the strings 'AB' and 'AB   ' are equivalent, 'AB' and '   AB' are not. In the jargon, the character strings are always *left justified,* and the *unset* characters are trailing blanks.

If we concatenate strings which have 'trailing blanks', the blanks, or spaces, are considered to be legitimate characters, and the concatenation begins after the end of the first string. Thus

```
CHARACTER (4) :: C2,C3
CHARACTER (8) :: JJ
C2='A'
C3='MAN'
JJ=C2//C3
PRINT*, 'THE CONCATENATION OF ',C2,' AND ',C3,' IS'
PRINT*,JJ
```

would appear as

THE CONCATENATION OF A   AND MAN GIVES

A   MAN

at the terminal.

Sometimes we need to be able to extract parts of character variables – sub-strings. The actual notation for doing this is a little strange at first, but it is very powerful. To extract a sub-string we must reference two items:

- (i) the position in the string at which the sub-string begins,

and

- (ii) the position at which it ends

e.g.

```
STRING='SHARE AND ENJOY'
```

16.3 Character sub-strings

We may extract parts of this string

```
BIT=STRING(3:5)
```

would place the characters 'ARE' into the variable BIT. This may be manipulated further

```
BIT1=STRING(2:4)//STRING(9:9)
BIT2=STRING(5:5)  // &
STRING(3:3)//STRING(1:1)//STRING(15:15)
```

Note that to extract a *single* character we reference its beginning position and its end (i.e. repeat the same position), so that

```
STRING(3:3)
```

gives the single character 'A'. The sub-string reference can cut out either one of the two numerical arguments. If the first is omitted, the characters up to and including the reference are selected, so that

```
SUB=STRING(:5)
```

would result in SUB containing the characters 'SHARE'. When the second argument is omitted, the characters from the reference are selected, so that

```
SUB=STRING(11:)
```

would place the characters 'ENJOY' in the variable SUB. In these examples it would also be necessary to declare STRING, SUB, BIT, BIT1 and BIT2 as CHARACTER type, of some appropriate length.

Character variables may also form arrays:

```
CHARACTER (10) , DIMENSION(20) :: A
```

sets up a character array of twenty elements, where each element contains ten characters. In order to extract sub-strings from these array elements, we need to know where the array reference and the sub-string reference are placed. The array reference comes first, so that

```
DO I=1,20
   FIRST=A(I)(1:1)
ENDO
```

places the first character of each element of the array into the variable FIRST. The syntax is therefore 'position in array, followed by position within string'.

Any argument can be replaced by a variable:

```
STRING(I:J)
```

This offers interesting possibilities, since we can, for example, strip out blanks from a string

```
PROGRAM Chapter16_05
IMPLICIT NONE
   CHARACTER(80) :: String, Strip
   INTEGER :: IPOS,I,Length=80
   IPOS=0
   PRINT *,' Type in a string'
   READ '(A)',String
   DO I=1,Length
      IF(String(I:I) /= ' ') THEN
         IPOS=IPOS+1
         Strip(IPOS:IPOS)=String(I:I)
      ENDIF
   END DO
   PRINT*,String
   PRINT*,Strip
END PROGRAM Chapter16_05
```

16.4 Character functions

There are special functions available for use with character variables: INDEX will give the starting position of a string within another string. If, for example we were looking for all occurrences of the string 'Geology' in a file, we could construct something like

```
PROGRAM Chapter16_03
IMPLICIT NONE
CHARACTER (80) :: Line
INTEGER :: I
   DO
      READ '(A)', Line
      I=INDEX(Line,'Geology')
      IF (I /= 0) THEN
         PRINT *, ' String Geology found at position ', I
         PRINT *, ' in line ', Line
         EXIT
      ENDIF
   ENDDO
END PROGRAM Chapter16_03
```

There are two things to note with the INDEX function. Firstly, it will only report the first occurrence of the string in the line; any later occurrences in any particular line will go unnoticed, unless you account for this in some way. Secondly, if the string does not occur, the result is zero, and hence the form of the logical expression in the IF THEN ENDIF statement.

LEN provides the length of a character string. This function is not immediately useful, since you really ought to know how many characters there are in the string. However, as later examples will show, there are some cases where it can be useful. Remember that trailing blanks do count as part of the character string, and contribute to the length.

The following example illustrates the use of both LEN and LEN_TRIM.

```
PROGRAM Chapter16_04
IMPLICIT NONE
CHARACTER (LEN=20) :: Name
INTEGER :: Name_Length
   PRINT *,' Type in your name'
   READ   '(A)',Name
!
! show LEN first
!
   Name_length=LEN(Name)
   PRINT *,' Name length is ',Name_length
   PRINT *,' ',Name(1:Name_length),'<-end is here'
```

```
Name_length=LEN_TRIM(Name)
PRINT *,' Name length is ',Name_length
PRINT *,' ',Name(1:Name_Length),'<-end is here'
END PROGRAM Chapter16_04
```

16.5 Collating sequence

The next group of functions need to be considered together. They revolve around
the concept of a collating sequence. In other words, each character used in Fortran
is ordered as a list, and given a corresponding *weight*. No two weights are equal.
Although Fortran has only 58 defined characters, the machine you use will generally have more; 95 printing characters are a typical minimum number. On this type
of machine the weights would vary from zero to 94. There is a defined collating
sequence, the ASCII sequence, which is likely to be the default. The parts of the
collating sequence which are of most interest are fairly standard throughout all collating sequences.

In general, we are interested in the numerals (0–9), the alphabetics (A–Z) and a few
odds and ends like the arithmetic operators (+ − / *), some punctuation (. and ,) and
perhaps the prime ('). As you might expect, 0–9 carry successively higher weights
(though not the weights 0 to 9), as do A to Z. The other odds and ends are a little
more problematic, but we can find out the weights through the function ICHAR.
This function takes a single character as argument, and returns an integer value. The
ASCII weights for the alphanumerics are as follows:

0–9	48–57
A–Z	65–90

One of the exercises is to determine the weights for other characters. The reverse of
this procedure is to determine the character from its weighting, which can be
achieved through the function CHAR. CHAR takes an integer argument and returns
a single character. Using the ASCII collating sequence, the alphabet would be generated from

```
DO  I=65,90
    PRINT*,CHAR(I)
ENDDO
```

This idea of a weighting may then be used in four other functions:

Function	Action
LLE	lexically less than or equal to
LGE	lexically greater than or equal to
LGT	lexically greater than
LLT	lexically less than

In the sequence we have seen before, A is lexically less than B, i.e. its weight is less. Clearly, we can use ICHAR and get the same result. For example

```
IF(LGT('A','B')) THEN
```

is equivalent to

```
IF(ICHAR('A') > ICHAR('B')) THEN
```

but these functions can take character string arguments of any length. They are not restricted to single characters.

These functions provide very powerful tools for the manipulation of characters, and open up wide areas of non-numerical computing through Fortran. Lots of text formatting and word processing applications may now be tackled (conveniently ignoring the fact that lower case characters may not be available).

There are many problems that require the use of character variables. These range from the ability to provide simple titles on reports, or graphical output, to the provision of a natural language interface to one of your programs, i.e. the provision of an English-like command language. *Software Tools*, Kernighan and Plauger, contains many interesting uses of characters in Fortran.

16.6 Summary

Characters represent a different data type to any other in Fortran, and as a consequence there is a restricted range of operations which may be carried out on them.

A character variable has a length which must be assigned in a CHARACTER declaration statement.

Character strings are delimited by apostrophes (') or quotation marks ("). Within a character string, the blank is a significant character.

Character strings may be joined together (concatenated) with the // operator.

Sub-strings, occurring within character strings, may be also be manipulated. There are a number of functions especially for use with characters:

- ACHAR
- ADJUSTL
- ADJUSTR
- CHAR
- IACHAR
- INDEX
- LEN
- LEN_TRIM
- LLE
- LGE
- LGT
- LLT
- REPEAT
- SCAN
- TRIM
- VERIFY.

16.7 Problems

1. Suggest some circumstances where PRIME='''' might be useful. What other alternative is there and why do you think we use that instead?

2. Write a program to write out the weights for the Fortran character set. Modify this program to print out the weights of the complete implementation defined character set for your version of Fortran 90. Is it ASCII? If not, how does it differ?

3. Use the INDEX function in order to find the location of all the strings 'IS' in the following data;

IF A PROGRAMMER IS FOUND TO BE INDISPENSABLE, THE BEST THING TO DO IS TO GET RID OF HIM AS QUICKLY AS POSSIBLE.

4. Find the 'middle' character in the following strings. Do you include blanks as characters? What about punctuation?

PRACTICE IS THE BEST OF ALL INSTRUCTORS. EXPERIENCE IS A DEAR TEACHER, BUT FOOLS WILL LEARN AT NO OTHER.

5. In English, the order of occurrence of the letters, from most frequent to least is:

E, T, A, O, N, R, I, S, H, D, L, F, C, M, U, G, Y, P, W, B, V, K, X, J, Q, Z.

Use this information to examine the two files given in Appendix D (one is a translation of the other) to see if this is true for these two extracts of text. The second text is in medieval Latin (c. 1320). Note that a fair amount of compression has been achieved by expressing the passage in Latin rather than modern English. Does this provide a possible model for information compression?

6. A very common cypher is the substitution cypher, where, for example, every letter A is replaced by (say) an M, every B is replaced by (say) a Y, and so on. These encyphered messages can be broken by reference to the frequency of occurrence of the letters (given in the previous question).

Since we know that (in English) E is the most commonly occurring letter, we can assume that the most commonly occurring letter in the encyphered message represents an E; we then repeat the process for the next most common and so on. Of course, these correspondences may not be exact, since the message may not be long enough to develop the frequencies fully.

However, it may provide sufficient information to break the cypher.

The file given in Appendix E contains an encoded message. Break it. Clue — *Pg Fybdujuvef jo Tdjfodf,* Jorge Luis Borges.

17

Complex

Make it as simple as possible, but no simpler.

Albert Einstein

'Can you do addition?' the White Queen asked. 'What's one and one and one and one and one and one and one and one and one and one?' 'I don't know' said Alice. 'I lost count.' 'She can't do addition,' the Red Queen interrupted.

Lewis Carroll, *Through the Looking Glass and What Alice Found There.*

Aims

The aims of this chapter are:

- to introduce the last predefined numeric data type in Fortran;
- to illustrate with examples how to use this type.

17 Complex

This variable type reflects an extension of the real data type available in Fortran — the COMPLEX data type, where we can store and manipulate complex variables. Problems that require this data type are restricted to certain branches of mathematics, physics and engineering. Complex numbers are defined as having a *real* and *imaginary* part, i.e.

$$a = x + iy$$

where i is the square root of -1.

They are not supported in many programming languages as a base type. This therefore makes Fortran the language of first choice for many people.

To use this variable type we have to write the number as two parts, the real and imaginary elements of the number, for example:

```
COMPLEX :: U
   U=(1.0,2.0)
```

represents the complex number 1+i2. Note that the complex number is enclosed in brackets. We can do arithmetic on variables like this, and most of the intrinsic functions like LOG, SIN, COS, etc. accept a complex data type as argument.

All the usual rules about mixing different variable types, like reals and integers, also apply to complex. Complex numbers are read in and written out in a similar way to real numbers, but with the provision that, for each single complex value, two format descriptors must be given. You may use either E or F formats (or indeed, mix them), as long as there are enough of them. Although you use brackets around the pairs of numbers in a program, these must not appear in any input, nor will they appear on the output.

Fortran has a number of functions which help to clarify the intent of *mixed mode* expressions. The functions REAL, CMPLX and INT can be used to 'force' any variable to real, complex or integer type.

There are a number of intrinsic functions to enable complex calculations to be performed. For example if we have:

```
COMPLEX:: Z, Z1,Z2,Z3,ZBAR
REAL :: X,Y,X1,Y1,X2,Y2,X3,Y3,ZMOD
   Z1 = CMPLX (1.0, 2.0)      !  1 + i 2
   Z2 = CMPLX(X2, Y2)         ! X2 + i Y2
   Z3 = CMPLX (X3, Y3)        ! X3 + i Y3
   Z  = Z1*Z2 / Z3
```

```
X    = REAL(Z)                    ! real part of Z
Y    = AIMAG (Z)                  ! imaginary part of Z
ZMOD = ABS(Z)                     ! modulus of Z
ZBAR = CONJG(Z)                   ! complex conjugate of Z
```

17.1 Example

The second order differential equation:

$$\frac{d^2 y}{d t^2} + 2\frac{dy}{dt} + y = x(t)$$

could describe the behaviour of an electrical system, where $x(t)$ is the input voltage and $y(t)$ is the output voltage and dy/dt is the current. The complex ratio

$$\frac{y(w)}{x(w)} = 1 / (-w^2 + 2jw + 1)$$

is called the frequency response of the system because it describes the relationship between input and output for sinusoidal excitation at a frequency of w and where j is $\sqrt{-1}$. The following program segment reads in a value of w and evaluates the frequency response for this value of w together with its polar form (magnitude and phase).

```
PROGRAM Complex_numbers
IMPLICIT NONE
!
! Program to calculate frequency response of a system
! for a given Omega
! and its polar form (magnitude and phase).
!
REAL :: Omega ,Real_part , Imag_part , Magnitude, Phase
COMPLEX:: Frequency_response
!
! Input frequency Omega
!
   PRINT *, 'Input frequency'
   READ *,Omega
!
   Frequency_response = 1.0 / &
      CMPLX( - Omega * Omega + 1.0 , 2.0 * Omega)
   Real_part = REAL(Frequency_response)
   Imag_part = AIMAG(Frequency_response)
!
```

```
! Calculate polar coordinates (magnitude and phase)
!
   Magnitude = ABS(Frequency_response)
   Phase = ATAN2 (Imag_part, Real_part)
!
   PRINT *, ' At frequency ',Omega
   PRINT *, 'Response = ', Real_part,' + I ',Imag_part
   PRINT *, 'in Polar form'
   PRINT *, ' Magnitude = ', Magnitude
   PRINT *, ' Phase = ', Phase
END PROGRAM Complex_numbers
```

17.2 Complex and kind type

The standard requires that there be a minimum of two kind types for real numbers
and this is also true of the complex data type. Chapter 8 must be consulted for a full
coverage of real kind types. We would therefore use something like the following
to select a complex kind type other than the default:

```
INTEGER , PARAMETER ::
Long_Complex=SELECTED_REAL_KIND(15,307)
COMPLEX (Long_Complex) :: Z
```

Chapter 24 contains a good example of how to use modules to define and use
precision throughout a program and sub-program units.

17.3 Summary

COMPLEX is used to store and manipulate complex numbers: those with a real and
imaginary part.

There are standard functions which allow conversion between the numerical data
types – CMPLX, REAL and INT.

17.4 Problems

1. The program used in Chapter 15 which calculated the roots of a quadratic had to
abandon the calculation if the roots were complex. You should now be able to
remedy this, remembering that it is necessary to declare any complex variables.
Instead of raising the expression to the power 0.5 in order to square root it, use the
function SQRT. If you manage this to your satisfaction, try your skills on the roots
of a cubic (see the problems in Chapter 15).

18

Logical

A messenger yes/no semaphore
her black/white keys in/out whirl of morse
hoopooe signals salvation deviously

Nathaniel Tarn, *The Laurel Tree*

Aims

The aims of this chapter are:

- to examine the last predefined type available in Fortran: logical

- to introduce the concepts necessary to use logical expressions effectively; namely

  - logical variables

  - logical operators

  - the hierarchy of operations

  - truth tables.

18 Logical

Often we have situations where we need ON/OFF, TRUE/FALSE or YES/NO switches, and in such circumstances we can use LOGICAL type variables: e.g.

```
LOGICAL :: FLAG
```

Logicals may take only two possible values, as shown in the following:

```
FLAG=.TRUE.
```

or

```
FLAG=.FALSE.
```

Note the full stops, which are essential. With a little thought you can see why they are needed. You will already have met some of the ideas associated with logical variables from IF statements.

```
IF(A == B) THEN
     .
ELSE
     .
ENDIF
```

The logical expression (A == B) returns a value *true* or *false,* which then determines the route to be followed; if the quantity is true, then we execute the next statement, else we take the other route.

Similarly, the following example is also legitimate:

```
LOGICAL :: ANSWER
   ANSWER=.TRUE.
   ...
   IF (ANSWER) THEN
      ...
   ELSE
      ...
   ENDIF
```

Again the expression IF (ANSWER) is evaluated; here the variable ANSWER has been set to .TRUE., and therefore the statements following the THEN are executed. Clearly, conventional arithmetic is inappropriate with logicals. What does 2 times true mean? (very true?). There are a number of special operators for logicals:

.NOT. which negates a logical value (i.e. changes *true* to *false* or vice versa)

.AND. logical intersection

.OR. logical union

To illustrate the use of these operators, consider the following program extract:

```
LOGICAL :: A,B,C
   A=.TRUE.
   B=.NOT.A
!                       (B now has the value 'false')
   C=A.OR.B
!                       (C has the value 'true')
   C=A.AND.B
!                       (C now has the value 'false')
```

To gauge the effect of these operators on logicals, we can consult a truth table:

X1	X2	.NOT.X1	X1.AND.X2	X1.OR.X2
true	true	false	true	true
true	false	false	false	true
false	true	true	false	true
false	false	true	false	false

As with arithmetic operators, there is an order of precedence associated with the logical operators.

.AND. is carried out before

.OR. and .NOT.

In dealing with logicals, the operations are carried out within a given level, from left to right. Any expressions in brackets would be dealt with first. The logical operators are a lower order of precedence to the arithmetic operators, i.e. they are carried out later. A more complete operator hierarchy is therefore:

- expressions within brackets

- exponentiation

- multiplication/division

- addition/subtraction

- relational logical (= =, >, <, >=, <= /=)

- .AND.

- .OR. and .NOT.

Although you can build up complicated expressions with mixtures of operators, these are often difficult to comprehend, and it is generally more straightforward to break '*big*' expressions down into smaller ones, whose purpose is more readily appreciated.

Historically, logicals have not been in evidence extensively in Fortran programs, although clearly there are occasions on which they are of considerable use. Their use often aids considerably in making programs more modular and comprehensible. They can be used to make a complex section of code involving several choices much more transparent by the use of one logical function, with an appropriate name. Logicals may be used to control output, e.g.

```
LOGICAL :: DEBUG
   . . .
   DEBUG=.TRUE.
   . . .
   IF(DEBUG)THEN
      . . .
      PRINT *,'LOTS OF PRINTOUT'
      . . .
   ENDIF
```

ensures that, while de-bugging a program you have more output. Then, when the program is *correct*, run with DEBUG=.FALSE.

Note that Fortran does try to protect you while you use logical variables. You cannot do this:

```
LOGICAL :: UP, DOWN
   UP=DOWN+.FALSE.
```

or

```
LOGICAL :: A2
   REAL DIMENSION(10):: OMEGA
   .
   A2=OMEGA(3)
```

The compiler will note that this is an error, and will not permit you to run the program. This is an example of *strong typing*, since only a limited number of predetermined operations are permitted. The real, integer and complex variable types are much more weakly typed (which helps to lead to the confusion inherent in mixing variable types in arithmetic assignments).

18.1 I/O

Since logicals may take only the values .TRUE. and .FALSE., the possibilities in reading and writing logical values are clearly limited. The L format allows logicals to be input and output. On input, if the first non-blank characters are either T or .T, the logical value .TRUE. is stored in the corresponding list item; if the first non-blank characters are F or .F, then .FALSE. is stored. (Note therefore that reading, say, TED and FAHR in an L4 format would be acceptable.) If the first non-blank character is not F, T, .F or .T, then an error message will be generated. On output, the value T or F is written out, right justified, with blanks (if appropriate). Thus,

```
LOGICAL :: FLAG
   FLAG=.TRUE.
   PRINT 100, FLAG, .NOT.FLAG
100 FORMAT(2L3)
```

would produce

```
T   F
```

at the terminal.

Assigning a logical variable to anything other than a .TRUE. or .FALSE. value in your program will result in errors. The 'shorthand' forms of .T, .F, F and T are not acceptable in the program.

18.2 Summary

Another type of data – logical – is also recognised. A LOGICAL variable may take one of two values – *true* or *false*.

- There are special operators for manipulating logicals:
  - .NOT.
  - .AND.
  - .OR..
- Logical operators have a lower order of precedence than any others.

18.3 Problems

1. Why are the full stops needed in a statement like A = .TRUE.?

2. Generate a truth table like the one given in this chapter.

3. Write a program which will read in numerical data from the terminal, but will *flag* any data which is negative, and will also turn these negative values into positive ones.

19

User Defined Types

Russell's theory of types leads to certain complexities in the foundations of mathematics,... Its interesting features for our purposes are that types are used to prevent certain erroneous expressions from being used in logical and mathematical formulae; and that a check against violation of type constraints can be made purely by scanning the text, without any knowledge of the value which a particular symbol might happen to have.

C.A.R. Hoare, *Structured Programming.*

Aims

The aim of this chapter is to introduce the concepts and ideas involved in using the facilities offered in Fortran 90 for the construction and use of user defined types:

- the way in which we define our own types;
- the way in which we declare variables to be of a user defined type;
- the way in which we manipulate variables of our own types;
- the way in which we can nest types within types.

The examples are simple and are designed to highlight the syntax. More complex and realistic examples of the use of user defined data types are to be found in later chapters.

19 User Defined Types

In the coverage so far we have used the intrinsic types provided by Fortran. The only data structuring technique available has been to construct arrays of these intrinsic types. Whilst this enables us to solve a reasonable variety of problems, it is inadequate for many purposes. In this chapter we look at the facilities offered by Fortran for the construction of our own types, and how we manipulate data of these new, user defined types.

With the ability to define our own types we can now construct aggregate data types that have components of a variety of base types. These are often given the name records in books on data structures. In mathematics the term cartesian product is often used, and this is the terminology adopted by Hoare. We will stick to the term records, as it is the one that is most commonly used in computing and texts on programming.

There are two stages in the process of creating and using our own data types, we must first define the type, and secondly create variables of this type.

19.1 Example 1: Dates

```
PROGRAM Record_01
IMPLICIT NONE
TYPE Date
   INTEGER :: Day=1
   INTEGER :: Month=1
   INTEGER :: Year=2000
END TYPE Date
TYPE (Date) :: D
   PRINT *,D%Day, D%Month, D%Year
   PRINT *,' Type in the date, day, month, year'
   READ *,D%Day, D%Month, D%Year
   PRINT *,D%Day, D%Month, D%Year
END PROGRAM Record_01
```

This complete program illustrates both the definition and use of the type. It also shows how you can define initial values within the type definition.

19.2 Type definition

The type *Date* is defined to have three component parts, comprising a *day*, a *month* and a *year*, all of integer type. The syntax of a type construction comprises:

```
TYPE Typename
  Data Type :: Component_name
  etc
END TYPE Typename
```

Reference can then be made to this new type by the use of a single word, *Date*, and we have a very powerful example of the use of abstraction.

19.3 Variable definition

This is done by:

```
TYPE (Typename) :: Variablename
```

and we then define a variable *D* to be of this new type. The next thing we do is have a READ * statement that prompts the user to type in three integer values, and the data is then echoed straight back to the user. We use the notation `Variable-name%Component_Name` to refer to each component of the new data type.

19.4 Example 2: Address lists

```
PROGRAM Record_02
IMPLICIT NONE
TYPE Address
   CHARACTER (LEN=40)  ::  Name
   CHARACTER (LEN=60)  ::  Street
   CHARACTER (LEN=60)  ::  District
   CHARACTER (LEN=60)  ::  City
   CHARACTER (LEN=8)   ::  Post_Code
END TYPE Address
INTEGER , PARAMETER :: N_of_Address=78
TYPE (Address) , DIMENSION(N_of_Address):: Addr
INTEGER :: I
   OPEN(UNIT=1,FILE="ADDRESS.DAT")
   DO I=1,N_of_Address
      READ(UNIT=1,FMT='(A40)') Addr(I)%Name
      READ(UNIT=1,FMT='(A60)') Addr(I)%Street
      READ(UNIT=1,FMT='(A60)') Addr(I)%District
      READ(UNIT=1,FMT='(A60)') Addr(I)%City
      READ(UNIT=1,FMT='(A8)') Addr(I)%Post_Code
   END DO
   DO I=1,N_of_Address
      PRINT *,Addr(I)%Name
      PRINT *,Addr(I)%Street
```

```
      PRINT *,Addr(I)%District
      PRINT *,Addr(I)%City
      PRINT *,Addr(I)%Post_Code
   END DO
END PROGRAM Record_02
```

In this example we define a type Address which has components that one would expect for a person's address. We then define an array Addr of this type. Thus we are now creating arrays of our own user defined types. We index into the array in the way we would expect from our experience with integer, real and character arrays. The complete example is rather trivial in a sense in that the program merely reads from one file and prints the file out to the screen. However it highlights many of the important ideas of the definition and use of user defined types.

19.5 Example 3: Nested user defined types

The following example builds on the two data types already introduced. Here we construct nested user defined data types based on these types and construct a new data type containing them both, plus additional information.

```
PROGRAM C19_03
IMPLICIT NONE
TYPE Address
   CHARACTER (LEN=60)    :: Street
   CHARACTER (LEN=60)    :: District
   CHARACTER (LEN=60)    :: City
   CHARACTER (LEN=8 )    :: Post_Code
END TYPE Address
TYPE Date_Of_Birth
   INTEGER :: Day
   INTEGER :: Month
   INTEGER :: Year
END TYPE Date_Of_Birth
TYPE Personal
   CHARACTER (LEN=20)       :: First_Name
   CHARACTER (LEN=20)       :: Other_Names
   CHARACTER (LEN=40)       :: Surname
   TYPE (Date_Of_Birth) :: DOB
   CHARACTER (LEN=1)        :: Sex
   TYPE (Address)           :: Addr
END TYPE Personal
INTEGER , PARAMETER :: N_People=2
TYPE (Personal) , DIMENSION(N_People) :: P
```

```
INTEGER :: I
   OPEN(UNIT=1,FILE='PERSON.DAT')
   DO I=1,N_People
      READ(1,FMT=10)  P(I)%First_Name,&
                      P(I)%Other_Names,&
                      P(I)%Surname,&
                      P(I)%DOB%Day,&
                      P(I)%DOB%Month,&
                      P(I)%DOB%Year,&
                      P(I)%Sex,&
                      P(I)%Addr%Street,&
                      P(I)%Addr%District,&
                      P(I)%Addr%City,&
      P(I)%Addr%Post_Code
      10 FORMAT(  A20,/,&
                  A20,/,&
                  A40,/,&
                  I2,1X,I2,1X,I4,/,&
                  A1,/,&
                  A60,/,&
                  A60,/,&
                  A60,/,&
                  A8)
   END DO
   DO I=1,N_People
      WRITE(*,FMT=20)   P(I)%First_Name,&
                        P(I)%Other_Names,&
                        P(I)%Surname,&
                        P(I)%DOB%Day,&
                        P(I)%DOB%Month,&
                        P(I)%DOB%Year,&
                        P(I)%Sex,&
                        P(I)%Addr%Street,&
                        P(I)%Addr%District,&
                        P(I)%Addr%City,&
                        P(I)%Addr%Post_Code
      20 FORMAT(        A20,A20,A40,/,&
                        I2,1X,I2,1X,I4,/,&
                        A1,/,&
                        A60,/,&
                        A60,/,&
                        A60,/,&
```

```
                              A8)
      END DO
END PROGRAM C19_03
```

Here we have a date of birth data type (Date_Of_Birth) based on the Date data type from the first example, plus a slightly modified address data type, incorporated into a new data type comprising personal details. Note the way in which we reference the component parts of this new, aggregate data type.

19.6 Problems

1. Modify the last example to include a more elegant printed name. The current example will pad with blanks the first name, other names and surname and span 80 characters on one line, which looks rather ugly.

Add a new variable name which will comprise all three sub-components and write out this new variable, instead of the three sub-components.

19.7 Bibliography

Dahl O.J., Dijkstra E.W., Hoare C.A.R., *Structured Programming*, Academic Press, 1972.

- This is one of the earliest and best introductions to data structures and structured programming. The whole book hangs together very well, and the section on data structures is a must for serious programmers.

Fortran 90 is a relatively young language, and there are a lack of books that look at data structuring using Fortran 90 as the vehicle. This is not the problem that it might appear at first sight, as there are a wealth of books that are in the Algol, Pascal, Modula 2 family of languages and that are cheap and widely available. Some of these are given below.

Vowels R.A., *Algorithms and Data Structures in F and Fortran*, Unicomp, 1989.

- One of the few books looking at algorithms and data structures using Fortran.

Wirth N., *Algorithms + Data Structures = Programs*, Prentice Hall.

Wirth N., *Algorithms + Data Structures*, Prentice Hall.

- The first is in Pascal, and the second in Modula 2.

Wood D., *Paradigms and Programming in Pascal*, Computer Science Press.

- Contains a number of examples of the use of recursion in problem solving. Also provides a number of useful case studies in problem solving.

20

Dynamic Data Structures

The question naturally arises whether the analogy can be extended to a data structure corresponding to recursive procedures. A value of such a type would be permitted to contain more than one component that belongs to the same type as itself; in the same way that a recursive procedure can call itself recursively from more than one place in its own body.

C.A.R. Hoare, *Structured Programming.*

Aims

The primary aims of the chapter are to introduce the facilities offered by Fortran 95 for the construction and use of dynamic data types. These additional features enable us to solve a much wider range of problems using simple and straightforward algorithms. Examples include the use of pointers in user defined data types, in particular:

- singly linked lists;
- trees;
- using singly linked lists to store sparse vectors.

The secondary aims are to provide a summary of what can be achieved with the correct choice of data structures and algorithms, and the bibliography contains details sources of data structures and algorithms.

20 Dynamic Data Structures

All of the data types introduced so far, with the exception of the allocatable array, have been static. Even with the allocatable array a size has to be set at some stage during program execution. The facilities provided in Fortran by the concept of a pointer combined with those offered by a user defined record enable us to address a completely new problem area, previously extremely difficult to solve in Fortran.

There are many problems where one genuinely does not know what requirements there are on the size of a data structure. Anyone who has used a word processing package or editor would not like to have to provide information at the start about the size of their document or file.

A pointer is an alias (another name) for something. It can be an alias for another variable or a piece of memory. A pointer must have the pointer attribute and must be of the same type of the variable or memory for which it is going to be an alias.

20.1 Simple pointer concepts

With the introduction of pointers as a data type into Fortran 95 we also have the introduction of a new assignment statement, the pointer assignment statement. Consider the following example:

```
PROGRAM C2001
   INTEGER , POINTER :: A,B
   INTEGER , TARGET :: C
   INTEGER :: D
   C = 1
   A => C
   C = 2
   B => C
   D = A + B
   PRINT *,A,B,C,D
END PROGRAM C2001
```

The first declaration defines A and B to be variables, with the POINTER attribute. This means we can use A and B to refer or point to integer values.

The second declaration defines C to be an integer, with the TARGET attribute, i.e. we can use pointers to refer or point to the value of the variable C.

The last declaration defines D to be an ordinary integer variable.

Let us now look at the various executable statements in the program, one at a time:

C = 1

This is an example of the normal assignment statement that we are already familiar with. We use the variable name C in our program and whenever we use that name we get the *value* of the variable C.

A => C
This is an example of a pointer assignment statement. This means that both A and C now refer to the same value, in this case 1.

C = 2
Conventional assignment statement, and C now has the value 2.

B = > C
Second example of pointer assignment. B now points to the value that C has, in this case 2.

D = A + B
Simple arithmetic assignment statement. The value that A points to is added to the value that B points to and the result is assigned to D.

The last statement prints out the values of A, B, C and D.

The output is:

2 2 2 4

20.2 Pointer assignment

Consider the following example:

```
PROGRAM C2002
IMPLICIT NONE
REAL  ,  TARGET  ::  T1  =  21
REAL  ,  TARGET  ::  T2  =  30
REAL  ,  POINTER  ::  P1,P2
   P1  =>  T1
   P2  =>  T2
   PRINT  *  ,  '  P1  =  '  ,  P1  ,  '  P2  =  '  ,  P2
   P1=P2
   PRINT  *  ,  '  P1  =  '  ,  P1  ,  '  P2  =  '  ,  P2
   PRINT  *  ,  '  T1  =  '  ,  T1  ,  '  T2  =  '  ,  T2
END  PROGRAM  C2002
```

This program produces the following output:

P1	=	21.00000	P2	=	30.00000
P1	=	30.00000	P2	=	30.00000
T1	=	30.00000	T2	=	30.00000

The statement:

```
P1  =  P2
```

is equivalent to

```
T1  =  T2
```

and whilst the above may seem artificial a later example will show it to be essential when working with dynamic memory.

These examples highlight the essentials of pointer usage, and also the difference between normal assignment and pointer assignment.

20.3 Using pointers to create dynamic variables

Consider the following example:

```
PROGRAM C2003
IMPLICIT NONE
REAL , POINTER :: P1 => NULL()
   ALLOCATE(P1)
   P1=21.0
! The value 21.0 is now stored in the
! memory location that P1 points to.
   PRINT *,P1
   DEALLOCATE(P1)
! This releases the memory and now P1 is
! disassociated.
END PROGRAM C2003
```

P1 is defined to be a pointer which can point to an area of memory that can hold a real value. The allocate statement allocates a memory location that P1 points to. We can then refer to this memory location by its alias P1.

20.3.1   Pointer states

We mentioned in an earlier chapter that variables were either defined or undefined. Pointers add one more level of complexity. They can also be associated or disassociated. In the earlier examples the initial states of the pointers were undefined. In the above example the initial status of the pointer P1 is defined but disassociated, by using the NULL intrinsic function.

Consider the following program example:

```
PROGRAM C2004
IMPLICIT NONE
REAL , POINTER :: P1 => NULL()
```

```
REAL  , POINTER :: P2 => NULL()
   ALLOCATE(P1)
   P1=21.0
! The value 21.0 is now stored in the
! memory location that P1 points to.
   P2=>P1
   PRINT *,P1
   PRINT *,P2
   P2=P2+1
   PRINT *,P1
   PRINT *,P2
   DEALLOCATE(P1)
! This releases the memory and now P1 is
! disassociated.
   PRINT *,P2
END PROGRAM C2004
```

Run this program. Take care with dangling pointers.

Let us look at a simple example that will read an arbitrary amount of text from the keyboard, and then echo it back to the user.

20.4 Singly linked list

Conceptually a singly linked lists consists of a sequence of boxes with compartments. In the simplest case the first compartment holds a data item and the second compartment contains directions to the next box. Graphically:

Figure 20.1 Singly linked list

We can construct a data structure in Fortran to work with a singly linked list by combining the concept of a record from the previous chapter with the new concept of a pointer. A complete program to do this is given below.

```
PROGRAM C2005
TYPE Link
   CHARACTER :: C
   TYPE (Link) , POINTER    :: Next
END TYPE Link
TYPE (Link) , POINTER :: Root , Current
INTEGER :: IO_Stat_Number=0
   ALLOCATE(Root)
   READ (UNIT = *, FMT = '(A)' , ADVANCE = 'NO' , &
     IOSTAT = IO_Stat_Number) Root%C
   IF (IO_Stat_Number == -1) THEN
      NULLIFY(Root%Next)
   ELSE
      ALLOCATE(Root%Next)
   ENDIF
   Current => Root
   DO WHILE (ASSOCIATED(Current%Next))
      Current => Current%Next
      READ (UNIT=*,FMT='(A)',ADVANCE='NO', &
      IOSTAT=IO_Stat_Number) Current%C
      IF (IO_Stat_Number == -1) THEN
         NULLIFY(Current%Next)
      ELSE
         ALLOCATE(Current%Next)
      ENDIF
   END DO
   Current => Root
   DO WHILE (ASSOCIATED(Current%Next))
      PRINT * , Current%C
      Current => Current%Next
   END DO
END PROGRAM C2005
```

The behaviour of this program is system specific. You will have to look at your compiler documentation regarding the IO_Stat_Number. The first thing of interest is the type definition for the singly linked list. We have:

```
TYPE Link
   CHARACTER :: C
   TYPE (Link) , POINTER :: Next
END TYPE Link
```

and we call the new type Link. It comprises two component parts, the first holds a character C, and the second holds a pointer called Next to allow us to refer to another instance of type Link. Remember we are interested in joining together several boxes or Links.

The next item of interest is the variable definition. Here we define two variables Root and Current to be pointers that point to items of type Link. In Fortran when we define a variable to be a pointer we also have to define what it is allowed to point to. This is a very useful restriction on pointers, and helps make using them more secure.

The first executable statement

```
ALLOCATE(Root)
```

requests that the variable Root be allocated memory. At this time the contents of both the character component and the pointer component are undefined.

The next statement reads a character from the keyboard. We are using a number of additional features of the READ statement, including:

```
ADVANCE='NO'
IOSTAT=IO_Stat_Number
```

and the two options combine to provide the ability to read an arbitrary amount of text from the user per line, and terminate only when end of file is encountered as the only input on a line, typically by typing CTRL Z. Please note that the numbers returned by the IOSTAT option are implementation specific. A small program would have to be written to test the values returned for each platform.

If an end of file is reached then the pointer Root%Next is nullified using the NULLIFY statement. This gives the pointer a status of disassociated, and this is a convenient way of saying that it doesn't point to anything valid.

If the end of file is not detected then the next link in the chain is created.

The statement

```
Current => Root
```

means that both Current and Root point to the same physical memory location, and this holds a character data item and a pointer. We must do this as we have to know where the start of the list is. This is now our responsibility, not the compilers. Without this statement we would not be able to do anything with the list except fill it up – hardly very useful.

The WHILE loop is then repeated until end of file is reached. If the user had typed an end of file immediately then Current%Next would not be ASSOCIATED, and the WHILE loop would be skipped.

This loop allocates memory and moves down the chain of boxes one character at a time filling in the links between the boxes as we go.

We then have

```
Current => Root
```

and this now means that we are back at the start of the list, and in a position to traverse the list and print out each character in the list.

There is thus the concept with the pointer variable Current of it providing us with a window into memory where the complete linked list is held, and we look at one part of the list at a time.

Both WHILE loops use the intrinsic function ASSOCIATED to check the association status of a pointer.

It is recommended that this program be typed in, compiled and executed. It is surprisingly difficult to believe that this program will actually read in a completely arbitrary number of characters from the user. Seeing is believing.

20.5 Other dynamic data structures

There are a wide range of dynamic data types and they include lists, queues, stacks and trees. Lists are a very commonly used data structure, especially in the doubly linked form where we can traverse in either direction. A queue is also a commonly used data structure and exists in a variety of forms, most noticeable *last in first out* (LIFO) and *first in first out* (FIFO). A stack is another quite widely used data structure. These three data structures are essentially one dimensional. A tree is a two dimensional data structure. It is one of the most widely used dynamic data structures and occurs in many algorithms. The Sedgewick book highlights the importance of the tree as a very versatile and powerful data structure.

20.6 Trees

The tree data structure occurs quite commonly in real life. One example is a family tree, shown below, another is in a knock-out competition. This is shown in figure 20.2.

Trees have a surprisingly wide range of use in computer related applications, e.g. the compiler will construct a parse tree during the compilation process.

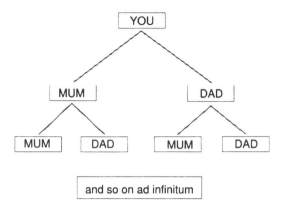

Figure 20.2 Family tree

20.6.1 Example 4: Perfectly balanced tree

Let us now look at a more complex example that builds a perfectly balanced tree
and prints the tree out. A loose definition of a perfectly balanced tree is a tree that
for *n* nodes has minimum depth. More accurately a tree is perfectly balanced if for
each node the number of nodes in its left and right sub-trees differ by at most 1.

```
MODULE Node_Type_Def
   TYPE Tree_Node
   INTEGER :: Number
   TYPE (Tree_Node) , POINTER :: Left,Right
   END TYPE Tree_Node
END MODULE Node_Type_Def


PROGRAM C20_06
! Construction of a perfectly balanced tree
USE Node_Type_Def
TYPE (Tree_Node) , POINTER :: Root
INTEGER :: N_of_Items

INTERFACE

   RECURSIVE FUNCTION Tree(N)  RESULT(Answer)
      USE Node_Type_Def
      TYPE (Tree_Node) , POINTER :: Answer
      INTEGER :: N
   END FUNCTION Tree
```

```
   SUBROUTINE Print_Tree(Trees,H)
      USE Node_Type_Def
      TYPE (Tree_Node) , POINTER :: Trees
      INTEGER :: H
   END SUBROUTINE Print_Tree

END INTERFACE

   PRINT *,' Enter number of items'
   READ *,N_Of_Items
   Root=>Tree(N_Of_Items)
   CALL Print_Tree(Root,0)

END PROGRAM C20_06

RECURSIVE FUNCTION Tree(N) RESULT (Answer)
USE Node_Type_Def
TYPE (Tree_Node) , POINTER :: Answer
TYPE (Tree_Node) , POINTER :: New_Node

INTEGER :: L,R,X
   IF (N == 0) THEN
      print *,' terminate tree'
      NULLIFY(Answer)
   ELSE
      L=N/2
      R=N-L-1
      PRINT *,L,R,N
      PRINT *,' Next item'
      READ *,X
      ALLOCATE(New_Node)
      New_Node%Number=X
      print *, ' left branch'
      New_Node%Left => Tree(L)
      print *, ' right branch'
      New_Node%Right => Tree(R)
      Answer => New_Node
   ENDIF
   PRINT *, ' Function tree ends'
END FUNCTION Tree
```

```
RECURSIVE SUBROUTINE Print_Tree(T,H)
USE Node_Type_Def
TYPE (Tree_Node) , POINTER :: T
INTEGER :: I
INTEGER :: H
   IF (ASSOCIATED(T)) THEN
      CALL Print_Tree(T%Left,H+1)
      DO I=1,H
         WRITE(UNIT=*,FMT=10,ADVANCE='NO')
         10 FORMAT('    ')
      ENDDO
      PRINT *,T%Number
      CALL Print_Tree(T%Right,H+1)
   ENDIF
END SUBROUTINE Print_Tree
```

There are a number of very important concepts contained in this example and they include:

- the use of a module to define a type: for user defined data types we must create a module to define the data type if we want it to be available in more than one program unit. We will look more formally at modules in later chapters.

- the USE statement to make this data type available in each program unit that requires it: in the above case in the main program, the function and the subroutine;

- a subroutine is an extension of the facilities provided by function. It does not return a result, but carries out a more complex action. We will look at the concepts involved here in more depth in the later chapters of subroutines and modules.

- the use of interface blocks to define the interfaces to the function and subroutine. We will look at the concepts of interface blocks more fully in later chapters.

- the use of a function that returns a pointer as a result;

- as the function returns a pointer we must determine the allocation status before the function terminates. This means that in the above case that we use the NULLIFY(Result) statement. The other option is to TARGET the pointer.

- the use of ASSOCIATED to determine if the node of the tree is terminated or points to another node;

Type the program in and compile, link and run it. Notice that the tree only has the minimal depth necessary to store all of the items. Experiment with the number of items and watch the tree change its depth to match the number of items. This will create a structure that is shown graphically below.

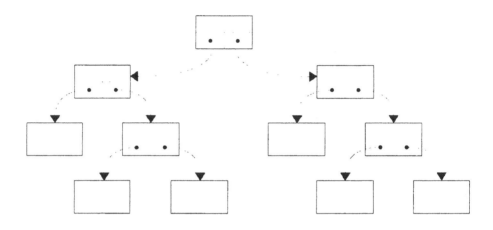

Figure 20.3 Perfectly balanced tree

20.7 Using linked lists for sparse matrix problems

A matrix is said to be sparse if many of its elements are zero. Mathematical models in areas such as management science, power systems analysis, circuit theory and structural analysis consist of very large sparse systems of linear equations. These systems would not be possible to solve if classical methods were applied because the sparsity would be lost and the eventual system too large to solve. Many of these systems consist of tens of thousands, hundreds of thousands and millions of equations. As the computer systems become ever more powerful with massive amounts of memory the solution of even larger problems becomes feasible.

Direct Methods for Sparse Matrices, Duff I.S. Erismon A.M., Reid J.K., looks at direct methods for solving sparse systems of linear equations.

Sparse matrix techniques lend themselves to the uses of dynamic data structures in Fortran 95. Only the non-zero elements of a sparse matrix need be stored, together with their position in the matrix. Other information also needs to be stored so that row or column manipulation can be performed without repeated scanning of a potentially very large data structure. Sparse methods may involve introducing some new non-zero elements, and a way is needed of inserting them into the data structure. This is where the Fortran 95 pointer construct can be used. The sparse matrix can be implemented using a linked list to which entries can be easily added and deleted.

As a simple introduction, consider the storage of sparse vectors. What we learn here can easily be applied to sparse matrices, which can be thought of as sets of sparse vectors.

20.7.1 Inner product of two sparse vectors

Assume that we have two sparse vectors x and y and their non-zero elements are stored in sequential order in two files, together with their indices, e.g.

File 1   File 2

x_i	i	y_l	l
x_j	j	y_m	m
x_k	k	y_n	n
.	.	.	.
.	.	.	.
.	.	.	.

and we wish to calculate the inner product $x^T y \equiv \sum_{i=1}^{n} x_i\, y_i$. There are a number of approaches to doing this and the one we use in the program below stores them as two linked lists.

```
PROGRAM C2007
!
! This program reads the non-zero elements of
! two sparse vectors x and y together with their
! indices, and stores them in two linked lists.
! Using these linked lists it then calculates
! and prints out the inner product.
! It also prints the values.
!
! updated 21/3/00 to initialise pointers to
! be disassociated using intrinsic function NULL
! plus minor updates
!
  IMPLICIT NONE
  CHARACTER (LEN=30):: Filename
```

```
   TYPE sparse_vector
   INTEGER :: index
   REAL:: value
   TYPE (sparse_vector), POINTER ::next=> NULL ( )
   END TYPE sparse_vector
   TYPE(sparse_vector), POINTER ::      Root_x,Current_x, &
                         Root_y,Current_y
   REAL :: Inner_prod=0.0
   INTEGER::IO_status
!
! Read non-zero elements of vector x together
! with indices into a linked list
!
   PRINT *,'input file name for vector x'
   READ '(A)',Filename
   OPEN(UNIT=1 , FILE=Filename , STATUS='OLD' &
   , IOSTAT=IO_status)
   IF(IO_status /= 0)THEN
     PRINT*,'Error opening file ',Filename
     STOP
   ENDIF
   ALLOCATE(Root_x)
   READ (UNIT=1 , FMT=* , IOSTAT=IO_status) &
     Root_x%value,Root_x%index
   IF(IO_status /= 0) THEN
     PRINT*,' Error when reading from file ' &
     , Filename, ' or file empty'
     STOP
   ENDIF
!
! Read data for vector x from file until eof
!
   Current_x => Root_x
   ALLOCATE(Current_x%next)
   DO WHILE(ASSOCIATED(Current_x%next))
     Current_x => Current_x%next
     READ (UNIT=1,FMT=*,IOSTAT=IO_status) &
       Current_x%value, Current_x%index
     IF(IO_status == 0)THEN
       ALLOCATE(Current_x%next)
       CYCLE
     ELSEIF(IO_status > 0 )THEN
```

```
!
! Error on reading
!
      PRINT * ,'Error occurred when reading from ' &
              , Filename
      STOP
    ELSE
!
! End of file
!
      NULLIFY (Current_x%next)
    END IF
  END DO

  CLOSE(UNIT=1)
!
! Read non-zero elements of vector y together
! with indices into a linked list
!
  PRINT *,'input file name for vector y'
  READ '(A)',Filename
  OPEN(UNIT=1 , FILE=Filename , STATUS='OLD' &
   , IOSTAT=IO_status)
  IF(IO_status /= 0)THEN
    PRINT*,'Error opening file ',Filename
    STOP
  ENDIF
  ALLOCATE(Root_y)
  READ (UNIT=1 , FMT=* , IOSTAT=IO_status) &
     Root_y%value,Root_y%index
  IF(IO_status /= 0) THEN
    PRINT*,' Error when reading from ' &
      , Filename, ' or file empty'
    STOP
  ENDIF
!
! Read data for vector y from file until eof
!
  Current_y => Root_y
  ALLOCATE(Current_y%next)
  DO WHILE(ASSOCIATED(Current_y%next))
    Current_y => Current_y%next
```

```
      READ (UNIT=1 , FMT=* , IOSTAT=IO_status) &
        Current_y%value, Current_y%index
      IF(IO_status == 0)THEN
        ALLOCATE(Current_y%next)
        CYCLE
      ELSEIF(IO_status > 0 )THEN
!
! Error on reading
!
        PRINT * , 'Error occurred when reading from' &
          , Filename
        STOP
      ELSE
!
! End of file
!
        NULLIFY (Current_y%next)
      END IF
    END DO
!
! Data has now been read and stored in 2 linked lists
! start at the beginning of x linked list and
! y linked list and compare indices
! in order to perform inner product
!
    Current_x => Root_x
    Current_y => Root_y
    DO WHILE (ASSOCIATED(Current_x%next))
      DO WHILE (Associated(Current_y%next) &
        .AND. Current_y%index < Current_x%index)
!
! move through 2nd list
!
        Current_y => Current_y%next
      END DO
!
! At this point Current_y%index >= Current_x%index
! or 2nd list is exhausted
!
      IF (Current_y%index == Current_x%index) THEN
        Inner_prod = Inner_prod &
          + Current_x%value * Current_y%value
```

```
      END IF
      Current_x => Current_x%next
   END DO
!
! Print out inner product
!
   PRINT *,'Inner product of two sparse vectors is :' &
    , Inner_prod
!
! Print non-zero values of vector x and indices
!
   PRINT*, 'non-zero values of vector x and indices:'
   Current_x => Root_x
   DO WHILE (ASSOCIATED(Current_x%next))
     PRINT*,Current_x%value,Current_x%index
     Current_x => Current_x%next
   END DO
!
! Print non-zero values of vector y and indices
!
PRINT*, 'non-zero values of vector y and indices:'
   Current_y => Root_y
   DO WHILE (ASSOCIATED(Current_y%next))
     PRINT*,Current_y%value,Current_y%index
     Current_y => Current_y%next
   END DO
!
END PROGRAM C2007
```

20.8 Arrays of pointers

Arrays in Fortran are rectangular, even when allocatable. So if you wish to set up a lower triangular matrix that uses minimal memory you have to use arrays of pointers. The following examples shows how to do this.

```
PROGRAM C2008
IMPLICIT NONE
TYPE Ragged
   REAL , DIMENSION(:) , POINTER :: Ragged_row
END TYPE
INTEGER :: I
INTEGER , PARAMETER :: N=3
TYPE (Ragged) , DIMENSION(1:N) :: Lower_Diag
```

```
   DO I=1,N
      ALLOCATE(Lower_Diag(I)%Ragged_Row(1:I))
      PRINT *,' Type in the values for row ' , I
      READ *,Lower_Diag(I)%Ragged_Row(1:I)
   END DO
   DO I=1,N
      PRINT *,Lower_Diag(I)%Ragged_Row(1:I)
   END DO
END PROGRAM C2008
```

The type Ragged has a component that is a pointer to an array. Within the first DO loop we allocate a row at a time and each time we go round the loop the array allocated increases in size.

20.9 Memory leak example

Dynamic memory brings greater versatility but requires greater responsibility. Consider the following example:

```
PROGRAM C2009
IMPLICIT NONE
REAL , DIMENSION(:) , POINTER :: X
REAL , DIMENSION(1:10) , TARGET :: Y
INTEGER , PARAMETER :: SIZE=10000
INTEGER :: I
   ALLOCATE(X(1:SIZE))
! initialise the memory that x points to
   DO I=1,SIZE
      X(I)=I
   END DO
! print out the first 10 values
   DO I=1,10
      PRINT *,X(I)
   END DO
! initialise the array y
   DO I=1,10
      Y(I)=I*I
   END DO
! print out y
   DO I=1,10
      PRINT *,Y(I)
   END DO
! x now points to y
```

```
   X=>Y
! print out what x now points to
   DO I=1,10
      PRINT *,X(I)
   END DO
! what has happened to the memory that x
! used to point to?
END PROGRAM C2009
```

20.10 Data structures summary

We have not been able to give examples of the wide range of data structuring techniques that exist. This is impossible in a book where the primary aim is to teach a working sub-set of a programming language, in this case Fortran 95. There are a whole range of data structures and algorithms we have not been able even to mention including:

- finite state machines

- string processing algorithms

- geometric algorithms

- graph algorithms

- neural network algorithms

- quad trees

- oct trees

- etc.

Quad trees and oct trees are used for the manipulation of spatial information. Use must be made of the material in the bibliographies at the end of each chapter. The choice of the correct algorithm and data structure can make a seemingly impossible task trivial. (Well, not quite trivial!).

The more you learn in this area the easier things become. It is surprising how ingenious man can be, and some of the solutions presented in the references are fascinating.

20.11 Problems

1. Type in the first example. Verify that the output is as stated, i.e.

2 2 2 4

2. There are a number of ways of handling exceptions with the READ statement, and we have used the IOSTAT option in this chapter. Consider the following program:

```
PROGRAM C2010
INTEGER :: IO_Stat_Number=0
INTEGER :: I
    DO
        READ (UNIT=* , FMT=10 , ADVANCE='NO' &
        , IOSTAT=IO_Stat_Number) I
        10 FORMAT(I3)

! 0    = no error
!         no end of file (eof)
!         no end of record (eor)
! -    = eor or eof
! +    = an error occurred

        PRINT *,' iostat=',IO_Stat_Number
        PRINT *,I
    END DO
END PROGRAM C2010
```

This program is a simple test of the iostat values of whatever system you work on. Try typing in a variety of values including minimally

- a valid 3 digit number + [RETURN] key

- a three digit number with an embedded blank, e.g. 1 2 + [RETURN] key

- [RETURN] key only

- [CTRL] + Z

- any other non-numeric character on the keyboard

- 100200300 + [RETURN] key

- [CTRL] + C

This will enable us to program exactly the kind of behaviour we want from I/O and can be used as a code segment for other programs.

3. Using the balanced tree example as a basis, modify it to work with a character array rather than an integer. The routine that prints the tree will also have to be modified to reflect this.

4. Use the program that calculated the inner product of two sparse vectors with the following vectors:

x

$$\begin{bmatrix} 6 \\ 5 \\ 4 \\ 0 \end{bmatrix}$$

y

$$\begin{bmatrix} 0 \\ 3 \\ 2 \\ 1 \end{bmatrix}$$

This should produce the answer of 23.

20.12 Bibliography

There are a number of books that are of use here. Many older sources will be Pascal based. We recommend looking at Modula 2 sources too. There should be little difficulty converting from one of these languages to Fortran 95.

For up to date information on Fortran sources visit the Fortran Market.

http://www.fortran.com/fortran/market.html

Duff I.S., Erismon A.M., Reid J.K., *Direct Methods for Sparse Matrices*, Oxford Science Publications.

- Authoritative coverage of this area. Relatively old, but well regarded. Code segments and examples are a mixture of Fortran 77 and Algol 60 (which of course do not support pointers) and therefore the implementation of linked lists is done using the existing features of these languages. The onus is on the programmer to correctly implement linked lists using fixed size arrays rather than using the features provided by pointers in a language. It is remarkable how elegant these solutions are, given the lack of dynamic data structures in these two languages.

Schneider G.M., Bruell S.C., *Advanced Programming and Problem Solving with Pascal*, Wiley.

- The book is aimed at computer science students and follows the curriculum guidelines laid down in *Communications of the ACM*, August 1985, Course CS2. The book is very good for the complete beginner as the examples are very clearly laid out and well explained. There is a coverage of data structures, abstract data types and their implementation, algorithms for sorting and searching, the principles of software development as they relate to the specification, design, implementation and verification of programs in an orderly and disciplined fashion – their words.

Sedgewick R., *Algorithms in Modula 3*, Addison Wesley, 1993.

- Good general algorithm source.

Vowels R.A., *Algorithms and Data Structures in F and Fortran*, Unicomp, 1998.

- The only book currently that uses Fortran 90/95 and F. Visit the Fortran web site for more details. They are the publishers.

  http://www.fortran.com/fortran/market.html

Wirth N., *Algorithms + Data Structures = Programs*, Prentice Hall, 1976.

- An early but illuminating book on the subject. Well worth a read. Pascal is used.

Wirth N., *Algorithms + Data Structures*, Prentice Hall, 1986.

- This is the Modula 2 version. Closer to Fortran than the Pascal version.

21

Files

It is a capital mistake to theorise before one has data.

Sir Arthur Conan Doyle.

Aims

The aims of this chapter are:

- to review the process of file creation at a terminal

- to introduce more formally the idea of the file as a fundamental entity

- to show how files can be declared explicitly by the OPEN and CLOSE statements

- to introduce the arguments for the OPEN and CLOSE statements

- to demonstrate the interaction between the READ/WRITE statements and the OPEN/CLOSE statements;

21 Files

While you are working interactively, on a terminal, you will be working with files; files that contain programs, files that contain data, and perhaps files that are libraries. The file is fundamental to most modern operating systems, and almost all operations are carried out on files.

In this chapter we are going to extend some of your ideas about files. Let us consider what kinds of files you have met so far:

1) Text files. These are the source of your programs, compilation listings, etc. They can be examined by printing them. They can also be transmitted round a computer system fairly easily. A file sent to a printer is a text file. Mail messages are generally plain text files. Note that when mail messages arrive in your mail box they will then typically contain additional non-printable information.

2) Data files. These exist in two main forms, firstly those prepared by using an editor, and hence a text file, and those prepared using a package or program, and in a computer readable form, but not directly readable by a human.

3) Binary, object or relocatable files, e.g. output from the compiler, satellite data. They cannot be printed. To examine files like these you need to use special utilities, provided by most operating systems.

The above categories account for the majority of files that you have met so far.

If you use a word processor then you will also have met files that are textual with additional non-printable information.

Let us now consider how we can manipulate files using Fortran. They will generally be data files, and will thus be text files. They can therefore be listed, etc., using standard operating system commands.

21.1 Files in Fortran

These allow us to associate a logical unit number with any arbitrary file name during the running of the program, e.g.

```
OPEN(UNIT=1,FILE='DATA')
```

would associate the name DATA and the logical unit 1, so that

```
READ(UNIT=1,FMT=100) X
```

would read from DATA. Note that for this to work on some operating systems the file DATA must have been *local* to the session; we specify the name as a character variable. If we then wanted to use a subsequent data file, we could have another

OPEN statement, but if we want to use the same logical unit number, we must first CLOSE the file.

```
CLOSE(UNIT=1,FILE='DATA')
```

before we

```
OPEN(UNIT=1,FILE='DATA2')
```

In this way we can keep referring to logical unit 1, but change the file associated with it. This can be useful in interactive programs where we wish to analyse different sets of data, e.g.

```
PROGRAM Flex
IMPLICIT NONE
REAL :: X
CHARACTER (7) :: WHICH
    OPEN(UNIT=5,FILE='INPUT')
    DO
        WRITE(UNIT=6,FMT='('' DATA SET NAME, OR END'')')
        READ(UNIT=5,FMT='(A)') WHICH
        IF(WHICH == 'END') EXIT
        OPEN(UNIT=1,FILE=WHICH)
        READ(UNIT=1,FMT=100) X
        ...
        CLOSE(UNIT=1,FILE=WHICH)
    END DO
END PROGRAM Flex
```

One useful feature of the OPEN statement is that there are other parameters. What would happen, for example, if the file was not there? To take care of this you can use the IOSTAT and STATUS keywords, e.g.

```
OPEN(UNIT=1,FILE='DATA',IOSTAT=FileStat,STATUS='OLD')
```

STATUS can be equated to one of four values:

```
STATUS='OLD'
STATUS='NEW'
STATUS='SCRATCH'
STATUS='UNKNOWN'
```

If we say STATUS='NEW', we are creating a new file and it should not matter whether a file of the same name is present; 'SCRATCH' does not concern us, while

'UNKNOWN' implies that, if a file of the correct name is present use it, if not create a 'NEW' one. If you omit the STATUS= keyword altogether, the value 'UNKNOWN' will be assumed. If we use STATUS='OLD' and the file is not present, this will cause an error and this will reflected in the value associated with the variable Open_File_Status, consider the following example:

```
. . .
OPEN(UNIT=1,FILE='DATA',IOSTAT=FileStat,STATUS='OLD')
IF (FileStat > 0) THEN
   PRINT *,' Error opening file, please check'
   STOP
END IF
READ(UNIT=1,FMT=100) X
. . .
```

The program will terminate after printing an appropriate error message. The standard defines that if an error occurs then IOSTAT will return a positive integer value. A value of zero is returned if no error occurs.

21.2 Summary of options on OPEN

UNIT The unit number of the file to be opened.

IOSTAT Integer variable given the value zero if there are no errors.

FILE Character expression specifying the file name.

STATUS Character expression specifying the file status. It can be one of 'OLD', 'NEW', 'SCRATCH' or 'UNKNOWN'.

ACCESS Character expression specifying whether the file is to be used in a sequential or random fashion. Valid values are *SEQUENTIAL* (the default), or *DIRECT*.

The two most common access mechanisms for files are sequential and direct. Consider a file with 1000 records. To get at record 789 in a sequential file means reading or processing the first 788 records. To get at record 789 in a direct access file means using a record number to immediately locate record 789.

FORM Character expression specifying one of:

FORMATTED if the file is opened for formatted I/O

UNFORMATTED if the file is opened for unformatted I/O.

The default is formatted for sequential access files and unformatted for direct access files. If the file exists, FORM must be consistent with its present characteristics.

As was stated in earlier chapters data is maintained internally in a binary format, not immediately comprehensible by humans. When we wish to look at the data we must write it out in a formatted fashion, i.e. as a sequence of printable ASCII characters – text, or the written word. This formatting will carry with it an overhead in terms of the time required to do the formatting. It will also carry with it the penalty of conversion from one number base (internally binary) to another and also loss of significance due to rounding with whatever edit descriptors are used, e.g. writing out as F7.4.

If we are interested in reusing data on the same system and compiler then we can use the unformatted option and avoid both the time overhead (as there is no conversion between the internal and external formats) and the loss of significance associated with formatted data.

Please note that unformatted files are rarely portable between different computer systems, and sometimes even between different compilers on the same system.

We will look again at the use of unformatted files in Chapter 28 when we look at efficiency and the space time trade off.

RECL Integer variable or constant specifying the record length for a direct access file. It is specified in characters for a formatted file, and words for an unformatted file.

BLANK Character expression having one of the following values:

'NULL' if blanks are to be ignored on reading. Note that a field of all blanks is treated as 0!

'ZERO' if blanks are to be treated as zeros.

21.3 More foolproof I/O

Fortran provides a way of writing more foolproof programs involving I/O. This is done via the IOSTAT keyword on the READ statement. Consider the program given as a problem at the end of Chapter 20:

```
PROGRAM C21_01
IMPLICIT NONE
INTEGER :: IO_Stat_Number=-1
INTEGER :: I
  DO
    READ (UNIT=*,FMT=10,&
      IOSTAT=IO_Stat_Number) I
    10 FORMAT(I3)
    PRINT *,' iostat=',IO_Stat_Number
    PRINT *,I
```

```
   IF (IO_Stat_Number==0) EXIT
  END DO
END PROGRAM C21_01
```

If you didn't attempt this problem then the above program should be typed in and run on whatever system you use. There are aspects of it that are implementation specific. The following data input should be tried and the values of:

```
IO_Stat_Number
```

should be examined:

1. a valid 3 digit number + [RETURN] key

2. a three digit number with an embedded blank, e.g. 1 2 + [RETURN] key

3. [RETURN] key only

4. [CTRL] + Z

5. any other non-numeric character on the keyboard

6. 100200300 + [RETURN] key=

7. [CTRL] + C

This will then enable us to write programs that handle common I/O errors. Consider the following:

```
PROGRAM C21_02
INTEGER , DIMENSION(10) :: A =&
   (/-1,-1,-1,-1,-1,-1,-1,-1,-1,-1/)
INTEGER :: IO_Stat_Number=0
INTEGER :: I
  OPEN(UNIT=1,FILE='DATA.DAT',STATUS='OLD')
  DO I=1,10
     READ (UNIT=1,FMT=10,IOSTAT=IO_Stat_Number) A(I)
     10 FORMAT(I3)
     IF (IO_Stat_Number == 0) THEN
        CYCLE
     ELSEIF (IO_Stat_Number == -1) THEN
        PRINT *,' End of file detected at line ',I
        PRINT *,' Please check data file'
        EXIT
     ELSEIF (IO_Stat_Number > 0 ) THEN
        PRINT *,' Non numeric data in file at line ',I
        PRINT *,' Please correct data file'
```

```
      EXIT
    ENDIF
  END DO
  DO I=1,10
    PRINT * , ' I = ',I,' A(I) = ',A(I)
  DNDDO
END PROGRAM C21_02
```

The above program is system specific but interestingly the following compilers return the same value for end of file. They return different values for non-numeric data:

- NAG/Salford compiler
- DEC Alpha OPENVMS compiler
- NagAce Fortran 90 under Solaris
- Sun F90 compiler (release 2.x)
- Nag F95 compiler under Solaris
- Compaq/Dec F95, 6.01A

What happens with a completely blank line?

Note that in the above example the testing for the various conditions only exits the DO loop for reading data from the file. This means that execution would continue with the statement immediately after the END DO statement. This may not be what we want in all cases, and the EXIT may be replaced with a STOP statement to terminate execution immediately.

21.4 Summary

- The file is a fundamental entity within the operating system.

- Files may be manipulated in Fortran by associating their name with a unit number. All subsequent communication within the program is through the unit number.

- When a file is opened there are a large number of equatable keywords which may be employed to establish its characteristics.

- The default file type used in Fortran is *sequential formatted,* but several other esoteric types may be used.

21.5 Problems

1. Write a program to write the first 500 integers to a file using formatted I/O. Put 10 values on a line, with a blank as the first character of the line, and 8 columns allowed for each integer, with two spaces between each integer field.

Now write a program to read this file into an array, and write the numbers in reverse order over the original data, i.e. the data file now contains the first 500 numbers in descending order.

Now modify the first program to add the next 500 integers to the same file, so that the file now comprises the first 500 numbers in descending order, and the next 500 numbers in ascending order.

2. To write and maintain a crude database of student details, we might do the following; create separate files for each year – CLAS1, CLAS2, CLAS3, or COF84, COF85, COF86, and so on. In either case there is an unchanging prefix, CLAS or COF, and a variable suffix, which identifies membership within the overall group. In each of the files we may wish to record details like; name, date of birth, address, courses taken, etc. Such files will require updating as details change, or as errors are noted. Write (or sketch out) a program which would select and maintain such records, and which would allow corrected files to be printed out. While you might feel that the most appropriate tool for this job is an editor, you might find this too powerful a tool. An editor can leave files in a sorry state. Naturally, any program like this should be helpful (so called 'user friendly'). Is this sort of information sensitive enough to require security checks and passwords?

22

Introduction to Subroutines

A man should keep his brain attic stacked with all the furniture he is likely to use, and the rest he can put away in the lumber room of his library, where he can get at it if he wants.

Sir Arthur Conan-Doyle, *Five Orange Pips.*

Aims

The aims of this chapter are:

- to consider some of the reasons for the inclusion of subroutines in a programming language;

- to introduce with a concrete example some of the concepts and ideas involved with the definition and use of subroutines:

  - the INTERFACE statement and interface blocks;

  - parameters;

  - the INTENT attribute for parameters;

  - the CALL statement;

  - scope of variables;

  - local variables and local variables and the SAVE attribute;

  - the use of parameters to report on the status of the action carried out in the subroutine.

22 Introduction to Subroutines

In the earlier chapter on functions we introduced two types of function:

- intrinsic functions – which are part of the language
- user defined functions – by which we extend the language.

We now introduce subroutines which collectively with functions are given the name procedures. Procedures provide a very powerful extension to the language by:

- providing us with the ability to break problems down into simpler more easily solvable sub-problems.

- allowing us to concentrate on one aspect of a problem at a time.

- avoiding duplication of code.

- hiding away messy code so that a main program is a sequence of calls to procedures.

- providing us with the ability to put together collections of procedures that solve commonly occurring sub-problems, often given the name libraries, and generally compiled.

- allowing us to call procedures from libraries written, tested and documented by experts in a particular field. There is no point in re-inventing the wheel!

There are a number of concepts required for the successful use of subroutines and we met some of them in the chapter on functions when we looked at user defined functions. We will extend the ideas introduced there of parameters and introduce the additional concept of an interface block. The ideas are best explained with a concrete example.

Note that we use the terms parameters and arguments interchangeably.

22.1 Simple subroutine example

This example is one we met earlier that solves a quadratic equation, i.e. solves

$$a x^2 + b x + c = 0$$

The program to do this originally was just one program. In the example below we break that problem down into smaller parts, and make each part a subroutine. The components are

- main program or driving routine;
- interaction with user to get the coefficients of the equation;

- solution of the quadratic.

Let us look now at how we do this with the use of subroutines.

```
PROGRAM C22_01
IMPLICIT NONE
! Simple example of the use of a main program and two
! subroutines. One interacts with the user and the
! second solves a quadratic equation,
! based on the user input.
INTERFACE

   SUBROUTINE Interact(A,B,C,OK)
      IMPLICIT NONE
      REAL , INTENT(OUT) :: A
      REAL , INTENT(OUT) :: B
      REAL , INTENT(OUT) :: C
      LOGICAL , INTENT(OUT) :: OK
   END SUBROUTINE Interact

   SUBROUTINE Solve(E,F,G,Root1,Root2,IFail)
      IMPLICIT NONE
      REAL , INTENT(IN) :: E
      REAL , INTENT(IN) :: F
      REAL , INTENT(IN) :: G
      REAL , INTENT(OUT) :: Root1
      REAL , INTENT(OUT) :: Root2
      INTEGER , INTENT(INOUT) :: IFail
   END SUBROUTINE Solve

END INTERFACE

REAL :: P, Q, R, Root1, Root2
INTEGER :: IFail=0
LOGICAL :: OK=.TRUE.
   CALL Interact(P,Q,R,OK)
   IF (OK) THEN
      CALL Solve(P,Q,R,Root1,Root2,IFail)
      IF (IFail == 1) THEN
         PRINT *,' Complex roots, calculation abandoned'
      ELSE
         PRINT *,' Roots are ',Root1,' ',Root2
      ENDIF
```

```
   ELSE
      PRINT*,' Error in data input program ends'
   ENDIF
END PROGRAM C22_01
SUBROUTINE Interact(A,B,C,OK)
   IMPLICIT NONE
   REAL , INTENT(OUT) :: A
   REAL , INTENT(OUT) :: B
   REAL , INTENT(OUT) :: C
   LOGICAL , INTENT(OUT) :: OK
   INTEGER :: IO_Status=0
   PRINT*,' Type in the coefficients A, B AND C'
   READ(UNIT=*,FMT=*,IOSTAT=IO_Status)A,B,C
   IF (IO_Status == 0) THEN
      OK=.TRUE.
   ELSE
      OK=.FALSE.
   ENDIF
END SUBROUTINE Interact

SUBROUTINE Solve(E,F,G,Root1,Root2,IFail)
   IMPLICIT NONE
   REAL , INTENT(IN) :: E
   REAL , INTENT(IN) :: F
   REAL , INTENT(IN) :: G
   REAL , INTENT(OUT) :: Root1
   REAL , INTENT(OUT) :: Root2
   INTEGER , INTENT(INOUT) :: IFail
! Local variables
   REAL :: Term
   REAL :: A2
   Term = F*F - 4.*E*G
   A2 = E*2.0
! if term < 0, roots are complex
   IF(Term < 0.0)THEN
      IFail=1
   ELSE
      Term = SQRT(Term)
      Root1 = (-F+Term)/A2
      Root2 = (-F-Term)/A2
   ENDIF
END SUBROUTINE Solve
```

22.2 Defining a subroutine

A subroutine is defined as:

SUBROUTINE subroutine_name(optional list of dummy arguments)

IMPLICIT NONE

dummy argument type definitions with INTENT

...

END SUBROUTINE subroutine_name

and from the earlier example we have the subroutine:

```
SUBROUTINE Interact(A,B,C,OK)
   IMPLICIT NONE
   REAL, INTENT(OUT)::A,B,C
   LOGICAL, INTENT(OUT)::OK


END SUBROUTINE Interact
```

22.3 Referencing a subroutine

To reference a subroutine you use the CALL statement:

CALL subroutine_name(optional list of actual arguments)

and from the earlier example the call to subroutine Interact was of the form:

```
CALL Interact(P,Q,R,OK)
```

When a subroutine returns to the calling program unit control is passed to the statement following the CALL statement.

22.4 Dummy arguments or parameters, and actual arguments

Procedures and their calling program units communicate through their arguments. We often use the terms parameter and arguments interchangeably throughout this text. The SUBROUTINE statement normally contains a list of dummy arguments, separated by commas and enclosed in brackets. The dummy arguments have a type associated with them, for example in subroutine Solve X is of type REAL, but no space is put aside for this in memory. When the subroutine is referenced e.g. CALL Solve(P,Q,R,Root1,Root2,Ifail) then the dummy argument *points* to the actual argument P which is a variable in the calling program unit. The dummy argument and the actual argument must be of the same type, in this case REAL.

22.5 Interface

We strongly recommend the use of interface blocks in the calling routine to provide us with information about the called routine. These provide us with the ability to do type checking between the calling routine and the called routine. One of the most common errors in programming is getting the sequence and type of the parameters wrong between sub-programs.

There are times when the use of interface blocks is mandatory in Fortran and we will cover this as and when required. However it is a good working practice to always provide interface blocks.

We will look at additional ways of providing explicit interfaces in a later chapter.

```
INTERFACE

    SUBROUTINE Interact(A,B,C,OK)
        IMPLICIT NONE
        REAL , INTENT(OUT) :: A
        REAL , INTENT(OUT) :: B
        REAL , INTENT(OUT) :: C
        LOGICAL , INTENT(OUT) :: OK
    END SUBROUTINE Interact

    SUBROUTINE Solve(E,F,G,Root1,Root2,IFail)
        IMPLICIT NONE
        REAL , INTENT(IN) :: E
        REAL , INTENT(IN) :: F
        REAL , INTENT(IN) :: G
        REAL , INTENT(OUT) :: Root1
        REAL , INTENT(OUT) :: Root2
        INTEGER , INTENT(INOUT) :: IFail
    END SUBROUTINE Solve

END INTERFACE
```

The subroutine Interact takes four arguments, A, B, C and OK, and the first three are of REAL type and the fourth is of type LOGICAL.

The subroutine Solve takes six arguments, E,F,G, Root1, Root2 and IFail and the first five are of REAL type and the sixth is of INTEGER type.

As Fortran 95 libraries become more widely available interface blocks for library routines will be provided by the supplier on line, and this minimizes much of the effort in using them. NAG for example already has interface blocks available for its library for many platforms.

22.6 Intent

It is recommended that dummy arguments have an INTENT attribute. In the earlier example subroutine Solve has a dummy argument E with INTENT(IN), which means that when the subroutine is referenced or called it is expecting E to have a value , but its value cannot be changed inside the subroutine. This acts as an extra security measure besides making the program easier to understand. For each parameter it may have one of three attributes:

- INTENT(IN), where the parameter already has a value and cannot be altered in the called routine;

- INTENT(OUT), where the parameter does not have a value, and is given one in the called routine;

- INTENT(INOUT), where the parameter already has a value and this is changed in the called routine;

22.7 Local variables

We saw with functions that variables could be essentially local to the function and unavailable elsewhere. The concept of local variables also applies to subroutines. In the example above Term and A2 are both local variables to the subroutine Solve.

22.7.1 Local variables and the SAVE attribute

Local variables are usually created when a procedure is called and their value lost when execution returns to the calling program unit. To make sure that a local variable retains its values between calls to a sub-program the SAVE attribute can be used on a type statement, e.g.

```
INTEGER , SAVE :: I
```

means that when this statement appears in a sub-program the value of the local variable I is saved between calls.

22.8 Scope of variables

In most cases variables are only available within the program unit that defines them. The introduction of argument lists to functions and subroutines immediately opens up the possibility of data within one program unit becoming available in one or more program units.

In the main program we declare the variables P, Q, R, Root1, Root2, IFail and OK.

Subroutine `Interact` has no variables locally declared. It works on the arguments A, B, C and OK which map onto P, Q, R and OK from the main program, i.e. it works with those variables.

Subroutine `Solve` has two locally defined variables Term and A2. It works with the variables E, F, G, Root1, Root2 and IFail, which map onto P, Q, R, Root1, Root2 and IFail from the main program.

22.9 Status of the action carried out in the subroutine

It is also useful to use parameters that carry information regarding the status of the action carried out by the subroutine. With the subroutine `Interact` we use a logical variable OK to report on the status of the interaction with the user. In the subroutine `Solve` we use the status of the integer variable Ifail to report on the status of the solution of the equation.

22.10 Why bother?

Given the increase in the complexity of the overall program to solve a relatively straightforward problem one must ask why bother. The answer lies in our ability to manage the solution of larger and larger problems. We need all the help we can get if we are to succeed in our task of developing large scale reliable programs.

We need to be able to break our problems down into manageable sub-components and solve each in turn. We are now in a very good position to be able to do this. Given a problem that requires a main program, one or more functions and one or more subroutines we can work on each sub-component in relative isolation, and know that by using things like interface blocks that we will be able to glue each of the components together into a stable structure at the end. We can independently compile the main program and functions and subroutines and use the linker to generate the overall executable and then test that. Providing we keep our interfaces the same we can alter the actual implementations of the functions and subroutines and just recompile the changed procedures.

22.11 Summary

We now have the following concepts for the use of subroutines:

- INTERFACE blocks;
- INTENT attribute for parameters;
- Dummy parameters;
- the use of the CALL statement to invoke a subroutine;

- the concepts of variables that are local to the called routines and are unavailable elsewhere in the overall program;

- communication between program units via the argument list;

- the concept of parameters on the call that enable us to report back on the status of the called routine.

22.12 Problems

1. Type in the program example in this chapter as three files. Compile each individually. When you have successfully compiled each routine (there will be the inevitable typing mistakes) look at the file sizes of the object file. Now use the linker to produce one executable. Look at the file size of the executable. What do you notice?

The development of large programs is eased considerably by the ability to compile small program units and eradicate the compilation errors from one unit at a time.

The linker obviously also has an important role to play in the development process.

2. Write a subroutine to calculate new coordinates (x' , y') from (x,y) when the axes are rotated counterclockwise through an angle of **a** radians using:

$$x' = x \cos a + y \sin a$$

$$y' = -x \sin a + y \cos a$$

Hint:

The subroutine would look something like

SUBROUTINE ChangeCoordinate(X,Y,A,XD,YD)

Write a main program to read in values of x,y,a and call the subroutine and print out the new coordinates.

3. Look at the following program:

```
program test
real  ::  a,b,c
   a=100.0
   b=20.0
   call  divide(a,b,c)
   print  *,c
end program test
subroutine  divide(a,b,c)
integer  ::  a,b,c
  c=a/b
```

```
   return
end subroutine divide
```

The first thing to note is the mismatch between the argument types in the main program and the subroutine.

Do you get a compilaton warning about this mismatch?

What do you think the output will be?

What was the value of *c* when you ran the program?

23

Subroutines: 2

It is one thing to show a man he is in error, and another to put him possession of the truth.

John Locke

Aims

The aims of this chapter are to extend the ideas in the earlier chapter on subroutines by using concrete examples that:

- look at passing rank one arrays as parameters, rather than simple scalars;
  - to introduce explicit shape dummy arrays;
- look at passing character variables as parameters;
  - to introduce assumed-length dummy arguments;
- uses the Quick Sort algorithm which in turn;
  - introduces recursive subroutines;
  - introduces the use of an internal subroutine;
  - looks at the way in which we can maintain a consistent interface between a program and a subroutine and actually re-implement the algorithm that solves the particular sub-problem;
  - looks at the use of the timing routines available in Fortran to determine where the program actually spends its time;
- look at passing rank two arrays as parameters;
  - to introduce assumed-shape dummy arrays.

23 Subroutines: 2

23.1 Example 1: Introduction to arrays as parameters

23.1.1 Explicit shape dummy arrays

So far we have seen scalar parameters. We will now look at array parameters, initially rank one arrays.

A fundamental rule in Fortran 95 is that the shape of an actual array argument and its associated dummy arguments are the same, i.e., they must both have the same rank and the same extents in each dimension.

Consider a simple program which calls a subroutine to add up the square and the cube of each element in a real array, to produce:

$$\sum_{i=1}^{n} x_i^2$$

and

$$\sum_{i=1}^{n} x_i^3$$

```
PROGRAM Ch23_1
IMPLICIT NONE
REAL, DIMENSION (1:50)::A
REAL:: Sum_A_2,Sum_A_3
INTEGER::Number
INTERFACE
   SUBROUTINE Stats(X,Sum_x_2,Sum_x_3,N)
      IMPLICIT NONE
      INTEGER,INTENT(IN)::N
      REAL,INTENT(IN),DIMENSION(1:50)::X
      REAL,INTENT(OUT)::Sum_x_2,Sum_x_3
   END SUBROUTINE Stats
END INTERFACE
!  ...
   CALL Stats(A,Sum_A_2,Sum_A_3,Number)
!  ...
END PROGRAM Ch23_1

SUBROUTINE Stats(X,Sum_x_2,Sum_x_3,N)
```

```
IMPLICIT NONE
INTEGER,INTENT(IN)::N
REAL,INTENT(IN),DIMENSION(1:50)::X
REAL,INTENT(OUT)::Sum_x_2,Sum_x_3
INTEGER::I
REAL:: Temp
!
    Sum_x_2=0.0
    Sum_x_3=0.0
    DO I=1,N
        Temp=X(I)*X(I)
        Sum_x_2=Sum_x_2+Temp
        Sum_x_3=Sum_x_3+X(I)*Temp
    END DO
END SUBROUTINE Stats
```

In both the subroutine and the main program the dummy argument X and the actual argument A are the same shape. In subroutine Stats the dummy argument X is declared with explicit bounds, and is known as an explicit shape dummy array. This program and subroutine will work with arrays of up to and including 50 elements. To allow for larger problems the upper bounds of the actual and dummy array arguments must be increased. This doesn't make the program and subroutine very general. One way round this is to give the actual argument a deferred shape by making it an allocatable array in the main program and to make the dummy argument N the upper bound for the dummy array X in the subroutine, e.g. in the main program use:

```
REAL, DIMENSION (:), ALLOCATABLE:: A
    READ *, Number
    ALLOCATE(A(1:Number))
    CALL Stats(A,Sum_A_2,Sum_A_3,Number)
```

and in the subroutine use:-

```
REAL, INTENT(IN), DIMENSION(1:N) ::X
```

The dummy argument X still has explicit shape, but now the bounds depend on the value of the dummy argument N and its size is determined when the subroutine is called. Even though it is not mandatory it is recommended that interface blocks are used so that the shape and size of actual and dummy arguments can be checked explicitly.

23.2 Example 2: Characters as parameters and assumed-length dummy arguments

The types of parameters considered so far have been REAL, INTEGER and LOGI-CAL. CHARACTER variables are slightly different because they have a length associated with them. In the simplest form consider a subroutine which, given the name of a file, opens it and reads values into two REAL arrays X and Y.

```
SUBROUTINE Readin(Name,X,Y,N)
IMPLICIT NONE
INTEGER , INTENT(IN) :: N
REAL,DIMENSION(1:N),INTENT(OUT)::X,Y
CHARACTER (LEN=20),INTENT(IN)::Name
INTEGER::I
   OPEN(UNIT=10,STATUS='OLD',FILE=Name)
   DO I=1,N
      READ(10,*)X(I),Y(I)
   END DO
   CLOSE(UNIT=10)
END SUBROUTINE Readin
```

A main program to call this subroutine could look like the following:

```
PROGRAM Ch23_2
IMPLICIT NONE
REAL,DIMENSION(1:100)::A,B
INTEGER :: Nos,I
CHARACTER(LEN=20)::Filename
INTERFACE
   SUBROUTINE Readin(Name,X,Y,N)
      IMPLICIT NONE
      INTEGER , INTENT(IN) :: N
      REAL,DIMENSION(1:N),INTENT(OUT)::X,Y
      CHARACTER (LEN=20),INTENT(IN)::Name
   END SUBROUTINE Readin
END INTERFACE
!  ...
   PRINT *,' Type in the name of the data file'
   READ '(A)' , Filename
   PRINT *,' Input the number of items in the file'
   READ * , Nos
   CALL Readin(Filename,A,B,Nos)
   PRINT * , ' Data read in was'
```

```
DO I=1,Nos
   PRINT *,' ',A(I),' ',B(I)
ENDDO
END PROGRAM Ch23_2
```

The main program reads the file name from the user and passes it to the subroutine that reads in the data. If we wanted to allow longer filenames then we would have to change both the main program and the subroutine. To minimize the number of places where we have to make changes we can use assumed-length dummy arguments and their use is strongly recommended for character arguments. The type statement in the subroutine should be therefore changed to

```
CHARACTER (LEN=*) , INTENT(IN) :: Name
```

and the dummy argument Name then takes on the size of the actual argument Filename. An interface block **must** be used when we are using assumed-shape dummy arguments.

23.3 Example 3: Using Hoare's Quick Sort algorithm

This example highlights several important issues involved in the use of subroutines. The overall problem is to read in and sort a file of real numbers. This can be broken down into several steps:

- interact with the user and find out the file name and how many items there are in the file;
- sort these items
- write out the sorted data to a second file.

We will add an additional step of producing timing information regarding each subroutine in the overall problem solution.

We will solve the problem by writing the following routines:

- a driving routine or main program with calls to the timing routines and a print out of the times spent in each subroutine. We will use the intrinsic subroutine CPU_TIME to produce the timing information;
- a subroutine to read the data from a file;
- a subroutine to sort the data;
- a subroutine to write the data to a second file.

In the problem at the end we will look at replacing the actual routine that does the sort with another routine. If you have the NAG library or similar available, use one of the sort routines in that library, and see what timing that routine provides.

```fortran
PROGRAM Sort_Example01
!
!
! This program is a simple example of how
! to construct larger programs
! using some of the new features introduced
! with Fortran 95. The program
! comprises 4 routines,
!
! 1. a driving routine, which interacts with the user
! and requests the number of data items,
! and file name.
! 2. a routine to read in the data, from a file.
! 3. a routine to sort the data.
! 4. a routine to print out the sorted data to a file
!
! The program attempts to highlight the
! importance of the modular nature of the solution,
! and how we can simply replace one component,
! without affecting the other routines.
IMPLICIT NONE
INTEGER                                 :: How_Many
CHARACTER      (LEN=20)                  :: File_Name
REAL , ALLOCATABLE , DIMENSION(:)        :: Raw_Data
REAL                                     :: cputime
REAL                                     :: T1,T2,T3,T4,T5
INTERFACE
   SUBROUTINE Read_Data(File_Name,Raw_Data,How_Many)
     IMPLICIT NONE
     CHARACTER (LEN=*) , INTENT(IN) :: File_Name
     INTEGER , INTENT(IN) :: How_Many
     REAL , INTENT(OUT) , &
     DIMENSION(How_Many) :: Raw_Data
   END SUBROUTINE Read_Data
END INTERFACE

INTERFACE
   SUBROUTINE Sort_Data(Raw_Data,How_Many)
```

```
      IMPLICIT NONE
      INTEGER , INTENT(IN) :: How_Many
      REAL , INTENT(INOUT) , &
      DIMENSION(How_Many) :: Raw_Data
   END SUBROUTINE Sort_Data
END INTERFACE

INTERFACE
   SUBROUTINE Print_Data(Raw_Data,How_Many)
      IMPLICIT NONE
      INTEGER , INTENT(IN) :: How_Many
      REAL , INTENT(IN) , &
      DIMENSION(How_Many) :: Raw_Data
   END SUBROUTINE Print_Data
END INTERFACE

   PRINT * , ' How many data items are there?'
   READ  * , How_Many
   PRINT * , ' What is the file name?'
   READ '(A)',File_Name


   CALL CPU_TIME(cputime)
   t1=cputime
   PRINT 100 , cputime
   100 FORMAT(' Initial cpu time    = ',F7.3)

   ALLOCATE(Raw_Data(How_Many))

   CALL CPU_TIME(cputime)
   t2=cputime-t1
   PRINT 110 , cputime
   110 FORMAT(' Allocate cpu time   = ',F7.3)

   CALL Read_Data(File_Name,Raw_Data,How_Many)

   CALL CPU_TIME(cputime)
   t3=cputime-t2-t1
   PRINT 120 , cputime
   120 FORMAT(' Read data cpu time  = ',F7.3)

   CALL Sort_Data(Raw_Data,How_Many)
```

```
   CALL CPU_TIME(cputime)
   t4=cputime-t3-t2-t1
   PRINT 130 , cputime
   130 FORMAT(' Quick sort cpu time = ',F7.3)

   CALL Print_Data(Raw_Data,How_Many)

   CALL CPU_TIME(cputime)
   t5=cputime-t4-t3-t2-t1
   PRINT 140 , cputime
   140 FORMAT(' Write data cpu time = ',F7.3)


   PRINT *,' '
   PRINT *,' Initial    Memory    Read       Sort
Print'
   PRINT *,' '
   PRINT 150, t1,t2,t3,t4,t5
   150 FORMAT(5(2x,F7.3))

   PRINT * , ' '
   PRINT *, ' Data written to file SORTED.DAT'

END PROGRAM Sort_Example01
SUBROUTINE Read_Data(File_Name,Raw_Data,How_Many)
IMPLICIT NONE
CHARACTER (LEN=*) , INTENT(IN) :: File_Name
INTEGER , INTENT(IN) :: How_Many
REAL , INTENT(OUT) , DIMENSION(How_Many) :: Raw_Data

INTEGER :: I

   OPEN(FILE=File_Name,UNIT=1)
   DO I=1,How_Many
     READ (UNIT=1,FMT=*) Raw_Data(I)
   ENDDO

END SUBROUTINE Read_Data
SUBROUTINE Sort_Data(Raw_Data,How_Many)
IMPLICIT NONE
INTEGER , INTENT(IN) :: How_Many
```

```
REAL , INTENT(INOUT) , DIMENSION(How_Many) :: Raw_Data

   CALL QuickSort(1,How_Many)

CONTAINS

   RECURSIVE SUBROUTINE QuickSort(L,R)
   IMPLICIT NONE
   INTEGER , INTENT(IN) :: L,R
   INTEGER :: I,J
   REAL :: V,T

! The original quick sort algorithm taken
! from Sedgewick failed when the pivot is the
! smallest element in the array.
! This is clearly stated by Sedgewick
! in the text that follows the algorithm.
!
! In the light of the subsequent changes he made
! to this algorithm (including the removal
! of recursion) we decided to look for an
! alternate recursive source.
!
! We used Wirths "algorithms and data structures"
! as a source
!

   i=1
   j=r
   v=raw_data( int((l+r)/2) )
   do
      do while (raw_data(i) < v )
          i=i+1
      enddo
      do while (v < raw_data(j) )
          j=j-1
      enddo
      if (i<=j) then
        t=raw_data(i)
        raw_data(i)=raw_data(j)
        raw_data(j)=t
        i=i+1
```

```
    j=j-1
  endif
  if (i>j) exit
enddo

if (l<j) then
  call quicksort(l,j)
endif

if (i<r) then
  call quicksort(i,r)
endif


END SUBROUTINE QuickSort

END SUBROUTINE Sort_Data
SUBROUTINE Print_Data(Raw_Data,How_Many)
IMPLICIT NONE
INTEGER , INTENT(IN) :: How_Many
REAL , INTENT(IN) , DIMENSION(How_Many) :: Raw_Data
INTEGER :: I
  OPEN(FILE='SORTED.DAT',UNIT=2)
  DO I=1,How_Many
    WRITE(UNIT=2,FMT=*) Raw_Data(I)
  ENDDO
  CLOSE(2)
END SUBROUTINE Print_Data
```

23.3.1   Note 1 – Interface Blocks

Each subroutine has an interface block in the main program. This enables us to compile the main program and each subroutine independently and have the benefit of cross routine type checking for each of the parameters. In the earlier chapter the parameters were scalars; in this example we have a mix of arrays and scalars.

It is good programming practice to get in the habit of using interface blocks when writing programs that contain several procedures, i.e. either functions or subroutines. The likelihood of errors decreases with the use of interface blocks.

Interface blocks are **mandatory** under the following situations:

- the procedure has optional arguments;
- when a function returns an array;

- when a function returns a pointer. The balanced tree example in Chapter 20 uses a recursive function that returns a pointer;

- for character functions a result that is dynamic;

- when the procedure has assumed-shape dummy arguments;

- when the procedure has dummy arguments with the pointer attribute;

- when the procedure has dummy arguments with the target attribute;

- when the procedure has keyword arguments and/or optional arguments;

- when the procedure is generic. You have already seen that some of the intrinsic procedures have this status, e.g. SINE will return a result when the argument is of a variety of types. This means that we can construct procedures that will accept arguments of a variety of types and all we need to do is provide a procedure that manipulates data of that type. We will look at the construction of a procedure that is generic in a later chapter;

- when the procedure provides a user defined operator;

- when the procedure provides user defined assignment.

23.3.2   Note 2 – Intent attribute

There is the use of the INTENT attribute for each parameter. This clarifies the actions of the various routines, and decreases the likelihood of a mistake.

23.3.3   Note 3 – Explicit shape dummy array

An explicit shape dummy array is used for the data array. Its upper bound is passed as a dummy argument and is hence used to dimension the Read_Data array.

23.3.4   Note 4 – Assumed length dummy argument

The subroutine Read_Data has an assumed-length dummy character argument through which the file name is passed.

23.3.5   Note 5 – Recursive subroutine

The actual sorting is done in the recursive subroutine QuickSort. This is a direct translation of Hoare's original algorithm. Recursion is said to be inefficient. In the light of the timing figures do you think that that statement is true?

Recursion provides us with a very clean and expressive way of solving many problems. There will be instances where it is worthwhile removing the overhead of recursion, but the first priority is the production of a program that is correct. It is pointless having a very efficient but incorrect problem solution.

We will look again at recursion and efficiency in a later chapter and under what criteria we can replace recursion with iteration.

23.3.6   Note 6 – Internal subroutines and scope

The routine that actually performs the sort is an internally declared subroutine. We first came across internal sub programs in the chapter on functions, using Stirling's approximation. Let us look at the complete program now and consider fully the whole issue of the scope of variables.

In the main program we declare the variables How_Many, File_Name, Raw_Data, T1, T2, T3, T4, T5 and cputime.

How_Many, File_Name and Raw_Data are arguments to Read_Data and are therefore available to that routine.

How_Many and Raw_Data are arguments to both Sort_Data and Print_Data and are therefore available to those two routines.

T1, T2, T3, T4, T5 and cputime are used to produce timing information and are purely local to the main program.

Subroutine Read_Data has one locally declared variable I, and this exists completely independently of I in the main routine.

Subroutine Print_Data has one locally declared variable I, and again this exists completely independently of I in both the main program and the Read_Data routine.

Subroutine Sort_Data and the recursive subroutine QuickSort introduce a number of important extensions to the concept of scope.

Within the Sort_Data routine the Raw_Data array is a variable that is available to the QuickSort subroutine as QuickSort is **contained** within the Sort_Data routine.

QuickSort has its own local variables I, J, V and T. Note that as QuickSort is recursive that there will be multiple versions of this routine in existence as the sorting is undertaken. Thus there will be multiple instances of the local variables I, J, V and T in existence, and they are all separate from one another.

Thus we have the use of variables called I and J throughout three program units and they are all distinct from one another and altering one of them has no effect at all on the others. This ability to hide information is a very powerful tool, and without it we would find it very difficult to construct large secure bug free programs.

23.3.7   Note 7 – Flexible design

The QuickSort recursive routine can be replaced with another sorting algorithm and we can maintain the interface to Sort_Data. We can thus decouple the implementation of the actual sorting routine from the defined interface. We would only need to recompile the Sort_Data routine and we could relink using the already compiled main routine, read data routine and print data routines.

23.3.8   Note 8 – Timing information

In this example we call the system intrinsic CPU_TIME to produce timing details. This will provide implementation dependent timing. On two platforms this returned timing information in hundredths of a second.

Timing information can also be obtained from the system intrinsic:

- SYSTEM_CLOCK

and you can find a variant of the above program using calls to SYSTEM_CLOCK on our Fortran 95 web pages. The time slice is given below for three compilers:

- Sun F90, Sun UltraSparc- 1/1,000,000

- Nag F95, As above 1/1,000

- Compaq/Dec f95, PC - 1/10,000

Care should therefore be taken when using timing information, especially on different platforms.

23.4   Example 4: Assumed shape arrays

When we introduced subroutines we only used scalar parameters. The three preceding examples introduced parameters that were rank one arrays and used explicit-shape dummy array arguments. Explicit-shape dummy arrays have their shape explicitly specified in a procedure, or just their rank specified, the bounds depending on the value of one or more dummy arguments. Either way this is not very flexible, especially for rank two or higher arrays where extra arguments may be needed to specify the bounds of the dummy arrays. Consider the following program and subroutine:

```
PROGRAM Rain
   IMPLICIT NONE
   REAL,DIMENSION(1:12)::Rainfall
   REAL::Average,Total
   INTEGER::  I,N=12
   INTERFACE
     SUBROUTINE Rainfall_stats(Rf,Average,Sum,Nf)
       IMPLICIT NONE
       REAL,DIMENSION  (:),INTENT(IN)::Rf
       REAL,INTENT(OUT)::Average,Sum
       INTEGER,INTENT(IN)::Nf
```

```
    END SUBROUTINE Rainfall_stats
  END INTERFACE
    PRINT *, 'Input the rainfall for 12 months:'
    DO I=1,N
        READ*,Rainfall(I)
    END DO
    CALL Rainfall_stats(Rainfall,Average,Total,N)
    PRINT*,'The total rainfall = ',Total
    PRINT*,'The average rainfall = ',Average
    END PROGRAM Rain

SUBROUTINE Rainfall_stats(Rf,Average,Sum,Nf)
  IMPLICIT NONE
  REAL,DIMENSION (:),INTENT(IN)::Rf
  REAL,INTENT(OUT)::Average,Sum
  INTEGER,INTENT(IN)::Nf
  INTEGER::I
    Sum=0.0
    DO I=1,Nf
      Sum = Sum+Rf(I)
    END DO
    Average=Sum/Nf
END SUBROUTINE Rainfall_stats
```

In this example dummy array argument Rf in the subroutine Rainfall_stats is an assumed-shape array, i.e. it takes the shape of the actual argument Rainfall when the subroutine is called.

There are several restrictions when using assumed-shape arrays:-

- The ranks is equal to the number of colons, in this case one;

- The lower bounds of the assumed-shape array are the specified lower bounds, if present, and 1 otherwise. In the example above it is 1 because we haven't specified a lower bound;

- The upper bounds will be determined on entry to the procedure and will be whatever values are needed to make sure that the extents along each dimension of the dummy argument are the same as the actual argument. In this case the upper bound will be 12;

- An assumed-shape array must not be defined with the POINTER or AL-LOCATABLE attribute;

- When using an assumed-shape array an interface block is mandatory.

23.5 Example 5: Rank two and higher arrays as parameters

23.5.1 Assumed shape arrays

Assumed-shape arrays come into their own when using rank two or higher dummy array arguments. Consider the following example:

```
PROGRAM Matrix_works
  IMPLICIT NONE
  REAL , ALLOCATABLE , DIMENSION &
  (:,:)::One,Two,Three,One_T
  INTEGER :: I,N
  INTERFACE
    SUBROUTINE Matrix_bits(A,B,C,A_T)
      IMPLICIT NONE
      REAL, DIMENSION (:,:), INTENT(IN) :: A,B
      REAL, DIMENSION (:,:), INTENT(OUT) :: C,A_T
    END SUBROUTINE Matrix_bits
  END INTERFACE
    PRINT *,'Input size of matrices'
    READ*,N
    ALLOCATE(One(1:N,1:N))
    ALLOCATE(Two(1:N,1:N))
    ALLOCATE(Three(1:N,1:N))
    ALLOCATE(One_T(1:N,1:N))
    DO I=1,N
      PRINT*, 'Input row ', I,' of One'
      READ*,One(I,1:N)
    END DO
    DO I=1,N
      PRINT*, 'Input row ', I,' of Two'
      READ*,Two(I,1:N)
    END DO
    CALL Matrix_bits(One,Two,Three,One_T)
    PRINT*,' Matrix Three:'
    DO I=1,N
      PRINT *,Three(I,1:N)
    END DO
    PRINT *,' Matrix One_T:'
    DO I=1,N
      PRINT *,One_T(I,1:N)
    END DO
END PROGRAM Matrix_works
```

```
SUBROUTINE Matrix_bits(A,B,C,A_T)
  IMPLICIT NONE
  REAL, DIMENSION (:,:), INTENT(IN)  :: A,B
  REAL, DIMENSION (:,:), INTENT(OUT) :: C,A_T
    C=MATMUL(A,B)
    A_T=TRANSPOSE(A)
END SUBROUTINE Matrix_bits
```

23.5.2 Notes

The dummy array and actual array arguments look the same but there is a difference:

- The dummy array arguments A, B, C, A_T are all assumed-shape arrays and take the shape of the actual array arguments One, Two, Three and One_T respectively.

- The actual array arguments One, Two, Three and One_T in the main program are allocatable arrays or deferred-shape arrays. An allocatable array is an array that has an allocatable attribute. Its bounds and shape are declared when the array is allocated, hence deferred-shape.

23.6 Summary

We now have a lot of the tools to start tackling problems in a structured and modular way, breaking problems down into manageable chunks and designing subprograms for each of the tasks.

23.7 Problems

1. Using the following formulae:

$$\text{mean} = \quad \bar{x} = \left(\sum_{i=1}^{n} x_i \right) \Big/ n$$

$$\text{variance} \quad \frac{\sum_{i=1}^{n} (x_i - \bar{x})^2}{n-1}$$

and the standard deviation is the square root of the variance. Firstly write a subroutine to calculate the mean and standard deviation of a set of numbers x_i, $i=1..n$. Secondly, write a main program to read in the numbers, call the subroutine and then print out the mean and standard deviation.

2. Here is a program that will create a data file comprising random numbers. Run the program to generate a data file with at least 20,000 real data values. We will use this file as input to the second example.

```
PROGRAM Random
IMPLICIT NONE
INTEGER :: I
REAL :: X
   CALL RANDOM_SEED
   OPEN(UNIT=1,FILE='RANDOM.DAT')
   DO I=1,32767
      CALL RANDOM_NUMBER(X)
      X=X*100
      WRITE (1,FMT='(F6.2)') X
   END DO
END PROGRAM Random
```

3. Run the Quick_Sort program in this chapter with the data file as input. Obtain timing details.

What percentage of the time does the program spend in each subroutine? Is it worth trying to make the sort much more efficient given these timings?

4. Find out if there is a subroutine library like the NAG library available. If there is replace the Quick_Sort recursive subroutine with a suitable routine from that library. What times do you obtain?

5. Try using the operating system SORT command to sort the file. What timing figures do you get now?

Was it worth writing a program?

6. Consider the following program.

```
program test02
!
! Program to test array subscript checking
! when the array is passed as an argument.
!
implicit none
integer , parameter :: array_size=10
integer :: i
integer , dimension(array_size) :: a
   do i=1,array_size
     a(i)=i
```

```
  end do
  call sub01(a,array_size)
end program test02

subroutine sub01(a,array_size)
implicit none
integer , intent(in) :: array_size
integer , intent(in) , dimension(array_size) :: a
integer :: i
integer :: atotal=0
integer :: rtotal=0
  do i=1,array_size
    rtotal=rtotal+a(i)
  end do
  do i=1,array_size+1
    atotal=atotal+a(i)
  end do
  print *,' Apparent total is ' , atotal
  print *,'      real total is ' , rtotal
end subroutine sub01
```

The key thing to note is that we haven't used interface blocks and we have an error in the subroutine where we go outside the array. Run this program. What answer do you get for the apparent total?

Are there any compiler flags or switches which will enable you to trap this error?

23.8 Bibliography

So far we have been able to work with a relatively natural language description of the rules and syntax of Fortran. The problems in this and subsequent chapters now require a much more tight and unambiguous syntax definition. One source of this is obviously the standard itself. This is for most people not an option through cost. Given that the standard is itself some 400 pages it is not possible or desirable to duplicate the whole of the standard in this work, copyright permitting (which it is not).

ISO/IEC 1539:1991 (E), *Fortran 90*, 1991

ISO/IEC, *Technical Corrigendum 1 to ISO/IEC 1539:1991*, 1994.

ISO/IEC, *Technical Corrigendum 2 to ISO/IEC 1539:1991*, 1994.

ISO/IEC 1539-1:1997, *Information technology, Programming languages, Fortran - Part 1: Base language*, 1997

ISO/IEC 1539-2:1994 *Information technology -- Programming languages -- FOR-TRAN -- Part 2: Varying length character strings.*

ISO/IEC 1539-3:1999 *Information technology -- Programming languages -- Fortran -- Part 3: Conditional compilation.*

ISO/IEC TR 15580:1998 *Information technology Programming languages Fortran -- Floating-point exception handling*

ISO/IEC TR 15581:1998 *Information technology -- Programming languages -- Fortran -- Enhanced data type facilities.*

The above comprise the definition of the language. They are aimed more at language lawyers and compiler implementors, rather than the end user. They are in the end the definitive statement regarding the language.

The ISO url is:

http://www.iso.ch/

Use the search facility to locate the information you require.

We thus have to look for alternate sources of this information. The best compiler implementations will provide both user documentation and reference documentation. You are strongly urged to see what is supplied with the compiler you use.

Compaq provide very comprehensive documentation on CDs with their compiler. The two key documents are:

- Programmers Guide
- Language Reference

It is essential to install the above and they can then be browsed on-line. They can also be printed.

There are a number of books on Fortran that are more reference orientated than user orientated. The following are two of them.

Adams J.C., Brainerd W.S., Martin J.T., *Fortran 95 Handbook: Complete ANSI/ISO Reference,* McGraw Hill.

- Highly recommended. Several of the authors were on the X3J3 committee, and this shows in the authority of the contents.

Gehrke W., *Fortran 95 Reference Handbook*, Springer Verlag, 1996.

- Comprehensive coverage of the standard. Very reasonably priced source of information.

23.9 Commercial numerical and statistical subroutine libraries

There are two major suppliers of commercial libraries and these are:

- NAG: Numerical Algorithms Group

and

- Visual Numerics.

They can be found at:

- http://www.nag.co.uk/

and

- http://www.vni.com/index.html

respectively. Their libraries are written by numerical analysts, and are fully tested and well documented. They are under constant development and available for a wide range of hardware platforms and compilers. Parallel versions are also available.

24

An Introduction to Modules

Common sense is the best distributed commodity in the world, for every man is convinced that he is well supplied with it.

Descartes.

Aims

The aims of this chapter are to look at the facilities provided in Fortran provided by modules, in particular:

- the use of a module to aid in the consistent definition of precision throughout a program and sub-programs;

- the use of modules for global data;

- the use of modules for derived data types;

- the use of modules for explicit procedure interfaces;

- the use of modules to package procedures;

- a complete numerical example solving systems of linear equations using Gaussian elimination.

24 An Introduction to Modules

As summarized in the previous chapter we now have the tools to solve many problems just using a main program and one or more external and internal subprograms. Both external and internal subprograms communicate through their argument lists, whilst internal subprograms have access to data in their host program units.

We now introduce another type of program unit, the module, which is probably one of the most important features of Fortran 90. The purpose of modules is quite different from subprograms. In their simplest form they exist so that anything required by more than one program unit may be packaged in a module and made available where needed.

The form of a module is:

```
MODULE module_name
...
END MODULE module_name
```

and the information contained within it is made available in the program units that need to access it by the following: ⸳ · ·

```
USE module_name
```

The USE statement must be the first statement after the PROGRAM or SUBROUTINE or FUNCTION statement.

In this chapter we will look at:

- modules for global data;
- modules for derived types;
- modules for explicit interfaces;
- modules containing procedures.

Modules are another program unit and exist so that anything required by more than one program unit maybe packaged in a module and made available where needed.

24.1 Modules for global data

So far the only way that a program unit can communicate with a procedure is through the argument list. Sometimes this is very cumbersome, especially if a number of procedures want access to the same data and it means long argument lists. The problem can be solved using modules. For example defining the precision to which you wish to work and any constants defined to that precision which maybe needed by a number of procedures.

24.1.1 Example 1: Modules for precision specification and constant definition

In the following example we use a module to define a parameter Long to specify the precision to which we wish to work, and a value for the parameter π. Note that the parameter π is defined to this working precision. We then import the module defining these parameters into the program units that need them.

```
MODULE Precision_defs
   IMPLICIT NONE
   INTEGER , PARAMETER:: Long=SELECTED_REAL_KIND(15,307)
   REAL (Long) , PARAMETER::Pi=3.14159265358979_Long
END MODULE Precision_defs
PROGRAM Main
   USE Precision_defs
   IMPLICIT NONE
   INTERFACE
      SUBROUTINE Sub1(Radius,Area,Circum)
      USE Precision_defs
      IMPLICIT NONE
      REAL(Long),INTENT(IN)::Radius
      REAL(Long),INTENT(OUT)::Area,Circum
      END SUBROUTINE Sub1
   END INTERFACE
   REAL(Long)::R,A,C
   INTEGER ::I
   DO I=1,10
      PRINT*,'Radius?'
      READ*,R
      CALL Sub1(R,A,C)
      PRINT *,' For radius   = ',R
      PRINT *,' Area         = ',A
      PRINT *,' Circumference = ',C
   END DO
END PROGRAM Main

SUBROUTINE Sub1(Radius,Area,Circum)
   USE Precision_defs
   IMPLICIT NONE
   REAL(Long),INTENT(IN)::Radius
   REAL(Long),INTENT(OUT)::Area,Circum
   Area=Pi*Radius*Radius
   Circum=2.0_Long*Pi*Radius
END SUBROUTINE Sub1
```

24.1.2   Note

In this example we wish to work with the precision specified by the kind type parameter Long in the module Precision_defs. In order to do this we use the statement

```
USE Precision_defs
```

inside the program unit before any declarations. The kind type parameter Long is then used with all the REAL type declaration, e.g.

```
REAL (Long):: R ,A,C
```

To make sure that all floating point calculations are performed to the working precision specified by Long any constants such as 2.0 in subroutine Sub1 are specified as const_Long, e.g.

```
2.0_Long
```

Note also that we define things once and use them on two occasions, i.e. we define the precision once and use this definition in both the main program and the subroutine.

24.1.3   Example 2: Constant definition and array definition

The following example uses one module containing a number of constants and a second module containing an array definition. We have again the use of modules to define once and used on two or more occasions.

```
MODULE Consts
   IMPLICIT NONE
   REAL,PARAMETER:: A=15.0,B=22.7,C=3.691
END MODULE Consts

MODULE Data
   IMPLICIT NONE
   INTEGER,PARAMETER::No_of_Readings=100
   REAL,DIMENSION(1:No_of_readings)::X,Y
END MODULE Data

SUBROUTINE Stat(Arg1,Arg2,Arg3)
   USE Data
   IMPLICIT NONE
   REAL,INTENT(OUT)::Arg1,Arg2,Arg3
   INTEGER::I
   Arg1=0.0;  Arg2=0.0;  Arg3=0.0
```

```
   DO I=1,No_of_readings
      Arg1 = Arg1+X(I)*X(I)
      Arg2 = Arg2+Y(I)*Y(I)
      Arg3 = Arg3+X(I)*Y(I)
   END DO
   Arg3=Arg3*Arg3
END SUBROUTINE Stat

PROGRAM Main
USE Consts
USE Data
IMPLICIT NONE

INTERFACE
   SUBROUTINE Stat(Arg1,Arg2,Arg3)
      USE Data
      IMPLICIT NONE
      REAL,INTENT(OUT)::Arg1,Arg2,Arg3
   END SUBROUTINE Stat
END INTERFACE

   CHARACTER (LEN=40):: File_name
   INTEGER:: I
   REAL:: Sum,SUM_x_2,Sum_y_2,Sum_xy_2
!
   PRINT *,'Data file name?'
   READ(*,'(A)')File_name
   OPEN(UNIT=10,FILE=File_name,STATUS='OLD')
   DO I=1,No_of_readings
      READ(10,*)X(I),Y(I)
   END DO
   CALL Stat(Sum_x_2,Sum_y_2,Sum_xy_2)
   Sum= (A*Sum_x_2 + B*Sum_y_2) / (C*Sum_xy_2)
   PRINT *,'Sum = ',Sum
!
END PROGRAM Main
```

24.2 Modules for derived data types

When using derived data types and passing them as arguments to subroutines, both the actual arguments and dummy arguments must be of the same type, i.e. they must be declared with reference to the same type definition. The only way this can be achieved is by using modules. The user defined type is declared in a module and each program unit that requires that type **uses** the module.

24.2.1   Example 3: Person data type

In this example we have a user defined type Person which we wish to use in the main program and pass arguments of this type to the subroutines Read_data and Stats. In order to have the type Person available to two subroutines and the main program we have defined Person in a module Personal_details and then made the module available to each program unit with the statement:

```
USE Personal_details
```

We also have the use of an interface block to provide the ability to develop the overall solution in stages.

```
MODULE Personal_details
   IMPLICIT NONE
   TYPE Person
      REAL:: Weight
      INTEGER :: Age
      CHARACTER :: Sex
   END TYPE Person
END MODULE Personal_details

PROGRAM Survey
   USE Personal_details
   IMPLICIT NONE
   INTEGER ,PARAMETER:: Max_no=100
   TYPE (Person), DIMENSION(1:Max_no) :: Patient
   INTEGER :: I,No_of_patients
   REAL :: Male_average, Female_average
INTERFACE

   SUBROUTINE Read_data(Data,Max_no,No)
      USE Personal_details
      IMPLICIT NONE
      TYPE (Person), DIMENSION (:), INTENT(OUT):: Data
      INTEGER, INTENT(OUT):: No
      INTEGER, INTENT(IN):: Max_no
   END SUBROUTINE Read_Data

   SUBROUTINE Stats(Data,No,M_a,F_a)
      USE Personal_details
```

```
      IMPLICIT NONE
      TYPE(Person), DIMENSION (:) :: Data
      REAL:: M_a,F_a
      INTEGER :: No
   END SUBROUTINE Stats

END INTERFACE
!
   CALL Read_data(Patient,Max_no,No_of_patients)
   CALL Stats( Patient , No_of_patients , &
               Male_average , Female_average)
   PRINT*, 'Average male weight is ',Male_average
   PRINT*, 'Average female weight is ',Female_average
END PROGRAM Survey

SUBROUTINE Read_Data(Data,Max_no,No)
   USE Personal_details
   IMPLICIT NONE
   TYPE (PERSON), DIMENSION (:), INTENT(OUT)::Data
   INTEGER, INTENT(OUT):: No
   INTEGER, INTENT(IN):: Max_no
   INTEGER :: I
   DO
      PRINT *,'Input number of patients'
      READ *,No
      IF ( No > 0 .AND. No <= Max_no) EXIT
   END DO
   DO I=1,No
      PRINT *,'For person ',I
      PRINT *,'Weight ?'
      READ*,Data(I)%Weight
      PRINT*,'Age ?'
      READ*,Data(I)%Age
      PRINT*,'Sex ?'
      READ*,Data(I)%Sex
   END DO
END SUBROUTINE Read_Data

SUBROUTINE Stats(Data,No,M_a,F_a)
   USE Personal_details
   IMPLICIT NONE
   TYPE(Person), DIMENSION(:)::Data
```

```
REAL  ::  M_a,F_a
INTEGER::  No
INTEGER  ::  I,No_f,No_m
M_a=0.0;  F_a=0.0;No_f=0;  No_m =0
DO  I=1,No
    IF ( Data(I)%Sex == 'M' &
    .OR. Data(I)%Sex == 'm') THEN
        M_a=M_a+Data(I)%Weight
        No_m=No_m+1
    ELSEIF(Data(I)%Sex == 'F' &
        .OR. Data(I)%Sex == 'f') THEN
        F_a=F_a +Data(I)%Weight
        No_f=No_f+1
    ENDIF
END DO
IF (No_m > 0 ) THEN
    M_a = M_a/No_m
ENDIF
IF (No_f > 0 ) THEN
    F_a = F_a/No_f
ENDIF
END SUBROUTINE Stats
```

24.3 Modules for explicit procedures interfaces

When we introduced subroutines we also introduced the interface block, and have seen how useful it is as an extra security measure at compile time, to check that actual and dummy arguments agree. Interface blocks are mandatory under the following conditions:

- for argument types like pointers, assumed-shape arrays and assumed- shape dummy arguments;

- when defining generic procedures – see Chapter 27;

- when operator overloading – see Chapter 27;

- when defining new meaning to the assignment symbol.

When programs start to become larger with many procedure references it becomes tedious and time consuming to keep repeating interface blocks. One way round this is to place one or more procedure interfaces in a module and then use the module in each program unit as required. This is also strongly recommended for programs where we use the same interface in two or more places. The golden rule is define once and use many times.

A good example of this in practice has been provided by NAG. For some of their Fortran 77 libraries they have automatically generated a suite of precompiled modules containing interface blocks for every subroutine and function organized on a chapter by chapter basis.

24.3.1 Example: Using QuickSort

Using the QuickSort example in the previous chapter we have:

```
MODULE Read_Interface
INTERFACE
   SUBROUTINE Read_data ( File_name,Raw_Data,How_Many)
      IMPLICIT NONE
      CHARACTER (LEN=*),INTENT(IN)       :: File_Name
      INTEGER, INTENT(IN) :: How_Many
      REAL, INTENT (OUT), &
         DIMENSION (How_Many) :: Raw_Data
   END SUBROUTINE Read_Data
END INTERFACE
END MODULE Read_Interface


MODULE Sort_Interface
INTERFACE
   SUBROUTINE Sort_Data(Raw_Data, How_Many)
      IMPLICIT NONE
      INTEGER , INTENT(IN) :: How_Many
      REAL , INTENT(IN), &
         DIMENSION (How_Many) :: Raw_Data
   END SUBROUTINE Sort_Data
END INTERFACE
END MODULE Sort_Interface


MODULE Print_Interface
INTERFACE
   SUBROUTINE Print_Data (Raw_Data,How_Many)
      IMPLICIT NONE
      INTEGER , INTENT(IN)     :: How_Many
      REAL , INTENT(IN), &
         DIMENSION (How_Many) :: Raw_Data
   END SUBROUTINE Print_Data
END INTERFACE
END MODULE Print_Interface
```

and then the main program would look like:

```
PROGRAM Sort_Example01
USE Read_Interface
USE Sort_Interface
USE Print_Interface
IMPLICIT NONE
INTEGER :: How_many
    . . .
    CALL Read_Data(File_Name, Raw_Data, How_Many)
    . . .
END PROGRAM Sort_Example01
```

24.4 Modules containing procedures

A module can also contain one or more procedures, and takes the form:

```
MODULE Procs
. . .
. . .
CONTAINS
    . . .
    . . .
    SUBROUTINE sub
    . . .
    . . .
    END SUBROUTINE sub
    . . .
    . . .
END MODULE Procs
```

This is a very powerful feature. The procedures inside the module are called **module procedures**. Like internal procedures they have access to any data and type definitions declared in the module, and their interfaces are explicit to each other.

When designing a suite of subprograms, related subroutines and functions can be packed into one module.

For example, if you are designing a suite of sub-programs to solve ordinary differential equations you may want to offer three methods:-

- Runge-Kutta
- Adams-Bashforth
- Gear

The subroutines implementing these three algorithms could be packaged into one module:

```
MODULE Odes
IMPLICIT NONE
INTEGER, PARAMETER:: Long=SELECTED_REAL_KIND(15,307)
REAL (Long) :: Step_interval = 100.0_Long
REAL (Long) :: Smallest_step = 1.0E-6_Long
!...
CONTAINS
   SUBROUTINE RK(...)
!   .
   END SUBROUTINE RK
   SUBROUTINE AB(...)
!   .
   END SUBROUTINE AB
   SUBROUTINE Gear(...)
!   .
   END SUBROUTINE Gear
END MODULE Odes
```

All the subroutines in the module have access to the Kind type parameter Long and the two variables Step_interval and Smallest_step.

A main program to call any of these subroutines could be of the form:-

```
PROGRAM Diff_Eqns
USE Odes
IMPLICIT NONE
REAL (Long), DIMENSION (:), ALLOCATABLE :: Y,F
REAL (Long) ::T,A,B
CHARACTER (LEN=2) :: Method
   PRINT*,'Method? (RK, AB or G)'
   READ(*,'(A)')Method
   SELECT CASE (Method)
      CASE ('RK','rk','Rk','rK')
         CALL RK(...)
!         ...
      CASE ('AB','ab', 'Ab','aB')
         CALL AB(...)
!         ...
      CASE ('G','g')
         CALL Gear(...)
```

```
!         . . . .
       CASE DEFAULT
          PRINT*,'No valid method chosen'
    END SELECT
END PROGRAM Diff_Eqns
```

This is how Fortran 90 libraries will be designed in the future. The Numerical Algorithms Group (NAG) have been the providers of a Fortran numerical and statistical library for a number of years. They have released a completely redesigned Fortran 90 library, albeit a subset of the popular Fortran 77 library. The Fortran 90 library, fl90, is organised into chapters and within each chapter there are:

- one or more modules

- each module contains one of more procedures

  - each module may contain type definitions

  - each module may contain global data

For instance in release 1 chapter 3 - *Special Functions* has seven modules. One such module is called nag_gamma_fun which contains four procedures:

Procedure Name	Action
nag_gamma	Gamma function
nag_log_gamma	Log gamma function
nag_polygamma	Polygamma function
nag_incompl_gamma	Incomplete gamma functions

Up to date information can be found at their web site.

24.5 Example 4 – The solution of linear equations using Gaussian elimination

At this stage we have introduced many of the concepts needed to write numerical code, and so we have included a popular algorithm, Gaussian elimination, together with a main program which uses it, and a module, to bring together many of the features covered so far.

Finding the solution of a system of linear equations is very common in scientific and engineering problems, either as a direct physical problem or indirectly for example as the result of using finite difference methods to solve a partial differential equation. We will restrict ourselves to the case where the number of equations and the number of unknowns are the same. The problem can be defined as:

$$
\begin{aligned}
a_{11}x_1 + a_{12}x_2 \ldots + a_{1n}x_n &= b_1 \\
a_{21}x_2 + a_{22}x_2 \ldots + a_{n2}x_n &= b_2 \\
\cdot \qquad \cdot \qquad \ldots \quad \cdot \qquad \cdot \ \cdot \\
a_{n1}x_1 + a_{n2}x_n \cdots + a_{nn}x_n &= b_n
\end{aligned}
\tag{1}
$$

or

$$
\begin{pmatrix}
a_{11} & a_{12} & \ldots & a_{1n} \\
a_{21} & a_{22} & \ldots & a_{2n} \\
\cdot & \cdot & \ldots & \cdot \\
a_{n1} & a_{n2} & \ldots & a_{nn}
\end{pmatrix}
\begin{pmatrix}
x_1 \\ x_2 \\ \cdot \\ x_n
\end{pmatrix}
=
\begin{pmatrix}
b_1 \\ b_2 \\ \cdot \\ b_n
\end{pmatrix}
$$

which can be written as:

$$
A x = b
\tag{2}
$$

where A is the $n \times n$ coefficient matrix, b is the right hand side vector and x is the vector of unknowns. We will also restrict ourselves to the case where A is a general real matrix.

Note, there is a unique solution to (2) if the inverse, A^{-1}, of the coefficient matrix A, exists. However the system should never be solved by finding A^{-1} and then solving $A^{-1} b = x$ because of the problems of rounding error and the computational costs.

A well known method for solving (2) is Gaussian elimination, where multiples of equations are subtracted from others so that the coefficients below the diagonal become zero, producing a system of the form:

$$
\begin{pmatrix}
a_{11}^* & a_{12}^* & a_{13}^* & \ldots & a_{1n}^* \\
0 & a_{22}^* & a_{23}^* & \ldots & a_{2n}^* \\
0 & 0 & a_{33}^* & \ldots & a_{3n}^* \\
\cdot & \cdot & \cdot & \ldots & \cdot \\
0 & 0 & 0 & 0 & a_{nn}^*
\end{pmatrix}
\begin{pmatrix}
x_1 \\ x_2 \\ x_3 \\ \cdot \\ x_n
\end{pmatrix}
=
\begin{pmatrix}
b_1^* \\ b_2^* \\ b_3^* \\ \cdot \\ b_n^*
\end{pmatrix}
$$

where A has been transformed into an upper triangular matrix. By a process of *backward substitution* the values of *x drop* out.

The subroutine Gaussian_Elimination implements the Gaussian elimination algorithm with *partial pivoting* which makes sure that the multipliers are less than 1 in magnitude, by interchanging rows if necessary. This is to try and prevent the build up of errors.

This implementation is based on two LINPACK routines SGEFA and SGESL and a Fortran 77 subroutine written by Tim Hopkins and Chris Phillips in their excellent book *Numerical Methods in Practice.*

The matrix A and vector B are passed to the subroutine Gaussian_Elimination and on exit both A and B are overwritten. Mathematically Gaussian elimination is described as working on rows, and using partial pivoting row interchanges may be necessary. Due to Fortran's row element ordering, to implement this algorithm efficiently it works on columns rather than rows by interchanging elements within a column if necessary.

```
MODULE Precisions
INTEGER,PARAMETER:: Long=SELECTED_REAL_KIND(15,307)
END MODULE Precisions

PROGRAM Solve

   USE Precisions
   IMPLICIT NONE
   INTEGER :: I,N
   REAL (Long), ALLOCATABLE:: A(:,:),B(:),X(:)
   LOGICAL:: Singular

INTERFACE

   SUBROUTINE Gaussian_Elimination(A,N,B,X,Singular)
      USE Precisions
      IMPLICIT NONE
      INTEGER, INTENT(IN)::N
      REAL (Long), INTENT (INOUT) :: A(:,:),B(:)
      REAL (Long), INTENT(OUT)::X(:)
      LOGICAL, INTENT(OUT) :: Singular
   END SUBROUTINE Gaussian_Elimination

END INTERFACE

   PRINT *,'Number of equations?'
   READ *,N
   ALLOCATE(A(1:N,1:N),B(1:N),X(1:N))
   DO I=1,N
```

```
      PRINT *,'Input elements of row ',I,' of A'
      READ*,A(I,1:N)
      PRINT*,'Input element ',I,' of B'
      READ *,B(I)
   END DO
   CALL Gaussian_Elimination(A,N,B,X,Singular)
   IF(Singular) THEN
      PRINT*, 'Matrix is singular'
   ELSE
      PRINT*, 'Solution X:'
      PRINT*,X(1:N)
   ENDIF
END PROGRAM Solve

SUBROUTINE Gaussian_Elimination(A,N,B,X,Singular)
! Routine to solve a system Ax=b
! using Gaussian Elimination
! with partial pivoting
! The code is based on the Linpack routines
! SGEFA and SGESL
! and operates on columns rather than rows!
   USE Precisions
   IMPLICIT NONE
! Matrix A and vector B are over-written
! Arguments
   INTEGER, INTENT(IN):: N
   REAL (Long),INTENT(INOUT):: A(:,:),B(:)
   REAL (Long),INTENT(OUT)::X(:)
   LOGICAL,INTENT(OUT)::Singular
! Local variables
   INTEGER::I,J,K,Pivot_row
   REAL (Long):: Pivot,Multiplier,Sum,Element
   REAL (Long),PARAMETER::Eps=1.E-13_Long
!
! Work through the matrix column by column
!
   DO K=1,N-1
!
!  Find largest element in column K for pivot
!
   Pivot_row = MAXVAL( MAXLOC( ABS( A(K:N,K) ) ) ) &
      + K - 1
```

```
!
! Test to see if A is singular
! if so return to main program
!
      IF(ABS(A(Pivot_row,K)) <= Eps)  THEN
         Singular=.TRUE.
         RETURN
      ELSE
         Singular = .FALSE.
      ENDIF
!
! Exchange elements in column K if largest is
! not on the diagonal
!
      IF(Pivot_row /= K)  THEN
         Element=A(Pivot_row,K)
         A(Pivot_Row,K)=A(K,K)
         A(K,K)=Element
         Element=B(Pivot_row)
         B(Pivot_row)=B(K)
         B(K)=Element
      ENDIF
!
! Compute multipliers
! elements of column K below diagonal
! are set to these multipliers for use
! in elimination later on
!
      A(K+1:N,K)  =  A(K+1:N,K)/A(K,K)
!
! Row elimination performed by columns for efficiency
!
      DO J=K+1,N
         Pivot = A(Pivot_row,J)
         IF(Pivot_row /= K)  THEN
!          Swap if pivot row is not K
            A(Pivot_row,J)=A(K,J)
            A(K,J)=Pivot
         ENDIF
         A(K+1:N,J)=A(K+1:N,J)-Pivot* A(K+1:N,K)
      END DO
!
```

```
! Apply same operations to B
!
    B(K+1:N)=B(K+1:N)-A(K+1:N,K)*B(K)
  END DO
!
! Backward substitution
!
  DO I=N,1,-1
    Sum = 0.0
    DO J= I+1,N
      Sum=Sum+A(I,J)*X(J)
    END DO
    X(I)=(B(I)-Sum)/A(I,I)
  END DO
END SUBROUTINE Gaussian_Elimination
```

24.5.1   Notes

24.5.1.1 Module for kind type

A module, Precisions, has been used to define a kind type parameter, Long, to specify the floating point precision to which we wish to work. This module is then used by the main program and the subroutine, and the kind type parameter Long is used with all the REAL type definitions and with any constants, e.g.

```
REAL(Long), PARAMETER :: Eps=1.E-13_Long
```

24.5.1.2 Deferred shape arrays

In the main program matrix A and vectors B and X are declared as deferred shape arrays, by specifying their rank only and using the ALLOCATABLE attribute. Their shape is determined at run time when the variable N is read in and then the statement:

```
ALLOCATE(A(1:N,1:N), B(1:N), X(1:N))
```

is used.

24.5.1.3 Intrinisic functions

Using intrinsic functions MAXVAL and MAXLOC

In the context of subroutine Gaussian_Elimination we have used:-

```
MAXVAL ( MAXLOC (ABS ( A ( K:N,K ) ) ) ) + K - 1
```

Breaking this down:-

```
MAXLOC ( ABS ( A (K:N,K) ) )
```

takes the rank one array

$$(\, | A(K,K) | \, , \, | A(K+1,K) | \, , \, \dots \, | A(N,K) | \,) \tag{1}$$

where $| A(K,K) | = \text{ABS}(A(K,K))$ and of length $N- K + 1$. It returns the position of the largest element as a rank one array of size one, e.g. (L)

Applying MAXVAL to this rank one array (L) returns L as a scalar. L being the position of the largest element of array (1).

What we actually want is the position of the largest element of (1) , but in the Kth column of matrix A. We therefore have to add $K-1$ to L to give the actual position in column K of A.

24.6 Notes on module usage and compilation

If we only have one file comprising all of the program units (main program, modules, functions and subroutines) then there is little to worry about. However it is recommended that larger scale programs are developed as a collection of files with related program units in each file, or even one program unit per file. This is more productive in the longer term. This will however lead to problems with modules unless we compile each module **before** we use it in other program units.

Secondly we must use one directory or sub-directory so that the compiler and linker can find each program unit.

Thirdly we must be aware of the file naming conventions used by each compiler implementation we work with. Consider the following:

Fortran Module name	Compaq under DOS	NAG f95 Sun Ultra Sparc
Precisions_defs	Precisions_def.mod	Precisions_def.mod

Whilst in this case they are the same, this is not guaranteed.

24.7 Summary

We have now introduced the concept of a module, another type of program unit, probably one of of the most important features of Fortran 90. We have seen in this chapter how they can be used:

- define global data

- define derived data types

- contain explicit procedure interfaces

- package together procedures

This is a very powerful addition to the language, especially when constructing large programs and procedure libraries.

24.8 Problems

1. Write two functions, one to calculate the volume of a cylinder $\pi r^2 l$ where the radius is r and the length is l, and the other to calculate the area of the base of the cylinder πr^2. Define π as a parameter in a module which is used by the two functions. Now write a main program which prompts the user for the values of r and l, calls the two functions and prints out the results.

2. Make all the real variables in the above problem have 15 significant digits and a range of 10^{-307} to 10^{+307}. Use a module.

24.9 Bibliography

Dongarra, J., Bunch, J.R., Moler, C.B., and Stewart, G.W. *LINPACK User's Guide.* SIAM Publications, Philadelphia, 1979.

- This Fortran 77 package is for the solution of simultaneous systems of linear algebraic equations. Special subroutines are included for many common types of coefficient matrices. The source is available through NETLIB. See Chapter 28 for more details.

Hopkins T., Phillips C., *Numerical Methods in Practice, using the NAG Library.* Addison Wesley.

- This is a very good practical introduction to numerical analysis, with the aim of guiding users to the more commonly used routines in the NAG Fortran 77 library. It does this by introducing topics, giving some background, advantages and disadvantages, and the Fortran 77 code for some of the more well known algorithms. It then introduces the appropriate NAG routine with a brief discussion of its use, calling sequence and any error reporting facilities.
  We've found this invaluable for many of our students who are users of the NAG library but not well versed with numerical analysis.
  Maybe we will see a Fortran 90 version of this book in the near future?

NAG. Visit their web site for up to date details of their products

- http://www.nag.co.uk/

Visual Numerics. Visit their web site for details of their products.

- http://www.vni.com/index.html

25

ISO TR 15580
IEEE Arithmetic

'Can you do Addition?' the White Queen asked. 'What's one and one and one and one and one and one and one and one and one and one?'

'I don't know,' said Alice. 'I lost count.'

Lewis Carroll, *Through the Looking Glass and What Alice Found There*

Aims

The aims of this chapter are to look in more depth at arithmetic and in particular what support Fortran has for the IEEE 754 standard. There is a coverage of:

- Hardware support for arithmetic.

- Integer formats.

- Floating point formats: single and double.

- Special values: denormal, infinity and not a number - NAN.

- Exceptions and flags: divide by zero, inexact, invalid, overflow, underflow.

25 ISO TR 15580 – IEEE Arithmetic

The literature contains details of the IEEE 754 standard and the bibliography contains details of a number of printed and on-line sources.

25.1 History

When we use programming languages to do arithmetic two major concerns are the ability to develop reliable **and** portable numerical software. Arithmetic is done in hardware and there are number of things to consider:

- The range of hardware available both now and in the past.
- The evolution of hardware.

There has been a very considerable change in arithmetic units since the first computers. The following is a list of hardware and computing systems that the authors have some used or have heard of. It is not exhaustive or definitive. It reflects the authors' age and experience.

- CDC
- Cray
- IBM
- ICL
- Fujitsu
- DEC
- Compaq
- Gateway
- Sun
- Silicon Graphics
- Hewlett Packard
- Data General
- Honeywell
- Elliot
- Mostek
- National Semiconductors
- Intel

- Zilog
- Motorola
- Signetics
- Amdahl
- Texas Instruments
- Cyrix

Some of the operating systems include:

- NOS
- NOS/BE
- Kronos
- Unix
- VMS
- Dos
- Windows 3.x
- Windows 95
- Windows 98
- Windows NT
- Windows 2000
- MVS
- VM
- CP/M
- Macintosh
- OS/2

and again the list is not exhaustive or definitive. The intention is to provide with some idea of wide range of hardware, computer manufacturers and operating systems that have existed in the last 50 years.

To help with the anarchy that existed in this area Doctor Robert Stewart (acting on behalf of the IEEE) convened a meeting which led to the birth of IEEE 754.

The first draft was prepared by William Kahan, Jerome Coonen and Harold Stone, called the KCS draft and eventually adopted as IEEE 754. A fascinating account of the development of this standard can be found in *An Interview with the Old Man of Floating Point*, and the bibliography provides a web address of this interview. Kahan went on to get the ACM Turing Award in 1989 for his work in this area

This has become a de facto standard amongst arithmetic units in modern hardware. Note that it is not possible to precisely describe the answers a program will give and the authors of the standard knew this. This goal is virtually impossible to achieve when one considers floating point arithmetic. Reasons for this include:

- The conversions of numbers between decimal and binary formats.
- The use of elementary library functions.
- Results of calculations may be in hardware inaccessible to the programmer.
- Intermediate results in subexpressions or arguments to procedures.

The bibliography contains details of a paper that addresses this issue in much greater depth – *Differences Among IEEE 754 Implementations*.

Fortran is one of a small number of languages to provide access to IEEE arithmetic, and it achieves this via TR1880 which will become an integral part of Fortran 2000. The C standard (C9X) addresses this issue and Java offers limited IEEE arithmetic support. More information can be found in the references at the end of the chapter.

25.2 IEEE 754 Specifications

The standard specifies a number of things including:

- Single precision floating point format.
- Double precision floating point format.
- Two classes of extended floating point formats.
- Accuracy requirements on the following floating point operations:
  - Add.
  - Subtract.
  - Multiply.
  - Divide.
  - Square root.
  - Remainder.
  - Round numbers in floating point format to integer values.

- Convert between different floating point formats.

- Convert between floating point and integer format.

- Compare.

- Base conversion, i.e. when converting between decimal and binary floating point formats and vice versa.

- Exception handling for:

  - Divide by zero.

  - Overflow.

  - Underflow.

  - Invalid operation.

  - Inexact.

- Rounding directions.

- Rounding precisions.

and we will look briefly at each of these requirements.

25.2.1 Single precision floating point format

This is a 32-bit quantity made up of a sign bit, 8-bit biased exponent and 23-bit mantissa. The standard also specifies that certain of the bit patterns are set aside and do not represent normal numbers. This means that valid numbers are in the range 3.40282347E+38 to 1.17549435E-38 and the precision is between 6 and 9 digits depending on the numbers.

The special bit patterns provide the following:

- +0

- -0

- subnormal numbers in the range 1.17549421E-38 to 1.40129846E-45

- + infinity

- - infinity

- quiet NaN (Not a Number)

- signalling NaN

One of the first systems that the authors worked with that had special bits patterns set aside were the CDC 6000 range of computers that had negative indefinite and infinity. The ideas are not new therefore, as this was in the late 1970s.

The support of positive and negative zero means that certain problems can be handled correctly including:

- The evaluation of the log function which has a discontinuity at zero.

- The equation $\sqrt{1/z}=1/\sqrt{z}$ can be solved when $z = -1$.

See also the Kahan paper *Branch Cuts for Complex Elementary Functions, or Much Ado About Nothing's Sign Bit* for more details.

Subnormals, which permit gradual underflow, fill the gap between 0 and the smallest normal number.

Simply stated underflow occurs when the result of an arithmetic operation is so small that it is subject to a larger than normal rounding error when stored. The existence of subnormals means that greater precision is available with these small numbers than normal numbers. The key features of gradual underflow are:

- When underflow does occur there should never be a loss of accuracy any greater than from ordinary roundoff.

- The operations of addition, subtraction comparison and remainder are always exact.

- Algorithms written to take advantage of subnormal numbers have smaller error bounds than other systems.

- If x and y are within a factor of 2 then x-y is error free, which is used in a number of algorithms that increase the precision at critical regions.

The combination of positive and negative zero and subnormal numbers means that when x and y are small and x-y has been flushed to zero the evaluation of:

- $1/(x-y)$

can be flagged and located.

Certain arithmetic operations cause problems including:

- $0 * \infty$

- $0 / 0$

- $\sqrt{x}$ when $x < 0$

and the support for NaN handles these cases.

The support for positive and negative infinity allows the handling of:

- $x / 0$ when x is non-zero and of either sign

and the outcome of this means that we write our programs to take the appropriate action. In some cases this would mean recalculating using another approach.

For more information see the references in the bibliography.

25.2.2   Double precision floating point format

This is a 64 bit quantity made up of a sign bit, 11-bit biased exponent and 52-bit mantissa. As with single precision the standard specifies that certain of the bit patterns are set aside and do not represent normal numbers. This means we have valid numbers in the range 1.7976931348623157E308 to 2.2250738585072014E-308 and precision between 15 and 17 digits depending on the numbers.

As with single precision there are bit patterns set aside for the same special conditions.

Note that this does not mean that the hardware has to handle the manipulation of this 64-bit quantity in an identical fashion. The Sparc and Intel family handle the above as two 32-bit quantities but the order of the 2 component parts is reversed – so called big endian and little endian.

25.2.3   Two classes of extended floating point formats

These formats are not mandatory. A number of variants of double extended exist including:

- Sun – 4 32-bit words, one sign bit, 15-bit biased exponent and 112-bit mantissa, numbers in the range 3.362E-4932 to 1.189E4932, 33 to 36 digits of significance.

- Intel – 10 bytes – one sign bit, 15=bit biased exponent, 63-bit mantissa, numbers in the range 3.362E-4932 to 1.189E4932, 18-21 digits of significance.

- PowerPC – as Sun.

25.2.4   Accuracy requirements

Remainder and compare must be exact. The rest should return the exact result if possible. If not, there are well defined rounding rules to apply.

25.2.5   Base conversion - i.e. when converting between decimal and binary floating point formats and vice versa

These results should be exact if possible; if not the results must differ by tolerances that depend on rounding mode.

25.2.6   Exception handling

It must be possible to signal to the user the occurrence of the following conditions or exceptions:

- Divide by zero.

- Overflow.

- Underflow.

- Invalid operation.

- Inexact.

The ability to detect the above is a big step forward in our ability to write robust and portable code. These operations do occur in calculations and it is essential to have user programmer control over what action to take.

25.2.7   Rounding directions

Four rounding directions are available:

- nearest – the default

- down

- up

- chop.

Access to directed rounding can be used to implement interval arithmetic for example.

25.2.8   Rounding precisions

The only mandatory part here is that machines that perform computations in extended mode let the programmer control the precision via a control word. This means that if software is being developed on machines that support extended modes they can be switched to a mode that would enable the software to run on a system that didn't support extended mode. This area looks like a can of worms. Look at the Kahan paper for more information – *Lecture Notes on the Status of IEEE 754*.

25.3 Resumé

The above has provided a quick tour on IEEE 754. We'll now look at what Fortran has to offer to support the above.

25.4 ISO TR 15580

Fortran provides access to the facilities via the USE statement. The current standard does not have the concept of an intrinsic module. TR 15580 introduces this concept. Three modules are provided and they are:

- ieee_features
- ieee_exceptions
- ieee_arithmetic

The first thing to consider is the degree of conformance to the IEEE standard. It is possible that not all of the features are supported. Thus the first thing to do is run one or more test programs to determine the degree of support for a particular system.

25.4.1 ieee_features module

This module defines a derived type, IEEE_FEATURES_TYPE, and up to 11 constants of that type representing IEEE features:

- IEEE_DATATYPE – whether any IEEE datatypes are available.
- IEEE_DENORMAL – whether IEEE denormal values are available.
- IEEE_DIVIDE – whether division has the accuracy required by IEEE.
- IEEE_HALTING – whether control of halting is supported.
- IEEE_INEXACT_FLAG – whether the inexact exception is supported.
- IEEE_INF – whether IEEE positive and negative infinities are available.
- IEEE_INVALID_FLAG – whether the invalid exception is supported.
- IEEE_NAN – whether IEEE NaNs are available.
- IEEE_ROUNDING – whether all IEEE rounding modes are available.
- IEEE_SQRT – whether SQRT conforms to the IEEE standard.
- IEEE_UNDERFLOW_FLAG – whether underflow is supported.

25.4.2 ieee_exceptions module

This module provides data types, constants and generic procedures for IEEE exceptions.

TYPE IEEE_STATUS_TYPE

Variables of this type can hold a floating-point status value.

SUBROUTINE IEEE_GET_STATUS(STATUS_VALUE)

TYPE(IEEE_STATUS_TYPE),INTENT(OUT) :: STATUS_VALUE

Stores the current floating-point status into the STATUS_VALUE argument.

SUBROUTINE IEEE_SET_STATUS(STATUS_VALUE)

TYPE(IEEE_STATUS_TYPE),INTENT(IN) :: STATUS_VALUE

Sets the current floating-point status from the STATUS_VALUE argument.

TYPE IEEE_FLAG_TYPE

Values of this type specify individual IEEE exception flags; constants for these are available as follows:

TYPE(IEEE_FLAG_TYPE),PARAMETER :: IEEE_DIVIDE_BY_ZERO

TYPE(IEEE_FLAG_TYPE),PARAMETER :: IEEE_INEXACT

TYPE(IEEE_FLAG_TYPE),PARAMETER :: IEEE_INVALID

TYPE(IEEE_FLAG_TYPE),PARAMETER :: IEEE_OVERFLOW

TYPE(IEEE_FLAG_TYPE),PARAMETER :: IEEE_UNDERFLOW

In addition, two array constants are available for indicating common combinations of flags:

TYPE(IEEE_FLAG_TYPE),PARAMETER :: &

IEEE_USUAL(3) = (/&

IEEE_DIVIDE_BY_ZERO,&

IEEE_INVALID, &

IEEE_OVERFLOW /), &

IEEE_ALL(5) = (/&

IEEE_DIVIDE_BY_ZERO,&

IEEE_INEXACT, &

IEEE_INVALID,&

IEEE_OVERFLOW, &

IEEE_UNDERFLOW /)

LOGICAL FUNCTION IEEE_SUPPORT_FLAG(FLAG,X)

TYPE(IEEE_FLAG_TYPE),INTENT(IN) :: FLAG

REAL(kind),INTENT(IN),OPTIONAL :: X

Returns TRUE if detection of the specified IEEE exception is supported for the REAL kind of X (if X is present), or for all REAL kinds (if X is absent).

LOGICAL FUNCTION IEEE_SUPPORT_HALTING(FLAG)

TYPE(IEEE_FLAG_TYPE),INTENT(IN) :: FLAG

Returns TRUE if IEEE_SET_HALTING_MODE can be used to change whether the processor terminates the program on receiving the specified exception.

ELEMENTAL SUBROUTINE &
IEEE_GET_FLAG(FLAG,FLAG_VALUE)

TYPE(IEEE_FLAG_TYPE),INTENT(IN) :: FLAG

LOGICAL,INTENT(OUT) :: FLAG_VALUE

Sets (each element of) FLAG_VALUE to TRUE if the corresponding exception specified by FLAG is signalling, and to FALSE otherwise.

ELEMENTAL SUBROUTINE &
IEEE_GET_HALTING_MODE(FLAG,HALTING)

TYPE(IEEE_FLAG_TYPE),INTENT(IN) :: FLAG

LOGICAL,INTENT(OUT) :: HALTING

Sets (each element of) HALTING to TRUE if the corresponding exception specified by FLAG is signalling, and to FALSE otherwise.

ELEMENTAL SUBROUTINE IEEE_SET_FLAG(FLAG,FLAG_VALUE)

TYPE(IEEE_FLAG_TYPE),INTENT(OUT) :: FLAG

LOGICAL,INTENT(IN) :: FLAG_VALUE

Sets the exception flag specified by (each element of) FLAG to signalling or quiet according to the corresponding element of FLAG_VALUE.

ELEMENTAL SUBROUTINE &
IEEE_SET_HALTING_MODE(FLAG,HALTING)

TYPE(IEEE_FLAG_TYPE),INTENT(OUT) :: FLAG

LOGICAL,INTENT(IN) :: HALTING

Sets the halting mode for each exception specified by FLAG to the value of the corresponding element of HALTING (TRUE = halt).

25.4.3　ieee_arithmetic module

These are given below.

25.4.3.1 IEEE datatype selection

INTEGER FUNCTION SELECTED_REAL_KIND(P,R)

INTEGER(kind1),OPTIONAL :: P

INTEGER(kind2),OPTIONAL :: R

The same as the SELECTED_REAL_KIND intrinsic, but only returns numbers of of IEEE kinds of reals.

25.4.3.2 General support enquiry functions

LOGICAL FUNCTION IEEE_SUPPORT_DATATYPE(X)

REAL(kind),OPTIONAL :: X

Whether IEEE arithmetic is supported for the same kind of REAL as X (or for all REAL kinds if X is absent).

LOGICAL FUNCTION IEEE_SUPPORT_DENORMAL(X)

REAL(kind),OPTIONAL :: X

Whether IEEE denormal values are supported for the same kind of REAL as X (or for all REAL kinds if X is absent).

LOGICAL FUNCTION IEEE_SUPPORT_DIVIDE(X)

REAL(kind),OPTIONAL :: X

Whether division is carried out to the accuracy specified by the IEEE standard for the same kind of REAL as X (or for all REAL kinds if X is absent).

LOGICAL FUNCTION IEEE_SUPPORT_INF(X)

REAL(kind),OPTIONAL :: X

Whether IEEE infinite values are supported for the same kind of REAL as X (or for all REAL kinds if X is absent).

LOGICAL FUNCTION IEEE_SUPPORT_NAN(X)

REAL(kind),OPTIONAL :: X

Whether IEEE NaN (Not-a-Number) values are supported for the same kind of REAL as X (or for all REAL kinds if X is absent).

LOGICAL FUNCTION IEEE_SUPPORT_SQRT(X)

REAL(kind),OPTIONAL :: X

Whether SQRT conforms to the IEEE standard for the same kind of REAL as X (or for all REAL kinds if X is absent).

LOGICAL FUNCTION IEEE_SUPPORT_STANDARD(X)

REAL(kind),OPTIONAL :: X

Whether all the IEEE facilities specified by the TR are supported for the same kind of REAL as X (or for all REAL kinds if X is absent).

25.4.3.3 Rounding modes

TYPE IEEE_ROUND_TYPE

Values of this type specify the IEEE rounding mode.

TYPE (IEEE_ROUND_TYPE) , &
PARAMETER :: IEEE_DOWN

TYPE (IEEE_ROUND_TYPE) , &
PARAMETER :: IEEE_NEAREST

TYPE (IEEE_ROUND_TYPE) ,
PARAMETER :: IEEE_TO_ZERO

TYPE (IEEE_ROUND_TYPE) , PARAMETER :: IEEE_UP

LOGICAL FUNCTION IEEE_SUPPORT_ROUNDING(ROUND_VALUE,X)

TYPE(IEEE_ROUND_TYPE),INTENT(IN) :: ROUND_VALUE

REAL(kind),OPTIONAL :: X

Whether the specified IEEE rounding mode is supported for the same kind of REAL as X (or for all REAL kinds if X is absent).

SUBROUTINE IEEE_GET_ROUNDING_MODE(ROUND_VALUE)

TYPE(IEEE_ROUND_TYPE),INTENT(OUT) :: ROUND_VALUE

Sets the ROUND_VALUE argument to the current IEEE rounding mode.

SUBROUTINE IEEE_SET_ROUNDING_MODE(ROUND_VALUE)

TYPE (IEEE_ROUND_TYPE) , INTENT(IN) :: ROUND_VALUE

Sets the current IEEE rounding mode to that specified by ROUND_VALUE.

25.4.3.4 Number classification

TYPE IEEE_CLASS_TYPE

Values of this type indicate the IEEE class of a number.

TYPE (IEEE_CLASS_TYPE) , &
PARAMETER :: IEEE_NEGATIVE_DENORMAL

TYPE (IEEE_CLASS_TYPE) , PARAMETER :: IEEE_NEGATIVE_INF

TYPE (IEEE_CLASS_TYPE) , PARAMETER :: IEEE_NEGATIVE_NORMAL

TYPE (IEEE_CLASS_TYPE) , PARAMETER :: IEEE_NEGATIVE_ZERO

TYPE (IEEE_CLASS_TYPE) , PARAMETER :: IEEE_POSITIVE_DENORMAL

TYPE (IEEE_CLASS_TYPE) , PARAMETER :: IEEE_POSITIVE_INF

TYPE(IEEE_CLASS_TYPE) , PARAMETER :: IEEE_POSITIVE_NORMAL

TYPE(IEEE_CLASS_TYPE) , PARAMETER :: IEEE_POSITIVE_ZERO

TYPE(IEEE_CLASS_TYPE) , PARAMETER :: IEEE_QUIET_NAN

TYPE(IEEE_CLASS_TYPE) , PARAMETER :: IEEE_signalling_NAN

ELEMENTAL TYPE(IEEE_CLASS_TYPE) FUNCTION IEEE_CLASS(X)

REAL(kind),INTENT(IN) :: X

Returns the appropriate value of IEEE_CLASS_TYPE for the number X, which may be of any IEEE kind.

In addition to ISO/IEC TR 15580:1998(E), the module IEEE_ARITHMETIC defines the "==" and "/=" operators for the IEEE_CLASS_TYPE. These may be used to test the return value of the IEEE_CLASS function, e.g.

USE,INTRINSIC :: IEEE_ARITHMETIC, ONLY: IEEE_CLASS, &

IEEE_QUIET_NAN, OPERATOR(==)

    ...

IF (IEEE_CLASS(X)==IEEE_QUIET_NAN) THEN

    ...

ELEMENTAL REAL(kind) FUNCTION IEEE_VALUE(X,CLASS)

REAL(kind),INTENT(IN) :: X

TYPE(IEEE_CLASS_TYPE),INTENT(IN) :: CLASS

Returns a sample value of the specified class for the same kind of real as X, which may be of any IEEE kind.

ELEMENTAL LOGICAL FUNCTION IEEE_IS_FINITE(X)

REAL(kind),INTENT(IN) :: X

Returns TRUE if X is not infinite or NaN.

ELEMENTAL LOGICAL FUNCTION IEEE_IS_NAN(X)

REAL(kind),INTENT(IN) :: X

Returns TRUE if X is either a signalling or quiet NaN.

ELEMENTAL LOGICAL FUNCTION IEEE_IS_NEGATIVE(X)

REAL(kind),INTENT(IN) :: X

Returns TRUE if X is negative, including negative zero.

ELEMENTAL LOGICAL FUNCTION IEEE_IS_NORMAL(X)

REAL(kind),INTENT(IN) :: X

Returns TRUE if X is not an infinity, NaN, or denormal.

ELEMENTAL LOGICAL FUNCTION IEEE_UNORDERED(X,Y)

REAL(kind),INTENT(IN) :: X,Y

Returns TRUE if X is a NaN or if Y is a NaN.

25.4.3.5 Arithmetic operations

ELEMENTAL REAL(kind) FUNCTION IEEE_COPY_SIGN(X,Y)

REAL (kind) , INTENT(IN) :: X,Y

Returns X with the sign of Y, even for NaNs and infinities.

ELEMENTAL REAL (kind) FUNCTION IEEE_LOGB(X)

REAL (kind) , INTENT(IN) :: X

Returns the unbiased exponent as a REAL value;

if X is zero, IEEE_DIVIDE_BY_ZERO signals and the result is -infinity if IEEE infinities are supported for that kind, and -HUGE(X) if not;

if X is infinite, the result is +infinity;

if X is a NaN, the result is a quiet NaN (the same one if X is a quiet NaN); otherwise the result is EXPONENT(X)-1.

ELEMENTAL REAL (kind) FUNCTION IEEE_NEXT_AFTER(X,Y)

REAL (kind) , INTENT(IN) :: X,Y

The same as NEAREST(X,1.0_kind) for Y>X and NEAREST(X,-1.0_kind) for Y<X; if Y==X, the result is X, if either X or Y are NaNs the result is one of these NaNs.

ELEMENTAL REAL (kind) FUNCTION IEEE_REM(X,Y)

REAL (kind) , INTENT(IN) :: X,Y

X-Y*N exactly, where N is the integer nearest to the exact value X/Y. If the result is zero, it has the same sign as X.

This function is not affected by the rounding mode.

ELEMENTAL REAL (kind) FUNCTION IEEE_RINT(X)

REAL (kind) , INTENT(IN) :: X

Round to an integer according to the current rounding mode.

ELEMENTAL REAL (kind) FUNCTION IEEE_SCALB(X,I)

REAL (kind1) , INTENT(IN) :: X

INTEGER (kind2) , INTENT(IN) :: I

The same as SCALE(X,I).

25.5 Summary

Support for the above is relatively limited at the time of writing this book. There is always a time lag between the formal publication of a standard and the implementation in production compilers. As compiler support improves examples will be added to our web site. Our home page is:

- http://www.kcl.ac.uk/kis/support/cit//fortran/f90home.html

25.6 Bibliography

Hauser J.R., *Handling Floating Point Exceptions in Numeric Programs*, ACM Transaction on Programming Languages and Systems, Vol. 18, No. 2, March 1996, Pages 139–174.

- The paper looks at a number of techniques for handling floating point exceptions in numeric code. One of the conclusions is for better structured support for floating point exception handling in new programming languages, or of course later standards of existing languages.

IEEE, *IEEE Standard for Binary Floating-Point Arithmetic, ANSI/IEEE Std 754-1985*, Institute of Electrical and Electronic Engineers Inc.

- The formal definition of IEEE 754.

Knuth D., *Seminumerical Algorithms*, Addison Wesley.

- There is a coverage of floating point arithmetic, multiple precision arithmetic, radix conversion and rational arithmetic.

Sun, *Numerical Computation Guide*, SunPro.

- Very good coverage of the numeric formats for IEEE Standard 754 for Binary Floating-Point Arithmetic. All SunPro compiler products support the features of the IEEE 754 standard.

25.6.1   Web based sources

http://validgh.com/goldberg/addendum.html

- *Differences Among IEEE 754 Implementations.* The material in this paper will eventually be included in the Sun Numerical Computation Guide as an addendum to Appendix D, David Goldberg's *What Every Computer Scientist Should Know about Floating Point Arithmetic.*

http://docs.sun.com/

- Follow the links to the *Floating Point and Common Tools AnswerBook*. The *Numerical Computation Guide* can be browsed on-line or downloaded as a pdf file. The last time we checked it was about 260 pages. Good source of information if you have Sun equipment.

http://www.validgh.com/

- This web site contains technical and business information relating to the validgh professional consulting practice of David G. Hough. Contains links to the Goldberg paper and the above addendum by Doug Priest.

http://babbage.cs.qc.edu/courses/cs341/IEEE-754references.html

- Brief coverage of IEEE arithmetic with pointers to further sources. There is also a coverage of the storage layout and ranges of floating point numbers. Computer Science 341 is an introduction to the design of a computer's hardware, particularly the CPU and memory systems.

http://www.nag.co.uk/nagware/NP/TR.html

- NAG provide coverage of TR 15580 and TR 15581. The first is the support Fortran has for IEEE arithmetic.

http://www.cs.berkeley.edu/~wkahan/

- Willam Kahan home page.

http://www.cs.berkeley.edu/~wkahan/ieee754status/754story.html

- *An Interview with the Old Man of Floating Point.* Reminiscences elicited from William Kahan by Charles Severance, which appears in an issue of IEEE Computer - March 1998 (not confirmed).

http://www.cs.berkeley.edu/~wkahan/ieee754status/ieee754.ps

- Lecture Notes on the Status of IEEE Standard 754 for Binary Floating-Point Arithmetic. Well worth a read.

http://www.stewart.cs.sdsu.edu/cs575/labs/l3floatpt.html

- *CS 575 Supercomputing – Lab 3: Floating Point Arithmetic.* CS 575 is an interdisciplinary course to introduce students in the sciences and engineering to advanced computing techniques using the supercomputers at the San Diego Supercomputer Center (SDSC).

http://www.mathcom.com/nafaq/index.html

- *FAQ: Numerical Analysis and Associated Fields Resource Guide.* A summary of Internet resources for a number of fields related to numerical analysis.

http://www.math.psu.edu/dna/disasters/ariadne.html

- *The Explosion of the Ariane 5*: A 64-bit floating point number relating to the horizontal velocity of the rocket with respect to the platform was converted to a 16-bit signed integer. The number was larger than 32,768, the largest integer storeable in a 16-bit signed integer, and thus the conversion failed.

25.6.2 Hardware sources

Osbourne A., Kane G., *4-bit and 8-bit Microprocessor Handbook,* Osbourne/McGraw Hill.

- Good source of information on 4 and 8 bit microprocessors.

Osbourne A., Kane G., *16 Bit Microprocessor Handbook,* Osbourne/McGraw Hill.

- Ditto 16 bit microprocessors.

Intel, *386 DX Microprocessor Hardware Reference Manual*, Intel.

- The first Intel offering with 32 bit addressing.

Intel, *80386 System Software Writer's Guide,* Intel.

- Developer's Guide to the above.

http://www.intel.com/

- Intel's home page.

http://developer.intel.com/design/pentiumiii/

- Details of the Pentium III processor.

http://www.cyrix.com/

- Cyrix home page.

Bhandarkar D.P., *Alpha Implementations and Architecture: Complete Reference and Guide,* Digital Press

- Looks at some of the trade offs and design philosophy behind the alpha chip. The author worked with VAX, MicroVAX and VAX vectors as well as the Prism. Also looks at the GEM compiler technology that DEC/Compaq use.

http://www.digital.com/alphaserver/workstations/

- Home page for the Compaq/DEC Alpha systems.

http://www.sgi.com/

- Silicon Graphics home page.

http://www.sun.com/

- Sun home page.

http://www.ibm.com/

- IBM home page.

25.6.3 Operating Systems

Deitel H.M., *An Introduction to Operating Systems*, Addison Wesley, 1990.

- The revised first edition includes case studies of Unix, VMS, CP/M, MVS and VM. The second edition adds OS/2 and the Macintosh operating systems. There is a coverage of hardware, software, firmware, process management, process concepts, asynchronous concurrent processes, concurrent programming, deadlock and indefinite postponement, storage management, real storage, virtual storage, processor management, distributed computing, disk performance optimization, file and database systems, performance, coprocessors, risc, data flow, analytic modelling, networks, security and concludes with case studies of the above operating systems. The book is well written and an easy read.

25.6.4 Java and IEEE 754

http://www.cs.berkeley.edu/~darcy/Borneo/

- *Borneo Language Homepage*: Borneo is a dialect of the Java language designed to have true support for the IEEE 754 floating point standard. The status of arithmetic in Java is fluid. At the time of writing this book Sun had withdrawn from the formal language standardization process. Sun have a publication at their web site that addresses changes to the Java language specification for JDK Release 1.2 floating point arithmetic. Their home Java page is:

- http://www.java.sun.com/

25.6.5   C and IEEE 754

http://wwwold.dkuug.dk/JTC1/SC22/WG14/

- The official home of JTC1/SC22/WG14 - C. The C programming language standard ISO/IEC 9899 was adopted by ISO in 1990. ANSI then replaced their first standard X3.159 by the ANSI/ISO 9899 standard identical to ISO/IEC 9899:1990.

http://www.c9x.org/

- Another source of information regarding C9X. There is a draft of the standard available and Annex F, G and H contain details of the changes concerning arithmetic.

26

Formal Syntax and Some Additional Features

Once upon a time, a very long time ago now, about last Friday, Winnie-the-Pooh lived in a forest all by himself under the name of Sanders.

(*"What does 'under the name' mean" asked Christopher Robin, "It means he had the name over the door in gold letters and lived under it"*...)

A.A. Milne., *Winnie-the-Pooh*.

Aims

The aims of this chapter are to introduce formal definitions of a number of concepts and also look at some of the more advanced features of Fortran 95, in particular:

- program units
- functions
- subroutines
- modules
- scope
- modules and scope
  - public
  - private
  - rename
- optional arguments.

26 Formal Syntax and Some Additional Features

In the coverage so far we have relied on quite lax definitions of the concepts introduced, choosing to provide concrete examples, rather than overwhelm the reader
with rather indigestible chunks of grammar and syntax. In this chapter we look
more formally at some of the earlier concepts as the reliable construction of larger
programs requires a more thorough understanding of these concepts.

We will also look at a number of advanced features of Fortran 95.

This material draws on Chapter 2 of the standard (Fortran terms and concepts) and
Annex D of the standard.

26.1 Program units

Program units are the fundamental building block of Fortran 95. A program unit
may be one of:

- a main program
- a function
- a subroutine
- a module

and for the first three there will be a specification part, an execution part. A module
does not have an executable component, unless there is a **contain**ed subprogram.

26.2 Procedure – function or subroutine

A procedure is either a function or subroutine. A function is a procedure that is
invoked in an expression, whilst a subroutine is a procedure that is invoked by the
CALL statement.

26.2.1   Internal procedure

An internal procedure is one that is CONTAINed within a program unit. An internal procedure is local to its host. There are examples of this with the Stirling
function in Chapter 14 and the QuickSort recursive subroutine in Chapter 23.

26.3 Module

The module program unit is a very powerful feature of Fortran 95. They are used
to:

- provide access to type definitions;
- provide access to global data;

- provide user defined operators;
- provide the ability to manage data types and valid operations on those types – data abstraction;
- provide packaging of functions and subroutines.

Access to some or all of the components of modules can be controlled by the use of a number of additional extensions that we will cover later, namely PRIVATE, PUBLIC and RENAME.

26.4 Executable statements

Program execution is a sequence of computational actions.

26.5 Statement ordering

The following figure summarizes the statement ordering.

FORMAT statements may appear anywhere between the USE statement and the CONTAINS statement.

The following table summarizes the usage of the various statements within individual scoping units.

Kind of scoping unit	Main program	Module	External sub program	Module sub program	Internal sub program	Interface body
USE	Y	Y	Y	Y	Y	Y
FORMAT	Y	N	Y	Y	Y	N
Misc Dec [1]	Y	Y	Y	Y	Y	Y
Derived type definition	Y	Y	Y	Y	Y	Y
Interface block	Y	Y	Y	Y	Y	Y
Executable statement	Y	N	Y	Y	Y	N
CONTAINS	Y	Y	Y	Y	N	N

[1] Misc Dec (Miscellaneous declaration) are PARAMETER statements, IMPLICIT statements, type declaration statements and specification statements.

PROGRAM, FUNCTION, SUBROUTINE,
MODULE statement

USE statements

IMPLICIT NONE

| PARAMETER | IMPLICIT |
| statements | statements |

| FORMAT | PARAMETER | Derived-type definitions, interface blocks, type declaration statements, statement function statements, and specification statements |
| statements | statements | |

| DATA | Executable |
| statements | constructs |

CONTAINS statement

Internal subprograms
or module subprograms

END statement

Figure 26.1 Statement ordering

26.6 Entities

The Fortran standard uses the word entity rather loosely. An entity may be identified by:

- a name
- a label
- an external I/O unit number
- an operator symbol
- an assignment symbol

and by means of association an entity may be referred to by the same identifier or a different identifier in a different scoping unit, or by a different identifier in the same scoping unit. Some examples of entities are:

- a variable

- a program unit

- an expression value

and we'll look at this in more depth in the next section.

26.7 Scope and association

In the simplest case scope refers to the places within a program where a name has meaning. Where we only have one program unit then we do not have any problems with the concept of scope as all named entities are available within that program unit.

The problem becomes more complex when we start constructing programs that comprise one or more procedures and use internal procedures and external libraries of routines.

A program consists of one or more non-overlapping scoping units. A scoping unit is:

- a program unit or subprogram, excluding derived type definitions, proce-dure interface bodies, and subprograms contained within it;

- a procedure interface body, excluding any derived type definitions and pro-cedure interface bodies contained within it;

- a derived type definition;

and a scoping unit that encloses another scoping unit is called the host scoping unit.

The USE statement provides the means by which a scoping unit accesses named data objects, derived data types, procedures and generic identifiers in a module. The entities in the scoping unit are said to be use associated with the entities in the module.

Using the sorting program in Chapter 23 as an example we have:

- Main program

    Variables: How_Many, File_Name, Raw_Data, cputime, T1, T2, T3, T4, T5

- CPU_TIME(cputime)

    Duumy argument: cputime

    No accessible variables

- Read_Data(File_Name,Raw_Data,How_Many)

Dummy arguments: File_Name,Raw_Data,How_Many

Local variable: I

- Sort_Data(Raw_Data,How_Many)

    Dummy arguments: Raw_Data,How_Many

    Contains:

    Quick_Sort(L,R)

        Dummy arguments: L,R

        Local variables: I,J,V,T

- Print_Data(Raw_Data,How_Many)

    Dummy arguments: Raw_Data,How_Many

    Local variable: I

The variables How_Many, File_Name, Raw_Data, cputime are declared within the main program. We make them available in the four subroutines by argument association.

The variables T1, T2, T3, T4, T5 are declared within the main program. These variables are purely local to the main program.

The variable I in the Read_Data routine is local to that routine and is not available elsewhere.

The variables Raw_Data and How_Many in the Sort_Data subroutine are globally available to the Quick Sort subroutine as QuickSort is CONTAINed within the Sort Data subroutine. This is called host association.

The variables I, J, V and T are purely local to the QuickSort routine and not available elsewhere. Note also, as this routine is recursive, there will be multiple instances of this routine in existence as the sort proceeds and therefore multiple and completely separate instances of these four variables.

The Print_Data routine has How_Many and Raw_Data available via argument association and I is purely local.

Thus Fortran provides complete decoupling of entity names between program units automatically. The only way that communication can take place is via argument association and host association in the above example.

26.8 Modules and scope

Modules provide a very powerful way to make data available throughout program units. In the example at the start of the previous chapter we had a module that contained a definition for π. We then **used** this module in each subprogram unit that needed it. Thus we have the ability with modules to extend the way in which we make named entities available throughout program units.

The power of modules increases further when we use them to make data types available and operations on these data types.

When a module contains an executable procedure the problem immediately arises as to the accessibility of variables within the module, and potential name conflicts. Fortran provides a number of facilities to control things in a situation like this.

26.8.1 Public and private attributes

By default entities within a module are PUBLIC, i.e. they are visible to every program unit in which the module is made available. An entity is one of:

- type definition

- variable

- non-intrinsic procedure

- named constants.

Entities that are made available via the USE statement are said to be accessed by *use association.*

If we wished to hide some entities in a module we would add an attribute of PRIVATE to their declaration, e.g. in Section 24.4 in an earlier chapter we could make Step_Interval and Smallest_Step invisible to the main program in which the module is **used**. We could do this in the following way:

```
MODULE ODES
IMPLICIT NONE
INTEGER , PARAMETER :: Long=SELECTED_REAL_KIND(15,307)
REAL (Long) , PRIVATE :: Step_Interval =100.0_Long
REAL (Long) , PRIVATE :: Smallest_Step =1.0E-6_Long
. . .
END MODULE ODES
```

Step_Interval and Smallest_Step are now hidden from the main program in which the module is used but the parameter Long is available because by default it has PUBLIC attribute.

There is an additional form of PRIVATE that enables us to hide non-intrinsic procedures, generic names and operator and assignment overloading. See Chapter 27 for an example of operator and assignment overloading.

There are also additional forms of the USE statement that, together with the above two forms, provide most of the flexibility we require in this area.

26.8.2   USE, ONLY and Rename

In the examples so far we have only had simple forms of the USE statement, e.g.

```
USE Module_Name
```

There are a number of additional forms that are very useful. One provides the ability to import **only** a subset of the entities from the used module, and is of the form:

```
USE Module-Name , ONLY : access-list
```

where access-list is any of the **public** entities in the module, e.g.

```
USE String_Module , ONLY : X,Y
```

and only the variables X and Y in module String_Module are available to the program unit in which this USE statement appears.

The second form provides the ability to rename entities to avoid name conflicts, and is of the form:

```
USE Module-Name [local-name=>] module-entity-name
```

The local-name (if present) is the new name of that entity in the using program unit, e.g.

```
USE Tree_Module , Tree_Walk => TW
```

The module variable Tree_Walk is known as TW in the program unit in which the USE statement appears.

26.9   Keyword and optional arguments

The examples of procedures so far have assumed that the dummy arguments and the corresponding arguments are in the same position, i.e. we are using positional arguments. Fortran 95 also provides the ability to supply the actual arguments to a procedure by keyword, and hence in any order.

To do this the name of the dummy argument is referred to as the keyword and is specified in the actual argument list in the form:-

```
dummy-argument = actual-argument
```

To illustrate this, let us consider a subroutine to solve ordinary differential equations. The full subroutine and explanation are given in the next chapter.

```
SUBROUTINE Runge_Kutta_Merson(Y,FUN,IFAIL,N,A,B,TOL)
```

where A is the initial point, B is the end point at which the solution is required, TOL is the accuracy to which the solution is required and N is the number of equations. The rest of the dummy arguments are explained in the next chapter.

The subroutine can be called as follows:

```
CALL Runge_Kutta_Merson( Y , Fun1 , IFAIL , A=0.0 ,&
    B=8.0 , Tol=1.0E-6 , N=3)
```

where the dummy arguments A, B, Tol and N are now being used as keywords. The use of keyword arguments make the code easier to read and decreases the need to remember their precise position in the argument list.

Also with Fortran 95 comes the ability to specify that an argument is optional. This is very useful when designing procedures for use by a range of programmers. Inside a procedure defaults can be set for the optional arguments providing an easy-to-use interface, at the same time allowing sophisticated users a comprehensive interface.

To declare a dummy argument to be optional the OPTIONAL attribute can be used. For example the last dummy argument Tol for the subroutine Runge_Kutta_Merson could be declared to be optional (although internally in the subroutine the code would have to be changed to allow for this), e.g.

```
SUBROUTINE Runge_Kutta_Merson(Y,FUN,IFAIL,N,A,B,Tol)
USE Precisions
    REAL(Long), INTENT(INOUT), OPTIONAL :: Tol
```

and because it is at the end of the dummy argument list, calling the subroutine with a positional argument list, Tol can be omitted, e.g.

```
CALL Runge_Kutta_Merson(Y,Fun1,IFAIL,N,A,B)
```

The code of the subroutine will need to be changed to check to see if the argument Tol is supplied, the intrinsic function PRESENT being available for this purpose.

A number of points need to be noted when using keyword and optional arguments:

- If all the actual arguments use keywords they may appear in any order.

- When only some of the actual arguments use keywords the first part of the list must be positional followed by keyword arguments in any order.

- When using a mixture of positional and keyword arguments, once a keyword argument is used all subsequent arguments must be specified by keyword.

- If an actual argument is omitted the corresponding optional dummy argument must not be redefined or referenced, except as an argument to the PRESENT intrinsic function.

- If an optional dummy argument is at the end of the argument list then it can just be omitted from the actual argument list.

- Keyword arguments are needed when an optional argument not at the end of an argument list is omitted, unless all the remaining arguments are omitted as well.

- Keyword and optional arguments require explicit procedure interfaces, i.e. the procedure must be internal, a module procedure or have an interface block available in the calling program unit.

A number of the intrinsic procedures we have used have optional arguments. Consult Appendix D for details.

26.10 Syntax summary of some frequently used Fortran constructs

The following provides simple syntactical definitions for of some of the more frequently used parts of Fortran 95.

26.10.1 Main program

```
PROGRAM [ program-name ]
   [ specification-construct ] ...
   [ executable-construct ] ...
   [CONTAINS
   [ internal procedure ] ... ]
END [ PROGRAM [ program-name ] ]
```

26.10.2 Subprogram

```
procedure heading
   [ specification-construct ] ...
   [ executable-construct ] ...
   [CONTAINS
   [ internal procedure ] ... ]
```

```
procedure ending
```

26.10.3 Module

```
MODULE name
   [ specification-construct ] ...
   [CONTAINS
   subprogram
   [ subprogram ] ... ]
END [ MODULE   [ module-name ]
```

26.10.4 Internal procedure

```
procedure heading
   [ specification construct ] ...
   [ executable construct ] ...
procedure ending
```

26.10.5 Procedure heading

```
[ RECURSIVE ] [ type specification ] FUNCTION
function-name &
   ( [ dummy argument list ] ) [ RESULT ( result name ) ]
[ RECURSIVE ] SUBROUTINE subroutine name &
   [ ( [ dummy argument list ] ) ]
```

26.10.6 Procedure ending

```
END [ FUNCTION [ function name ] ]
END [ SUBROUTINE [ subroutine name ] ]
```

26.10.7 Specification construct

```
derived type definition
interface block
specification statement
```

26.10.8 Derived type definition

```
TYPE [[ , access specification ] :: ] type name
   [ PRIVATE ]
   [ SEQUENCE ]
   [ type specification [[ , POINTER ] :: ] component
specification list ]
   ...
   END TYPE [ type name ]
```

26.10.9 Interface block

```
INTERFACE [ generic specification ]
    [ procedure heading
      [ specification construct ] ...
  procedure ending ] ...
    [ MODULE PROCEDURE module procedure name list ] ...
END INTERFACE
```

26.10.10 Specification statement

```
ALLOCATABLE [ :: ] allocatable array list
DIMENSION array dimension list
EXTERNAL external name list
FORMAT ( [ format specification list ] )
IMPLICIT implicit specification
INTENT ( intent specification ) :: dummy argument
name list
INTRINSIC intrinsic procedure name list
OPTIONAL [ :: ] optional object list
PARAMETER ( named constant definition list )
POINTER [ :: ] pointer name list
PUBLIC [ [ :: ] module entity name list ]
PRIVATE[ [ :: ] module entity name list ]
SAVE[ [ :: ] saved object list ]
TARGET [ :: ] target name list
USE module name [ , rename list ]
USE  module name , ONLY : [ access list ]
type specification [ [ , attribute specification ]
...  :: &
      object declaration list
```

26.10.11 Type specification

```
INTEGER [ ( [ KIND= ] kind parameter ) ]
REAL[ ( [ KIND= ] kind parameter ) ]
COMPLEX[ ( [ KIND= ] kind parameter ) ]
CHARACTER[ ( [ KIND= ] kind parameter ) ]
CHARACTER[ ( [ KIND= ] kind parameter ) ] &
   [ LEN= ] length parameter )
LOGICAL[ ( [ KIND= ] kind parameter ) ]
TYPE ( type name )
```

26.10.12 Attribute specification

```
ALLOCATABLE
DIMENSION ( array specification )
EXTERNAL
INTENT ( intent specification )
INTRINSIC
OPTIONAL
PARAMETER
POINTER
PRIVATE
PUBLIC
SAVE
TARGET
```

26.10.13 Executable construct

```
action statement
case construct
do construct
if construct
where construct
```

26.10.14 Action statement

```
ALLOCATE ( allocation list ) [ ,STAT= scalar integer
variable ] )
CALL subroutinename [ ( [ actual argument
specification list] ) ]
CLOSE ( close specification list )
CYCLE [ do construct name ]
DEALLOCATE( name list ) [ , STAT= scalar integer
variable ] )
ENDFILE external file unit
EXIT [ do construct name ]
GOTO label
IF ( scalar logical expression ) action statement
INQUIRE ( inquire specification list ) [ output item
list ]
NULLIFY ( pointer object list )
OPEN ( connect specification list )
PRINT format [ , output item list ]
READ (i/o control specification list ) [ input item
list ]
READ format [ , output item list ]
```

```
RETURN [ scalar integer expression ]
REWIND ( position specification list )
STOP [ access code ]
WHERE ( array logical expression ) array assignment
expression
WRITE ( i/o control specification list ) [ output
item list ]
pointer variable => target expression
variable = expression
```

27

Case Studies

The good teacher is a guide who helps others to dispense with his services.

R. S. Peters, *Ethics and Education.*

Aims

The aims of this chapter are to look at several complete examples highlighting a variety of aspects of the use of Fortran 95:

- the solution of a set of ordinary differential equations using the Runga–Kutta–Merson method, with the use of a procedure as a parameter, and the use of work arrays;

- generic procedures;

- a function that returns a variable length array;

- operator and assignment overloading;

- diagonal extraction of a matrix;

- modules and packing;

- pure and elemental functions;

- elemental subroutines.

27 Case Studies

This chapter looks at more realistic case studies of the use of Fortran 95 and its new features. There are examples of:

- the solution of a set of ordinary differential equations using the Runga–Kutta–Merson method, with the use of a procedure as a parameter, and the use of work arrays;

- the construction of generic procedures in Fortran 95. Many of the internal functions will take arguments of a variety of data types and return a result of the same type, e.g. SINE will take an integer argument, real argument of whatever precision, complex argument and return the appropriate result;

- operator and assignment overloading and the use of a MODULE PROCEDURE;

- the extraction of the diagonal elements of a matrix;

- pure and elemental functions;

- elemental subroutines.

The examples have been chosen to highlight the better features of Fortran 95 and what is possible with a modern language.

27.1 Example 1 – Solving a system of first order ordinary differential equations using Runga–Kutta–Merson

Simulation and mathematical modelling of a wide range of physical processes often leads to a system of ordinary differential equations to be solved. Ordinary differential equations also occur when approximate techniques are applied to more complex problems. We will restrict ourselves to a class of ordinary differential equations called initial value problems. These are systems for which all conditions are given at the same value of the independent variable. We will further restrict ourselves to first order initial value problems of the form:

$$\dot{y}_1 = f_1(\underline{y}, t)$$
$$\dot{y}_2 = f_2(\underline{y}, t)$$
$$\cdot = \cdot$$
$$\dot{y}_n = f_n(\underline{y}, t)$$

or

$$\dot{\underline{y}} = \underline{f}(\underline{y}, t) \tag{1}$$

with initial conditions

$$\underline{y}(t_0) = \underline{y}_0$$

where

$$y = \begin{pmatrix} y_1 \\ \cdot \\ y_n \end{pmatrix} \qquad f = \begin{pmatrix} f_1 \\ \cdot \\ f_n \end{pmatrix} \qquad \underline{y}_0 = \begin{pmatrix} y_1(t_0) \\ \cdot \\ y_n(t_0) \end{pmatrix}$$

If we have a system of ordinary differential equations of higher order then they can be reformulated to a system of order one. See the NAG library documentation for solving ordinary differential equations.

One well known class of methods for solving initial value ordinary differential equations is Runge–Kutta. In this example we have coded the Runga–Kutta–Merson algorithm which is a fourth order method and solves (1) from a point $t = A$ to a point $t = B$.

It starts with a step length $h = (B - A)/100$ and includes a local error control strategy such that the solution at $t+h$ is accepted if:

$|error\ estimate| <\ user\ defined\ tolerance.$

If this isn't satisfied the step length h is halved and the solution attempt is repeated until the above is satisfied or the step length is too small and the problem left unsolved. Assuming the error criterion was satisfied the algorithm progresses with a suitable step length solving the equations at intermediate points until the end point B is reached. For a full discussion of the algorithm and the error control mechanism used see *Numerical Methods in Practice*, Tim Hopkins and Chris Phillips.

```
MODULE Precisions
INTEGER, PARAMETER:: Long=SELECTED_REAL_KIND(15,307)
END MODULE Precisions
SUBROUTINE Runge_Kutta_Merson(Y,FUN,IFAIL,N,A,B,Tol)
!
! Runge-Kutta-Merson method for the solution
! of a system of N
! 1st order initial value ordinary
! differential equations.
! The routine tries to integrate from T=A to T=B with
! initial conditions in Y, subject to the
! condition that the
! Absolute Error Estimate <= Tol. The step length is
! adjusted automatically to meet this condition.
! If the routine is successful it returns with
```

```
! IFAIL = 0,  T=B and
! the solution in Y.
!
USE Precisions
!
IMPLICIT NONE
! Define arguments
!
REAL (Long),INTENT(INOUT):: Y(:)
REAL(Long),  INTENT(IN)::A,B,Tol
INTEGER,INTENT(IN)::N
INTEGER,INTENT(OUT)::IFAIL
!
INTERFACE
   SUBROUTINE FUN(T,Y,F,N)
   USE Precisions
   IMPLICIT NONE
   REAL(Long),INTENT(IN),DIMENSION(:)::Y
   REAL(Long),INTENT(OUT),DIMENSION(:)::F
   REAL(Long),INTENT(IN)::T
   INTEGER,INTENT(IN)::N
   END SUBROUTINE FUN
END INTERFACE
!
! Local variables
!
REAL(Long), DIMENSION(1:SIZE(Y)):: &
            S1,S2,S3,S4,S5,New_Y_1,New_Y_2,Error
REAL(Long)::T,H,H2,H3,H6,H8,Factor=1.E-2_Long
REAL(Long)::Smallest_step=1.E-6_Long,Max_Error
INTEGER::No_of_steps=0
!
   IFAIL=0
!
! Check input parameters
!
   IF(N <= 0 .OR. A == B .OR. Tol <= 0.0) THEN
      IFAIL = 1
      RETURN
   ENDIF
!
! Initialize T to be start of interval and
```

```
! H to be 1/100 of interval
   T=A
   H=(B-A)/100.0_Long
   DO                            ! Beginning of Repeat loop
      H2=H/2.0_Long
      II3-II/3.0_Long
      H6=H/6.0_Long
      H8=H/8.0_Long
!
! Calculate S1,S2,S3,S4,S5
!
! S1=F(T,Y)

      CALL FUN(T,Y,S1,N)

      New_Y_1=Y+H3*S1

! S2 = F(T+H/3,Y+H/3*S1)

      CALL FUN(T+H3,New_Y_1,S2,N)
      New_Y_1=Y+H6*S1+H6*S2

! S3=F(T+H/3,Y+H/6*S1+H/6*S2)

      CALL FUN(T+H3,New_Y_1,S3,N)

      New_Y_1=Y+H8*(S2+3.0_Long*S3)

! S4=F(T+H/2,Y+H/8*(S2+3*S3))

      CALL FUN(T+H2,New_Y_1,S4,N)
      New_Y_1=Y+H2*(S1-3.0_Long*S3+4.0_Long*S4)

! S5=F(T+H,Y+H/2*(S1-3*S3+4*S4))

      CALL FUN(T+H,New_Y_1,S5,N)
!
! Calculate values at T+H
!
      New_Y_1=Y+H6*(S1+4.0_Long*S4+S5)
      New_Y_2=Y+H2*(S1-3.0_Long*S3+4.0*S4)
!
```

```
! Calculate error estimate
!
      Error=ABS(0.2_Long*(New_Y_1-New_Y_2))
      Max_Error=MAXVAL(Error)
      IF(Max_Error > Tol) THEN
!
! Halve step length and try again
!
          IF(ABS(H2) < Smallest_step) THEN
             IFAIL = 2
             RETURN
          ENDIF
          H=H2
      ELSE
!
! Accepted approximation so overwrite Y with Y_new_1,
! and T with T+H
!
          Y=New_Y_1
          T=T+H
!
! Can next step be doubled?
!
          IF(Max_Error*Factor < Tol)THEN
             H=H*2.0_Long
          ENDIF
!
! Does next step go beyond interval end B,
! if so set H = B-T
!
          IF(T+H > B) THEN
             H=B-T
          ENDIF
          No_of_steps=No_of_steps+1
      ENDIF
      IF(T >= B) EXIT                ! End of repeat loop
   END DO
END SUBROUTINE Runge_Kutta_Merson
```

A main program to use this subroutine is of the form:

```
PROGRAM Odes
USE Precisions
IMPLICIT NONE
REAL(Long),Dimension(:),Allocatable::Y
REAL(Long)::A,B,Tol
INTEGER::N,IFAIL,All_stat
INTERFACE
   SUBROUTINE Runge_Kutta_Merson(Y,FUN,IFAIL,N,A,B,Tol)
      USE Precisions
      IMPLICIT NONE
      REAL(Long),INTENT(INOUT)  ::  Y(:)
      REAL(Long),INTENT(IN)::A,B,Tol
      INTEGER,INTENT(IN)::N
      INTEGER,INTENT(OUT)::IFAIL
      INTERFACE
         SUBROUTINE FUN(T,Y,F,N)
            USE Precisions
            IMPLICIT NONE
            REAL(Long),  INTENT(IN),DIMENSION(:)::Y
            REAL(Long),  INTENT(OUT),DIMENSION(:)::F
            REAL(Long),  INTENT(IN)::T
            INTEGER,INTENT(IN)::N
         END SUBROUTINE FUN
      END INTERFACE
   END SUBROUTINE Runge_Kutta_Merson
END INTERFACE
!
INTERFACE
   SUBROUTINE Fun1(T,Y,F,N)
   USE Precisions
   IMPLICIT NONE
   REAL(Long),  INTENT(IN),DIMENSION(:)::Y
   REAL(Long),  INTENT(OUT),DIMENSION(:)::F
   REAL(Long),INTENT(IN)::  T
   INTEGER,  INTENT(IN)::  N
   END SUBROUTINE Fun1
END INTERFACE
!
   PRINT *,'Input no of equations'
   READ*,N
!
! Allocate space for Y - checking to see that it
```

```
! allocates properly
!
   ALLOCATE(Y(1:N),STAT=All_stat)
   IF(All_stat /= 0) THEN
       PRINT * , ' Not enough memory'
       PRINT * , ' array Y is not allocated'
       STOP
   ENDIF
   PRINT *,' Input start and end of interval over'
   PRINT *,' which equations to be solved'
   READ *,A,B
   PRINT *,"Input ic's"
   READ *,Y(1:N)
   PRINT *,'Input Tolerance'
   READ *,Tol
   PRINT *,'At T= ',A
   PRINT *,'Initial conditions are :',Y(1:N)
   CALL Runge_Kutta_Merson(Y,Fun1,IFAIL,N,A,B,Tol)
   IF(IFAIL /= 0) THEN
       PRINT *,'Integration stopped with IFAIL = ',IFAIL
   ELSE
       PRINT *,'at T= ',B
       PRINT*,'Solution is: ',Y(1:N)
   ENDIF
END PROGRAM Odes
```

Consider trying to solve the following system of first order ordinary differential equations:

$$\dot{y}_1 = \tan y_3$$

$$\dot{y}_2 = \frac{-0.032 \tan y_3}{y_2} - \frac{0.02\, y_2}{\cos y_3}$$

$$\dot{y}_3 = -\frac{0.032}{y_2^2}$$

over an interval $t = 0.0$ to $t = 8.0$ with initial conditions $y_1 = 0 \quad y_2 = 0.5 \quad y_3 = \frac{\pi}{5}$

The user supplied subroutine is:

```
Subroutine Fun1(T,Y,F,N)
   USE Precisions
```

```
    IMPLICIT NONE
    REAL(Long),INTENT(IN),DIMENSION(:)::Y
    REAL(Long),INTENT(OUT),DIMENSION(:)::F
    REAL(Long),INTENT(IN)::T
    INTEGER,INTENT(IN)::N
|
    F(1)=TAN(Y(3))
    F(2)=-0.032_Long*F(1)/Y(2)-0.02_Long*Y(2)/COS(Y(3))
    F(3)=-0.032_Long/(Y(2)*Y(2))
END SUBROUTINE Fun1
```

27.1.1 Note: Alternative form of the Allocate statement

In the main program Odes we have defined Y to be a deferred shape array, allocating it space after the variable N is read in. In order to make sure that enough memory is available to allocate space to array Y the ALLOCATE statement is used as follows:

ALLOCATE(Y(1:N),STAT=All_stat)

If the allocation is successful variable All_stat returns zero, otherwise it is given a processor dependent positive value. We have included code to check for this and the program stops if All_stat is not zero.

27.1.2 Note: Automatic arrays

The subroutine Runge_Kutta_Merson needs a number of local rank-one arrays S1, S2, S3, S4 and S5 for workspace, their shape and size being the same as the dummy argument Y. Fortran 95 supplies automatic arrays for this purpose and can be declared as:

REAL(Long), DIMENSION (1:SIZE(Y)) :: S1, S2, S3, S4, S5

The size of automatic arrays can depend on the size of actual arrays: in our example they are the same shape and size as the dummy array Y, or some other dummy arguments. Automatic arrays are created when the procedure is called and destroyed when control passes back to the calling program unit. They may have different shapes and sizes with different calls to the procedure, so because of this automatic arrays cannot be saved or initialized.

A word of warning should be given at this point. If there isn't enough memory available when an automatic array needs to be created problems will occur. There is no way of testing to see if an automatic array has been created successfully, unlike allocatable arrays. The general feeling is that even though they are nice, automatic arrays should be used with care and maybe shouldn't be used in production code!

27.1.3   Note: Dummy procedure arguments

In order to make the use of the subroutine Runge_Kutta_Merson as general as possible, one of its dummy arguments (FUN) is the name of a subroutine which the user supplies with the actual system of ordinary differential equations they wish to solve. This means that the main program which calls Runge_Kutta_Merson passes as an actual argument the name of the subroutine containing the definition of the equations they wish to solve. In this example the subroutine is called Fun1. In order to do this in the main program Odes we have an interface block for the Runge_Kutta_Merson subroutine and within this interface block we have another interface block for the dummy routine FUN. Also in the main program we have an interface block for the actual subroutine Fun1.

27.2   Example 2: Generic procedures

There has always been a degree of support in Fortran for the concept of a generic procedure. Simplistically a procedure is generic if it can handle arguments of more than data type. This concept is one that is probably taken for granted with the intrinsic procedures.

With Fortran 95 we can now define our own generic procedures. The example we will use is based on the earlier one of sorting. In the original example the program worked with real data. In the example below we have extended the program to handle both integer and real data.

What is not obvious from our use of the internal procedures is that there will be specific procedures that handle each data type, i.e. if a function can take integer, real and complex arguments then there will be one implementation of that function for each data type, i.e. three separate functions.

In the example below we add the ability to handle integer data. This means that where we had:

- read data
- sort data
- print data

and one subroutine to implement the above we now have **two** subroutines to do each of the above, one to handle integers and one to handle reals.

```
PROGRAM Generic_Example
! This is an example of the ability in Fortran 90
! to construct generic procedures. The earlier example
! of sorting is now extended to handle both integer
! and real arrays.
```

```
IMPLICIT NONE
INTEGER :: How_Many
CHARACTER (LEN=20) :: File_Name
INTEGER,ALLOCATABLE , DIMENSION(:) :: I_Data
REAL ,ALLOCATABLE , DIMENSION(:) :: R_Data

INTERFACE Read_Data
   SUBROUTINE RR(File_Name,Raw_Data,How_Many)
     IMPLICIT NONE
     CHARACTER (LEN=*) , INTENT(IN) :: File_Name
     INTEGER , INTENT(IN) :: How_Many
     REAL , INTENT(OUT) , &
       DIMENSION(How_Many) :: Raw_Data
   END SUBROUTINE RR
   SUBROUTINE RI(File_Name,Raw_Data,How_Many)
     IMPLICIT NONE
     CHARACTER (LEN=*) , INTENT(IN) :: File_Name
     INTEGER , INTENT(IN):: How_Many
     INTEGER , INTENT(OUT) , &
       DIMENSION(How_Many) :: Raw_Data
   END SUBROUTINE RI
END INTERFACE

INTERFACE Sort_Data
   SUBROUTINE RS(Raw_Data,How_Many)
     IMPLICIT NONE
     INTEGER , INTENT(IN) :: How_Many
     REAL , INTENT(INOUT) , &
       DIMENSION(How_Many) :: Raw_Data
   END SUBROUTINE RS
   SUBROUTINE IS(Raw_Data,How_Many)
     IMPLICIT NONE
     INTEGER , INTENT(IN) :: How_Many
     INTEGER , INTENT(INOUT) , &
       DIMENSION(How_Many) :: Raw_Data
   END SUBROUTINE IS
END INTERFACE

INTERFACE Print_Data
   SUBROUTINE PR(Raw_Data,How_Many)
     IMPLICIT NONE
     INTEGER , INTENT(IN) :: How_Many
```

```fortran
      REAL, INTENT(IN) , &
        DIMENSION(How_Many) :: Raw_Data
   END SUBROUTINE PR
   SUBROUTINE PI(Raw_Data,How_Many)
      IMPLICIT NONE
      INTEGER , INTENT(IN) :: How_Many
      INTEGER , INTENT(IN) , &
        DIMENSION(How_Many) :: Raw_Data
   END SUBROUTINE PI
END INTERFACE

   PRINT * , ' How many data items are there?'
   READ  * , How_Many
   PRINT * , ' What is the file name?'
   READ '(A)',File_Name
   ALLOCATE(I_Data(How_Many))
   CALL Read_Data(File_Name,I_Data,How_Many)
   CALL Sort_Data(I_Data,How_Many)
   CALL Print_Data(I_Data,How_Many)
   PRINT *, ' Phase 1 ends.'
   PRINT *, ' data written to file name ISORTED.DAT'
   DEALLOCATE(I_Data)

   PRINT * , ' How many data items are there?'
   READ  * , How_Many
   PRINT * , ' What is the file name?'
   READ '(A)',File_Name
   ALLOCATE(R_Data(How_Many))
   CALL Read_Data(File_Name,R_Data,How_Many)
   CALL Sort_Data(R_Data,How_Many)
   CALL Print_Data(R_Data,How_Many)
   PRINT *, ' Program ends.'
   PRINT *, ' data written to file name RSORTED.DAT'
END PROGRAM Generic_Example

SUBROUTINE RR(File_Name,Raw_Data,How_Many)
IMPLICIT NONE
CHARACTER (LEN=*) , INTENT(IN) :: File_Name
INTEGER , INTENT(IN) :: How_Many
REAL , INTENT(OUT) , &
   DIMENSION(How_Many) :: Raw_Data
INTEGER :: I
```

```
   OPEN(FILE=File_Name,UNIT=1)
   DO I=1,How_Many
     READ (UNIT=1,FMT=*) Raw_Data(I)
   ENDDO
END SUBROUTINE RR

SUBROUTINE RI(File_Name,Raw_Data,How_Many)
IMPLICIT NONE
CHARACTER (LEN=*) , INTENT(IN):: File_Name
INTEGER , INTENT(IN) :: How_Many
INTEGER , INTENT(OUT) , &
   DIMENSION(How_Many) :: Raw_Data
INTEGER :: I
   OPEN(FILE=File_Name,UNIT=1)
   DO I=1,How_Many
     READ (UNIT=1,FMT=*) Raw_Data(I)
   ENDDO
END SUBROUTINE RI

SUBROUTINE RS(Raw_Data,How_Many)
IMPLICIT NONE
INTEGER , INTENT(IN) :: How_Many
REAL , INTENT(INOUT)  , &
   DIMENSION(How_Many) :: Raw_Data
   CALL QuickSort(1,How_Many)

CONTAINS

RECURSIVE SUBROUTINE QuickSort(L,R)
IMPLICIT NONE
INTEGER , INTENT(IN) :: L,R
INTEGER :: I,J
REAL :: V,T

! The quick sort algorithm taken from Sedgewick
! fails when the pivot is the smallest element
! in the array. This is clearly stated by Sedgewick
! in the text that follows the algorithm.
!
! In the light of the subsequent changes he made
! to this algorithm (including the
! removal of recursion)
```

```
! we decided to look for an alternate
! recursive source.
!
! we have used wirths "algorithms and data structures"
! as a source
!

  i=1
  j=r
  v=raw_data( int((l+r)/2) )
  do
     do while (raw_data(i) < v )
          i=i+1
     enddo
     do while (v < raw_data(j) )
          j=j-1
     enddo
     if (i<=j) then
        t=raw_data(i)
        raw_data(i)=raw_data(j)
        raw_data(j)=t
        i=i+1
        j=j-1
     endif
     if (i>j) exit
  enddo

  if (l<j) then
     call quicksort(l,j)
  endif

  if (i<r) then
     call quicksort(i,r)
  endif

END SUBROUTINE QuickSort

END SUBROUTINE RS

SUBROUTINE IS(Raw_Data,How_Many)
IMPLICIT NONE
INTEGER , INTENT(IN) :: How_Many
```

```
INTEGER , INTENT(INOUT)   , &
   DIMENSION(How_Many) :: Raw_Data
   CALL QuickSort(1,How_Many)

CONTAINS

RECURSIVE SUBROUTINE QuickSort(L,R)
IMPLICIT NONE
INTEGER , INTENT(IN) :: L,R
INTEGER :: I,J
INTEGER :: V,T

! The quick sort algorithm taken from Sedgewick
! fails when the pivot is the smallest element
! in the array. This is clearly stated by Sedgewick
! in the text that follows the algorithm.
!
! In the light of the subsequent changes he made
! to this algorithm (including the
! removal of recursion)
! we decided to look for an alternate
! recursive source.
!
! we have used wirths "algorithms and data structures"
! as a source
!

   i=1
   j=r
   v=raw_data( int((1+r)/2) )
   do
      do while (raw_data(i) < v )
          i=i+1
      enddo
      do while (v < raw_data(j) )
          j=j-1
      enddo
      if (i<=j) then
        t=raw_data(i)
        raw_data(i)=raw_data(j)
        raw_data(j)=t
        i=i+1
```

```
      j=j-1
    endif
    if (i>j) exit
  enddo

  if (l<j) then
    call quicksort(l,j)
  endif

  if (i<r) then
    call quicksort(i,r)
  endif

END SUBROUTINE QuickSort

END SUBROUTINE IS

SUBROUTINE PR(Raw_Data,How_Many)
IMPLICIT NONE
INTEGER , INTENT(IN) :: How_Many
REAL , INTENT(IN) , &
   DIMENSION(How_Many) :: Raw_Data
INTEGER :: I
  OPEN(FILE='RSORTED.DAT',UNIT=2)
  DO I=1,How_Many
    WRITE(UNIT=2,FMT=*) Raw_Data(I)
  END DO
  CLOSE(2)
END SUBROUTINE PR

SUBROUTINE PI(Raw_Data,How_Many)
IMPLICIT NONE
INTEGER , INTENT(IN) :: How_Many
INTEGER , INTENT(IN) , &
   DIMENSION(How_Many) :: Raw_Data
INTEGER :: I
  OPEN(FILE='ISORTED.DAT',UNIT=2)
  DO I=1,How_Many
    WRITE(UNIT=2,FMT=*) Raw_Data(I)
  END DO
  CLOSE(2)
END SUBROUTINE PI
```

27.3 Example 3 – A function that returns a variable length array

```
PROGRAM Running
! this program has a function that returns an array
! that contains the running average for the array
! passed

IMPLICIT NONE

INTERFACE
   FUNCTION Running_Average(A,How_Many)
      IMPLICIT NONE
      INTEGER , INTENT(IN) :: How_Many
      REAL , DIMENSION (How_Many) , INTENT(IN) :: A
      REAL , DIMENSION(How_Many) :: Running_Average
   END FUNCTION Running_Average
END INTERFACE

INTERFACE Read_Data

   SUBROUTINE RR(File_Name,Raw_Data,How_Many)
      IMPLICIT NONE
      CHARACTER (LEN=*) , INTENT(IN) :: File_Name
      INTEGER , INTENT(IN) :: How_Many
      REAL , INTENT(OUT) , &
      DIMENSION(How_Many) :: Raw_Data
   END SUBROUTINE RR

   SUBROUTINE RI(File_Name,Raw_Data,How_Many)
      IMPLICIT NONE
      CHARACTER (LEN=*) , INTENT(IN) :: File_Name
      INTEGER , INTENT(IN) :: How_Many
      INTEGER , INTENT(OUT) , &
      DIMENSION(How_Many) :: Raw_Data
   END SUBROUTINE RI

END INTERFACE

INTEGER :: How_Many
CHARACTER (LEN=20) :: File_Name
REAL , ALLOCATABLE , DIMENSION(:)  :: Raw_Data
REAL , ALLOCATABLE , DIMENSION(:)  :: RA
INTEGER :: I
```

```
      PRINT * , ' How many data items are there?'
      READ   * , How_Many
      PRINT * , ' What is the file name?'
      READ '(A)',File_Name
      ALLOCATE(Raw_Data(How_Many))
      ALLOCATE(RA(How_Many))
      CALL Read_Data(File_Name,Raw_Data,How_Many)
      RA=Running_Average(Raw_Data,How_Many)
      DO I=1,How_Many
         PRINT *,Raw_Data(I),'    ' ,RA(I)
      END DO
END PROGRAM Running

FUNCTION Running_Average(R,How_Many)
INTEGER , INTENT(IN) :: How_Many
REAL , INTENT(IN) , DIMENSION(How_Many) :: R
REAL , DIMENSION(How_Many) :: Running_Average
INTEGER :: I
REAL :: Sum=0.0
   DO I=1,How_Many
      Sum = Sum + R(I)
      Running_Average(I)=Sum/I
   END DO
END FUNCTION Running_Average
```

27.4 Example 4: Operator and assignment overloading

It is sometimes convenient to extend the meaning of an operator and the assignment symbol beyond that provided by the language. This can be done in Fortran 95 using module procedures. The example below is based on moving round a three dimensional space.

```
MODULE T_Position
IMPLICIT NONE
TYPE Position
   INTEGER :: X
   INTEGER :: Y
   INTEGER :: Z
END TYPE Position


INTERFACE OPERATOR (+)
   MODULE PROCEDURE New_Position
```

```
END INTERFACE


CONTAINS

FUNCTION New_Position(A,B)
TYPE (Position) ,INTENT(IN) :: A,B
TYPE (Position) :: New_Position
   New_Position % X = A % X + B % X
   New_Position % Y = A % Y + B % Y
   New_Position % Z = A % Z + B % Z
END FUNCTION New_Position

END MODULE T_Position

PROGRAM Operator_Overload
USE T_Position
IMPLICIT NONE
TYPE (Position) :: A,B,C
   A%X=10
   A%Y=10
   A%Z=10
   B%X=20
   B%Y=20
   B%Z=20
   C=A+B
   PRINT *,A
   PRINT *,B
   PRINT *,C
END PROGRAM Operator_Overload
```

We have extended the meaning of the addition operator so that we can write simple expressions in Fortran based on the addition operator and have our new position calculated using a user supplied function that actually implements the calculation of the new position.

27.5 Example 5: A Subroutine to extract the diagonal elements of a matrix

A common task mathematically is to extract the diagonal elements of a matrix. For example if:

$$A = \begin{pmatrix} 21 & 6 & 7 \\ 9 & 3 & 2 \\ 4 & 1 & 8 \end{pmatrix}$$

The diagonal elements are (21, 3, 8)

This can be thought of as extracting an array section, but the intrinsic function PACK is needed. In its simplest form PACK (Array,Vector) packs an array, Array, into a rank one array, Vector, according to Array's array element order.

Here's a subroutine to demonstrate this:

```
SUBROUTINE Matrix_Diagonal (A, Diag, N)
   IMPLICIT NONE
   REAL, INTENT(IN), DIMENSION(:,:) ::A
   REAL, INTENT(OUT), DIMENSION(:) :: Diag
   INTEGER, INTENT(IN) ::N
   REAL, DIMENSION (1:SIZE(A,1)*SIZE(A,1)) :: Temp
!
! Subroutine to extract the diagonal elements of
! an N * N matrix A
!
    IF(SIZE(A,1) == N .AND. SIZE(A,2) == N) THEN
       Temp = PACK(A,.TRUE.)
       Diag=Temp(1:N*N:N+1)
    ELSE
       PRINT * , ' The matrix A is not (N,N)'
       PRINT * , ' where N = ',N
       PRINT * , ' Diagonal elements not extracted'
    END IF
END SUBROUTINE Matrix_Diagonal
```

27.6 Modules and packaging

The power of modules is demonstrated very clearly when we look at how we package and make available data types and operations on those data types. The earlier example in this chapter on operator and assignment overloading was quite straightforward. Let us consider the provision of a windowing interface, with both text and graphics modes. The following is one possible (very simple) solution:

MODULE Window, with procedures

    Open_Window
    Close_Window
    Draw_Title
    Redefine_Window

Place_On_Top
Place_Underneath
On_Top
Up_Window

MODULE Text_Window, with procedures

Open_Text_Window
Close_Text_Window
Redefine_Text_Window
Assign_Font
Assign_Restore_Procedure
Assign_EOW_Action
Draw_Title
Draw_Line
Scroll_Up
Scroll_Down
Get_Position
Set_Position
Read_from_Window
Write_To_Window

MODULE Graphic_Window, with procedures

Open_GraphicsWindow
Close_Graphics_Mode
Select_Graphics_Mode
Redefine_Graphics_Window
Set_Pen
Turn_To
Turn
Move_To
Move
Circle
Area
Copy_Area
etc.

MODULE Mouse_and_Cursor, with procedures

Get_Mouse
Set_Mouse
Read_Mouse
Move_Cursor
Erase_Cursor
etc.

Modules are the first choice to implement this kind of problem over a suite of functions and subroutines because they provide a very clean way of packaging the whole solution.

Consult the web addresses to see what has been done in this area. A number of people and organizations have made sample code publicly available.

27.7 Pure function example

We recommended in Chapter 14 that you should ensure that your functions did not have side effects, for safety reasons. With the ability of running your code on parallel systems we have the additional problem in that the code may not actually work! We would also like to be able to take advantage of automatic parallelization if possible. In the following example we show how to do this using the PURE function prefix.

```
PROGRAM GCDExample
IMPLICIT NONE
INTEGER :: I,J,Result
INTEGER :: GCD
  PRINT *,' Type in two integers'
  READ *,I,J
  Result=GCD(I,J)
  PRINT *,' GCD is ',Result
END PROGRAM GCDExample

PURE INTEGER FUNCTION GCD(A,B)
IMPLICIT NONE
INTEGER , INTENT(IN) :: A,B
INTEGER :: Temp
  IF (A < B) THEN
    Temp=A
  ELSE
    Temp=B
  ENDIF
  DO WHILE ((MOD(A,Temp) /= 0) .OR. (MOD(B,Temp) /=0))
    Temp=Temp-1
  END DO
  GCD=Temp
END FUNCTION GCD
```

Procedures can be made pure also.

27.7.1   Pure constraints

The following are some of the constraints on pure procedures:

- a dummy argument must be INTENT(IN) for a pure function

- a dummy argument must have an INTENT attribute in a pure subroutine.

- local variables may not have the save attribute

- no I/O must be done in the procedure

- any functions and procedures referenced must be pure

- you cannot have a stop statement with a pure procedure

and the above information should be enough to enable you to write simple pure functions and procedures.

27.8   Elemental function example

The intrinsic trigonometric functions are elemental in that they can take an argument that is scalar or array valued, and of any of the supported numeric kind types. With Fortran 95 we can make our own user defined functions elemental. Consider the following example, which is an extension of the earlier example that calculated e**x.

```
PROGRAM C2710
IMPLICIT NONE
!
! Elemental function example
!
INTEGER :: I
REAL :: X
REAL , DIMENSION(10) :: Y

INTERFACE
   ELEMENTAL REAL FUNCTION ETOX(X)
   IMPLICIT NONE
   REAL , INTENT(IN) :: X
   END FUNCTION ETOX
END INTERFACE

   X=1.0
   DO I=1,10
      Y(I)=I
   END DO
```

```
   PRINT *,Y
   X=ETOX(X)
   PRINT *,X
   Y=ETOX(Y)
   PRINT *,Y
END PROGRAM C2710

ELEMENTAL REAL FUNCTION ETOX(X)
IMPLICIT NONE
REAL , INTENT(IN) :: X
REAL :: TERM
INTEGER :: NTERM
REAL , PARAMETER :: TOL =1.0E-6
   ETOX=1.0
   TERM=1.0
   NTERM=0
   DO
      NTERM=NTERM+1
      TERM=(X/NTERM)*TERM
      ETOX=ETOX+TERM
      IF (TERM<=TOL) EXIT
   END DO
END FUNCTION ETOX
```

Note the following:

- we have added an interface block for the etox function
- we have added the ELEMENTAL prefix to the function header
- the dummy argument is scalar and INTENT(IN)
- the function result is scalar

In this example we call the function with a scalar argument and a rank one array. Run the program to see what happens.

You can have the PURE prefix but it is redundant as ELEMENTAL implies PURE.

27.8.1 Elemental constraints

Some of the restrictions include:

- an elemental procedure must not be recursive
- a dummy argument must not be a pointer
- the result of an elemental function must not be a pointer

- elemental procedures must have explicit interfaces in all program units that reference them

In a parallel environment this means that the array calculations could be carried out simultaneously on two or more processors.

27.9 Elemental subroutine example

It is also possible to make subroutines elemental. Consider the following example.

```
PROGRAM C2711
IMPLICIT NONE

INTERFACE
   ELEMENTAL SUBROUTINE SWAP(X,Y)
   INTEGER , INTENT(INOUT) :: X,Y
   END SUBROUTINE SWAP
END INTERFACE

INTEGER , DIMENSION(10) :: A,B
INTEGER :: I
   DO I=1,10
     A(I)=I
     B(I)=I*I
   END DO
     PRINT *,A
     PRINT *,B
     CALL SWAP(A,B)
     PRINT *,A
     PRINT *,B
END PROGRAM C2711

ELEMENTAL SUBROUTINE SWAP(X,Y)
INTEGER , INTENT(INOUT) :: X,Y
INTEGER :: TEMP
   TEMP=X
   X=Y
   Y=TEMP
END SUBROUTINE SWAP
```

Note the following:

- we have an interface block for the elemental subroutine

- the subroutine dummy arguments are scalar with an INTENT attribute, in this case INTENT(INOUT) as we are swapping them over.

In a parallel environment the swapping of array elements may be done simultaneously on two or more processors.

27.10 Problems

1. Type in the subroutine to extract the diagonal elements of a matrix. Write a main program to call it, and try running it with matrices of your own choice.

2. Write a generic subroutine Swap which two arguments a and b (real or integer) and swaps them. Write a main program that reads two real values and calls Swap and then reads two integer values and again calls Swap.

3. Using Example 4 as a starting point extend to overload the subtraction operator (-), for the user defined type position.

4. Rewrite the Stirling function example in Chapter 14 as a pure external function.

5. Modify the elemental function example to include usage of the function etox with a rank two or higher array.

Also add a call to the intrinsic function exp and compare the results.

27.11 Bibliography

Hopkins T., Phillips C., *Numerical Methods In Practice, Using the NAG Library.* Addison Wesley.

- Good adjunct to the NAG library documentation for the less numerate user.

http://www.nag.co.uk/

- Visit their site for up to date details of the products they have.

Web addresses

- http://www.kcl.ac.uk/kis/support/cit//fortran/f90home.html
- http://www.fortran.com/fortran/market.html
- http://www.lahey.com/other.htm

Converting from Fortran 77

Twas brillig, and the slithy toves
did gyre and gimble in the wabe;
All mimsy were the borogoves,
And the mome raths outgrabe.

Lewis Carroll.

Aims

The aims of this chapter are to provide some simple guidelines for the conversion
of existing Fortran 77 code to Fortran 95. In particular, to emphasize the better
features that exist in Fortran 95 in many areas.

- decremented features – candidates for deletion in future standards:

  > arithmetic if; real and double precision DO control variables;
  > shared DO termination; alternate RETURN; PAUSE statement;
  > ASSIGN and assigned GOTO statements; assigned FORMAT
  > statements; H editing;

- better alternatives – potential candidates for removal from future standards

  > double precision; fixed format; implicit typing; COMMON;
  > EQUIVALENCE; block data; entry statement; statement func-
  > tions; computed GOTO; alternate RETURN; INCLUDE; EXTER-
  > NAL, assumed-size array arguments;

28 Converting from Fortran 77

The aim here is to provide the existing Fortran 77 programmer (and in particular the person with legacy code) with some simple guidelines for conversion.

The first thing that one must have is a thorough understanding of the newer, better language features of Fortran 95. It is essential that the material in the earlier chapters of this book be covered, and some of the problems attempted. This will provide a feel for Fortran 95.

The second thing one must have is a thorough understanding of the language constructs used in this legacy code. Use should be made of the compiler documentation for whatever Fortran 77 compiler you are using as this will provide the detailed (often system specific) information required. The recommendations below are therefore brief.

It is possible to move gradually from Fortran 77 to Fortran 95. In many cases existing code can be quite simply recompiled by a suitable choice of compiler options. This enables us to mix and match old and new in one program. This process is likely to highlight non-standard language features in your old code. There will inevitably be some problems here.

The first thing to consider is what the standard says. The standard identifies two kinds of decremented features. These are deleted features and obsolescent features. It is extremely unwise to consider the long term use of these features as they are candidates for removal from future standards.

28.1 Deleted features

The list of deleted features for Fortran 95 is empty, i.e. there are none.

28.2 Obsolescent features

The obsolescent features are those for which better methods are available. They are given below with alternatives.

28.2.1 Arithmetic IF

Use the IF statement.

28.2.2 Real and double precision do control variables

Use integer.

28.2.3 Shared DO termination and non ENDDO termination

Use an END DO.

28.2.4 Alternate RETURN

Use a CASE statement on return. An error code has to be returned.

28.2.5 PAUSE Statement

System specific. Normally easily replaced with a suitable READ statement.

28.2.6 ASSIGN and assigned GOTO statements

Fortunately rarely used.

28.2.7 Assigned FORMAT statements

Use character arrays, arrays and constants.

28.2.8 H editing

Use character edit descriptor.

28.3 Better alternatives

Here we are looking at the new features of the Fortran 95 standard, and how we can replace our current coding practices with the better facilities that now exist.

- DOUBLE PRECISION – use KIND, see Chapter 8, and examples throughout the book.

- fixed format – use free format

- implicit typing – use IMPLICIT NONE

- BLOCK DATA – use modules

- COMMON statement – use modules

- EQUIVALENCE

  Invariably the use of this feature requires considerable system specific knowledge. There will be cases where there have been extremely good reasons why this feature has been used, normally efficiency related. However with the rapid changes taking place in the power and speed of hardware these reasons are diminishing.

- assumed-size / explicit shape dummy array arguments

  If a dummy argument is assumed-size or explicit shape (the only ones available in Fortran 77) then the ranks of the actual argument and the associated argument don't have to be the same. With Fortran 95 arrays are now objects instead of a linear sequence of elements, as was the case with Fortran 77, and now for array arguments the fundamental rule is that actual and dummy arguments have the same rank and same extents in each dimension, i.e. the same shape, and this is done using assumed-shape dummy array arguments. An interface block is mandatory for assumed-shape arrays.

- ENTRY statement - use module plus USE statement

- statement functions - use internal function, see Chapter 14.

- computed GOTO - use CASE statement, see Chapter 15.

- alternate RETURN - use error flags on calling routine

- INCLUDE - use modules plus USE statement

- EXTERNAL statement for dummy procedure arguments

  Use explicit interface blocks everywhere. See Chapter 27, Section 27.1 This also provides argument checking and other benefits.

28.4 Summary

There are a number of free and commercial conversion programs to help you move from Fortran 77. Have a look at the F90 FAQ and the Fortran Market.

Fortran 2000 and Various Fortran Dialects

Experience is a dear teacher, but fools will learn at no other.

Aims

The aim of this chapter is to provide a brief coverage of what developments are taking place with standard Fortran and look briefly at several of the so-called Fortran dialects.

29 Fortran 2000 and Various Fortran Dialects

Programming languages evolve. Fortran has been standardized several times and work is already underway for Fortran 2000. We look briefly here at developments in the standards area.

There are also a number of non-standard Fortrans'. We touch briefly on these in this chapter. More information can be found at the various web addresses that have been provided.

29.1 Fortran standards

The two key bodies involved are Working Group 5 (WG5) and Technical Committee J3. More details are given below.

The international standards organization responsible for the standardization of Fortran is WG5. They maintain web pages to inform interested parties about the development of the Fortran language. Their home page is:

*   http://www.nag.co.uk/sc22wg5/

J3 - Programming Language Fortran is the technical committee responsible for the development and interpretation of the United State and international standards for Programming Language Fortran. Their home page is

*   http://www.NCITS.org/tc_home/j3.htm

An amusing history of the Fortran 90 standard can be found at:

*   http://www.kcl.ac.uk/kis/support/cit//staff/brian/forsaga.html

29.2 ISO Technical Report (TR) 15580 Exception Handling

This has now been incorporated into a number of Fortran 95 compilers. It will be a formal part of the Fortran 2000 standard. We have covered this in an earlier chapter.

29.3 ISO TR 15581 Enhanced Data Types

This has now been incorporated into a number of Fortran 95 compilers. It will be a formal part of the Fortran 2000 standard.

29.3.0.1 Allocatable dummy arrays

The following is a complete example that illustrates its use. It is based on the quick sort example in Chapter 23. In this case we actually allocate the dummy array argument in the read subroutine.

```
PROGRAM Sort_Example01
!
! This program is a simple example of how to
! construct larger programs
! using some of the new features introduced
! with Fortran 90. The program
! comprises 4 routines,
! 1. a driving routine, which interacts with the user
! and requests the number of data items,
! and file name.
! 2. a routine to read in the data, from a file.
! 3. a routine to sort the data.
! 4. a routine to print out the sorted data to a file
!
! The program attempts to highlight the importance
! of the
! modular nature of the solution,
! and how we can simply
! replace one component,
! without affecting the other routines.
IMPLICIT NONE
INTEGER :: How_Many
CHARACTER (LEN=20) :: File_Name
REAL , ALLOCATABLE , DIMENSION(:) :: Raw_Data
INTEGER :: Count
INTEGER :: Count_Rate
INTEGER :: Count_Max
INTEGER :: T1,T2,T3,T4,I,J

INTERFACE
   SUBROUTINE Read_Data(File_Name,Raw_Data,How_Many)
     IMPLICIT NONE
     CHARACTER (LEN=*) , INTENT(IN) :: File_Name
     INTEGER , INTENT(IN) :: How_Many
     REAL , INTENT(OUT) , ALLOCATABLE , &
     DIMENSION(:) :: Raw_Data
   END SUBROUTINE Read_Data
END INTERFACE

INTERFACE
   SUBROUTINE Sort_Data(Raw_Data,How_Many)
     IMPLICIT NONE
```

```fortran
      INTEGER , INTENT(IN) :: How_Many
      REAL , INTENT(INOUT) , DIMENSION(:) :: Raw_Data
   END SUBROUTINE Sort_Data
END INTERFACE

INTERFACE
   SUBROUTINE Print_Data(Raw_Data,How_Many)
      IMPLICIT NONE
      INTEGER , INTENT(IN) :: How_Many
      REAL , INTENT(IN) , DIMENSION(:) :: Raw_Data
   END SUBROUTINE Print_Data
END INTERFACE

   PRINT * , ' How many data items are there?'
   READ * , How_Many
   PRINT * , ' What is the file name?'
   READ '(A)',File_Name

   CALL SYSTEM_CLOCK(Count,Count_Rate,Count_Max)
   I=Count
   J=I
   PRINT *,I,'   ',Count_Rate,'   ',Count_Max

   CALL SYSTEM_CLOCK(Count)
   T1=Count-I
   I=T1/Count_Rate
   PRINT *,T1,I

   CALL Read_Data(File_Name,Raw_Data,How_Many)

   CALL SYSTEM_CLOCK(Count)
   T2=Count-T1-J
   I=T2/Count_Rate
   PRINT *,T2,'   ',I

   CALL Sort_Data(Raw_Data,How_Many)

   CALL SYSTEM_CLOCK(Count)
   T3=Count-T2-J
   I=T3/Count_Rate

   PRINT *,T3,'   ',I
```

```
    CALL  Print_Data(Raw_Data,How_Many)

    CALL  SYSTEM_CLOCK(Count)
    T4=Count-T3-J
    I-T4/Count_Rate
    PRINT *,T4,'   ',I
    PRINT *,T1,'   ',T2,'   ',T3,'   ',T4
    PRINT *, ' Program ends'
    PRINT *, ' data written to file name SORTED.DAT'

END  PROGRAM Sort_Example01
SUBROUTINE Read_Data(File_Name,Raw_Data,How_Many)
IMPLICIT NONE
CHARACTER (LEN=*) , INTENT(IN) :: File_Name
INTEGER , INTENT(IN) :: How_Many
REAL , INTENT(OUT) , ALLOCATABLE , &
    DIMENSION(:) :: Raw_Data

INTEGER :: I
    ALLOCATE(Raw_Data(1:How_Many))
    OPEN(FILE=File_Name,UNIT=1)
    DO I=1,How_Many
        READ (UNIT=1,FMT=*) Raw_Data(I)
    ENDDO

END SUBROUTINE Read_Data
SUBROUTINE Sort_Data(Raw_Data,How_Many)
IMPLICIT NONE
INTEGER , INTENT(IN) :: How_Many
REAL , INTENT(INOUT) , DIMENSION(:) :: Raw_Data

    CALL QuickSort(1,How_Many)

CONTAINS

    RECURSIVE SUBROUTINE QuickSort(L,R)
    IMPLICIT NONE
    INTEGER , INTENT(IN) :: L,R
    INTEGER :: I,J,tt
    REAL :: V,T
```

```
! The quick sort algorithm taken from Sedgewick
! fails when the pivot is the smallest element
! in the array. This is clearly stated by Sedgewick
! in the text that follows the algorithm.
!
! In the light of the subsequent changes he made
! to this algorithm
! (including the removal of recursion)
! we decided to look for an alternate
! recursive source.
!
! we have used wirths "algorithms and data structures"
! as a source
!

  i=1
  j=r
  v=raw_data( int((l+r)/2) )
  do
     do while (raw_data(i) < v )
         i=i+1
     enddo
     do while (v < raw_data(j) )
         j=j-1
     enddo
     if (i<=j) then
       t=raw_data(i)
       raw_data(i)=raw_data(j)
       raw_data(j)=t
       i=i+1
       j=j-1
     endif
     if (i>j) exit
  enddo

  if (l<j) then
     call quicksort(l,j)
  endif

  if (i<r) then
     call quicksort(i,r)
  endif
```

```
  END SUBROUTINE QuickSort

END SUBROUTINE Sort_Data

SUBROUTINE Print_Data(Raw_Data,How_Many)
IMPLICIT NONE
INTEGER , INTENT(IN) :: How_Many
REAL , INTENT(IN) , DIMENSION(:) :: Raw_Data
INTEGER :: I
  OPEN(FILE='SORTED.DAT',UNIT=2)
  DO I=1,How_Many
    WRITE(UNIT=2,FMT=*) Raw_Data(I)
  ENDDO
  CLOSE(2)
END SUBROUTINE Print_Data
```

29.3.1 Allocatable function results

The following is based on an earlier example of a function that returned an array. This demonstrates that the result of a function can be declared to be an allocatable array.

```
PROGRAM Running

! this program has a function that returns an array
! that contains the running average for the array
! passed

IMPLICIT NONE

INTERFACE
  FUNCTION Running_Average(R,How_Many) RESULT(Rarray)
    IMPLICIT NONE
    INTEGER , INTENT(IN) :: How_Many
    REAL , ALLOCATABLE , DIMENSION (:) , &
      INTENT(IN) :: R
    REAL , ALLOCATABLE , DIMENSION(:) :: Rarray
  END FUNCTION Running_Average
END INTERFACE

INTERFACE
  SUBROUTINE Read_Data(File_Name,Raw_Data,How_Many)
```

```
      IMPLICIT NONE
      CHARACTER (LEN=*) , INTENT(IN) :: File_Name
      INTEGER , INTENT(IN) :: How_Many
      REAL , INTENT(OUT) , ALLOCATABLE , &
        DIMENSION(:) :: Raw_Data
    END SUBROUTINE Read_Data
  END INTERFACE

  INTEGER :: How_Many
  CHARACTER (LEN=20) :: File_Name

  REAL , ALLOCATABLE , DIMENSION(:)  :: Raw_Data
  REAL , ALLOCATABLE , DIMENSION(:)  :: RA

  INTEGER :: I

    PRINT * , ' How many data items are there?'
    READ  * , How_Many
    PRINT * , ' What is the file name?'
    READ '(A)',File_Name

    CALL Read_Data(File_Name,Raw_Data,How_Many)

    ALLOCATE(RA(1:How_Many))

    RA=Running_Average(Raw_Data,How_Many)

    DO I=1,How_Many
      PRINT *,Raw_Data(I),'    ' ,RA(I)
    END DO

  END PROGRAM Running

  FUNCTION Running_Average(R,How_Many) RESULT(Rarray)
  INTEGER , INTENT(IN) :: How_Many
  REAL , INTENT(IN) , ALLOCATABLE , DIMENSION(:) :: R
  REAL , ALLOCATABLE , DIMENSION(:) :: Rarray
  INTEGER :: I
  REAL :: Sum=0.0
    ALLOCATE(Rarray(1:How_Many))
    DO I=1,How_Many
      Sum = Sum + R(I)
```

```
      Rarray(I)=Sum/I
    END DO
END FUNCTION Running_Average

SUBROUTINE Read_Data(File_Name,Raw_Data,How_Many)
IMPLICIT NONE
CHARACTER (LEN=*) , INTENT(IN) :: File_Name
INTEGER , INTENT(IN) :: How_Many
REAL , INTENT(OUT) , ALLOCATABLE , &
    DIMENSION(:) :: Raw_Data
INTEGER :: I
    ALLOCATE(Raw_Data(1:How_Many))
    OPEN(FILE=File_Name,UNIT=1)
    DO I=1,How_Many
      READ (UNIT=1,FMT=*) Raw_Data(I)
    ENDDO

END SUBROUTINE Read_Data
```

29.3.2 Allocatable structure components

When working with user defined data types it is possible to make their components allocatable. This new feature provides a much safer way of working with dynamic memory than was previously possible. A very clear coverage can be found at the following address:

http://www.nag.co.uk/nagware/NP/TR.html

29.4 Fortran 2000

The next version of the language, possibly called Fortran 2000, has a target publication date of 2004.

This will include:

- Exception handling

- Facilities to simplify interoperability with the C language, in order to enable Fortran programs to access, and interact with, operating system features more easily

- Enhancements to derived data types to allow allocatable components and parametorized types

- Additional features to provide high performance numerical computing, possibly including facilities for interval arithmetic

- New input/output features such as asynchronous I/O and derived type I/O

- Features to allow object oriented programs to be written in Fortran

- Facilities to enable Fortran programs to take advantage of internationalization features provided through the operating system.

It is possible that not all of these will actually make it into the standard.

29.5 HPF

To quote their home page

- http://www.crpc.rice.edu/HPFF/home.html

'The High Performance Fortran Forum (HPFF), a coalition of industry, academic and laboratory representatives, works to define a set of extensions to Fortran 90 known collectively as High Performance Fortran (HPF). HPF extensions provide access to high-performance architecture features while maintaining portability across platforms.'

They also provide details of:

- Surveys of HPF compilers and tools;

- Currently available commercial HPF compilers;

- Public domain HPF compilation systems;

- Research prototypes of HPF and HPF-related compilation systems;

- Mailing list.

29.6 MPI

MPI (Message Passing Interface) is the standard for multicomputer and cluster message passing introduced by the Message Passing Interface Forum in April 1994.

- http://www.mpi-forum.org/index.html

Visit:

- http://www.tc.cornell.edu/

at Cornell University for details of the above in practice.

29.7 PVM

Parallel Virtual Machine consists of a library and a run-time environment which allow the distribution of a program over a network of (even heterogeneous) computers. Visit

- http://www.epm.ornl.gov/pvm/
- http://www.netlib.org/pvm3/

for more details.

29.8 Co–Array Fortran

Co-array Fortran (previously known as F--) is a small extension to Fortran 95. Visit:

- http://www.co-array.org/

for more details.

The syntax is architecture-independent and may be implemented on

- distributed memory machines
- shared memory machines
- clustered machines.

29.9 Openmp

To quote their home page '*The OpenMP Application Program Interface (API) supports multi-platform shared-memory parallel programming in C/C++ and Fortran on all architectures, including Unix platforms and Windows NT platforms. Jointly defined by a group of major computer hardware and software vendors, OpenMP is a portable, scalable model that gives shared-memory parallel programmers a simple and flexible interface for developing parallel applications for platforms ranging from the desktop to the supercomputer.*' Visit

- http://www.openmp.org/

for more information.

29.10 Elf

Elf is a clean Fortran 90 based subset. Visit

- http://www.lahey.com/

for more details.

29.11 F

F is another clean Fortran 90 based subset. Visit

- http://www.uni-comp.com/imagine1/

for more details.

29.12 Parallel programming and high performance computing

Have a look at:

- http://suparum.rz.uni-mannheim.de/docs/ind.html

for a lot of links to supercomputing centres and information on parallel computing in general.

For details of the US Accelerated Strategic Computing Initiative – ASCI – visit:

- http://www.sandia.gov/ASCI/
- http://www.lanl.gov/projects/asci/asci.html
- http://www.llnl.gov/asci/

The following are some useful UK sites:

- http://www.epsrc.ac.uk/hpc
- http://www.csar.cfs.ac.uk/

The following site lists the top 500 supercomputers in the world:

- http://www.netlib.org/benchmark/top500.html

To see what can be done with all this processing power visit:

- http://www.met-office.gov.uk/

29.12.1 Summary

Fortran is evolving and it has come a long way from the 1950s. It is now capable of solving quite a wide range of problems and work already in the pipeline is keeping it up to date.

A number of Fortran dialects have emerged, but is important to realize that they are dialects and not part of the Fortran standard, and hence using them cannot guarantee portability.

Computers capable of supporting multiple processors are dropping in price and becoming within the reach of most people. Developments in this area open up the possibilities of solving problems previously only possible on supercomputers.

Miscellanea

'The time has come,' the Walrus said,
  'To talk of many things:
of shoes–and ships–and sealing wax–
  of cabbages – and kings–
And why the sea is boiling hot–
  And whether pigs have wings.'

Lewis Carroll, *Through the Looking Glass, and What Alice Found There.*

Aims

The aim of this chapter is to provide a summary of what has been covered and help put some of the material into context. In particular:

- program development and software engineering;

- programming style – programs should be easy to read;

- programming style – programs should behave well;

- data structures;

- algorithms;

- recursion, and when not to use it;

- structured programming and the GOTO statement;

- efficiency, the space time trade off;

- simple debugging guidelines;

- numerical software sources.

There is much to be learnt concerning the discipline of programming that does appear rather nonsensical at first.

30 Miscellanea

By now it should be apparent that coding is only one small part of programming. A thorough knowledge of a programming language is however a prerequisite for long term success.

Fortran has, because of its history, a number of drawbacks in terms of its syntax and semantics. There are some features that are quite clumsy in comparison to other, more modern languages. However there are disadvantages too in starting afresh each time, and this is highlighted by the Algol W, Pascal, Modula, Modula 2, (Modula 3), Oberon, Oberon 2 development. Moving from one language to its successor requires code changes of varying degrees of effort.

30.1 Program development and software engineering

When one first starts programming the phrase software engineering will for many people appear meaningless. The problems that one solves when learning a programming language are by necessity small and amenable to fairly rapid solution and hence don't require too much thought and serious planning. This means that many people will initially have a rather simplistic attitude and approach to programming in the real world.

Consider the following classification, from Fairley (1985), *Software Engineering Concepts*:

Classification	Number of programmers	Time scale	Lines of code
Trivial	1	1–4 weeks	500
Small	1	1–6 months	1K–5K
Medium	2–5	1–2 years	5K-50K
Large	5–20	2–3 years	50K–100K
Very large	100–1000	4–5 years	1M
Massive	2000–5000	5–10 years	1M–10M

The development of reliable and correct programs requires increasing degrees of planning and organization as one moves from trivial, to small, to medium and beyond. It is worthwhile looking again at the earlier coverage of systems analysis and design to see what stages we need to go through in the process of software engineering.

There are some practical considerations that can be applied regarding our use of a programming language, in this case Fortran 90.

30.1.1 Modules

Modules have a very important role to play in software engineering. Their addition to Fortran has made the language a much better vehicle for the construction of large scale, reliable and easily maintainable programs. They enable us to adhere to the two guidelines of logical coherence and independence.

How big should a program unit be? The rather trite statement here is *small is beautiful*. Research has consistently shown that the time taken to test and debug a program unit grows exponentially with program size. Thus we have the following:

Program size	Testing and debugging time
1 unit	1 unit
2 units	4 units
3 units	8 units
4 units	32 units
etc.	

Experience also shows that most program units are between 60 and 120 lines of code. The reasons for this are to do with page size, rather than anything wonderfully technical. It is what we can fit on one or two pages, i.e. what we can examine and understand easily. If we have to flip back and for then we quickly lose track of what is happening.

30.1.2 Programming style – programs should be easy to read

Programs have to be read and understood by both computer systems (the compiler) and humans. Your time is a very valuable resource. It therefore pays to develop a good programming style. Clarity, simplicity and consistency are of the essence:

- meaningful names, not too long, not too short;
- comments should clarify the meaning of the code;

- indentation and formatting should be used to help structure the program and make it easier to read and understand; pretty print utilities may be available to help tidy up code.

The aim is not a Nobel prize for literature, rather a style that adds rather than detracts from understanding the meaning of the program.

30.1.3   Programming style – programs should behave well

Programs that behave badly will not be used, and most people reading this will know programs that they have stopped using precisely because they don't behave well. There are a number of things to consider here:

- robustness, e.g. a compiler should not abort at the first error, but rather continue until some error limit is reached, preferably under user control;

- input validation should be carried out, and the first criterion is legal input data. A second criteria is to allow correction of invalid data without forcing the user to have to retype everything. The phrase *'garbage in garbage out'* immediately springs to mind!

- defensive programming – carry out tests before undertaking an operation. This will trap many common run-time errors, e.g. inappropriate argument to a function like the tangent of 90 degrees;

- graceful degradation, e.g. ignore the one erroneous record in a file and carry on processing the rest of the file;

- stick to the standard – as was stated earlier this pays off in the protection of the investment in people, in portability and a known reference point. If you have to use non-standard features then learn fully what that entails. The *apparently* identical language extension in two compilers can quite legitimately produce completely different results. Let the buyer beware!

30.2 Data structures

Data structures have an enormous role to play in programming. An acquaintance with the wide range of data structuring techniques that is available is another skill that needs to be developed.

30.3 Algorithms

Algorithms have an important role to play in programming. The ability to choose the most appropriate algorithm for a particular problem is another skill that needs to be developed.

30.4 Recursion

Recursion is a very powerful tool in problem solving. However there are occasions when the overhead of recursion can be a problem. In this case it may be necessary to attempt to remove the recursion. There are a number of books that address this issue.

30.5 Structured programming and the goto statement

Consider the task of painting the floor boards in a room. Imagine getting a brush and a can of varnish and starting at the door. At some stage we end up in in the corner of the room and we have no way of leaving the room without walking over the recently painted boards. No problem: we GOTO the door.

Whilst the above may strike one as silly the intention is to highlight the problems that can be created by inadequate preparation and planning.

As Knuth makes clear in *Structured Programming with goto Statements* the real issue is structured programming, and structured programming is not the process of writing programs and then eliminating their goto statements. The comment by W.W. Peterson in this paper (regarding the teaching of PL/I, where he taught students to use the goto in exceptional circumstances) highlights this point: '*A disturbingly large percentage of the students ran into situations that require gotos, and sure enough, it was often because* **while** *didn't work well to their plan, but almost invariably because their plan was poorly thought out.*'

We have left the coverage of the GOTO statement until the last chapter to try and get people to think of solving problems without its use. The more astute reader may have already noticed that we have several examples throughout the notes that use an implied goto. These are the CYCLE and EXIT statements in loops. There is nothing wrong with using a goto providing its meaning is clear.

The syntax of the statement is:

```
GOTO label
```

where label is a string of one to five decimal digits. Any statement in a Fortran program may have a label, e.g.

```
GOTO 100
```

Commonly used with a logical IF statement, e.g.

```
IF (Error) GOTO 1000
```

30.6 Efficiency, space time trade off

Efficiency is important, but the first priority must always be program correctness. A good understanding of the capabilities of the language, combined with a reasonable breadth of knowledge in data structuring and algorithms is a necessary precursor to concerns regarding efficiency.

There is a simple trade off available with many problems: space versus time. This means that the program will require a large amount of memory to solve a problem, and this will be reflected in a time reduction. Memory cannot be infinite on any system, so there will be instances when a longer execution time has to be endured through lack of physical memory.

It will often be necessary therefore to have only part of the data in memory. We will have to use disk to store the rest of the data we are processing. In situations like this it is recommended that you use unformatted files. As was stated earlier they offer no loss of precision, and none of the overhead involved in formatting.

30.7 Program testing

Simplistically this means choosing a suite of data set inputs that test the following:

- one or more commonly occurring cases;
- limiting cases;
- pathological cases.

Just because it works on a small range of test data does not mean that there are no bugs.

30.8 Simple debugging techniques

The first choice is to switch on all error testing that can be provided by the compiler, and flag all non-standard language features. This will trap the most common error which is array indexing going beyond the declared bounds, for any array data type.

Use of interface blocks will trap another very common error which is parameter mismatch between the calling routine and called routine.

The simplest debugging technique is the inclusion of print statements to clearly identify where the problem lies, and the state of the variables of interest. There is no substitute for sitting down and working through a listing of the program with sample runs to try and determine where problems lie.

30.9 Software tools

There will be a range of tools available that aid in the program development process for the hardware and software platform that you use.

30.9.1 Cross referencing

Good compilers will offer cross reference compilation options. It is probable that standalone tools in this area will eventually become available over the Internet.

30.9.2 Pretty print

It is likely that tools to aid in consistent program style will become available in the near future over the Internet. NAG for example offers a tool to pretty print Fortran 90 programs.

30.9.3 NAGWare f90 Tools

The following tools are currently available:

- **Polisher**: Pretty prints Fortran 90 code.

- **Declaration Standardiser**: Standardizes declarations of variables and parameters.

- **Precision Standardiser**: Modifies software to use parameterized precision.

- **Name Changer**: Changes names.

Additional tools will be added with later releases.

30.10 Numerical software sources

This software exists in two main forms.

Firstly as coded algorithms, which can be obtained in a variety of source forms, which you as end user include in your own program and compile with your particular compiler. Some of these are verified, others are made available with no warranty!

Secondly as commercially pre-compiled libraries for a variety of compilers, operating systems and hardware platforms. These are subject to rigorous testing by the suppliers and very well documented.

ACM – TOMS Transactions on Mathematical Software

They publish mathematical software as part of their collected algorithms of the ACM, available on magnetic tape and diskette. Further information is available on the World Wide Web, URL, http://www.acm.org

Chapter 30

These sources are subject to validation and corrections and improvements are published.

30.10.1 Numerical Algorithms Group

This is one of the two major commercial providers of numeric and statistical software. Their home page is:

http://www.nag.co.uk/

30.10.2 Visual Numerics

Visual Numerics are the other major commercial provider of numeric and statistical software. Their home page is:

http://www.vni.com/index.html

The following is the library home page:

http://www.vni.com/products/imsl/index.html

30.10.3 Netlib

To quote their home page *'The Netlib repository contains freely available software, documents, and databases of interest to the numerical, scientific computing, and other communities. The repository is maintained by AT&T Bell Laboratories, the University of Tennessee and Oak Ridge National Laboratory, and by colleagues world-wide. The collection is replicated at several sites around the world, automatically synchronized, to provide reliable and network efficient service to the global community.'*

Home page is:

http://www.netlib.org/

The software is free but you use it at your own risk, no support offered, and their motto is, *Anything free comes with no guarantee!*

30.11 Coda

Good luck!

30.12 Bibliography: All sources (bar one) taken from comp.software-eng.

30.12.1 Software engineering

The best place to start is on USENET news. One of the FAQs is a comprehensive post on reading material for software engineers, and it is maintained by professional software engineers. The current top five are in order below, the sixth is recommended reading.

Pfleeger S., *Software Engineering: The Production of Quality Software*, Macmillan, 1991.

Pressman R., *Software Engineering. A Practitioner's Approach*, McGraw Hill, 1987.

Sage A., Palmer J.D., *Software Systems Engineering*, Not known.

Ghezzi C., Jayazeri M., Mandrioli D., *Fundamentals of Software Engineering*, Prentice Hall.

Berzins V., Luqi, *Software Engineering with Abstractions*, Addison Wesley, 1991.

Brooks Frederick P. Jr, *The Mythical Man Month: Essays of Software Engineering*, Addison Wesley.

30.12.2 Programming style

Anand N., *Clarify Function!*, ACM SigPLAN Notices, 23(6), 69–79.

Henry S., *A Technique for Hiding Proprietary Details While Providing Sufficient Information for Researchers; or, do you Recognise this Well Known Algorithm?*, Journal of Systems and Software, 8(1), 3–11.

Brooks R., *Studying Programmer Behaviour Experimentally: The Problems of Proper Methodology*, Communications of the ACM, 23(4), 207–213.

30.12.3 Software testing

Beizer Boris, *Software Testing Techniques*, Van Nostrand Reinhold, 1990.

Hetzel William C., *The Complete Guide to Software Testing*, 2nd edition, QED Information Services Inc, 1988.

Software Research Inc., *Testing Techniques Newsletter*, Software Research Inc.

30.12.4 Fun

Martin Gardner, *Lewis Carroll: The Annotated Alice*, Penguin.

- Martin Gardner has been writing articles on mathematics as fun for twenty years. Lewis Carroll, née Charles Lutwidge Dodgson was a lecturer in mathematics at Christ Church College, Oxford.

A Glossary

actual argument

A value (variable, expression or procedure) passed from a calling program unit to a sub-program unit.

adjustable array

An explicit shape array that is a dummy argument to a sub-program.

algorithm

Derived from the name of the 9th century Persian mathematician Abu Ja'far Mohammed ibn Musa al-Kuwarizmi (father of Ja'far Mohammed, son of Moses, native of Kuwarizmi), corrupted through western culture as Al-Kuwarizmi. Now a sequence of computations.

allocatable array

An array that has the ALLOCATABLE attribute.

argument

Exists in two forms; actual argument which is in the calling routine, and is one of a variable, expression or procedure, and dummy argument, which is in the called routine.

argument association

The process of matching up an actual argument and dummy argument during program execution.

array

An array is a data structure where each scalar element has the same type and kind. An array may be up to rank 7. It may be referenced by element (via subscripts), by section or as a whole.

array constructor

A mechanism used to initialize or give values to a one dimensional array. The RESHAPE function can then be used to handle rank 2 and above arrays.

array element

A scalar item of an array. An array element is picked out by a subscript.

array element ordering

the elements of an array, regardless of rank, form a linear sequence. The sequence is such that the subscripts along the first dimension vary most rapidly.

array section

A part of an array. The actual set depends on the subscripts.

ASCII

American Standard Code for Information Interchange. See Appendix C.

association

The means by which an entity can be referenced by different names in one scoping unit, or one or more names in multiple scoping units.

assumed length dummy argument

A dummy argument that inherits the length attribute of the actual argument.

assumed shape array

A dummy argument that inherits the shape of the associated argument.

assumed size array

A dummy array whose size is inherited from the associated actual argument.

attribute

A property of a data type, and specified in a type declaration statement.

automatic array

This is an explicit shape array that is a local variable in a sub-program unit.

bound

The bounds of an array are the upper and lower limits of the index in each dimension.

character constant

A constant that is a string of one or more printable ASCII characters, enclosed in ' (apostrophe) or " (quotation mark).

character string

A sequence of one or more characters. These are contiguous.

collating sequence

The order in which a set of characters is sorted by default. The standard does not require that a processor provide the ASCII encoding, but does require intrinsic functions that convert between the processor encoding and the ASCII encoding.

compilation unit

One or more source files that are compiled to form one object file.

component

Part of a derived type definition.

concatenate

join together two or more character items using the character concatenation operator //.

conformable

Two arrays are said to be conformable if they have the same shape.

constant

A constant is a data object whose value cannot be changed There are two kinds in Fortran: one is obtained using the PARAMETER statement, the other is a literal constant in an expression, e.g. with the expression 4*ATAN(1) both 4 and 1 are literal constants. It may be a scalar or an array.

contiguous

Normally applied to items that are adjacent in memory, e.g. characters in a character variable.

data entity

A data object that has a specific type.

data object

a data object is a constant, variable or part of a constant or variable.

data type

For each data type there is the following: 0. a name 1. a set of values from a domain; 2. a set of valid operations upon these values; 3. a display method There are five predefined data types in Fortran and these are integer, real, complex, character and logical.

For integers the values are drawn from the domain of integer numbers, the valid operations are addition, subtraction, multiplication, division and exponentiation, and they are displayed as a sequence of digits.

declaration

A declaration is a non-executable statement that specifies attributes of a program element, e.g. specifying the dimension of an array, and the type of a variable.

default kind

The kind type parameter which is used for one of Fortran's base types (integer, real, complex, character or logical) if one is not specified.

deferred shape array

An allocatable array or an array pointer. The bounds are specified with a colon, e.g. (:).

defined

For a data object having a valid value.

derived type

A data type that is user defined and not one of the five intrinsic types.

dimension

An array can be from one to seven dimensioned inclusive. Also called the rank.

dummy argument

A variable name that appears in the bracketed or parenthesized list following the procedure name. (e.g. function or subroutine name). Dummy arguments take on the actual values of the corresponding arguments in the calling routine.

elemental

An operation that applies independently to each element in an array.

entity

Rather vague term covering a constant, variable, program unit, etc.

exceptional values

Normally restricted to real numbers and typically one of non-normalized numbers, infinity, not-a-number (NaN) values, etc.

explicit interface

A mechanism to make information available between the calling routine and the called routine. This information includes the names of the procedures, the dummy arguments, the attributes of the arguments, the attributes of functions, and the order of the arguments.

explicit shape array

A named array that has its bounds specified in each dimension.

expression

An expression is a sequence of operands and operators that specifies a computation.

extent

The number of elements of one dimension of an array. Also called the size.

external subprogram

An external subprogram is one that is global to the whole program.

function

One of the two procedure mechanisms available in Fortran along with the subroutine. They effectively provide a way of invoking a computation by using the function name, and return a result. There is the concept of type and kind for the result.

function reference

A function is invoked by the use of its name in an expression.

function result

The result value(s) from invoking a function.

generic

Simplistically the ability of a procedure to accept arguments of more than type. This facility is taken for granted with the intrinsic procedures, and the user can now create their own generic procedures.

global

An entity that is available throughout the executable program. A global entity has global scope. See also scope and local scope.

host association

The mechanism by which a module procedure, internal procedure or derived type definition accesses entities of the host.

implicit interface

A procedure interface whose properties are not known within the scope of the calling routine.

inquiry function

A function whose result depends on the properties of the argument.

interface block

A sequence of statements starting with an INTERFACE statement and ending with an END INTERFACE statement.

interface body

The sequence of statements in an interface block between either a FUNCTION or SUBROUTINE statement and the corresponding END statement

internal procedure

A procedure that is contained within an internal subprogram. The program unit containing the internal procedure is called the host. The internal procedure is local to the host and inherits the host environment through host association.

intrinsic procedure

One of the standard supplied procedures.

kind

For each of the five Fortran types (integer, real, complex, logical and character) there is the concept of kind. For example for integers it is common to find 8 bit, 16 bit and 32-bit implementations. Each of these has an associated kind type.

For real and complex types this enables us to choose both the range and precision of the numbers we work with.

For characters we can chose between character sets, which is of considerable use for working with different languages.

kind type parameter

An integer value used to identify the kind of one of the five base types, see above.

language extension

Most compiler implementations will provide language extensions. These are NOT part of the standard, and make porting code suites between different hardware and software platforms difficult and sometimes impossible.

linker

A program that is normally the final stage in the process of going from Fortran source to executable.

local entity

An entity that is only available within the context of a sub-program.

main program

A program unit that contains a PROGRAM statement.

module

A program unit that contains specifications and definitions that other program units can access and use.

module procedure

A function or subroutine defined within a module

name

An entity with a program, e.g. constant, variable, function result, procedure, program unit, dummy argument.

name association

This provides access to the same entity (either data or a procedure) from different scoping units by the same or different name.

nesting

The placing of one entity within another, e.g. one loop within another or one subprogram within another.

nonexecutable statement

A language statement that describes program attributes, but does not cause any action when the program is executed.

object file

File created after successful compilation. Used by the linker to generate an executable.

parameter

Term used to describe two completely different things. 1. a named constant – and hence the PARAMETER attribute. 2. more generally equivalent to argument

pointer

A data object that has the POINTER attribute.

pointer association

The association of a part of memory to a pointer by means of a target.

precision

The number of significant digits in a real number.

procedure

A function or subroutine.

procedure interface

The statements that specify the name of a procedure, the characteristics of that procedure, the name of the dummy arguments, the attributes of the dummy arguments the generic identifier (optional) for the procedure.

program

A program is an entity that can be compiled and executed on its own. There must be at least a declaration block and execution block.

program unit

A main program or a subprogram. The subprogram can be a function, subroutine or module.

rank

The rank of an array is the number of dimensions.

recursion

A property of a function or subroutine, and it means that the function or subroutine references itself directly or indirectly.

reference

a data object reference is the appearance of a named entity in an executable statement requiring the value of the object.

relational expression

An expression containing one or more of the relational operators and operands of numeric or character type.

scalar

A single data object of any type. A scalar has a rank of zero.

scalar variable

A variable of scalar type.

scope and scoping unit

The part of a program in which a name has a defined meaning. The name may be a named constant, a variable, a function, a procedure, or dummy argument. The part of the program is one of a program unit or subprogram, a derived type definition or a procedure interface body. Scoping units cannot overlap, but one scoping unit may be contained in another. In the latter case we have an example of host association.

shape

The rank and extents of an array.

shape conformance

Generally means that two or more arrays have the same rank and extent.

size

The total number of elements in an array – the product of the extents.

source file

A file known to the operating system that contains the Fortran statements.

statement

An instruction in a programming language, and they are normally classified as executable and nonexecutable.

stride

The increment in subscript triplet.

structure

Either a scalar data object of derived type or a composite entity containing one or more subcomponents.

subprogram

A user written or supplied function or subroutine.

subroutine

A user subprogram that is invoked with the CALL statement. It can return one value, many values or no value at all to the calling program through the arguments.

subscript

a scalar integer expression used to select an element of an array

substring

a contiguous set of characters in a string.

target

A named data object associated with a pointer.

transformational function

An intrinsic function that is not elemental or inquiry.

truncation

For real numbers the approximation obtained by chopping off the fractional part of the number and working with the integer part.

For character variables removing one or more characters from a string.

type declaration

One of the nonexecutable statements in Fortran, and one of INTEGER, REAL, COMPLEX, CHARACTER, LOGICAL or TYPE.

underflow

A condition where the result of an arithmetic expression is smaller than the minimum value in the range for that data type.

user-defined type

A data type that is defined by the user and not one of the intrinsic types.

variable

A data object that has an associated memory location, whose value can be changed during program execution. A variable may be a scalar or an array.

B   Sample Program Examples

There is a coverage of the standard that applies, where appropriate. For the more curious and inquisitive user they may be interested in the information held at:

www.iso.ch

which is the International Standards Organisations world wide web page.

Ada: ISO/IEC 8652:1995
```
WITH TEXT_IO;USE TEXT_IO;
PROCEDURE Add IS
   X1   : FLOAT;
   X2   : FLOAT;
   Sum : FLOAT:=0.0;
BEGIN
PACKAGE FLT_IO IS NEW FLOAT_IO(FLOAT);
USE FLT_IO;
   PUT(" Type in the two numbers");
   GET(X1);
   GET(X2);
   Sum:=X1 + X2;
   NEW_LINE(1);
   PUT(X1);
   PUT(" + ");
   PUT(X2);
   PUT(" = ");
   PUT(Sum);
END Add;
```

Algol: Was ISO 1538, but this has been withdrawn.

Algol 68: No standard, but the major definition is in the Revised Report.

Apl: ISO 8485:1989

Basic: ISO/IEC 10279:1991, Full Standard; ISO 6373:1984, Minimal Conformance.
```
100 PRINT " Type in two numbers"
200 INPUT A, B
300 C = A + B
400 PRINT A, " + ", B, " = ", C
```

C: ISO/IEC 9899:1990

```c
# include <stdio.h>
main()
{ float a,b,sum;
  printf(" Type in two numbers ");
  ooanf("%f",&a);
  scanf("%f",&b);
  sum=a+b;
  printf("%f",a);
  printf(" + ");
  printf("%f",b);
  printf(" = ");
  printf("%f",sum);
  printf("\n"); }
```

C++: 1997–1998

```cpp
#include <iostream.hxx>
#include <math.h>
int main()
{    float a,b,sum;
  sum=0.0;
  cout < " Type in two numbers   " ;
  cin > a > b ;
  sum =   a + b ;
  cout < a < " + " < b < " = " < sum < "\n" ;
  return (0); }
```

Cobol: ISO/IEC 1989:1985

Fortran 90: ISO/IEC 1539:1990

```fortran
PROGRAM Example
IMPLICIT NONE
REAL :: A
REAL :: B
REAL :: Sum=0.0
  PRINT * , ' Type in two numbers'
  READ * , A,B
  Sum = A + B
  PRINT * , A ,' + ', B , ' = ', Sum
END PROGRAM Example
```

ICON: No standard.

Lisp

Logo: No standard.

Modula 2: ISO/IEC Draft 10514
```
MODULE Example;
   FROM InOut IMPORT Write,WriteLn,WriteString;
   FROM InOut IMPORT ReadReal,WriteReal;
   VAR
     A,B : REAL;
     Sum : REAL;
BEGIN
   Sum := 0.0;
   WriteString(" Type in two numbers");
   WriteLn;
   ReadReal(A);
   ReadReal(B);
   Sum := A + B;
   WriteReal(A,10);
   WriteString(" + ");
   WriteReal(B,10);
   WriteString(" = ");
   WriteReal(Sum,10);
   WriteLn;
END Example.
```

Oberon: No standard.

Pascal: Pascal – ISO 7185:1990; Extended Pascal – ISO/IEC 10206: 1991
```
PROGRAM Example(INPUT,OUTPUT);
VAR
   A : REAL;
   B : REAL;
   Sum : REAL;
BEGIN
   WRITELN(' Type in two numbers');
   READLN(A,B);
   Sum := A + B;
   WRITELN(A, ' + ' , B ,' = ' , Sum)
END.
```

Postscript:

Prolog: ISO/IEC Draft 13211-1

SQL: ISO 9075:1992(E)

Simula: No international standard, but a Swedish one does exist.

Smalltalk:

Snobol:

C   ASCII Character Set

0	nul	32		64	@	96	'
1	soh	33	!	65	A	97	a
2	stx	34	"	66	B	98	b
3	etx	35	#	67	C	99	c
4	eot	36	$	68	D	100	d
5	enq	37	%	69	E	101	e
6	ack	38	&	70	F	102	f
7	bel	39	'	71	G	103	g
8	bs	40	(	72	H	104	h
9	ht	41	)	73	I	105	i
10	lf	42	*	74	J	106	j
11	vt	43	+	75	K	107	k
12	ff	44	,	76	L	108	l
13	cr	45	-	77	M	109	m
14	so	46	.	78	N	110	n
15	si	47	/	79	O	111	o
16	dle	48	0	80	P	112	p
17	dc1	49	1	81	Q	113	q
18	dc2	50	2	82	R	114	r
19	dc3	51	3	83	S	115	s
20	dc4	52	4	84	T	116	t
21	nak	53	5	85	U	117	u
22	syn	54	6	86	V	118	v
23	etb	55	7	87	W	119	w
24	can	56	8	88	X	120	x
25	em	57	9	89	Y	121	y
26	sub	58	:	90	Z	122	z
27	esc	59	;	91	[	123	{
28	fs	60	<	92	\	124		
29	gs	61	=	93	]	125	}
30	rs	62	>	94	^	126	~
31	us	63	? l	95	_	127	del

D   Intrinsic Functions and Procedures

The following abbreviations and typographic conventions are used in this appendix.

Argument type and result type:

I	Integer
R	Real
C	Complex
N	Numeric (any of integer, real, complex)
L	Logical
P	Pointer
T	Target
DP	Double precision
Char	Character, length = 1.
S	Character

Class

E	elemental function
I	inquiry function
T	transformational function
S	subroutine

See Chapter 14 for more information on these classifications.

Arguments in italics

ALL(Mask,*Dim*)

are optional arguments, i.e. Dim may be omitted in the example above.

Double precision

Before Fortran 90 if you required real variables to have greater precision than the default real then the only option available was to declare them as double precision. With the introduction of kind types with Fortran 90 the use of double precision declarations is not recommended, and instead real entities with a kind type offering more than the default precision should be used.

Kind optional argument

There are several functions that have an optional argument Kind, e.g. AINT(A,Kind). If Kind is absent the result is the same kind type as the first argument, in this case A. If Kind is present the result has the kind type specified by this argument.

Result type

When the result type is as argument type then the result is not just the same type as the argument but also the same kind.

Miscellaneous rules

When the argument is Back it is of logical type.

When the argument is Count_Rate, Count_Max, Dim, Kind, Len, Order, N_Copies, Shape, Shift, Values it is of integer type.

When the argument is Mask it is of logical type.

When the argument is Target it is of pointer or target type.

ABS(A)

Yields the absolute value unless A is complex, see below.

Argument: A	**Type:** N
Result: As argument	**Class:** E

Note: If A is complex (x,y) then the functions returns $\sqrt{x^2 + y^2}$

Example: R1=ABS(A)

ACHAR(I)

Returns character in the ASCII character set.

Argument: I	**Type:** I
Result: Char	**Class:** E

Example: C=ACHAR(I)

ACOS(X)

Arccosine (inverse cosine).

Argument: X	**Type:** R
Result: As argument	**Class:** E

Note: $|x| \le 1$

Example: Y=ACOS(X)

ADJUSTL(String)

Adjust string left, removing leading blanks and inserting trailing blanks.

Argument: String	**Type:** S
Result: As argument	**Class:** E

Example: S=ADJUSTL(S)

ADJUSTR(String)

Adjust string right, removing trailing blanks and inserting leading blanks.

Argument: String	**Type:** S
Result: As argument	**Class:** E

Example: S=ADJUSTR(S)

AIMAG(Z)

Imaginary part of complex argument.

Argument: Z	**Type:** C
Result: As argument	**Class:** E

Example: Y=AIMAG(Z)

AINT(A,*Kind*)

Truncation.

Argument: A	**Type:** R
Result: As A	**Class:** E
Argument: Kind	**Type:** I

Example: Y=AINT(Z) and when Z=0.3 Y=0, when Z=2.73 Y=2.0, when Z=-2.73 Y=-2.0

ALL(Mask,*Dim*)

Determines whether all values are true in Mask along dimension Dim.

Argument: Mask	**Type:** L
Result: L	**Class:** T

Note: Dim must be a scalar in the range $1 \leq Dim \leq n$ where n is the rank of Mask. The result is scalar if Dim is absent or Mask has rank 1. Otherwise it works on the dimension Dim of Mask and the result is an array of rank n-1.

Example: T=ALL(M)

ALLOCATED(Array)

Returns true if array is allocated.

Argument: Array	**Type:** Any
Result: L	**Class:** I

Note: Array must be declared with the ALLOCATABLE attribute.

Example: IF (ALLOCATED(Array)) THEN ...

ANINT(A,*Kind*)

Rounds reals, i.e. returns nearest whole number.

Argument: A	**Type:** R
Result: As A	**Class:** E

Example: Z=ANINT(A), if A = 5.63 Z = 6, if A=-5.7 Z = -6.0

ANY(Mask,*Dim*)

Determines whether any value is true in Mask along dimension Dim.

Argument: Mask	**Type:** L
Result: L	**Class:** T

Note: Mask must be an array. The result is a scalar if Dim is absent or if Mask is of rank 1. Otherwise it works on the dimension Dim of Mask and the result is an array of rank n-1.

Example: T=ANY(A)

ASIN(X)

Arcsine.

Argument: X	**Type:** R
Result: As argument	**Class:** E

Example: Z=ASIN(X)

ASSOCIATED(Pointer,*Target)*

Returns the association status of the pointer.

Argument: Pointer	**Type:** P
Result: I,	**Class:** I

Note:

1. If Target is absent then the result is true if POINTER is associated with a target, otherwise false.
2. If Target is present and is a target, the result is true if Pointer is currently associated with Target and false if it is not.
3. If Target is present and is a pointer, the result is true if both Pointer and Target are currently associated with the same target, and is false otherwise. If either Pointer or Target is disassociated the result is false.

Example: T=ASSOCIATED(P)

ATAN(X)

Arctangent.

Argument: X	**Type:** R
Result: As argument	**Class:** E

Example: Z=ATAN(X)

ATAN2(Y,X)

Arctangent of Y / X.

Argument: Y	**Type:** R
Result: As arguments	**Class:** E

Example: Z=ATAN2(Y,X)

BIT_SIZE(I)

Returns the number of bits, as defined by the numeric model for integer numbers in Chapter 8.

Argument: I	**Type:** I
Result: As argument	**Class:** I

Example: N_Bits=SIZE(I)

BTEST(I,Pos)

Returns true if the bit is set in the integer argument at the position given by the second argument.

Argument: I   **Type:** I

Result: L   **Class:** E

Example: T=BTEST(I,Pos)

CEILING(A,*Kind*)

Returns the smallest integer greater than or equal to the argument.

Argument: A   **Type:** R

Result: I   **Class:** E

Note:

If kind is present the result has the kind type parameter Kind.

Otherwise the result of type default integer.

Example: I=CEILING(A) If A=12.21 then I=13, if A=-3.16 then I=-3

CHAR(I,*Kind*)

Returns the character in a given position in the processor collating sequence associated with the specified kind type parameter. Normally ASCII.

Argument: I   **Type:** I

Result: CHAR   **Class:** E

Example: C=CHAR(65) and for the ASCII character set C='A'.

CMPLX(X,*Y,Kind*)

Converts to complex from integer, real and complex.

Argument: X   **Type:** N

Result: C   **Class:** E

Note:
1. If X is complex and Y is absent it is as if Y were present with the value AIMAG(X).
2. If X is not complex and Y is absent, it is as if Y were present with the value 0.

Example: Z=CMPLX(X,Y)

CONJG(Z)

Conjugate of a complex argument.

Argument: Z	**Type:** C
Result: As Z	**Class:** E

Example: Z1=CONJG(Z)

COS(X)

Cosine.

Argument: X	**Type:** R, C
Result: As argument	**Class:** E

Note: The arguments of all trigonometric functions should be in radians, not degrees.

Example: A=COS(X)

COSH(X)

Hyperbolic cosine.

Argument: X	**Type:** R
Result: As argument	**Class:** E

Example: Z=COSH(X)

COUNT(Mask,*Dim*)

Returns the number of true elements in Mask along dimension Dim.

Argument: Mask	**Type:** L
Result: I	**Class:** T

Note: Dim must be a scalar in the range $1 \le Dim \le n$ where n is the rank of Mask. The result is scalar if Dim is absent or Mask has rank 1. Otherwise it works on the dimension Dim of Mask and the result is an array of rank n-1.

Example: N=COUNT(A)

CPU_TIME(Time)

Returns the processor time.

Argument: Time	**Type:** R
Result: N/A	**Class:** S

Example: CALL CPU_TIME(Time)

CSHIFT(Array,Shift,*Dim*)

Circular shift on a rank one array or rank one sections of higher rank arrays.

Argument: Array	**Type:** Any
Result: As Array	**Class:** T

Note: Array must be an array, Shift must be a scalar if Array has rank one, otherwise it is an array of rank *n*-1, where *n* is the rank of Array. Dim must be a scalar with a value in the range $1 \leq Dim \leq n$.

Example: Array=CSHIFT(Array,10)

DATE_AND_TIME(*Date,Time,Zone,Values*)

Returns the current date and time (compatible with ISO 8601:1988).

Argument: Date	**Type:** S
Result: N/A	**Class:** S

Time and Zone are of type S.

Note:
1. Date is optional and must be scalar and of length 8 characters in order to return the complete value of the form CCYYMMDD where CC is the century, YY is the year, MM is the month and DD is the day. It is INTENT(OUT).
2. Time is optional and must be scalar and of length 10 characters in order to return the complete value of the form hhmmss.sss where hh is the hour, mm is the minutes and ss.sss is the seconds and milliseconds. It is INTENT(OUT).
3. Zone is optional and must be scalar and must be of length 5 characters in order to return the complete value of the form ±hhmm where hh and mm are the time differences with respect to Coordinated Universal Time in hours and minutes. It is INTENT(OUT).
4. Values is optional and a rank one array of size 8. It is INTENT(OUT). The values returned are as follows:
Values(1) = the year
Values(2) = the month
Values(3) = the day
Values(4) = the time with respect to Coordinated Universal Time in minutes.
Values(5) = the hour (24 hour clock)
Values(6) = the minutes
Values(7) = the seconds
Values(8) = the milliseconds in the range 0–999.

Example: CALL DATE_TIME(D,T,Z,V)

DBLE(A)

Converts to double precision from integer, real, and complex

Argument: A   **Type:** N

Result: DP   **Class:** E

Example: D=DBLE(A)

DIGITS(X)

Returns the number of significant digits of the argument as defined in the numeric models for integer and reals in Chapter 8.

Argument: X   **Type:** I,R

Result: I   **Class:** I

Example: I=DIGITS(X)

DIM(X,Y)

Returns first argument minus minimum of the two arguments: X -MIN(X,Y).

Argument: X   **Type:** I

Result: As arguments   **Class:** E

Example: Z=DIM(X,Y)

DOT_PRODUCT(Vector_1,Vector_2)

Performs the mathematical dot product of two rank one arrays.

Argument: Vector_1   **Type:** Nt

Result: As arguments   **Class:** T

Vector_2 is as Vector_1.

Note:
1. If Vector_1 is of type integer or real the result has the value SUM(Vector_1*Vector_2).
2. If Vector_1 is complex the result has the value SUM(CONJG(Vector_1)*Vector_2).
3. If Vector_1 is logical the result has the value ANY(Vector_1 .AND. Vector_2).

Example: A=DOT_PRODUCT(X,Y)

DPROD(X,Y)

Double precision product of two reals.

| **Argument:** X | **Type:** R |
| **Result:** DP | **Class:** E |

Example: D=DPROD(X,Y)

EOSHIFT(Array,Shift,*Boundary,Dim*)

End off shift of a rank 1 array or rank one section of a higher rank array.

| **Argument:** Array | **Type:** Any |
| **Result:** As Array | **Class:** T |

Boundary is as Array.

Note: Array must be an array, Shift must be a scalar if Array has rank one, otherwise it is an array of rank n-1, where n is the rank of Array. Boundary must be scalar if Array has rank one, otherwise it must be either scalar or of rank n-1. Dim must be a scalar with a value in the range $1 \le Dim \le n$.

Example: A=EOSHIFT(A,Shift)

EPSILON(X)

Smallest difference between two reals of that kind. See Chapter 8 and real numeric model.

| **Argument:** X | **Type:** R |
| **Result:** As argument | **Class:** I |

Example: Tiny=EPSILON(X)

EXP(X)

Exponential, e^x.

| **Argument:** X | **Type:** R, C |
| **Result:** As argument | **Class:** E |

Example: Y=EXP(X)

EXPONENT(X)

Returns the exponent component of the argument. See Chapter 8 and the real numeric model.

| **Argument:** X | **Type:** R |

Result: I   **Class:** E

Example: I=EXPONENT(X)

FLOOR(A, *Kind).*

Returns the greatest integer less than or equal to the argument

Argument: A   **Type:** R

Result: I   **Class:** E

Note:

If kind is present the result has the kind type parameter Kind.

Otherwise the result of type default integer.

Example: I=FLOOR(A) and when A=5.2 I has the value 5, when A=-9.7 I has the value -10

FRACTION(X)

Returns the fractional part of the real numeric model of the argument See Chapter 8 and the real numeric model.

Argument: X   **Type:** R

Result: As X   **Class:** E

Example: F=FRACTION(X)

HUGE(X)

Returns the largest number for the kind type of the argument. See Chapter 8 and the real and integer numeric models.

Argument: X   **Type:** I,R

Result: As argument   **Class:** I

Example: H=HUGE(X)

IACHAR(C)

Returns the position of the character argument in the ASCII collating sequence.

Argument: C   **Type:** Char

Result: I   **Class:** E

Example: I=IACHAR('A') returns the value 65.

IAND(I,J)

Performs a logical AND on the arguments.

    Argument: I   **Type:** I

    Result: As arguments   **Class:** E

Example: K=IAND(I,J)

IBCLR(I,Pos)

Clears one bit of the argument to zero.

    Argument: I   **Type:** I

    Result: As I   **Class:** E

Note: $0 \leq Pos < BIT\_SIZE(I)$

Example: I=IBCLR(I,Pos)

IBITS(I,Pos,Len)

Returns a sequence of bits.

    Argument: I   **Type:** I

    Result: As I   **Class:** E

Note: $0 \leq Pos$ and $(Pos+Len) \leq BIT\_SIZE(I)$ and $Len \geq 0$.

Example: Slice=IBITS(I,Pos,Len)

IBSET(I,Pos)

Sets one bit of the argument to one.

    Argument: I   **Type:** I

    Result: As I   **Class:** E

Note: $0 \leq Pos < BIT\_SIZE(I)$.

Example: I=IBSET(I,Pos)

ICHAR(C)

Returns the position of a character in the processor collating sequence associated with the kind type parameter of the argument. Normally the position in the ASCII collating sequence.

    Argument: C   **Type:** CHAR

    Result: I   **Class:** E

Example: I=ICHAR('A') would return the value 65 for the ASCII character set.

IEOR(I,J)

Performs an exclusive OR on the arguments.

Argument: I	**Type:** I
Result: As I	**Class:** E

Example: I=IEOR(I,J)

INDEX(String,Substring,*Back*)

Locates one substring in another, i.e. returns position of Substring in character expression String.

Argument: String	**Type:** S
Result: I	**Class:** E

Substring is of type S.

Note:
1. If Back is absent or present with the value .FALSE. then the function returns the start position of the first occurrence of the substring. If LEN(Substring) = 0 then one is returned.
2. If Back is present with the value .TRUE. then the function returns the start position of the last occurrence of the substring. If LEN(Substring) = 0 then the value (LEN(String) + 1) is returned.
3. If the substring is not found the result is zero.
4. If LEN(String) < LEN(Substring) the result is zero.

Example:
Where=INDEX(' Hello world Hello','Hello')
The result 2 is returned.
Where=INDEX(' Hello world Hello','Hello',.TRUE.)
The result 14 is returned.

INT(A,*Kind*)

Converts to integer from integer, real, and complex.

Argument: A	**Type:** N
Result: I	**Class:** E

Example: I=INT(F)

IOR(I,J)

Performs an inclusive OR on the arguments.

Argument: I   **Type:** I

Result: As I   **Class:** E

Example: I=IOR(I,J)

ISHFT(I,Shift)

Performs a logical shift. The bits of I are shifted by Shift positions.

Argument: I   **Type:** I

Result: As I   **Class:** E

Note: $|Shift| \le BIT\_SIZE(I)$

Example: I=ISHIFT(I,Shift).

ISHFTC(I,Shift,*Size*)

Performs a circular shift of the rightmost bits. The Size rightmost bits of I are circularly shifted by Shift positions.

Argument: I   **Type:** I

Result: I   **Class:** E

Note:
$| Shift | \le Size$
$0 \le Size \le BIT\_SIZE(I).$
If Size is absent it is as if it were present with the value of BIT_SIZE(I).
If Shift is positive the shift is to the left.
If Shift is negative the shift is to the right.
If Shift is zero no shift is performed.

Example: I=ISHFTC(I,Shift,Size)

KIND(X)

Returns the KIND type parameter of the argument.

Argument: X   **Type:** Any

Result: I   **Class:** I

Example: I=KIND(X)

LBOUND(Array,*Dim*)

Returns the lower bounds for each dimension of the array argument or a specified lower bound.

Argument: Array   **Type:** Any

Result: I   **Class:** I

Note:

$1 \leq Dim \leq n$ where n is the rank of Array. The result is scalar if Dim is present otherwise the result is an array of rank one and size n.

The result is scalar if Dim is present otherwise a rank one array and size n.

Example: I=LBOUND(Array)

LEN(String)

Length of a character entity.

     Argument: String   **Type:** S

     Result: I   **Class:** I

Example: I=LEN(String)

LEN_TRIM(String)

Length of character argument less the number of trailing blanks.

     Argument: String   **Type:** S

     Result: I   **Class:** E

Example: I=LEN_TRIM(String)

LGE(String_1,String_2)

Lexically greater than or equal and this is based on the ASCII collating sequence.

     Argument: String_1   **Type:** S

     Result: L   **Class:** E

String_2 is of type S.

Example: L=LGE(S1,S2)

LGT(String_1,String_2)

Lexically greater than and this is based on the ASCII collating sequence.

     Argument: String_1   **Type:** S

     Result: L   **Class:** E

Example: L=LGT(S1,S2)

LLE(String_1,String_2)

Lexically less than or equal and this is based on the ASCII collating sequence.

Argument: String_1   **Type:** S

Result: L   **Class:** E

String_2 is of type S.

Example: L=LLE(S1,S2)

LLT(String_1,String_2)

Lexically less than and this is based on the ASCII collating sequence.

Argument: String_1   **Type:** S

Result: L   **Class:** E

Example: L=LLT(S1,S2)

LOG(X)

Natural logarithm, $\log_e x$.

Argument: X   **Type:** R, C

Result: As argument   **Class:** E

Example: Y=LOG(X)

LOG10(X)

Common logarithm, $\log_{10}$.

Argument: X   **Type:** R

Result: As argument   **Class:** E

Example: Y=LOG10(X)

LOGICAL(L,*Kind*)

Converts between different logical kind types, i.e. performs a type cast.

Argument: L   **Type:** L

Result: L   **Class:** E

Example: L=LOGICAL(K,Kind)

MATMUL(Matrix_1,Matrix_2)

Performs mathematical matrix multiplication of the array arguments.

Argument: Matrix_1   **Type:** N,L

Result: As arguments   **Class:** T

Matrix_2 is as Matrix_1.

Note:

1. Matrix_1 and Matrix_2 must be arrays of rank one or two. If Matrix_1 is of numeric type so must Matrix_2.
2. If Matrix_1 has rank one, Matrix_2 must have rank two.
3. If Matrix_2 has rank one, Matrix_1 must have rank two.
4. The size of the first dimension of Matrix_2 must equal the size of the last dimension of Matrix_1.
5. If Matrix_1 has shape (n,m) and Matrix_2 has shape (m,k) the result has shape (n,k).
6. If Matrix_1 has shape (m) and Matrix_2 has shape (m,k) the result has shape (k).
7. If Matrix_1 has shape (n,m) and Matrix_2 has shape (m) the result has shape (n).

Example: R=MATMUL(M_1,M_2)

MAX(A1,A2,*A3*,...)

Returns the largest value.

Argument: A1	**Type:** I,R
Result: As arguments	**Class:** E

A2, A3,.. are as A1.

Example: A=MAX(A1,A2,A3,A4)

MAXEPONENT(X)

Returns the maximum exponent. See Chapter 8 and numeric models.

Argument: X	**Type:** R
Result: I	**Class:** I

Example: I=MAXEXPONENT(X)

MAXLOC(ARRAY,*Dim,Mask*)

Determine the location of the first element of Array having the maximum value of the elements identified by Mask if present.

Argument: Array	**Type:** I,R
Result: I	**Class:** T

Note:

0. Normally in Fortran 95 if you omit an optional argument you must use keywords for the rest. This intrinsic breaks this rule and DIM can be omitted and it is not necessary to use a keyword with Mask.

1. Array must be an array.
2. Mask must be conformable with Array
3. The result is an array of rank one and of size equal to the rank of Array.
4. If DIM is present the result is an array of the rank of Array reduced by one and with the shape of Array without the dimension DIM.

Example:

A=(/5,6,7,8/)

I=MAXLOC(A)

is (4), which is the subscript of the location of the first occurrence of the maximum value in the rank-one array.

$$If\ A\ =\ \begin{pmatrix} 1 & 8 & 5 \\ 9 & 3 & 6 \\ 4 & 2 & 7 \end{pmatrix}$$

I = MAXLOC(A,dim=1)

is (2,1,3) returning the position of the largest in each column.

I = MAXLOC(A,dim=2)

is (2,1,3) returning the position of the largest in each row.

MAXVAL(Array,_Dim,Mask_**)**

Returns the maximum value of the elements of Array along dimension Dim corresponding to the true elements of Mask.

Argument: Array	**Type:** I,R
Result: As argument	**Class:** T

Note:
$1 \leq Dim \leq n$ where n is the rank of Array. The result is scalar if Dim is absent, or Array has rank one. Otherwise the result is an array of rank n-1.
If Array has size zero then the result is the largest negative number supported by the processor for the corresponding type and kind of Array.

Example:

MAXVAL((/1,2,3/)) returns the value 3.

MAXVAL(C,MASK=C < 0.0) returns the maximum of the negative elements of C.

$$For\ B = \begin{pmatrix} 1 & 3 & 5 \\ 2 & 4 & 6 \end{pmatrix}$$

MAXVAL(B,DIM=1) returns (2,4,6)

MAXVAL(B,DIM=2) returns (5,6)

MERGE(True,False,Mask)

Chooses alternative values according to the value of a mask.

Argument: True   **Type:** Any

Result: As True   **Class:** E

Example: for

For $True = \begin{pmatrix} 2 & 6 & 10 \\ 4 & 8 & 12 \end{pmatrix}$, $False = \begin{pmatrix} 1 & 5 & 9 \\ 3 & 7 & 11 \end{pmatrix}$ and $Mask = \begin{pmatrix} T & F & T \\ F & T & F \end{pmatrix}$

The result is $\begin{pmatrix} 2 & 5 & 10 \\ 3 & 8 & 11 \end{pmatrix}$

MIN(A1,A2,A3,...)

Chooses the smallest value.

Argument: A1   **Type:** I, R

Result: As arguments   **Class:** E

Example: Y=MIN(X1,X2,X3,X4,X5)

MINEXPONENT(X)

Returns the minimum exponent. See Chapter 8 and numeric models.

Argument: X   **Type:** R

Result: I   **Class:** I

Example: I=MINEXPONENT(X)

MINLOC(Array,Dim,Mask)

Determine the location of the first element of Array having the minimum value of the elements identified by Mask.

Argument: Array   **Type:** I,R

Result: I   **Class:** T

Note:

0. Normally in Fortran 95 if you omit an optional argument you must use keywords for the rest. This intrinsic breaks this rule and dim can be omitted and it is not necessary to use a keyword with Mask.
1. Array must be an array.
2. Mask much be conformable with Array.
3. The result is an array of rank one and of size equal to the rank of Array.

4. If DIM is present the result is an array of the rank of Array reduced by one and with the shape of Array without the dimension DIM.

Example: I=MINLOC(Array)

In the above example if Array is a rank two array of shape (5,10) and the smallest value is in position (2,1) then the result is the rank one array I with shape (2) and I(1)=2 and I(2)=1.

See MAXLOC for further examples.

MINVAL(Array,*Dim,Mask)*

Returns the minimum value of the elements of Array along dimension Dim corresponding to the true elements of Mask.

Argument: Array	**Type:** I,R
Result: As Array	**Class:** T

Note: $1 \leq Dim \leq n$ where n is the rank of Array. The result is scalar if Dim is absent, or Array has rank one. Otherwise the result is an array of rank n-1.
If Array has size zero then the result is the largest negative number supported by the processor for the corresponding type and kind of Array.

Example:

MINAL((/1,2,3/)) returns the value 1.

MINVAL(C,MASK=C > 0.0) returns the minimum of the positive elements of C.

For $B = \begin{pmatrix} 1\ 3\ 5 \\ 2\ 4\ 6 \end{pmatrix}$

MINVAL(B,DIM=1) returns (1,3,5).

MINVAL(B,DIM=2) returns (1,2).

MOD(A,B)

Returns the remainder when first argument divided by second.

Argument: A	**Type:** I, R
Result: As arguments	**Class:** E

Note: If B=0 the result is processor dependent. For B $\neq$ 0 the result is A - INT(A/B) * B.

Example: R=MOD(A,B)
If A=8 and B=5 then R=3
If A=-8 and B=5 then R=-3

If A=8 and B=-5 then R=3
If A=-8 and B=-5 then R=-3

MODULO(A,B)

Returns the modulo of the arguments.

Argument: A	Type: I,R
Result: As A	Class: E

Note:
1. If B=0 then the result is processor dependent.
2. Integer A
The result is R where A= Q * B + R and Q is integer
for B>0, $0 \leq R < B$
for B < 0, $B < R \leq 0$
3. Real A
The result is A - FLOOR(A/B) * B.

Example: R=MODULO(A,B)
If A=8 and B=5 then R=3
If A=-8 and B=5 then R=2
If A=8 and B=-5 then R=-2
If A=-8 and B=-5 then R=-3

MVBITS(From,F_Pos,Len,To,T_Pos)

Copies a sequence of bits from one data object to another.

Argument: From	Type: I
Result: N/A	Class: S

All arguments are of integer type.

Note:
From must be INTENT(IN).
F_Pos must be INTENT(IN), F_Pos $\geq$ 0, F_Pos+Len $\leq$ BIT_SIZE(From).
Len must be INTENT(IN), Len $\geq$ 0.
To must be INTENT(INOUT).
T_Pos must be INTENT(IN), T_Pos $\geq$ 0, T_Pos + Len $\leq$ BIT_SIZE(To).

Example: CALL MVBITS(F,FP,L,T,TP)

NEAREST(X,Next)

Returns the nearest different number. See Chapter 8 and the real numeric model.

Argument: X	Type: R

Result: As X   **Class:** E

Next is of type R.

Example: N=NEAREST(X,Next).

NINT(A,*Kind***)**

Yields nearest integer.

    Argument: A   **Type:** RI

    Result: I   **Class:** E

Note:
1. A > 0, the result is INT(A+0.5).
2. A ≤ 0, the result is INT(A-0.5).

Example: I=NINT(X)

NOT(I)

Returns the logical complement of the argument.

    Argument: I   **Type:** I

    Result: As I   **Class:** E

Example: I=NOT(I)

NULL(*Mold***)**

Returns a disassociated pointer.

    Argument: Mold   **Type:** P

    Result: As argument   **Class:** T

Note:

If the argument Mold is present the result is the same as Mold.

Otherwise it is determined by context.

Example: REAL , POINTER :: P=>NULL()

PACK(Array,Mask,*Vector***)**

Packs an array into an array of rank one, under the control of a mask.

    Argument: Array   **Type:** Any

    Result: As Array   **Class:** T

Note:
1. Array must be an array.
2. Mask be conformable with Array.
3. Vector must have rank one and have at least as many elements as there are TRUE elements in Mask.
4. If Mask is scalar with the value TRUE. Vector must have at least as many elements as there are in Array.
5. The result is an array of rank one.
6. If Vector is present the result size is that of Vector.
7. If Vector is not present the result size is t, the number of TRUE elements in Mask, unless Mask is scalar with a value TRUE in which case the result size is the size of Array.

Example: R=PACK(A,M)

PRECISION(X)

Returns the decimal precision of the argument. See Chapter 8 and numeric models.

Argument: X	**Type:** R, C
Result: I	**Class:** I

Example: I=PRECISION(X)

PRESENT(A)

Returns whether an optional argument is present.

Argument: A	**Type:** Any
Result: L	**Class:** I

Note: A must be an optional argument of the procedure in which the PRESENT function reference appears.

Example: IF (PRESENT(X)) THEN ...

PRODUCT(Array,*Dim,Mask*)

The product of all of the elements of Array along the dimension Dim corresponding to the TRUE elements of Mask.

Argument: Array	**Type:** N
Result: As Array	**Class:** T

Note:
1. Array must be an array.
2. $1 \leq Dim \leq n$ where n is the rank of Array.

3. Mask must be conformable with Array.

4. Result is scalar if Dim is absent, or Array has rank one, otherwise the result is an array of rank n-1.

Example:

1. PRODUCT((/1,2,3/)) the result is 6.

2. PRODUCT(C,Mask=C > 0.0) forms the product of the positive elements of C.

3. If $B = \begin{pmatrix} 1 & 3 & 5 \\ 2 & 4 & 6 \end{pmatrix}$

PRODUCT(B,DIM=1) is (2,12,30) and

PRODUCT(B,DIM=2) is (15,48)

RADIX(X)

Returns the base of the numeric argument. See Chapter 8 and numeric models.

Argument: X	**Type:** I,R
Result: I	**Class:** I

Example: Base=RADIX(X)

RANDOM_NUMBER(X)

Returns one pseudo-random number or an array of pseudo-random numbers from the uniform distribution over the range $0 \le x < 1$

Argument: X	**Type:** R
Result: N/A	**Class:** S

Note: X is INTENT(OUT).

Example: CALL RANDOM_NUMBER(X)

RANDOM_SEED(*Size,Put,Get*)

Restarts (seeds) or queries the pseudo-random generator used by RANDOM_NUM-BER.

Argument: Size	**Type:** I
Result: N/A	**Class:** S

All arguments are of integer type.

Note:

1. Size is INTENT(OUT). It is set to the number N of integers that the processor uses to hold the value of the seed.

2. Put is INTENT(IN). It is an array of rank one and size $\ge$ N. It is used by the processor to set the seed value.

3. Get is INTENT(OUT). It is an array of rank one and size $\geq$ N. It is set by the processor to the current value of the seed.

Example: CALL RANDOM_SEED

RANGE(X)

Returns the decimal exponent range of the real argument. See Chapter 8 and the numeric model representing the argument.

Argument: X	**Type:** N
Result: I	**Class:** I

Example: I=RANGE(N)

REAL(A,*Kind*)

Converts to real from integer, real or complex.

Argument: A	**Type:** N
Result: R	**Class:** E

Example: X=REAL(A)

REPEAT(String,N_Copies)

Concatenates several copies of a string.

Argument: String	**Type:** S
Result: S	**Class:** T

Example: New_S=REPEAT(S,10)

RESHAPE(Source,Shape,*Pad,Order*)

Constructs an array of a specified shape from the elements of a given array.

Argument: Source	**Type:** Any
Result: As Source	**Class:** T

Note:
1. Source must be an array. If Pad is absent or of size zero the size of Source must be $\geq$ PRODUCT(Shape).
2. Shape must be a rank one array and $0 \leq$ size < 8.
3. Pad must be an array.
4. Order must have the same shape as Shape and its value must be a permutation of $(1,2,... ,n)$ where n is the size of Shape. If absent it is as if it were present with the

value $(1,2,...,n)$.
5. The result is an array of shape, Shape.

Example:

RESHAPE$((/1,2,3,4,5,6/),(/2,3/))$ has the value $\begin{pmatrix} 1 & 3 & 5 \\ 2 & 4 & 6 \end{pmatrix}$

RESHAPE$(\ (/1,2,3,4,5,6/)\ ,\ (/2,4/)\ ,\ (/0,0/)\ ,\ (/2,1/)\ )$ has the value $\begin{pmatrix} 1 & 2 & 3 & 4 \\ 5 & 6 & 0 & 0 \end{pmatrix}$

RRSPACING(X)

Returns the reciprocal of the relative spacing of model numbers near the argument value. See Chapter 8 and the real numeric model.

Argument: X   **Type:** R

Result: As X   **Class:** E

Example: Z=RRSPACING(X)

SCALE(X,I)

Returns $X * b^I$ where b is the base in the model representation of X. See Chapter 8 and the real numeric model.

Argument: X   **Type:** R

Result: As X   **Class:** E

I is of integer type.

Example: Z=SCALE(X,I)

SCAN(String,Set,Back)

Scans a string for any one of the characters in a set of characters.

Argument: String   **Type:** S

Result: I   **Class:** E

Note:
1. The default is to scan from the left, and will only be from the right when Back is present and has the value TRUE.
2. Zero is returned if the scan fails.

Example: W=SCAN(String,Set)

SELECTED_INT_KIND(R)

Returns a value of the kind type parameter of an integer data type that represents all integer values n with $-10^R < n < 10^R$

Argument: R   **Type:** I

Result: I   **Class:** T

Note:

R must be scalar.

If a kind type parameter is not available then the value -1 is returned.

Example: I=SELECTED_INT_KIND(2)

SELECTED_REAL_KIND(*P*,*R*)

Returns a value of the kind type parameter of a real data type with decimal precision of at least *P* digits and a decimal exponent range of at least *R*.

Argument: P and R   **Type:** I

Result: I   **Class:** T

Note:

1. *P* and *R* must be scalar.
2. The value -1 is returned if the precision is not available, the value -2 if the exponent range is not available, and -3 if neither is available.

Example: I=SELECTED_REAL_KIND(P,R)

SET_EXPONENT(X,I)

Returns the model number whose fractional part is the fractional part of the model representation of X and whose exponent part is I.

Argument: X   **Type:** R

Result: As X   **Class:** E

I is of integer type.

Example: Exp_Part=SET_EXPONENT(X,I)

SHAPE(Source)

Returns the shape of the array argument or scalar.

Argument: Source   **Type:** Any

Result: I   **Class:** I

Note:

1. Source may be array valued or scalar. It must not be a pointer that is disassociated or an allocatable array that is not allocated. It must not be an assumed size array.
2. The result is an array of rank one whose size is equal to the rank of Source.

Example: S=SHAPE(A(2:5,-1:1)) yields S=(4,3)

SIGN(A,B)

Absolute value of A times the sign of B.

Argument: A	**Type:** I, R
Result: As A	**Class:** E

Note:

In the special case where B is zero normally the result would have the value ABS(A), but if B is one of the real kind types and the processor is able to distinguish between plus zero and minus zero then the result is ABS(A) if B is plus zero and the result is - ABS(A) if B is minus zero.

B is as A.

Example: A=SIGN(A,B)

SIN(X)

Sine.

Argument: X	**Type:** R, C
Result: As argument	**Class:** E

Note: The argument is in radians.

Example: Z=SIN(X)

SINH(X)

Hyperbolic sine.

Argument: X	**Type:** R
Result: As argument	**Class:** E

Example: Z=SINH(X)

SIZE(Array,*Dim*)

Returns the extent of an array along a specified dimension or the total number of elements in an array.

Argument: Array	**Type:** Any
Result: I	**Class:** I

Note:

1. Array must be an array. It must not be a pointer that is disassociated or an

allocatable array that is not allocated. If Array is an assumed size array Dim must be present with a value less than the rank of Array.

2. Dim must be scalar and in the range $1 \leq$ Dim $\leq n$ where n is the rank of Array.

3. Result is equal to the extent of dimension Dim of Array, or if Dim is absent, the total number of elements of Array.

Example: A=SIZE(Array)

SPACING(X)

Returns the absolute spacing of model numbers near the argument value. See Chapter 8 and the real numeric model.

Argument: X	**Type:** R
Result: As X	**Class:** E

Example: S=SPACING(X)

SPREAD(Source,Dim,N_Copies)

Creates an array with an additional dimension, replicating the values in the original array.

Argument: Source	**Type:** Any
Result: As Source	**Class:** T

Note:

1. Source may be array valued or scalar, with rank less than 7.

2. Dim must be scalar and in the range $1 \leq$ Dim $\leq n+1$ where n is the rank of Source.

3. N_Copies must be scalar.

4. The result is an array of rank $n+1$.

Example:

If A is the array (2,3,4) then SPREAD(A,DIM=1,NCOPIES=3) then the result is the array $\begin{pmatrix} 2 & 3 & 4 \\ 2 & 3 & 4 \\ 2 & 3 & 4 \end{pmatrix}$

SQRT(X)

Square root.

Argument: X	**Type:** R, C
Result: As argument	**Class:** E

Example A=SQRT(B)

SUM(Array,*Dim,Mask*)

Returns the sum of all elements of Array along the dimension Dim corresponding to the true elements of Mask.

Argument: Array	**Type:** N
Result: As Array	**Class:** T

Note:
1. Array must be an array.
2. $1 \leq$ Dim $\leq n$ where n is the rank of Array.
3. Mask must be conformable with Array.
4. Result is scalar if Dim is absent, or Array has rank one, otherwise the result is an array of rank n-1.

Example:
1. SUM((/1,2,3/)) the result is 6.
2. SUM(C,Mask=C > 0.0) forms the arithmetic sum of the positive elements of C.
3. If $B = \begin{pmatrix} 1 & 3 & 5 \\ 2 & 4 & 6 \end{pmatrix}$

SUM(B,Dim=1) is (3,7,11)
SUM(B,Dim=2) is (9,12)

SYSTEM_CLOCK(*Count,Count_Rate,Count_Max*)

Returns integer data from a real time clock.

Argument: Count	**Type:** I
Result: N/A	**Class:** S

Note:
1. Count is INTENT(OUT) and is set to a processor dependent value based on the current value of the processor clock or to -HUGE(0) if there is no clock. $0 \leq$ Count $\leq$ Count_Max.
2. Count_Rate is INTENT(OUT) and it is set to the number of processor clock counts per second, or zero if there is no clock.
3. Count_max is INTENT(OUT) and is set to the maximum value that Count can have or to zero if there is no clock.

Example: CALL SYSTEM_CLOCK(C,R,M)

TAN(X)

Tangent.

Argument: X	**Type:** R

Result: As argument   **Class:** E

Note: X must be in radians.

Example: Y=TAN(X)

TANH(X)

Hyperbolic tangent.

Argument: X   **Type:** R

Result: As argument   **Class:** E

Example: Y=TANH(X)

TINY(X)

Returns the smallest positive number in the model representing numbers of the same type and kind type parameter as the argument.

Argument: X   **Type:** R

Result: As X   **Class:** I

Example: T=TINY(X)

TRANSFER(Source,Mold,*Size*)

Returns a result with a physical representation identical to that of Source, but interpreted with the type and type parameters of Mold.

Argument: Source   **Type:** Any

Result: As Mold   **Class:** T

Warning: A thorough understanding of the implementation specific internal representation of the data types involved is necessary for successful use of this function. Consult the documentation that accompanies the compiler that you work with before using this function.

TRANSPOSE(Matrix)

Transposes an array of rank two.

Argument: Matrix   **Type:** Any

Result: As argument   **Class:** T

Note: Matrix must be of rank two. If its shape is (n,m) then the resultant matrix has shape (m,n)

Example: For $A = \begin{pmatrix} 1 & 2 & 3 \\ 4 & 5 & 6 \\ 7 & 8 & 9 \end{pmatrix}$ TRANSPOSE(A) yields $\begin{pmatrix} 1 & 4 & 7 \\ 2 & 5 & 8 \\ 3 & 6 & 9 \end{pmatrix}$

TRIM(String)

Returns the argument with trailing blanks removed.

    Argument: String   **Type:** S

    Result: As String   **Class:** T

Note: String must be a scalar.

Example: T_S=TRIM(S)

UBOUND(Array,*Dim*)

Returns all the upper bounds of an array or a specified upper bound.

    Argument: Array   **Type:** Any

    Result: I   **Class:** I

Note:
$1 \le Dim \le n$ where n is the rank of Array. The result is scalar if Dim is present otherwise the result is an array of rank one and size n.
Result is a scalar if Dim is present otherwise is an array of rank one, and size n.

Example: Z=UBOUND(A)

UNPACK(Vector,Mask,Field)

Unpacks an array of rank one into an array under the control of a mask.

    Argument: Vector   **Type:** Any

    Result: As Vector   **Class:** T

Note:
1. Vector must have rank one. Its size must be at least t, where t is the number of true elements in Mask.
2. Mask must be array valued.
3. Field must be conformable with Mask. Result is an array with the same shape as Mask.

Example:
With $Vector = (1,2,3)$ and $Mask = \begin{pmatrix} F & T & F \\ T & F & F \\ F & F & T \end{pmatrix}$ and $Field = \begin{pmatrix} 1 & 0 & 0 \\ 0 & 1 & 0 \\ 0 & 0 & 1 \end{pmatrix}$

The result is $\begin{pmatrix} 1 & 2 & 0 \\ 1 & 1 & 0 \\ 0 & 0 & 3 \end{pmatrix}$

VERIFY(String,Set,*Back*)

Verify that a set of characters contains all the characters in a string by identifying the position of the first character in a string of characters that does not appear in a given set of characters.

Argument: String   **Type:** S

Result: I   **Class:** E

Note:

1. The default is to scan from the left, and will only be from the right when Back is present and has the value TRUE.

2. The value of the result is zero if each character in String is in Set, or if String has zero length.

Example: I=VERIFY(String,Set)

E   English and Latin Texts

YET IF HE SHOULD GIVE UP WHAT HE HAS BEGUN, AND AGREE TO MAKE US OR OUR KINGDOM SUBJECT TO THE KING OF ENGLAND OR THE ENGLISH, WE SHOULD EXERT OURSELVES AT ONCE TO DRIVE HIM OUT AS OUR ENEMY AND A SUBVERTER OF HIS OWN RIGHTS AND OURS, AND MAKE SOME OTHER MAN WHO WAS ABLE TO DEFEND US OUR KING; FOR, AS LONG AS BUT A HUNDRED OF US REMAIN ALIVE, NEVER WILL WE ON ANY CONDITIONS BE BROUGHT UNDER ENGLISH RULE. IT IS IN TRUTH NOT FOR GLORY, NOR RICHES, NOR HONOURS THAT WE ARE FIGHTING, BUT FOR FREEDOM - FOR THAT ALONE, WHICH NO HONEST MAN GIVES UP BUT WITH LIFE ITSELF.

QUEM SI AB INCEPTIS DIESISTERET, REGI ANGLORUM AUT ANGLICIS NOS AUT REGNUM NOSTRUM VOLENS SUBICERE, TANQUAM INIMICUM NOSTRUM ET SUI NOSTRIQUE JURIS SUBUERSOREM STATIM EXPELLERE NITEREMUR ET ALIUM REGEM NOSTRUM QUI AD DEFENSIONEM NOSTRAM SUFFICERET FACEREMUS. QUIA QUANDIU CENTUM EX NOBIS VIUI REMANSERINT, NUCQUAM ANGLORUM DOMINIO ALIQUATENUS VOLUMUS SUBIUGARI. NON ENIM PROPTER GLORIAM, DIUICIAS AUT HONORES PUGNAMUS SET PROPTER LIBERATEM SOLUMMODO QUAM NEMO BONUS NISI SIMUL CUM VITA AMITTIT.

from *'The Declaration of Arbroath'* c.1320. The English translation is by Sir James Fergusson.

F Coded Text Extract

OH YABY NSFOUN, YAN DUBZY LZ DBUYLTUBFAJ BYYBOHNX GPDA
FNUZNDYOLH YABY YAN SBF LZ B GOHTMN FULWOHDN DLWNUNX
YAN GFBDN LZ BH NHYOUN DOYJ, BHX YAN SBF LZ YAN NSFOUN
OYGNMZ BH NHYOUN FULWOHDN. OH YAN DLPUGN LZ YOSN,
YANGN NKYNHGOWN SBFG VNUN ZLPHX GLSNALV VBHYOHT, BHX
GL YAN DLMMNTN LZ DBUYLTUBFANUG NWLMWNX B SBF LZ YAN
NSFOUN YABY VBG YAN GBSN GDBMN BG YAN NSFOUN BHX YABY
DLOHDOXNX VOYA OY FLOHY ZLU FLOHY. MNGG BYYNHYOWN YL
YAN GYPXJ LZ DBUYLTUBFAJ, GPDDNNXOHT TNHNUBYOLHG DBSN
YL RPXTN B SBF LZ GPDA SBTHOYPXN DPSENUGLSN, BHX, HLY VOY-
ALPY OUUNWNUNHDN, YANJ BEBHXLHNX OY YL YAN UOTLPUG LZ
GPH BHX UBOH. OH YAN VNGYNUH XNGNUYG, YBYYNUNX
ZUBTSNHYG LZ YAN SBF BUN GYOMM YL EN ZLPHX, GANMYNUOHT
BH LDDBGOLHBM ENBGY LU ENTTBU; OH YAN VALMN HBYOLH, HL
LYANU UNMOD OG MNZY LZ YAN XOGDOFMOHN LZ TNLTUBFAJ.